# Stars of David

# Stars of David
# Rock 'n' Roll's
# Jewish Stories

**SCOTT R. BENARDE**

BRANDEIS UNIVERSITY PRESS

Published by University Press of New England

Hanover and London

BRANDEIS UNIVERSITY PRESS
Published by University Press of New England,
37 Lafayette St., Lebanon, NH 03766
© 2003 by Brandeis University Press
All rights reserved
Printed in the United States of America
5 4 3 2 1

Library of Congress Cataloging-in-Publication Data
Benarde, Scott R.
Stars of David : rock 'n' roll's Jewish stories /
Scott R. Benarde.
  p.   cm.
ISBN 1-58465-303-5 (pbk. : alk. paper)
1. Jewish rock musicians—Biography. I. Title
ML385B377 2003
782.42166'092'3924—dc21
2003010772

"Hannibal," by Dan Bern
    Copyright © Dan Bern/Kababa Music (ASCAP)
    1993
"Jerusalem," by Dan Bern
    Copyright © Dan Bern/Kababa Music (ASCAP)
    1992
"Kids' Prayer," by Dan Bern
    Copyright © Dan Bern/Kababa Music (ASCAP)
    1999
"Lithuania," by Dan Bern
    Copyright © Dan Bern/Kababa Music (ASCAP)
    2002
"One Thing Real," by Dan Bern
    Copyright © Dan Bern/Kababa Music (ASCAP)
    1997
"I'm Glad I'm Jewish," by Michael Bloomfield
    Courtesy of the estate of Michael Bloomfield
"God & The FBI"
    Written by Janis Ian
    © 2000 RUDE GIRL PUBLISHING
    (BMI)/Administered by BUG
    All Rights Reserved. Used by Permission.
"Honor Them All"
    Written by Janis Ian
    © 1998 RUDE GIRL PUBLISHING
    (BMI)/Administered by BUG
    All Rights Reserved. Used by Permission.
"Tattoo"
    Written by Janis Ian
    © 1992 RUDE GIRL PUBLISHING
    (BMI)/Administered by BUG
    All Rights Reserved. Used by Permission.
"Jewish"
    Words and Music by Randy California
    Copyright © 1968 HOLLENBECK MUSIC
    Copyright Renewed
    All Rights Controlled and Administered by
    IRVING MUSIC, INC.
    All Rights Reserved. Used by Permission.
"From a Distance"
    Words and Music by Julie Gold
    Copyright © 1986, 1987 Julie Gold Music (BMI)
    and Wing & Wheel Music (BMI)
    Julie Gold Music Administered Worldwide by
    Irving Music, Inc.
    International Copyright Secured. All Rights
    Reserved.

(continued on page 373)

For
Mindi Dawn and Michael Dov,
my bedrock rhythm section, without whom
there is no song.
And for Shirah Beth, the newest member of the band.

In memory of rockers
Andy Kulberg, Zal Yanovsky, and
rocket man Ilan Ramon.

"The Jewish contribution [to rock music] has been

kind of a stealth one, hasn't it?"

Producer, songwriter, musician Kenny Edwards

# CONTENTS

Preface  xi

Acknowledgments  xv

Overture  1

## 1950s–1960s

Jerry Leiber and Mike Stoller  17

Carol Kaye  23

The Tokens  29

Al Kooper  34

Jay and the Americans  41

Barry Mann and Cynthia Weil  48

Peter Yarrow  56

Bob Dylan  62

David Grisman  68

Genya Ravan  73

Manfred Mann  78

Zal Yanovsky of the
    Lovin' Spoonful  84

P. F. Sloan  89

Michael Bloomfield  95

Barry Goldberg  102

Harvey Brooks  109

The Blues Project/Blood, Sweat and
    Tears/Seatrain  116

Country Joe and the Fish  123

Pete Brown  128

Janis Ian  134

Chuck E. Weiss  140

Jerry Kasenetz and Jeffry Katz
    The Kasenetz-Katz Singing
    Orchestral Circus  145

Keith Reid of Procol Harum  152

Randy Newman  157

Randy California  164

Leslie West and Corky Laing
    of Mountain  170

## 1970s–1980s

Lee Oskar of WAR  179

Norman Greenbaum  185

Marc Bolan  190

Steve Goodman  197

Kinky Friedman and the
    Texas Jewboys  203

Mike Garson  209

Wendy Waldman  214

Mickey Raphael of Willie Nelson
    and Family  219

Billy Joel  225

Phoebe Snow  230

Max Weinberg  236

Marcy Levy, a.k.a.
    Marcella Detroit  241

Graham Gouldman of 10cc  247

David Lee Roth  254

Stan Lynch of Tom Petty and the
    Heartbreakers  260

Melissa Manchester  267

Trevor Rabin  273

Johnny Clegg  279

Billy Steinberg  285

Don Was of Was (Not Was)  290

David Bryan of Bon Jovi  298

Diane Warren  303

Eric Bazilian and Rob Hyman of
    the Hooters  308

Peter Himmelman  316

**1990s and beyond**

Victoria Shaw  325

Julie Gold  330

Marc Cohn  335

Mike Gordon of Phish  340

Lisa Loeb  345

Dan Bern, a.k.a. Bernstein  350

Rami Jaffee of the Wallflowers  356

Remedy  363

Evan and Jaron  368

In 1986, for his bar mitzvah present, I took my cousin Russell to see a David Lee Roth concert. Diamond Dave, as Roth calls himself, was an arena-filling attraction at the time. He was only a year or so removed as the acrobatic, wickedly (with a wink) flamboyant frontman for the rock band Van Halen, and was on the charts with the Top Twenty hit "Yankee Rose." I used my connections as the rock music critic for a local newspaper to get us backstage before the show. Russell was too shy to approach Roth on his own, so with Russell in tow, I walked over to Roth, who was sitting outside his dressing room, and announced to him that he, the great rock showman David Lee, was my cousin's bar mitzvah gift. Upon hearing that, Roth's face lit up, and he declared, "Bar mitzvah! That's when I started learning how to sing, when I was studying for my bar mitzvah." I don't remember Russell's reaction to Roth's remarks, but I remember mine. I wrote them down, and filed them away, never completely getting over the impact of those words. Roth had said, in effect, that being Jewish mattered. It wasn't until ten years later that I began to wonder about the scope of the contribution Jews had made to rock 'n' roll, blues, folk, pop and country music, and, more important to me, whether being Jewish meant anything to those who wrote, played and sang the songs. Jews *kvell* (gush with pride) when they discover that someone famous or accomplished in any field is a member of the tribe, but wouldn't it really be something if these famous folks cared about being Jewish? Outside of the Christian rock genre, the media had rarely, if ever (with the exception of Bob Dylan), dealt with a rock star's religion or spirituality. That time-honored omission of religious beliefs had probably led fans to believe that rock stars had no such beliefs or faith. And while a good number of books extol the substantial contributions of Jewish actors, comedians, sports heroes, politicians, and others, the Jews of rock 'n' roll, and rock's contemporary musical cousins, had not been chronicled and credited. They deserved to be, especially with the genre reaching fifty. As non-Jewish songwriter, producer, and musician Kenny Edwards remarked to me, "The Jewish contribution has been kind of a stealth one, hasn't it?" It was time to unveil the big secret and light up radar screens—for several reasons: for the historical record; for doling out proper credit after decades of silence, even for letting anti-Semites know that so many of their most cherished songs were written, sung and/or played by Jews. Or that—say it ain't so—their favorite performers were Jewish. But most of all, for young rock fans like my cousin Russell, who, a lifetime later, hasn't forgotten his bar mitzvah encounter with David Lee Roth.

But, you wonder, and might rightly ask, how did I define "Jew" for this book? It may be helpful to know that I approached my subjects not by trying to discover how Jewish they were, but how they were Jewish. I had no measuring rod, per se. Rather, I used the following passage from *The Simple Guide to Judaism* by David Starr-Glass as my guide. "A Jew may intellectually renounce his Jewish identity, but it is considered that he cannot alter the state of his *neshama* (soul), nor ultimately his spiritual identity. Even Jews who are far from participating in religious observance are spiritually connected with the people of the nation of Israel and have the potential to return. As the late Rabbi Yosef Itzhak Schneerson remarked: 'A Jew is a lamp-lighter. The light is never extinguished.'" In the end, if a noted singer, songwriter or musician identified as a Jew, negatively or positively, culturally or religiously, that was good enough for me. As always, there are exceptions to the rule. I could not ask the late Marc Bolan of T. Rex about his Jewish identity. But the Jewish side of his family (paternal) claims him; he is on many lists of famous Jews, and is such a legendary figure in rock (especially in England and Europe), that I felt compelled to ferret out his Jewish roots for the record. On the other hand, with so many to track down and research, I did not pursue an interview with a noted British pop star from the sixties when I discovered that, in 1987, she found Jesus and refers to herself as a Messianic Jew. That said, she probably has an intriguing Jewish story.

Which brings us to the book's title. It went through several permutations before resolving itself to define and fit the material as the book took shape. All the people in this book are "Stars of David," musical descendants of King David, whom I view as the world's first Jewish rock star. Before becoming a king, he was an accomplished harpist and songwriter, with a voice so soothing he was known as "the sweet singer of Israel." He also was known to enjoy a good many, shall we say, groupies. (Nothing, it appears, is new.)

The depth and breadth of the Jewish contribution to rock 'n' roll may come as a surprise (and I am only dealing with songwriters, musicians, and singers in less than encyclopedic scope), but the fact that Jews and music get along so famously should not. Music has been an essential part of Judaism since Moses sang a song of thanks to God for leading the Hebrews out of Egypt. (And, as several rockers interviewed for this book noted, the Torah was made to be sung.) The power and importance of music and song are extolled throughout the Torah. Psalm 150 is a shining example:

> Praise Him with the blast of the horn
> Praise Him with the psaltry and the harp
> Praise Him with the timbrel and dance
> Praise him with the loud-sounding cymbals.
> Let everything that has breath praise the Lord, Hallelujah.

The Psalms, most of them attributed to King David, still resonate, with Psalm 33, ("Hinei Ma' Tov"), making it onto a rock album—in Hebrew—by Spirit in 1969, nearly three thousand years after it was composed. Even the *Zohar*, the guide to Jewish mysticism, declares that "There are halls in heaven that open only to the voice of song."

The second part of the title, *Rock 'n' Roll's Jewish Stories*, was a natural. As I began exploring the Jewish contribution to the canon of rock 'n' roll, and as the interviews piled up, it became clear that I had a collection of Jewish stories; everyone had a unique Jewish inspiration, influence or experience to recount. These stories are fascinating enough individually; collectively, however, they amount to a phenomenal discovery. Pious Jew, angry Jew, atheist Jew, assimilated Jew, cultural Jew, all validate what I had inferred from David Lee Roth in 1986: being Jewish mattered.

*Summer 2003* S.B.

## ACKNOWLEDGMENTS

I don't know if every author needs an army, but I had mine. *Stars of David: Rock 'n' Roll's Jewish Stories* would not have become a reality without a battalion of supporters and believers.

My family marched in the front lines. My wife, Mindi, read and corrected first drafts. My father, Mel, author of some ten books on health and environmental sciences; my mother, Anita, a book illustrator and children's book author; and my sister Dana, a graphic artist and marketing director, added their critical eyes, dramatically improving my work. My sister Andrea played cheerleader. Cousin Rachel Ginsberg, a book editor wise to the ways of the publishing world, provided literary advice.

My friend Randy Fuchs was onboard early, gladly emptying his Rolodex and sending me e-mails filled with possible "Jews I could use." Sam Sokolove was an informed, helpful, guiding soul and kindred spirit from beginning to end. Pat Baird at BMI (Broadcast Music International) and Jim Steinblatt of ASCAP (American Society of Composers, Authors and Publishers) were vital resources, who graciously answered my frequent queries and calls for help and served as go-betweens for numerous subjects in this book. They deserve Mensch awards. Steve Morse of the *Boston Globe* also deserves an award for not only providing contact numbers, but going the extra mile and making calls on my behalf. Longtime friends Thom Duffy and John Lannert of *Billboard* magazine were sources of encouragement, as were kindred spirits Sheldon Voss and Stuart Posin. Well into the project, I had the pleasure of "meeting" the Webmaster of *Jewhoo!* The Web site is an ever-growing repository of lists of famous Jews and their contributions. When I was stuck, I often turned to "NTeibloom." And when he came across information he thought I could use, he let me know about it. He also promoted my work on the *Jewhoo!* Web site, and for that I am grateful.

My co-workers in the communications department at my "day job" at the Jewish Federation of South Palm Beach County demonstrated their *menschlekeit* throughout. Department director Debbie Stern understood my passion for this book, and allowed me the leeway to work on it when time permitted. Deborah

Bibey and Steve Sicherman helped with photos and graphics amd provided technical support; Steve's help organizing the manuscript was invaluable. Department secretary Joyce Cippolla kept an eye on the fax machine for me. No one sacrificed more than my colleague, Ken Swart. Our sharing an office for much of the duration subjected him to more book-related phone conversations and interviews than any human deserved. Colleague Liz Feinstein provided moral support. I offer special thanks to philanthropist Larry Phillips, the mensch of Boca Raton, who believed in *Stars of David* and convinced Peter Yarrow of its importance.

Much of the strength of *Stars* comes from the recollections and anecdotes of many Jewish mothers. My sincerest gratitude to Nettie Becker, Hannah Blumenfeld, Minette Goodman, Regine Benyayer Jaffee, Bernice Pearl, Dorothy Shinderman, and Ida Rosenbaum (I did not forget Rico, Ida). Chuck Lowenstein, father of Evan and Jaron Lowenstein, represented the pride and kindness of fathers. A heartfelt thanks to Michael Bloomfield's brother, Allen, who provided encouragement as well as insight, vignettes, photographs, and music. I also owe a debt to Marc Bolan's brother Harry Feld and first cousin Caroline, who endured lengthy telephone interviews and numerous follow-up calls. Barry Smith, the co-director of the Official Marc Bolan Fan Club, also was a cheerful, invaluable sounding board and source of information.

Bob Merlis, former vice president of media relations at Warner Brothers Records greeted my calls for help with, "It's the least I can do for a landsman!" Music business publicists Barbara Shelley, Ida Langsom, Veronique Cordier, and Susan Stewart arranged interviews, provided photos and music, and shared their knowledge. Randy Haeker at Sony/Legacy, Kathy Williams and Jeff White at Rhino Records, Jill Christiansen at Rykodisc, and Jim Baltutis at Warner Brothers provided photos, music or arranged interviews. Dave A. Stein of All the Best Records was a repository of difficult-to-find music, and put me in touch with singer-songwriter P. F. Sloan. Joe and Sky at the now defunct Sid's Music in Margate, Florida, helped me find elusive vinyl Long Players. Arnie Goodman and Paul Aronson also shared their knowledge and provided out-of-print CDs. When I was stuck, the folks at the concert industry trade publication *Pollstar* provided contact numbers even though my subscription had expired. Photographer Henry Diltz, one of the legendary lensmen of rock 'n' roll, happily provided photos and encouragement.

Songwriters and musicians Richie Supa, Henry Gross, and Bob Glaub were generous with their time and paved the way for some of the interviews included here, though their own interviews were victims of limited time and space. (You're in the second edition, I promise!) My apologies to those who also gave me their time, but are not found in detail here: Kenny Aronoff, David Berman of Silver Jews, Karla Bonoff, Aaron Comess, Taylor Dayne, Judith Edelman, Bruce Gary of the Knack, Gerry Goffin, Hillary Kanter, Artie Kaplan, Lucy Kaplansky, Scott Kempner of the Dictators and the Del Lords, Artie Kornfeld, Danny Kortchmar, Isaac "Jacky" Bitton and Marco Tobaly of the Morrocan-French rock band Les Variations, Eleni Mandell, Mark Naftalin of the Paul Butterfield Blues Band, New Found Glory members Ian Grushka and Jordan Pundik, Novi Novog, Dan Pritzker of Sonia Dada, Eddie Schwartz, Ben Sidran, Josh Silver of Type O Negative, Derek Shulman of Gentle Giant, and Lauren Wood.

Scott Quittem, who runs a fan Web site for Gypsy, perhaps the seventies' most underrated American band, came through with photos and information about band co-founder, guitarist and songwriter Enrico Rosenbaum. Again, space and time prevented me from including the talented but unheralded Rosenbaum, who died much too young. Spirit fan Bruce Pates provided me with Randy California photos and insight, and passed along comments from former Spirit lead singer Jay Ferguson. Roland Clare, Webmaster of the Procol Harum fan Web site, Beyond the Pale, was also helpful to a stranger. When I couldn't find biographical information I needed, I turned to Steve Posti, a researcher at the *Palm Beach Post* library.

*Stars of David* is about Judaism as well as music, and I offer a "todah rabah" to the rabbis of Aish HaTorah's "Ask the Rabbi" for their prompt answers to questions about Jewish history, holidays, and ritual. My thanks also go to my friend and colleague Leon Weissberg, director of the Jewish Federation of South Palm Beach County's Jewish Education Commission, and Jack Rosenbaum for Hebrew translations and biblical research. One of the surprises of this project was how directly the Holocaust affected the lives of many performers profiled here. Peter Black, senior historian at the United States Holocaust Memorial Museum in Washington, D.C., tackled questions relating to the Shoah.

A grateful nod goes to Janis Ian, the first artist to consent to an interview and start me on what she described as "a daunting task." My gratitude to all the singers, songwriters, and musicians who also shared their Jewish stories (and their family photo albums), giving *Stars of David* a heart and soul. Others who provided all manner of aid and comfort: John Thornton, David Spero, Stuart Wax, Richie Pachter, Chuck Gaspari, Bob Rossi, Scott Gartner, and Roy Trakin. Thanks to Jack Boyle, Ron Cohen, Jon Stoll, and John Valentino for an unforgettable behind-the-scenes rock 'n' roll education long before the idea for this book was born. I must again thank my wife, not just for her fine copyeditor's eye, but for her patience, encouragement, and love. My mother and father deserve another loving embrace, not only for their time and constructive criticism, but for their unwavering belief in me.

My son, Michael Dov, was six months old when I began this labor of love, and five years old when I finished. (His sister, Shirah, was born as this project came to a conclusion.) Along with all those "why" questions preschoolers incessantly pose, he repeatedly asked, "Are you done with the book yet, Daddy?" I can finally answer, "Yes!" Thank you, Michael, for somehow understanding, and for your habit of yanking me from the computer by my shirttail for much-needed playtime. I couldn't have undertaken and completed this "daunting task" without you and Mommy. I love you both from Australia up to God.

# Stars of David

# Overture

In 1995, while on the Florida leg of a concert tour, Bob Dylan walked into Temple Beth El in West Palm Beach and attended Yom Kippur services. You would have thought Elijah had come through the door. Say what you want about Bob "Robert Zimmerman" Dylan's late seventies–early eighties experience as a born-again Christian, the enigmatic superstar's real roots were showing. Dylan's synagogue appearance made local news. It also made local Jews proud. Throughout the rock era, most Jewish performers, songwriters, and musicians preferred keeping their Jewishness out of the spotlight. The Jewish contribution to rock, blues, folk, country, and pop music, and the influence of Judaism on these performers, musicians, and songwriters has been substantial, but little publicized. Identifying as a Jew was considered bad for business. Some performers, as you shall see in the coming pages, have, for years, been singing Judaism's praises louder than we have realized. They just weren't doing it in front of an audience or mentioning it in fan magazines.

Nor were journalists asking them about it. If they had, the media might have discovered (and reported) that, along with Dylan attending synagogue, Bon Jovi's David Bryan blows the shofar at his temple during the High Holidays. And that during his nearly twenty-year tenure as the drummer with Tom Petty and the Heartbreakers, Stan Lynch took his *hanukkiah* on the road during concert tours to celebrate the Festival of Light. We might have known earlier that, from 1976 through at least 1980, the Jewish cast, crew, and guests of the hit NBC program *Saturday Night Live*, who were far from home, gathered for a Passover seder led by band member Paul Shaffer (who subsequently became music director for David Letterman). The seders were attended by Gilda Radner, Laraine Newman, Al Franken, and many of the show's writers, as well as musical guests. Participants still talk about the 1978 seder during which Art Garfunkel sang the Four Questions.

North American Jews weren't the only ones making an impact on pop music and trying to maintain a bond with their Judaism. This was occurring throughout the Diaspora. In the mid-sixties, Moroccan Jews Isaac "Jacky" Bitton (drums),

Marco Tobaly (guitar), and singer Jo Leb (replaced by Tunisian Jew Robert Fitoussi), who were living in France, co-founded Les Variations. The band sang in English and melded rock guitar and song structure with the indigenous rhythms and instrumentation of North Africa and the Sephardic melodies and Hebrew songs of their youth. Throughout the first half of the seventies, Les Variations was turning heads in the States with the albums *Moroccan Roll* and *Café de Paris* and were opening shows for the likes of Kiss and Aerosmith before personnel problems broke up the band in 1975. (Bitton wore a formidable Star of David around his neck during concerts.) Today, Bitton lives in the Crown Heights section of Brooklyn and leads a band that plays "Jewish rock 'n' roll." Tobaly and his family live in Paris (his wife is Israeli) and are *shomer Shabbos*.

From 1970 through 1980, trendsetting progressive British rock band Gentle Giant released a dozen albums of imaginative, trailblazing (and often uncommercial) progressive rock. Although the band wasn't big in its own backyard, and had only a cult following in the United States, it was one of the hottest concert attractions in Europe. Band founders and brothers Phil, Derek, and Ray Shulman, all multi-instrumentalists, also had scored an international hit, "Kites," in 1967 with their previous band, a psychedelic-rock outfit known as Simon Dupree and the Big Sound. The brothers were the sons of a Scottish bandleader and trumpeter who donned tefillin and *davened* daily before going off to play in Britain's jazz clubs. The brothers grew up in a liberal, observant home but attended a strict Hebrew school where they were nearly turned off by the intense ritual. Still, Gentle Giant never performed on Rosh Hashanah or Yom Kippur, though the band included several non-Jewish members. Derek Shulman, the band's lead singer, most closely followed in his father's observant footsteps, taking a *siddur* on the road during concert tours. After moving to the United States where he became a record company executive, he help found the Abraham Joshua Heschel School in New York, and bought a home in Jerusalem, which the family uses several times a year. Commenting on Gentle Giant's music, he says, "Our Judaism and the good ideological values of it did affect the musical and lyrical content of what Gentle Giant was. It was a little more of a thinking man's band . . . Looking back, Judaism probably affected our music more than I realized at the time."

By the mid-eighties, Yemen-born Israeli singer Ofra Haza had become an international star. Her music, initially inspired by ancient Sephardic melodies, was filled with stories and images of her Jewish heritage, her love of country and a yearning for peace in the Middle East. She even wrote a song called "Kaddish," about the importance and beauty of the Jewish prayer for the dead. She described the mourner's kaddish as "a small prayer holding all of the world's sorrow on the wings of an angel." A veteran of the Israeli army, her popularity broadened when she began experimenting with dance and techno rhythms in the late eighties and singing in English as well as Hebrew, Arabic, and Aramaic. Haza began to break through in America after rap acts began "sampling" her songs on their albums. Even after her untimely death in 2000 at age forty-one, Haza remains an Israeli icon.

South African singer, songwriter, and bandleader Johnny Clegg rebelled against his Jewish roots as a child and reclaimed them as an adult. Since the late seventies, he has used his music, a blend of rock and various forms of South African folk music, as a vehicle to pursue justice, and he is credited with helping erode the country's racist system of apartheid. He is as knowledgeable and embracing of Zulu culture as he is of Judaism and Jewish culture, singing many of his songs in Swahili and incorporating Zulu dance into his concerts. The Torah and Jewish history, however, influence songs such as "Jericho," "Jerusalema," and "Warsaw 1943." His integrated band, topical songs, dramatic performances, and international popularity helped shine a light of condemnation on South Africa's racist regime.

South African musician Sharon Katz, the daughter of Zionists who moved to Israel while she stayed to pursue her love of *mbaqanga, kwela* and reggae music, also wrote songs that were beacons of unity and social justice. In 1993, she campaigned for Nelson Mandela and helped teach formerly disenfranchised blacks, "coloreds," and Indians to vote. Her creation and direction of an integrated five-hundred-person choir called When Voices Meet, and her "Peace Train" performances at railroad stops throughout the country in support of Mandela, made her a household name in South Africa. Like Clegg, Katz sings many of her songs in Swahili, but she is also fluent in Hebrew. Her first U.S. release, *Imbizo*, in 2002, was filled with songs of hope and optimism.

During the past decade, as Dylan unintentionally illustrated by attending Yom Kippur services, an increasing number of Jewish rockers have been trumpeting their Jewishness a little louder than before. What changed? The passage of time? The increasing success of pop stars who are Jewish? The nothing-to-lose-attitude of performers who are the children of Holocaust survivors? The fact that gentile pop icons such as Madonna think Kabbalah is cool? Whatever it is, even veteran Jewish rockers from the sixites and seventies—observant or not—have become less reluctant to discuss their Jewishness. Longtime record producer Brooks Arthur (born Arnold Brodsky), who began his career as the studio engineer on most of Neil Diamond's hit singles and who also produced Adam Sandler's "Chanukah Song," observed in 1998 that among Jews in the music business, "your [Jewish] pride was more covert back then, and now it's overt."

Why? "Our parents' cry to us was 'Be American. Fit in.' So we were changing our ways. We realized twenty years later it wasn't working. For the last fifteen years or so, many people have been realizing that assimilation and intermarriage haven't been working," says Arthur, who also engineered and/or produced albums by Van Morrison, Blues Project, Bruce Springsteen, Janis Ian, Bette Midler, Liza Minelli, and comedians Jackie Mason and Robin Williams. It's also a question of mortality. "You realize you're a couple of steps closer to God, so we're cleaning up our acts. We're picking up where we left off after our bar mitzvahs," adds Arthur, who became *bal t'shuvah* in 1982. "I go to shul as often as I can, but my work and career don't allow me to get away all the time." Even so, he lays tefillin and davens every morning.

Rising new stars rarely think twice about talking about Judaism. Singer-songwriter Lisa Loeb, whose career was launched when her song "Stay (I Missed You)" from the *Reality Bites* soundtrack reached No. 1 in 1994, mentions starring in plays at the Dallas Jewish Community Center in her official record company bio. That's something few performers would have included in an official bio a dozen years ago. During a December 1997 television interview when asked what she would be doing for Christmas, Loeb boldly and honestly answered that she celebrated Hanukkah. Singer-songwriter Marc Cohn, winner of the 1991 Grammy Award for Best New Artist, whose parents died before he was of bar mitzvah age, has been re-examining his Jewish heritage to the point of participating on the critically acclaimed 1996 Hanukkah compilation CD, *Festival of Light*. He sings the lead track, a soulful version "Rock of Ages/Ma'oz Tzur." His 1998 album, *Burning the Daze*, is full of spiritual yearning and soul searching. And what of Adam Sandler's 1996 novelty tune, "The Chanukah Song"? Something must have changed not only for Sandler to write and record it, but for mainstream radio to play it frequently enough for the album on which it appears to sell well over one million copies.

But society, we know, was not always so tolerant. At the dawn of the rock era in the fifties even though the owners of many of the major record labels were Jewish, "Hanukkah" remarks such as Loeb's were no-nos. Like many film stars, she might have been compelled to change her name to increase her appeal to the masses—or simply to fit in. Many performers did. The members of Jay and the Americans, who had a string of hits between 1962 and 1970 ("Only in America," "Come a Little Bit Closer"), went through wholesale name changes early in the group's career. Kenny Rosenberg became Vance; Howie Kirschenbaum became Kane; Sandy Yaguda became Dean, Marty Kupersmith became Sanders, and David Blatt became Jay Black. Do you think keyboard player-arranger Manfred Mann, a self-described cultural Jew from South Africa best known for taking Bob Dylan and Bruce Springsteen songs to the top of the pop charts ("The Mighty Quinn," "Blinded By the Light"), would have been easier to market as Manfred Lubowitz? Would J. Geils Band harmonica player Magic Dick have sounded as sexy being introduced as Richard Salwitz, or lead singer Peter Wolf as Peter Blankfield? How about Cars lead guitarist Elliot Easton? Isn't that name hipper (that is to say, less ethnic), than Elliot Steinberg? Phoebe Snow is cooler than Phoebe Laub; Janis Ian hipper than Janis Fink; ditto Carole King who was born Carole Klein, and Taylor Dayne, born Leslie Wundermann. And which rocks more for the co-founder of Jane's Addiction, Porno For Pyros and the Lollapaloza festival, Perry Farrell or Perry Bernstein? British blues guitarist Peter Greenbaum simply dropped "baum" to become Peter Green before co-founding Fleetwood Mac in 1967 and writing the now-classic song, "Black Magic Woman," which became a huge hit for Santana in 1970.

Some names just don't "rock," or were "too Jewish" (though that attitude is changing). So Haifa-born Chaim Witz and New Yorker Stanley Eisen respectively became Gene Simmons and Paul Stanley of Kiss. You get the picture.

Al Kooper's parents changed the family name from Kuperschmidt long before their son became a Dylan sideman, joined the Blues Project, then founded Blood, Sweat and Tears. "My parents must have known I was destined for greatness," Kooper joked of the name change. Mountain guitarist Leslie West's mother gave her sons the choice of West or Winston when she decided to leave behind her married name of Weinstein after a divorce. Had Lou Reed's father, Sidney, not changed the family name to Reed before son Lou was born, the co-founder of the Velvet Underground would have been Lou Rabinowitz. (His birth name was never Louis Firbank as many music reference books have erroneously reported.) The fathers of songwriters P. F. Sloan ("Eve of Destruction," "Secret Agent Man") and Diane Warren ("Un-Break My Heart," "If I Could Turn Back Time") changed their family names in the 1950s to get work. Sloan had been Schlein; Warren had been Wolfberg. To be fair about name changes, Lollapalooza co-founder Farrell has discussed his Judaism during concerts, not tried to hide it, and in the late nineties announced that his return to Torah study helped him overcome a heroin addiction. (Farrell, who often uses his Hebrew name, Peretz, gave his child the biblical name of Yovel and based his 2001 album *Songs Yet to Be Sung* on the biblical concept of the jubilee year.) And keyboard player Manfred Mann never legally changed his name. "I think of myself as Lubowitz," he says. "There are two of me. I'm only Mann on stage." Songwriter Eddie Schwartz, best known for penning the 1979 Pat Benatar clasic, "Hit Me with Your Best Shot," says he isn't sure if he would have changed his name earlier in his career. He admits he "agonized over it a lot." Since he had written "Best Shot" under his own name, he kept Schwartz. It didn't seem to hurt him when as singer Eddie Schwartz he had his own Top Thirty hit, "All Our Tomorrows," in 1982. Even so, he says, "I wondered if it impaired my career, though I'm very proud of who I am."

Another reason Jewish performers kept their pedigree quiet was, of course, fear of anti-Semitism and the accompanying possibility of losing work and fans. Nashville-based singer-songwriter Henry Gross, a transplanted New Yorker (and a yeshiva graduate), said in 1996 that many of his Jewish colleagues were reluctant to discuss the subject because being Jewish in the Bible Belt could be a career death warrant. Gross, best known as a founding member of Sha Na Na, and for the 1976 Top Ten hit "Shannon," is an outspoken Zionist but has a sense of humor about the situation. He jokes about starting a Nashville TV show called *Heeb Haw*. In his spare time, he and his friends try to give classic rock song titles a Jewish flavor–remember, for example, the 1968 Iron Butterfly hit "In-A-Haggadah-Da-Vida."

And try being the only Yid on the tour bus. Mickey Raphael, the harmonica player in Willie Nelson's band has had that distinction since the early seventies. Fortunately, like his friend Henry Gross, Raphael has a sense of humor, too. When asked what it's like to be the only Jew in the band, Texas-born Raphael, who also lives in Nashville, often responds, "Well, besides manipulating the press and controlling world banking, I've got my hands full." New York City–born bass player Harvey Goldstein was nineteen when he took the stage name

Harvey Brooks after he "got into a Jewboy scenario" and was attacked during a
break at a gig in Michigan in the early sixties. "I took that name to avoid con-
flicts," says Brooks. "I thought, 'Just let me get a professional name without any
connotations, the blandest name I can find.'" If Brooks was a bland name, his
bass playing was anything but. He got his break working on the classic Bob Dylan
album, *Highway 61 Revisited*, in 1965.

Not every Jewish rocker acquiesced to a name change or was intimidated by
anti-Semitism. Singer-songwriter-keyboard player Barry Goldberg and his best
friend guitarist Michael Bloomfield, out of sheer pride, would not change their
names. But then they had a role model—Goldberg's uncle, Supreme Court Justice Arthur Goldberg. "It hurt me, not changing my name," says Goldberg, who
along with Bloomfield did stints with Dylan and the Electric Flag, as well as his
own Barry Goldberg Reunion. "Bloomfield and I were really into our heritage,
and traditions, and proud of our names, and if people didn't like them it was
tough shit. We were emphatic about keeping our real names." Goldberg also released an album of electric blues in 1969 called *2 Jews Blues*. Executives at Goldberg's record company, most of them Jewish, opposed the album title for being,
of course, "too Jewish." (The year also saw the release of another album that
didn't hide its Jewish influence. The second album by the rock band Spirit, *The
Family That Plays Together*, featured the song "Jewish," a rock version of Psalm 133,
"Hinei Ma'Tov." The previous year, the Electric Prunes put out what might be
considered the first two albums to marry religion and rock, *Mass in F-Minor*, and
*Release of an Oath: The Kol Nidre*. The band included no Jews. The idea for these religious rock albums came from the band's Jewish manager, Len Poncher, who
hired Jewish composer David Axelrod to write the music.)

During the seventies, Richard "Kinky" Friedman took a somewhat defiant approach to Jewish pride by calling his satire-soaked country band the Texas Jewboys. The name was a play on legendary country swing band Bob Wills and the
Texas Playboys and, Friedman says, it represented "the twin cultures from which
I spring forth: Jewish and Texas." His approach, in which he tried to defuse the
epithet "Jewboy," was misunderstood by some, including the Jewish Defense
League, which threatened his life. Where does that Texas Jewboy defiance come
from? It could be, says the singer-songwriter turned crime novelist, that "the
independent Texas spirit makes for a stronger Jew. It could be that we're not intimidated." That concept is exemplified by one of his best-known songs, "They

Ain't Making Jews Like Jesus Anymore," in which the protagonist fails to turn
the other cheek. (Nearly twenty years after Friedman's debut, singer-songwriter
Dan Bern embarked on a concert tour with a backup band dubbed the International Jewish Banking Conspiracy.)

Not every Jewish pop star's behavior was as exemplary as his or her art or craft.
Then again, the Torah is filled with flawed leaders and kings. "It was a chaotic,
crazy time," Barry Goldberg says of sixties rock-and-rebel culture. "We were like
guinea pigs for chemists and drug dealers." Some converted, or practiced other
religions. Many have intermarried (though many of that number have retained
their Jewish identity and are raising Jewish children). Rockers observing Shabbat? Not many. In fact, many Jewish pop singers have recorded best-selling
Christmas albums. Neil Diamond has recorded two. Credit contemporary jazz
saxophonist Kenny G (Gorelick), who recorded one of the hottest-selling Christmas albums of the nineties, for also releasing "The Jazz Service," music for
Shabbat eve, though he did that in 1986 before he became a superstar. (Producer
Brooks Arthur explains the Jews-making-Christmas-albums trend this way:
"Christmas is American now, a national holiday that on a lot of levels no longer
is religious, and Christmas sales are 60 to 70 percent of annual sales at retail, so
why not get on the ride? And if you make some money from a Christmas album,
give *tzedakah*, give money to your shul.")

Many Jewish rockers *are* role models, whether they intend to be or not. They
try to acknowledge, observe, or worship as best as they can in an industry in
which it is difficult to do so.

Bob Dylan did take time out to observe Yom Kippur. His son-in-law, rocker
Peter Himmelman, best known for scoring the TV show *Judging Amy*, is the Sandy
Koufax of rock 'n' roll. He does not perform on Shabbat, let alone Rosh Hashanah or Yom Kippur. The three Jewish members of the Jakob Dylan–led Wallflowers, who catapulted to fame in 1997 with the Grammy-winning album *Bringing Down the Horse*, make an effort to recite the blessings over the wine and bread
to acknowledge Shabbat, before performing on Friday nights. The band's secret
weapon is keyboard player Rami Jaffee, who the others refer to as "Rabbi Rami."

These days, Himmelman and Jaffee are far from alone. Something is beginning to stir in the hearts and minds of Jews—young and old—in the music
business. They are more willing to discuss their Jewishness and, in many cases,
less reluctant to let it show. Even the acerbic Lou Reed took part in the third an-

nual nonsectarian Knitting Factory Cyber-Seder on April 12, 1998 ("the third night") in the promenade at Avery Fisher Hall at New York's Lincoln Center. All 640 seats were sold for what was also a United Jewish Appeal (now called United Jewish Communities) fund-raiser. And organizers estimate between six thousand and eight thousand people visited the Cyber-Seder Web site. Reed performed the part of the wise child. Sandra Bernhard, John Zorn, the Klezmatics, Hannah Fox of the band Babe the Blue Ox, as well as a host of avant garde New York musicians, also participated in the performance Seder. Knitting Factory owner Michael Dorf (who opened the club in 1988 using money saved from his bar mitzvah) has turned his place into a flagship performance space for Jewish musicians, especially those playing jazz, klezmer, and experimental music. In 1998, he released the debut CD on his new Jewish Alternative Movement (JAM) record label, *The Jewish Alternative Movement: A Guide for the Perplexed*, featuring the Klezmatics, Hasidic New Wave, and former Captain Beefhart guitarist Gary Lucas.

Spin Doctors drummer Aaron Comess says he didn't realize until recently that studying for his bar mitzvah was one of the musical highlights of his life. This from a guy who co-wrote a pair of Top Twenty hits, "Little Miss Can't Be Wrong," and "Two Princes," and whose band's debut album in 1992 sold five million copies. "I was brought up in a kosher home," Comess says. "I was playing piano at five, and always knew music was what I wanted to do. Studying the tropes, the melody notations of the Torah, was an amazing musical experience. We had an incredible cantor at our temple and he made me learn the hardest melodies, and the melodies they use on a lot of these prayers are incredible. I learned how to sing and read Hebrew. It was a real drag then, but looking back it was a pretty cool thing." (Spin Doctors co-founder and singer Christopher Barron — whose last name is Gross — is also Jewish. The band even included an Israeli guitairst, Eron Tabib, for a while.) If Janis Ian's newer songs received the radio play songs such as "Society's Child" and "At Seventeen" received in the sixties and seventies, more people would have discovered "Tattoo," her song about the Holocaust, which was on her 1993 album *Breaking Silence.*

The Holocaust, in fact, has served as a dark influence for many Jewish (and some non-Jewish) songwriters. Aside from Ian, Bob Dylan, Procol Harum's Keith Reid, Dan Bern, Peter Himmelman, Kinky Friedman, Jill Sobule, Dan Pritzker of the funk 'n' roll band Sonia Dada, David Draiman of hardcore band

Disturbed, the rapper Remedy (Ross Filler), and non-Jewish Captain Beefheart (Don Van Vliet), are among those who have grappled in song with the ultimate calamity of the twentieth century. Reid and Bern, as well as Billy Joel, Kiss founder Gene Simmons, Rush singer and bass player Geddy Lee (born Gary Lee Weinreb), are children of Holocaust survivors. So are Lee Oskar of WAR, Ten Wheel Drive lead singer Genya Ravan, and Bob Glaub, one of rock's most respected bass players. Disturbed's Draiman is the grandson of survivors.

Receiving a Jewish education was influential, too. Toronto-born songwriter and singer Eddie Schwartz credits attending Zionist summer camps from ages nine through fifteen for helping him develop his musicianship and songwriting themes. "I learned lots of Hebrew folk songs and dances of modern Israel. I think the wonderful spirit of those songs, the spirit of strength through adversity had an influence on me and is thematic to what I do as a writer. I have tremendous pride about that," Schwartz says.

As Jewish musicians and songwriters reached their forties, more began to reflect on their heritage. Mickey Raphael, who traces his family to Sephardic Jews of Spain, spends much of his free time on tour with Willie Nelson reading about Jewish history and Kabbalah. Many of his books were provided by a Reform rabbi he met after a Willie Nelson concert at the kosher Concord Hotel in New York in 1991. "I'm really interested in Judaism now. I love the history," says Raphael, a Reform Jew. "I think when I turned forty I wanted to find out more. Maybe it's because your mortality comes into focus and you begin to look for some meaning in life."

Something keeps pulling people back to reconnect with their Judaism.

Take tough-as-nails record executive Henry Stone (born Epstein). He started in the record business in 1948, made some of the first records by Ray Charles, James Brown, and Sam and Dave, and gave a break to a couple of eager kids who would go on to form KC and the Sunshine Band. Unable to have a bar mitzvah at thirteen, he finally became an official son of the commandments in 1992 when he traveled from Miami to Israel with his rabbi and was bar mitzvahed on Masada—at the age of seventy-one. He simply felt compelled to do it. "In my later years, I got more Jewish," says the semiretired record mogul. Just two years before that, Stone's son Joe scored a novelty hit with 2 Live Jews and the album *As Kosher As They Wanna Be*, a parody of the X-rated rap act 2 Live Crew and its controversial album *As Nasty As They Wanna Be*. Included on the comedy record, however, was a more serious song called "Young Jews Be Proud." The younger Stone included a thought-provoking song about Judaism on several subsequent 2 Live Jews releases because, to him, Judaism wasn't just a laughing matter.

In 1991, a Chicago poet named David Berman formed an alternative rock band, and named it Silver Jews to do what Kinky Friedman had tried to do twenty years earlier, which was to reclaim the word Jew, "a beautiful word," says Berman, which anti-Semites had turned into a pejorative one. In 1993, Phish, one of the most popular concert attractions of the nineties, began performing "Avinu Malcanu" and "Yerushalayim Shel Zahav (Jerusalem of Gold)" in concert. Bass player Mike Gordon, one of the band's two Jewish members (drummer Jonathan Fishman is the other) brought the songs to the band to include in its vast repertoire.

In 1995, Judith Edelman, a bright talent and compelling songwriter based in Nashville, released *Perfect World*, the first of three albums melding bluegrass and pop that she recorded through 2000. "I think Judaism manifests itself in my music," said Edelman, the New York–born daughter of 1972 Nobel Prize winner (in medicine) Gerald Edelman. "My whole approach to lyric writing is informed by the way I was brought up, which is with the feeling of being a Jew. When I think of what it feels like to be a Jew, it's with a little bit of sadness in every ounce of happiness. It's never fully light. Jews are not reckless in their happiness. There's always the sense that the other shoe could drop, so pay a little attention to the left hand of God, or to the darker side of life." She added that there's a little bit of redemption in every situation, so her songs, "don't leave things without the possibility of a little bit of sweetness."

In 1997, former Van Halen lead singer David Lee Roth released his autobiography, *Crazy from the Heat*, in which he devoted a whole chapter to Judaism's influence on his life. In 1998, a white, Jewish rapper from Staten Island calling himself Remedy garnered international attention with his gripping hip-hop-style history of the Holocaust. Titled "Never Again," it was featured on a compilation album produced by members of the rap act Wu-Tang Clan. In 1999, singer-songwriter Dan Bern, a purveyor of a combination of folk, rock, and punk styles and stream-of-conscious lyrics, began referring to himself by his original family name Bernstein, reclaiming a part of his Jewish heritage that had become a victim of the Holocaust.

By the end of the nineties, an acoustic rock trio from Boston called Guster, all of whose members are Jewish, had released three albums and gained a national

following. The band's Web site unabashedly, and with great humor, offered clues
as to the band's collective Jewish background. The band's "FAQ" page began
with "Q: Are you guys a Christian band? A: Rather than answer this with a simple
'Yes' or 'No,' we suggest you check the following sources for clues. 1) Brian's last
name is Rosenworcel. 2) Any photo of Ryan where you can see his profile. 3) The
(band's) . . . contract . . . where we stipulate that 'the dressing room must be
furnished with plenty of borscht, noodle kugels, potato latkes, gefilte fish, and
homemade rugulah for dessert.'" If that answer didn't offer enough clues, their
more than occasional performance of "The Dreidel Song" in concert, or the time
one of the band members incorporated a shofar into a show in Vancouver,
should have clinched it. In 2000, the Atlanta-bred duo of Evan and Jaron (Lowenstein) made music history, becoming as far as can be determined, the first observant Jewish pop act to score a Top Twenty hit. The twin brothers, who observe
Shabbat and keep kosher, climbed the charts with a guitar- and harmony-laden
pop-rock song in which they declared they were "Crazy for This Girl." The
Lowensteins proved that the term "religious rocker" wasn't an oxymoron, and
that rock and religion could coexist.

In 2001, a young band from the New York area released its major label debut,
*mission: you*. The band's name overshadowed the album's title, and was spelled
proudly in large type across the cover: The ROSENBERGS. Though not all the
members of the band are Jewish, the band name is a billboard for where the
group's leader, David Fagin, is coming from. He is the product of a Jewish upbringing and proud of it. The name was inspired by a friend's hip, octogenarian
grandparents. Asked how the non-Jewish members of the band feel about the
name, he replied, "A previous member wanted us to change the band name, so
we changed him." (Names can send the wrong signal as well. Because of its
name, many fans of the punk-pop band New Found Glory believe the members
are born-again Christians. In fact, three of the band's five members are Jewish.
Says NFG bass player Ian Grushka, "Sometimes when people ask, I just say,
'Yeah, we're a Christian band.' They'll figure it out sooner or later.")

Even rock's old guard has come a long way. Bassist Harvey Brooks, who
changed his professional name from Goldstein all those years ago, now says this
of the switch: "If I had to do it again, I wouldn't."

These are shining examples of rock 'n' roll's Jewish stories; for the most part
untold tales, but tales that command telling. They are the undercurrents and

subplots that give the music fascinating new context, and in many cases, new meaning. Some of the stories hinted at in this "Overture" are found in detail in the coming pages. You'll also find many other revealing stories. Either way, the singers, songwriters, and musicians gathered here have contributed mightily to the vast ocean that Jewish disc jockey Alan Freed dubbed rock 'n' roll. My hope is that collectively they tell the big story of the all-encompassing role Jews and Judaism have played in making this music. I can't imagine what rock 'n' roll would be without the Stars of David.

# 1950s-1960s

**"The song shall testify before them as a witness."**

DEUTERONOMY 31:21

# Jerry Leiber and Mike Stoller

**Songwriter and producer Jerry Leiber, born April 25, 1933, Baltimore, Maryland. Songwriter, producer, and pianist Mike Stoller, born March 13, 1933, Belle Harbor, Long Island, New York. Created one of the most influential and beloved song catalogs in popular music, and helped define rock 'n' roll. Songs include "Hound Dog," "Jailhouse Rock," "On Broadway," and "Stand By Me." Inducted into the Songwriters Hall of Fame in ?985 and the Rock and Roll Hall of Fame in 1987.**

*Mike Stoller, left, and Jerry Leiber review the sheet music to their song "Jailhouse Rock" with Elvis Presley at MGM Studios in Culver City, California, in 1957. (Photo from the collection of Leiber and Stoller.)*

Jerry Leiber and Mike Stoller met in 1950, after their families moved to Los Angeles. A high school friend had tipped Leiber to a piano player who might provide the music for the lyrics Leiber kept scribbling in a notebook. Stoller wasn't interested when Leiber phoned. He thought Leiber was just another wannabe pop music hack who wouldn't appreciate his love of Charlie Parker, Bartok, and Stravinsky. Not to be denied, the persistent Leiber went to Stoller's house. When Stoller realized that Leiber's poems were really twelve bar blues he quickly changed his tune. The two teens discovered they had much in common. They were East Coast transplants who had a stronger passion for black culture than for their own Jewish roots.

By the time Jerry Leiber discovered that his father, Jake, had been a *hazan* in a shul in Poland before coming to America, his father had been dead for more than sixty years and Jerry had been a songwriting legend for more than forty. Learning of his father's musical background tied Jerry to a tradition he had not known he was a part of. His father, who opened a grocery store after coming to America, died from a cerebral hemorrhage when Jerry was five. His mother, Manya, dismissed Jerry's love of songwriting as child's play. Even when Jerry became rich and famous from penning and producing hit songs and running record labels, his mother never encouraged or congratulated him. So in 1997, when a dying cousin told Jerry about his father's life in Poland, it was especially meaningful. "It was very reassuring in the sense that I didn't make it up myself out of whole cloth, and that I came from some kind of history of music," Leiber says.

His parents had arrived in the United States aboard the Lusitania in 1925 and settled in Baltimore. Jerry was born April 25, 1933. The family, which included two daughters, spoke Yiddish and attended synagogue on holidays. Mrs. Leiber kept a kosher home and lit candles on Shabbat. Jerry remembers being sent to the kosher butcher for chicken and getting blood splattered on his shirt. Jerry, who didn't learn to speak English until he was about five, went to Hebrew school. But it was not a pleasant experience. Leiber remembers the rabbi who taught him as unkempt, autocratic and punishing. To make matters worse, after class, Leiber often had to navigate his way through an anti-Semitic gang in his neighborhood. He carried his books in a brown paper bag so strangers on the street couldn't see the Hebrew lettering. He got beat up so frequently that he signed up for boxing lessons being taught by a priest at a Catholic church. As a child, Leiber equated being Jewish with always having to be on your guard. His bar mitzvah, which he initially viewed as an honor, did not help matters. In front of his family, a substitute rabbi cuffed him on the head for wrapping tefillin on the wrong arm. "I felt humiliated," Leiber recalls. "I was about to hit him when my mother jumped up and said, 'Jerome.'"

In spite of threatening rabbis and street gangs, losing his father at a young age, and growing up poor, Leiber maintained a hardy sense of humor. "There was lots of humor in my house; poor people survive hardship with humor," he says. He also became a mensch, delivering five-gallon cans of kerosene and ten-pound bags of soft coal from his mother's grocery store to black families in the adjoining neighborhood (No other business would deliver to the neighborhood, according to Leiber). The boys in the 'hood never gave him any trouble. "I was trusted and therefore untouchable," Leiber says. "I think they saw me as a bringer of light, the white boy who was serving black people." Walking through the neighborhood, he heard the music and the language that would change his life. He heard the blues. And for Jerry Leiber the blues became "the Bible, the gospel, the truth about almost any subject."

Mike Stoller was born March 13, 1933, grew up in Queens, and was raised with his sister in an atheist household. His father, Abraham, was a draftsman who, during World War II, worked two eight-hour jobs a day and was rarely home. His mother, Adelyn, a model and sometime actress, was a friend of George and Ira Gershwin and had been a schoolmate of their sister Frances. Adelyn's brother was the blacklisted novelist and screenwriter Guy Endore (born Goldberg). Neither parent was particularly religious, nor were Stoller's paternal grandparents. (His maternal grandparents died before he was born.) The family also lived in a Jewish-Italian-Irish neighborhood where many of the resident Jews weren't very observant. Around 1940, some of the Jewish parents in the neighborhood began to feel guilty about depriving their children of a Jewish education and briefly established Jewish culture classes in a storefront to give their kids some Jewish identity. The one-month course included a seder. Stoller did not have a bar mitzvah. Seders at Leiber's house led in Hebrew by Leiber's stepfather, Abe Stein, would provide Stoller with much of his Jewish knowledge and identity. Anti-Semites also reminded Stoller of his roots. "I don't think I experienced anything like Jerry did," Stoller says, " but my sister and I got beaten up by Catholic kids because they said we killed Jesus. I guess that was taught back then." Stoller was taught a Jewish sense of morality and justice. His parents made sure he understood that all people were created equal, and that blacks were just as good as whites, and, like Jews, should not be discriminated against.

Stoller knew since the age of three that he wanted to be an artist; he just didn't know what kind. Even at that age he knew he didn't want "a job," which he equated with keeping his father away from home. Stoller found direction at Camp Wo Chi Ca, an integrated summer camp in Hacketstown, N.J., where he discovered black music. He was seven when he first went off to camp, and heard black teenagers playing boogie-woogie music on piano. Stoller was impressed by one of the teens in particular, would watch him practice, then try to replicate what he had observed. At the end of camp, Stoller continued practicing on the baby grand piano at home and began taking lessons. "By the time I was eight, I could play pretty good boogie-woogie," says Stoller. Around age ten, a neighbor introduced him to the composer and pre-eminent stride pianist (and Queens resident), James P. Johnson. Johnson was amused enough by the eager and determined Stoller to give him lessons. Back at camp, Stoller was introduced to the music of Dizzy Gillespie and Charlie Parker, among others, and fell in love with jazz as well as blues.

Though Leiber and Stoller were crazy about the blues, they also had deep respect and reverence for the great Tin Pan Alley songwriters: the Gershwins, Irving Berlin, Cole Porter, Rogers and Hart, and others. Those were the writers whose songs were timeless, the pair thought. They expected their own songs to be quite disposable with a shelf life of a few months if they were lucky. Their writing chemistry clicked instantly. Stoller called it "spontaneous combustion." He'd start pounding on the piano and Leiber would start shouting words, and if they both liked it, they'd write it down. It wasn't always easy. They had different opinions about everything. But they had a common vision: write authentic blues for blues singers.

Their big-break hit came in 1953 when the duo was asked to write a song for a blues singer named "Big Mama" Thornton. They came up with "Hound Dog." Three years later, unbeknownst to the duo, a young, sexy, fast-rising star named Elvis Presley recorded a version of "Hound Dog." It became a No. 1 hit, established a long and fruitful relationship with Presley, and launched the twin careers of Leiber and Stoller. They initially were unhappy with Presley's version of their song, but that opinion was short-lived as it flew up the charts.

The Leiber–Stoller hit machine was almost silenced before it got started.

Stoller, then twenty-three, was aboard the Italian ocean liner Andrea Doria when it collided with the Swedish cruise ship Stockholm off the coast of Massachusetts on July 26, 1956. Dozens were killed in the disaster. As the ship went down, Stoller thought it was the end. He also thought about praying, but decided not to since he didn't believe in God. His atheism, however, never diminished his Jewish identity. "There's no question that I am Jewish, and proud of it, and would never deny it," he says.

Leiber met a shaken Stoller (because of the Andrea Doria sinking Stoller was afraid to sail or fly for years) and greeted him with the news that "Hound Dog" was a huge hit by some white kid named Elvis Presley. Presley's publishing company asked them for more songs and they obliged. From late 1956 through early 1958, Presley had incredible success recording the duo's songs. "Love Me," "Jailhouse Rock," "Don't," "Loving You," and "Treat Me Nice," were big hits for Presley.

Leiber and Stoller were just getting warmed up. They had moved back to New York in 1957 to work for Atlantic Records, writing and producing for an array of artists. Their most notable post-Elvis success came with a West Coast group called the Coasters, with which they had started recording in Los Angeles before they moved east. Between mid 1957 and 1959, the Leiber-Stoller team wrote half a dozen Top Ten hits for the black vocal group: "Searchin'," "Young Blood," "Yakety Yak," "Charlie Brown," "Along Came Jones," and "Poison Ivy." There was mutual respect and admiration between the singing group and the producers that endured long after their hit-making days had passed. According to Coasters leader Carl Gardner, Leiber and Stoller attended the funerals of group members, and helped their families financially.

Leiber and Stoller productions grew more innovative and complex, with string sections and Latin rhythms, when the pair began producing records by another black vocal group called the Drifters. "There Goes My Baby," "Dance With Me," "On Broadway," "This Magic Moment," "Save the Last Dance For Me," "Up on the Roof," remain classics. Leiber and Stoller also had great success with Drifters lead singer Ben E. King when he opted for a solo career. King scored a pair of Top Ten hits in 1961 with "Spanish Harlem," and the immortal "Stand By Me," which he co-wrote with Leiber and Stoller. (King had a Top Ten hit with the song again in 1986 when it was used as the title of the Rob Reiner–directed film *Stand By Me*.) King scored another hit with a Leiber-Stoller song in 1963, the dramatic "I (Who Have Nothing)." The same year, a song about the nation's limitless opportunity called "Only in America," which the duo co-wrote and produced, became a hit for the all-Jewish vocal group Jay and the Americans. LaVern Baker, Ruth Brown, Edith Piaf, Dion, and Peggy Lee all struck gold with Leiber-Stoller songs. Of the incredibly fertile period from 1953 through 1963, Leiber says, "We were writing from blind intuition. We didn't know where it was coming from. We wrote for each other. We were each other's audience." In 1964, the duo launched Red Bird Records, the label for which the female vocal groups the Dixie Cups ("Chapel of Love") and the Shangri-Las ("Leader of the Pack") recorded.

With the exception of "Is That All There Is?" new material and hit-bound songs became scarce by the late sixties as the duo's interests and responsibilities changed, not to mention the country's tastes. Record companies, however, continued to issue numerous Coasters, Drifters, and Elvis Presley compilations, keeping Leiber-Stoller songs in the public consciousness. Besides being great songwriters, the two also were good businessmen, retaining the rights to their compositions through their own publishing company. Over the years, they also acquired the rights to rock classics such as "Good Lovin'," "Hanky Panky," "Happy Together," "If I Were A Carpenter," "The Twist," and the tunes to the Broadway evergreen, *Fiddler on the Roof*. One of the duo's greatest successes came in 1995 with the Broadway opening of *Smokey Joe's Café: The Songs of Leiber and Stoller*, a smartly produced retrospective of the pair's hits. The show was an enduring hit in England and Australia, as well as the United States, where it surpassed two thousand performances to become the longest-running musical revue in Broadway history.

Throughout the nineties, Leiber watched his two sons, Oliver and Jed, write for, produce, and tour with a variety of acts, including Paula Abdul, Hall and Oates, Jeff Beck, and Rod Stewart. Asked how he felt about his sons following in his footsteps, Leiber, sounding ever the Jewish parent, replied with a wink, "I wish they had become doctors or lawyers."

# Carol Kaye

**Bass and guitar player. Born Carol Smith, Everett, Washington, March 24, 1935. Recording session musician best known for playing on literally hundreds of hit records by Sam Cooke, Elvis Presley, the Beach Boys, Frank Sinatra, Simon and Garfunkel, Stevie Wonder, Sonny and Cher, the Doors, Barbra Streisand, the Supremes, the Temptations, Four Tops, Marvin Gaye, the Monkees, and other acts, as well as the themes to numerous hit TV shows, including *Mission: Impossible, M\*A\*S\*H, Hawaii Five-0,* and *The Brady Bunch.* Kaye is also a prominent bass teacher with a line of instructional books and videos.**

*Carol Kaye, shown here at a recording session in Los Angeles in 1974, says Judaism made her a better musician as well as person. (Photo courtesy of Carol Kaye.)*

In 1960, Carol Kaye, already a sought-after studio musician who had built her industry reputation playing guitar on hit records such as Richie Valens's "La Bamba," began taking classes to convert to Judaism. She had been dating a Jewish businessman named David Fireman and had become fascinated by Judaism's laws, customs, and holidays, as well as a fan of Jewish food and humor. Before her conversion was complete, she learned to cook kreplach soup and tzimmes, made a seder meal, celebrated Hanukkah instead of Christmas, and occasionally attended a Reform temple. Kaye often could be found studying Jewish textbooks during studio breaks. Her diligence impressed Jewish colleagues like fabled drummer Hal Blaine (born Chaim Zalmon Belsky, February 5, 1929, Holyoke, Massachusetts) and distinguished piano player Michael Melvoin (original family name Mehlworm, born May 10, 1937, Oshkosh, Wisconsin). Kaye was born a Baptist, but thought Judaism "made so much more sense." At the end of her conversion course she had a bat mitzvah and was given the name Ruth. She was twenty-five years old. In 1961, she married Fireman. The marriage, her second, ended in 1964, but her affection for Judaism didn't. Upset over the divorce, and looking to distance herself from any ties to her husband, Kaye tried to return to Christianity, but couldn't. She had become rooted to Judaism, and she raised her daughter from that marriage as a Jew. Kaye especially was moved by Judaism's commandments to pursue justice and welcome the stranger. "The word tolerance comes to mind," says Kaye. "I got the feeling that Jews were tolerant toward everybody, and that it was too bad other religions didn't have that same feeling toward others. Judaism was not out to grab your thinking or frighten you. It gave me a feeling of home, like I belonged." Kaye also appreciated Judaism's respect for women, the genius of Yom Kippur and its annual offer of a second chance, and the honesty of the Torah, which was unafraid to illuminate the flaws of Judaism's great leaders. "What better love from God than to recognize the human condition," Kaye says. Kaye also credits Judaism with improving her playing and making her a more soulful musician. "I play better because I have more tolerance in my heart. I'm sure Judaism gave me that tolerance," she says.

Carol Kaye was born Carol Smith in Everett, Washington, and raised in a home filled with music. Her father, Clyde, had played trombone in a World War I military band, Dixieland bands, and theater orchestras. Her mother, Dot, a ragtime and classical pianist, had provided piano accompaniment in silent movie houses during the twenties. Carol was six when her parents moved to southern Califor-

nia in December of 1941 after the bombing of Pearl Harbor. By age nine, however, her parents had divorced. When Carol was thirteen, her mother bought her
a ten-dollar guitar, which came with several free lessons. By then, Carol was
drawn to the music of Duke Ellington, Count Basie, Benny Goodman and Artie
Shaw (born Arthur Jacob Arshawsky, May 23, 1910, in New York City). She was
such a quick study, perhaps from having grown up surrounded by music, that
after only four months of taking lessons her guitar teacher hired her as an instructor. By age fourteen, Carol was transcribing band parts from Shaw's records
and was on the road performing in swing bands. By the mid-fifties, Kaye was
working in Los Angeles area bebop jazz clubs.

One night in late 1957, noted record producer Bumps Blackwell heard Kaye
and offered her a job on a Sam Cooke recording session. She initially was reluctant to lower herself to play pop music, but the money for pop recording sessions
was too good for lesser-paid jazz musicians to refuse. (By then Carol also was
working a day job as a 110-word-a-minute typist to support two children from her
first marriage to musician Al Kaye.) "I came into the studios with a pretty big
name," Carol recalls. "I was a bit of a snob with the attitude of 'Oh, I've got to
play rock now.'" Her first taste of playing on a hit song came in early 1959 when
she contributed rhythm guitar to the Richie Valens hit "La Bamba." In 1960 she
played on the Sam Cooke hit "Wonderful World," and did some sessions with
Lou Rawls. For the next ten years the phone rarely stopped ringing. Some of the
other hits Kaye contributed guitar to early in her career as a studio musician include: The Crystal's "He's a Rebel," "Johnny Angel" by Shelly Fabares, the Beach
Boys' "Surfin' USA," the Searchers' "Needles and Pins," "Little Old Lady from
Pasadena" and "Dead Man's Curve" by Jan and Dean, and the Righteous Brothers' "You've Lost That Lovin' Feelin'." Kaye also played on most of the hits by
Sonny and Cher, contributing the twelve-string guitar parts that became integral
to the duo's sound.

The lucrative studio work allowed her to quit her day job and leave the alcohol-
and smoke-filled nightclubs. She spent five years as a studio guitar player until
1963 when she was asked to fill in for an electric bass player who had failed to
show for a recording session. She found herself at ease with the instrument, enjoyed the greater creative freedom that producers allowed bass players, and loved
the fact that she didn't have to schlep a trunk full of guitars to recording sessions. Kaye's instinct for what a song required, her ability to improvise and com-

pose parts on the fly, the tones she coaxed from her instrument, and her integrity and reliability kept her on Hollywood's studio musician A-list. She was a favorite of producer Phil Spector, helping define his panoramic "wall of sound" approach to making records, and of Beach Boys creative brain trust Brian Wilson. Kaye played bass on numerous recording sessions for the Wilson-led group and is featured on most of the songs on the band's legendary *Pet Sounds* album. Though Brian Wilson wrote most of the bass parts, that's Kaye playing on classics such as "Good Vibrations," "California Girls," "Wouldn't It Be Nice," "God Only Knows," and "Caroline No," among many others.

Motown Records, which had its own celebrated in-house band in Detroit, quietly turned to Kaye and her colleagues to record basic tracks for its acts. Kaye graces such hits as "Ain't Nothing Like the Real Thing" by Marvin Gaye and Tammi Terrell, "Love Child," "Baby Love," "Stop in the Name of Love," "You Can't Hurry Love," and numerous others by the Supremes, and Stevie Wonder's 1967 smash "I Was Made to Love Her." She is also featured on the Glen Campbell hits "Witchita Lineman," "Galveston," and "Rhinestone Cowboy," and she added her touch to "Something Stupid" by Frank and Nancy Sinatra, "The Way We Were" by Barbra Streisand, "I Am a Rock" and "Scarborough Fair" by Simon and Garfunkel, "River Deep, Mountain High" by Tina Turner, and, perhaps most surprisingly, was the bass player on the Doors' No. 1 hit "Light My Fire." Her inventive sixteen-note bass pattern on the Joe Cocker hit "Feelin' Alright," had other bass players scrambling to imitate it. The list goes on and on. Kaye was one of a core group of about 350 musicians, an impressive number of them Jews from the jazz world, who played on most of the pop and rock records made on the West Coast from the late fifties through the early seventies. Pianists Don Randi, Artie Butler, Mike Lang, and Michael Melvoin (his daughter Wendy was a guitarist with Prince and the Revolution, and his late son Jonathan toured with Smashing Pumpkins); guitarist Don Peake, bass player Alf Clausen (who also composed the scores for *The Simpsons* and *Moonlighting* television shows), trumpeters Jules Chaiken and Jack Sheldon, were among the Jewish musicians constantly in demand to play on rock and R&B recording sessions. Many were also talented arrangers. (Beginning in the mid-seventies a new generation of Jewish studio musicians and touring sidemen began to make a reputation for themselves. They included guitarists Danny Kortchmar, Waddy Wachtel and Michael Landau, drummer Kenny Aronoff, bass players Bob Glaub, Tony Levin and Lee Sklar, viola player Novi Novog, and singer Kate Markowitz, among many others.)

Aside from Kaye, perhaps the most prolific and best-known studio musician was the versatile and inventive drummer Hal Blaine. Blaine's credits include playing on six consecutive records that won the Grammy Award for Record of the Year. The records were "A Taste of Honey" by Herb Alpert and the Tijuana Brass ("the Tijuana Brass were all Jewish," Blaine says); "Strangers in the Night" by Frank Sinatra, "Up, Up and Away" by the Fifth Dimension, "Mrs. Robinson" by Simon and Garfunkel, "Aquarius/Let the Sun Shine" by the Fifth Dimension, and "Bridge Over Troubled Water" by Simon and Garfunkel. He also played on most of the hits produced by Phil Spector, including "Be My Baby" in 1963, as well as many Beach Boys classics beginning with "I Get Around" in 1964. His resume includes playing on forty-one No. 1 hits. Blaine grew up poor in a *Yiddishkeit* household in Hartford, Connecticut. His father, Meyer Zabielski (Americanized to Belsky), earned five dollars a week as a shoemaker. To support the family, Meyer worked Saturdays, dropping Hal at a vaudeville theater in downtown Hartford on his way to the shoe shop. Hal saw every major singer, band, dance act, and comedian of the late thirties and early forties, including drummers Gene Krupa and Buddy Rich. By nine, Hal knew he wanted to be a professional drummer. By thirteen, he had his first drum set. At fifteen, his family moved to the West Coast, and by twenty-two he was using Blaine as a stage name and touring with Patti Page and Tommy Sands before the phrase "rock 'n' roll" had been coined. In 1995, Blaine joined mandolin player David Grisman and clarinet and mandolin player Andy Statman for a critically acclaimed album of traditional Jewish music called *Songs of Our Fathers.* In 2000, Blaine was inducted into the Rock and Roll Hall of Fame, the first musician to be inducted in the Hall's new "Sideman" category.

One can only wonder what so many hits would have sounded like without the creative touch of these studio musicians. "Very few rockers played on their own records," Kaye says. "We were all very experienced, and were able to create nice lines and make the songs groove. In the sixties, when Beach Boys fans went out to see them in concert, if the music and the vocals were close enough, it was OK." Unfortunately, most studio musicians rarely received credit for their performances because record companies didn't want fans to know that many of their favorite rock musicians weren't playing on their records. In some cases, non-credited studio musicians improvised the rhythmic or melodic lines that gave the songs their identity. (In 1973, the record industry adopted a policy of giving credit where credit was due.)

In 1969, Kaye wrote her first in a long line of instructional books and later added videos to her repertoire of teaching tools. The list of prominent bass players who have publicly credited Kaye as an influence includes Sting, John Paul Jones of Led Zeppelin, Badfinger's Stu Hamm, Will Lee of the David Letterman Show band, Tiran Porter of the Doobie Brothers, and jazz great Jaco Pastorius. Throughout the seventies, eighties and nineties Kaye gave private lessons, delivered seminars at schools across the country, and performed in various jazz combos with esteemed musicians such as guitarist Joe Pass and the late pianist Hampton Hawes. More recently, she's played California clubs and released several independently produced tapes with a trio called Thumbs Up. In 1998, the Experience Music Project Museum in Seattle, founded by billionaire Paul Allen, sent a film crew to Kaye's home to interview her for its music history archives. She also was hired to record bass for some of its exhibits and present music seminars, and she performed at the museum's opening in June of 2000. Kaye received a Lifetime Achievement Award from Duquesne University in Pittsburgh, and Women in Music presented Kaye with its Touchstone Award for her "pioneering spirit of service to the music industry" in 2000. Kaye continues to teach bass at the Henry Mancini Institute at UCLA, give private lessons, and play on selected recording sessions.

Her life is still guided by the lessons she learned in her conversion classes all those years ago. "My ideas of faith are more closely aligned to Judaism than anything else," Kaye says, adding that, "I will not stand for prejudice against anybody, whether they're black or Jewish or Asian, but especially Jews. 'Never Again' rules me in my dealings with people. The Jewish people practically saved the world with their contribution to science, and art, and music, and psychology, and psychiatry."

# The Tokens

**An all Jewish fifties and sixties doo-wop pop group best known for the
international No. 1 hit "The Lion Sleeps Tonight." Members: Jay Siegel,
born October 20, 1939, Brooklyn, New York; Hank Medress, born
November 19, 1938, Brooklyn, New York; Phil Margo, born April 1,
1942, Brooklyn, New York; Mitch Margo, born May 25, 1947, Brooklyn,
New York. The group's first lineup consisted of Medress, Neil Sedaka,
Eddie Rabkin, and Cynthia Zoliton.**

*The Tokens line up that sang the 1961 classic "The Lion Sleeps Tonight." From top to bottom:
Jay Siegel, Phil Margo, Hank Medress, and Mitch Margo. (Photo courtesy of Jay Siegel.)*

*Tokens lead singer Jay Siegel at the Western Wall in Jerusalem in 1997. (Photo courtesy of Jay Siegel.)*

Everybody thought Jay Siegel should be a cantor. His parents did. Abraham Scheinberg, his rabbi at the Hebrew Alliance Synagogue on Brighton Sixth Street in Brooklyn did; the synagogue's cantor did. Rabbi Scheinberg even announced to the congregation that "One day this boy will be a great cantor." Siegel's voice was so good so soon that by age ten, he was one of just two children in the synagogue's dozen-person choir. Not only did the boy soprano get to sing solos during the High Holidays, he was paid fifty dollars as a choir member. Siegel probably would have done it for free. He was mesmerized by the choir harmony that filled the synagogue during services. "I'll always remember hearing those twelve voices and that beautiful harmony and my big solo in the bridge of 'Avinu Malcanu.' "I got great reviews," recalls Siegel, who would achieve rock 'n' roll immortality as the lead vocalist on the Tokens' No. 1 hit "The Lion Sleeps Tonight."

Siegel grew up in a kosher home. The family lit candles on Friday night and celebrated all the Jewish holidays. Jay followed in his older (by eleven years) brother Jerry's footsteps, and reluctantly attended Hebrew school. His father, Louis, had emigrated from Vienna at age sixteen, arriving in New York stuffed in steerage of an ocean liner. He was Louis Siegenreich before the name was changed to Siegel on Ellis Island, according to family history. Louis worked as a stitcher for a furrier in what son Jay calls sweatshop conditions and made a minimal living. His mother, Yetta, was a housewife. The family was too poor to pay for High Holiday tickets. To hear their son sing, Jay the choirboy would sneak them into the Grand Concourse of the Concourse Plaza Hotel in the Bronx where the congregation held High Holiday services. Even then, Jay didn't sing the parts note-for-note, preferring to follow his heart and do some improvising. For him, music was the most important part of Judaism. "The religious part of Judaism, well," says Siegel, "I wasn't going to be going to yeshiva, but the music got me. Judaism had a major impact on me musically."

A variety of contemporary music could always be heard in the Siegel house in Brooklyn as well, including Tommy Dorsey, Hank Williams, and Bill Monroe. A favorite radio show was the Hometown Frolics program on WJZ in New Jersey. Siegel pursued his growing interest in music at Lincoln High School where he joined the chorus and met a kindred spirit in Neil Sedaka (born March 13, 1939).

In 1955, Sedaka formed a vocal group called the Linc-Tones that would later become the Tokens. When one of the members left in 1956, Sedaka asked Siegel to audition for the group. In those days singing groups were on every corner, but what elevated the Tokens (who were all Jewish) above the rest, says Siegel, was Sedaka's songwriting. Sedaka, the grandson of a cantor, had shown musical talent as early as kindergarten and had a natural affinity for the piano. Throughout his childhood, while his neighborhood friends played ball Neil practiced piano. Sedaka, collaborating with childhood friend Howard Greenfield, would go on to have a stellar solo career with nearly two dozen Top Forty hits between 1958 and 1980, including "Calendar Girl," "Happy Birthday, Sweet Sixteen," "Laughter in the Rain," and the classic "Breaking Up Is Hard to Do." The latter was a No. 1 hit in 1962 and reached the Top Ten again, as a ballad, in late 1975.

But from 1956 through 1958, while all the other street corner doo-wop groups were singing the radio hits of the day, the Tokens were singing Sedaka originals, getting noticed, and signing recording contracts. Sedaka's songwriting and Siegel's soaring falsetto made for a potent combination. The name Tokens was selected by a manager and had nothing to do with subway or bus tokens, but tokens of affection. "I disliked the name," says Siegel, "until we had a No. 1 record."

By the time the Tokens first hit the charts, Sedaka was a half-dozen hits into a successful solo career. When the Tokens had their first hit in the spring of 1961 with "Tonight I Fell in Love," the group consisted of Siegel, Hank Medress, and brothers Phil and Mitch Margo. (The Margo brothers' father had changed the family name to Margo from Margulies.) The members, still in their teens and early twenties, made a point of being home for the Jewish holidays. The Siegel and Phil Margo families continue to celebrate holidays together.

The Tokens got their first taste of anti-Semitism on a tour of the South to support "Tonight I Fell in Love." Recalls Siegel: "We were refused hotel rooms between New York and Florida. We couldn't find any temples in South Carolina and Georgia. Being Jews from New York was a double problem. They looked down on us right away."

Throughout their singing career all the members continued their education and all graduated from college. Siegel got a degree in market research; the others earned degrees in economics and physical education, in case fame was fleeting. "In Jewish households, education was the most important," Siegel says. Besides, Siegel never actually thought he could make a living singing; it was too much fun. His father had worked in a sweatshop. His brother was an architectural draftsman. Neither could wait for Friday, and both hated Monday. To be in the music business and make money was a dream come true. In late 1961, at the age of twenty-two, Siegel was about to make his dream-come-true last a lifetime. The Tokens reworked the South African folk song "Mbube" (Zulu for lion), a hit for the Weavers in 1952 as "Wimoweh." The noted RCA Victor Records production team of "Hugo and Luigi" retitled it "The Lion Sleeps Tonight."

The Tokens version opened with Siegel doing some instantly grabbing sky-high vocal gymnastics more akin to yodeling than doo-wop. Siegel took the Weavers' version, which was almost a *niggun* with the sole lyric "a wimoweh, a wimoweh, a wimoweh," a step farther, adding lyrics about a mighty jungle, a sleeping lion, a peaceful village, and a darling asked to "hush." He also rewrote the melody of the second half of each verse. With its tom-tom drum fills, loping rhythm, ghostly, opera-like trilling in the background, soprano saxophone solo coming out of nowhere, pumped up vocal arrangements, Siegel practically growling—and all of that occurring simultaneously at one point—the Tokens reinvented the song. The result: a couple of minutes of magic that hit No. 1 in thirty-six countries, including Israel, stayed in the Top Ten on the *Billboard* charts for three months, and sold three million copies. The Tokens became one of the first American pop groups to tour Europe. The irony of "four poor Jewish kids" being cheered by adoring fans as they rode in limousine luxury through Spain in the early sixties did not escape them.

Since 1961, the Tokens' version of "Mbube/Wimoweh" has been used in eleven films, numerous commercials, and the TV sitcom *Friends*. When RCA Records re-released the song in 1994 in conjunction with its appearance in the film *The Lion King*, it became a hit a second time around, selling 250,000 copies in the United States. "Thirty seconds of the song sung by a warthog and a miercat, and it became a hit all over again," Siegel says. Not surprisingly, the group made no money on the hit in 1961; they were young, and they say they "got ripped off." But they were smart enough to learn about the music business. The Tokens found themselves back in the Top 40 twice more with lesser hits "I Hear Trumpets Blow," No. 30 in 1966, and "Portrait of My Love," No. 36 in 1967. By then, however, the group had formed its own record label (B. T. Puppy, a take off on RCA Victor's dog Nipper) and publishing and production companies, Bright Tunes Music and Bright Tunes Productions. The quartet became the first vocal group to produce a hit by another vocal group. Under the Tokens' guidance, the Chiffons' "He's So Fine" reached No. 1 in 1963. The Tokens also scored big in the mid-sixties, producing all the hits by the Happenings, including "See You in September," and "I Got Rhythm." The latter was a catchy rearrangement of George and Ira Gershwin's tune from the 1930 musical, *Girl Crazy.* Throughout the seventies, the Tokens' production company also was involved in all the hits for Tony Orlando and Dawn, including "Candida," "Knock Three Times," and "Tie a Yellow Ribbon 'Round the Ole Oak Tree." The group also wrote, produced, and sang on a number of national radio and TV commercials.

Siegel still tours with a version of the Tokens but is the only original member from the group's "Lion" heyday. Phil and Mitch Margo operate B. T. Music and B. T. Productions from California and occasionally perform as "the Tokens featuring Phil and Mitch Margo." Hank Medress runs Bottom Line Records, a boutique record label distributed by entertainment behemoth BMG. "We didn't break up because we hated each other," Siegel says. "It was just geographical. We still work together, and we're good friends."

# Al Kooper

**Songwriter. Producer. Arranger. Keyboard player. Guitar player. Singer. College professor. Born Alan Peter Kuperschmidt, February 5, 1944, Brooklyn, New York. Member of the Royal Teens; co-writer of the hit "This Diamond Ring"; originator and player of Hammond organ part on Bob Dylan's "Like a Rolling Stone"; member of the Blues Project, founder of Blood, Sweat and Tears; Lynyrd Skynyrd producer.**

*Playing a Hasidic Jew in the 1985 music video "Born in East L.A." came easily for Al Kooper, left, on the set with guitarist Jeff Beck and actor Cheech Marin. Marin was spoofing the Bruce Springsteen hit "Born in the USA." (Photo by Henry Diltz.)*

Al Kooper is the Forrest Gump of rock 'n' roll. He's been there and done that in just about every capacity there is in the music business. He joined his first national act at age fourteen, the Royal Teens ("Short Shorts"), and just kept on going, later co-writing "This Diamond Ring," and the Gene Pitney hit "I Must Be Seeing Things." He was part of Bob Dylan's studio band for the recording of the classic 1965 *Highway 61 Revisited* album and played in Dylan's backing band at the Newport Folk Festival in 1965 when Dylan "went electric." He even served as assistant stage manager for the watershed 1967 Monterey Pop Festival. He was the creative soul behind the Blues Project and Blood, Sweat and Tears. He played on, arranged and/or produced records by dozens of folk, pop, and rock acts, including the Who (*The Who Sell Out*), Jimi Hendrix (*Electric Ladyland*), the Rolling Stones (*Let It Bleed*), and former Beatles George Harrison (*Somewhere in England*) and Ringo Starr (*Starr Struck: The Best of Ringo Starr*). As a talent scout for MCA Records, he nurtured, signed to a recording contract, and produced the first three albums of one of the great American rock bands, Lynyrd Skynyrd. He became an author, penning an entertaining autobiography in 1977, *Backstage Passes and Backstabbing Bastards: Memoirs of a Rock 'n' Roll Survivor*, which was updated and reissued in 1998.

He became a music professor spending a couple of years in the late nineties teaching songwriting and record production at the Berklee College of Music in Boston, and he also began writing a monthly column for EQ magazine, a trade publication for audio professionals. All the while, he never stopped making records, or playing concerts with his latest band, the Rekooperators, or doing one-man club shows. As Kooper explains in Backstage Passes, "My philosophy was that you couldn't afford the luxury of being in the right place at the right time. You had to try and be every place at every time, and hope that you might wind up anyplace at all." Al Kooper, in other words, was the prototypical, fast-talking self-promoter, with one major factor separating him from so many others: he had an incredible amount of talent. He also had vision, and a passion for all kinds of music.

Kooper was born in Brooklyn but grew up in Queens. His father, Sam, was an attorney. His mother, Natalie, was a housewife and travel agent. They changed the family name from Kuperschmidt shortly after Al was born. ("I guess they knew I was destined for greatness," Kooper jokes of the name change.) Kooper attended Hebrew school, was bar mitzvahed, then had the life-changing experience of hearing Elvis Presley. Early thoughts of following in his father's legal footsteps, and any distant thoughts of pursuing more Jewish education, ended where Elvis began.

Kooper was already a music fan. His father had an impressive jazz and blues record collection, and his mother played the radio in the house all the time. In 1955, when rock was in its birthing stage, eleven-year-old Kooper bought his first 45 rpm single. The choice boiled down to "The Closer You Are" by the Channels and "Autumn Leaves" by Roger Williams, "and the Channels won," he says. Kooper discovered his own musical gift even earlier. When he was six he sat down at a piano at a friend's house and played the instrument without a lesson, tapping out "Tennessee Waltz" (a No. 1 hit for Patti Page in 1950), on the black keys, "like Irving Berlin," he says. For the rest of his life, he remained, with few exceptions, self-taught.

How divine his musical gift was didn't strike him until much later. Though Kooper is not an observant Jew, he has a strong belief in a supreme being and credits God with his musical abilities. "There's religion involved in this; there's belief in God," Kooper says. "There are things I can do, and I don't understand how I'm able to do them—play instruments, arrange music instantly . . . so I have to think that [God] is at work here. That's the way I look at it. I don't understand where else it could have come from."

By the time Kooper discovered Elvis around age thirteen, he was confident of his musical abilities. He'd also taught himself guitar and joined his first band, the Aristo-Cats, which earned a few bucks playing temple and church dances. He eventually graduated to the Royal Teens. (Kooper admits that this was not the life his parents had envisioned for him, and says, "There was a lot of sneaking around going on at this time.") His brief tenure in the Royal Teens, however, directed the rest of his life. He'd become a rock musician, and he'd stay a rock musician, though actually earning a living from it at that stage of the game was far from a sure thing. Kooper tried just about everything to earn a living in the business, and in the process learned engineering and production as well as songwriting craft.

Around 1963, he was teamed with a pair of lyricists named Bob Brass and Irwin Levine. Kooper calls the collaboration a very Jewish experience. "We spoke a lot of Yiddish," he says, "but by now we're smoking pot, and matzahs just don't get it." The partnership was successful. The trio penned an R&B-flavored song with the Drifters in mind. The Drifters were on a roll with hits such as "Up on the Roof," "On Broadway," and "Under the Boardwalk" (all written by Jewish songwriting teams). Instead, the song by Kooper and company was reworked and recorded by a new band called Gary Lewis and the Playboys. Released in late 1964, "This Diamond Ring" reached No. 1 in early 1965. A few months later, singer Gene Pitney took a Kooper-Brass-Levine song, "I Must Be Seeing Things," to No. 31 on the charts. (Kooper and Levine also wrote "I Can't Quit Her," which ended up on the first Blood, Sweat and Tears album and became a staple of Kooper concerts and recordings.) Of the trio, Levine would go on to have the most commercial songwriting success, co-authoring the Tony Orlando and Dawn smashes "Candida," "Knock Three Times," and "Tie a Yellow Ribbon 'Round the Ole Oak Tree." Later in 1965, producer Tom Wilson invited Kooper to observe a Bob Dylan recording session for Dylan's next album, *Highway 61 Revisited*. In a story that is now part of rock legend, Kooper, ever the chutzpah-charged angler, arrived early and set up his guitar in the studio with his eye on participating. His hopes of playing guitar were torpedoed when Dylan arrived with a precocious guitarist who was so impressive while warming up that Kooper lost all guitar-playing courage. But he wasn't deterred completely. When the session's keyboard player, Paul Griffin, was shifted from Hammond organ to piano to record a song called "Like a Rolling Stone," Kooper, who wasn't very experienced on the Hammond organ (he didn't even know how to turn it on), bluffed his way into playing it on the recording session. Kooper claimed (falsely, of course), that he had come up with a great organ part for the tune. Dylan liked what he heard. The organ was turned up in the mix, the song reached No. 2 in August of 1965, and Kooper's organ playing became one of rock's most recognizable sounds. Even before the song became a hit, Dylan invited Kooper to join his backing group (members of the Paul Butterfield Blues Band, among others) for his landmark performance at the Newport Folk Festival in July. In one bold move Kooper had joined rock's A-list. He was twenty-one years old. When asked what possessed him to make a grab for the empty organ seat, Kooper simply replied, "Ambition." Kooper backed Dylan on at least a half dozen more albums throughout the pair's intertwined careers, including the classic *Blonde on Blonde* in 1966, *New Morning* and *Self Portrait* in 1970, and *Empire Burlesque* in 1985. Kooper also performed numerous concerts with him well into the nineties. Producer Wilson next invited Kooper to play keyboards on an audition tape by a new band called the Blues

Project. Invited to join the band, Kooper became the group's primary songwriter, arranger and driving musical force. More than thirty years after the band's 1968 demise, Hannah Blumenfeld, mother of Project drummer Roy Blumenfeld remarked of Kooper, "Now, that boy had talent"—not that her son didn't. The band released three critically acclaimed albums between 1966 and 1968—*Live at the Café au Go Go, Projections,* and *Live at Town Hall.* Ego clashes and the proverbial "creative differences" caused Kooper to leave in 1967, before the release of *Town Hall.* The Blues Project never had a Top Forty hit, but the Kooper-penned songs "Flute Thing," "Wake Me, Shake Me," and his arrangement of "I Can't Keep From Crying Sometimes," from the *Projections* album became FM radio favorites. (More than two decades later, the Beastie Boys and MC Serch, both Jewish hip-hop acts, would "sample" the original "Flute Thing" on their records.)

Kooper had written a new batch of songs with a horn section in mind. He wanted to add horns to rock's basic lineup of guitar, bass, drums and keyboards. With members of Blues Project vetoing the idea, he fulfilled that vision by putting together Blood, Sweat and Tears. With its propulsive big band–like horns, classical string arrangements, orchestral overture, and psychedelic electric guitar, not to mention fine songs, the band's debut album, *Child Is Father to the Man* (Columbia Records), was, like some of the Blues Project's work, groundbreaking and exhilarating. And like the Blues Project before it, all the wonderful reviews in the world couldn't help Blood, Sweat and Tears sell records and attain hit status. The weakness of both bands, critics claimed, was also the strength: Al Kooper. He could write, play, and arrange, but he wasn't considered a great singer. He wasn't a terrible singer, either. Like Michael Bloomfield's bluesier Electric Flag debut, *A Long Time Comin',* which also married horns to rock and was also on Columbia Records, Kooper's *Child* sounds as vital today as it did in 1968. Resisting pressure to give Blood, Sweat and Tears a more commercial pop sound, Kooper left. He took a job as a staff producer with Columbia Records, and some of his song selections and arrangements were included on Blood, Sweat and Tears' self-titled follow up. The record included the hits "You've Made Me So Very Happy," "Spinning Wheel," and "And When I Die," and it became a commercial smash with all three songs reaching No. 2 on the record charts.

One of his early projects as a staff producer was *Super Session,* featuring Michael Bloomfield and Stephen Stills. (Keyboard player Barry Goldberg and bass player Harvey Brooks also played prominent roles on the record.) Released in

1968, the record was a hit. The following year, Kooper also tasted success as a talent scout when he signed the Zombies ("She's Not There," "Tell Her No"), whose fortunes had been flagging, to a one-album recording contract. The deal resulted in the album *Odyssey and Oracle*, and the No. 3 hit "Time of the Season" in early 1969. Kooper also released *I Stand Alone*, the first in a long line of solo albums. Again, reviews were favorable, but sales were not. Also released that year was the double album, *The Live Adventures of Mike Bloomfield and Al Kooper*, taken from a series of concerts at the Fillmore West in San Francisco.

Kooper's career continued to be one of the most eclectic in all of popular music, as he wrote, produced, arranged, served as a backup musician on recording sessions, and released his own records. In the early seventies, he formed his own record label, Sounds of the South in conjunction with MCA Records. In 1972, he heard Lynyrd Skynyrd in an Atlanta bar, signed the band to a record deal, and produced the group's first three albums. The first, *Pronounced Leh-'Nerd Skin-'Nerd*, released in 1973, included the rock classic "Free Bird," as well as radio staples "Gimme Three Steps" and "Simple Man." The band's 1974 follow up, *Second Helping*, included the Top Ten hit "Sweet Home Alabama." Skynyrd's third release in 1975, *Nuthin' Fancy*, included the Top Thirty hit "Saturday Night Special."

Kooper also managed to record another solo album that year, *Act Like Nothing's Wrong*. Between the first and second Skynyrd records, Kooper also put together a Blues Project reunion in New York's Central Park, which was released as an album. During the second half of the seventies the tireless Kooper also produced albums by The Tubes and Nils Lofgren, played keyboards on albums by Roger McGuinn, the Nitty Gritty Dirt Band, Leo Sayer, and Bill Wyman, and wrote an autobiography. He stayed busy in the eighties recording with the likes of B. B. King, Was (Not Was), Roy Orbison, and Ringo Starr. Between 1987 and 1989, he scored the TV cop show *Crime Story*. In the nineties, much of it based out of Nashville, Kooper worked with a wide variety of acts that included the Byrds, Trisha Yearwood, Taj Mahal, Gloria Estafan, Neil Diamond, and Phoebe Snow. Back in New York, he began playing with a band he dubbed the Rekooperators, which featured members of the bands from late night TV's *David Letterman Show* and *Conan O'Brien Show*. In 1992, he participated in Columbia Record's star-studded thirtieth anniversary tribute to Bob Dylan at Madison Square Garden in New York, playing Hammond organ on "Like a Rolling Stone." In 1994, to celebrate his fiftieth birthday, Kooper once again reunited the Blues Project, as well as much of the original Blood, Sweat and Tears, and, with the Rekooperators on board as well, recorded a series of performances at New York's Bottom Line. The resulting thirty-six song, two-CD set was released in 1995. Titled *Soul of a Man: Al Kooper Live*, it reprised the best work of Kooper's career, and showcased him as an engaging live act.

In 1998, he became a visiting professor at the Berklee College of Music in Boston. Amidst this flurry of activity, Kooper found time to finish and record a gospel-flavored song he'd been working on for years. It was called "Living in My Own Religion," and explained Kooper's spiritual outlook. While he has yet to include the song on a record, he said this about being Jewish: "I don't really consider myself a member of any religious sect, but I have a healthy belief in, and respect for God, although I'm definitely Jewish. My roots are Jewish. I'm Jewish, there's no mistaking that, but post–bar mitzvah, my religion changed to simply a love of God."

# Jay and the Americans

**All-Jewish vocal group from New York City. Members included Kenny Vance, born Kenny Rosenberg, December 9, 1943; Jay Black, born David Blatt, born November 2, 1938; Howie Kane, born Howard Kirschenbaum, June 6, 1940; Sandy Deane, born Sandy Yaguda, January 30, 1940, and Marty Sanders, born Marty Kupersmith, February 28, 1941. Best known for the hits "Only America," "Come a Little Bit Closer," "Lets Lock the Door and Throw Away the Key," "Cara, Mia," "This Magic Moment," and, with original lead singer John "Jay" Traynor, "She Cried."**

*Jay and the Americans circa 1963. Back row from left, Jay Black (b. David Blatt), Howie Kane (b. Howie Kirshenbaum), and Sandy Deane (b. Sandy Yaguda); seated in front, Kenny Vance (b. Kenny Rosenberg) and Marty Sanders (b. Marty Kupersmith). (Photo courtesy Bob Nemser.)*

The story of Jay Black and Kenny Vance could be titled "Trading Places." Vance grew up Kenny Rosenberg in a somewhat assimilated American Jewish household in Brooklyn. He disliked going to synagogue and couldn't wait to get through Hebrew school, get his bar mitzvah over with, and pursue his dream of becoming a singer. He describes his behavior in Hebrew school as "pathetic." By the age of forty, however, long after achieving stardom with Jay and the Americans, he was laying tefillin, davening every day, and keeping kosher. "At thirteen, I heard Frankie Lyman," Vance says. "Those records inspired me in a way that made me crazy, in an emotional way that touched me that is difficult to explain. I think as time went by, and I was exposed to an authentic form of Judaism rooted in spirituality, that Judaism touched me the way rock 'n' roll touched me when I was thirteen, fourteen, fifteen. That's the way Judaism affected me."

Jay Black was born David Blatt in Queens, and grew up in a strict Orthodox household in Brooklyn. He wore payess, spoke Yiddish fluently, davened every day, attended yeshiva, and sang in a synagogue choir. By the age of fourteen, however, long before achieving stardom with Jay and the Americans, he was acting like a thug and was thrown out of more than one religious school. "I was always entertaining the guys in my class at the expense of the teachers, and the rabbis hated me," Black says, admitting to setting a rabbi's chair on fire on one occasion. He was angry at all the restrictions he felt Judaism placed on him and felt cheated at not being able to do things other kids did such as celebrate Christmas or play ball on Saturday. Though he disliked school, at home he read several newspapers a day, as well as books on American history. He also loved listening to music on the radio and imitating everyone he heard, including his greatest influence, operatic tenor Mario Lanza. The one place he felt comfortable was singing in the choir of Temple Beth-El in Boro Park when he was twelve and thirteen; the music reminded him of the operatic voices he heard on the radio. By the time Black reached adulthood, however, he was a card-carrying member of the National Rifle Association, and Jewish observance had dwindled to refraining from working on the High Holy Days in deference to his father's wishes. Still, identifying as a Jew remained important to him, and he worked to make sure that his four children maintained pride in being Jewish. "It's a little hypocritical in way," he admits, "I don't observe the holidays except for what my dad instilled in me."

For teenage Kenny Vance, spirituality in the 1950s was a Frankie Lyman record (Lyman is best known for the 1956 hit "Why Do Fools Fall In Love"). Vance spent hours in the basement of his home analyzing the songs of Frankie Lyman and the Teenagers and the other hit records by primarily black doo-wop and R&B groups. He learned the various vocal parts, then performed the songs with friends on Brooklyn street corners and on the boardwalk at Brighton Beach. By age fifteen, Vance had begun hanging out in the Brill Building (actually several buildings on Broadway that housed the offices of music publishing and record companies). He also attended disc jockey Alan Freed's rock 'n' roll revues in Brooklyn, joined a group with Sandy Yaguda called the Harbor-Lites, and in 1959 released a single on Ivy Records, "Is That Too Much to Ask?"

In 1961, along with Yaguda, Howie Kirschenbaum and John "Jay" Traynor, the quartet auditioned for the hot songwriter/producer team of Jerry Leiber and Mike Stoller. The producers liked what they heard, but before recording the group, wanted to rename it Binky Jones and the Americans. Group members successfully lobbied for Jay and the Americans, then recorded a new version of "Tonight" from *West Side Story*. Though the group's roots and influences were in streetcorner doo-wop and rhythm and blues, it evolved into a cleancut pop group that featured impeccable harmonies over string-sweetened Latin rhythms. The group had a knack for reinterpreting popular Broadway show tunes, and "Brill Building" songs that previously were hits for black acts and turning them into hits again. "Tonight" was a regional hit, doing well enough to merit another release. A song called "Dawning" was released in 1962, but it was the flip side of the single, "She Cried," that became the group's first Top Ten hit, reaching No. 5 in the spring of 1962. After the success of the song, Traynor left the group for an ill-fated solo career. In the meantime, the group had added guitarist Marty Sanders to the lineup, and Sanders recommended his songwriting partner, David Blatt, to fill the lead singer void. Blatt and Sanders had recorded with little success as the Two Chaps, and later as the Empires. Blatt auditioned for the Americans and his booming voice easily won him the job. (Blatt didn't tell anyone he had to overcome stage fright. It took a year before he stopped getting nauseous before every show.) Older by six years, Blatt became Vance's "irreverent mentor." The group's first hit (after several misfires), with its new "Jay," was "Only in America," written by Leiber and Stoller, and Barry Mann and Cynthia Weil. The song originally was intended for, and recorded by, the Drifters. Atlantic Records, however, didn't think it was appropriate for a black group in the early sixties to be singing a song about all the opportunities America afforded its citizens. (Leiber and Stoller wanted the Drifters to do the song to point out such hypocrisy.) Jay and the Americans lobbied to record the song. The Drifters' voices were erased from the tape, Jay and the Americans' were added, and the song reached No. 25 in September of 1963.

The Jewish quintet followed "Only in America" with one of its most popular songs, "Come a Little Bit Closer," which reached No. 3 in 1964. Though it's unclear exactly when and why all the group members changed their names (Vance recalls it was around 1962 after having a difficult time during a tour through the south), David Blatt accidentally became Jay Black during a 1964 appearance on *The Mike Douglas Show.* After the group's performance, Blatt sat down for a chat, and Douglas said, "Great performance Jay. What's your last name?" Douglas interpreted the mumbled response of "Blatt" as "Black" on national television, and Blatt embraced the error.

The group also became the answer to a trivia question earlier that year: Who was the opening act for the Beatles' first concert in the United States, held in Washington, D.C.? Jay and the Americans played the same role for the Rolling Stones in 1965, a year that found "Jay" and friends in the Top Twenty with "Let's Lock the Door (and Throw Away the Key)," "Cara, Mia," "Some Enchanted Evening," and "Sunday and Me." The latter song has the distinction of being the first Neil Diamond-penned song to become a hit. In 1967, in a nod to their collective Jewish roots, Jay and the Americans recorded a Barry Sisters song, "Vi iz dus Gesele," ("Where is the Village") that Black adapted and translated from the Yiddish. Black also adapted one of his mother's favorite songs, "It's a Big, Wide Wonderful World," a pre–World War II hit for Buddy Clark (born Samuel Goldberg). The songs appeared on the group's album, *Try Some of This,* which was a commercial disappointment. The Americans bounced back when their version of "This Magic Moment," a hit for the Drifters in 1960, reached No. 6 in 1969. Their version of the Ronettes' "Walking in the Rain" reached No. 19 in 1970, and turned out to be the group's Top Forty swan song. By the end of 1971, the original Jay and the Americans were rock 'n' roll history. (Its backup band at this time included Donald Fagen and Walter Becker, the founders of Steely Dan.)

Jay Black kept the group's music and name alive touring as Jay Black and the Americans, or as Jay Black. In 1971, Kenny Vance produced the first pre–Steely Dan album for Becker and Fagen, a film soundtrack album called *You Gotta Walk*

*It Like You Talk It.* Vance released a solo album in 1975, then became a music supervisor for films. In 1978, he not only selected the music for *American Hot Wax*,
he created a band called the Planotones to be in the film, a loose biography of DJ
Alan Freed, the man credited with coining the term "rock 'n' roll." Vance also
was in charge of the music for the 1978 hit film, *Animal House.* In 1979, after
wrapping up work as music supervisor for the film *The Warriors*, thirty-six-year-
old Kenny Vance joined a friend's film crew as a sound technician to make a documentary in Israel about teenage immigrants. In Israel, Vance suffered an identity crisis. He had been immersed in rock 'n' roll since he was thirteen; his whole
world was predicated on making records, performing, and playing the role of
pop star. In Israel, Vance was humbled. "I discovered I didn't know who I was,"
he recalls. "Israel made me feel threatened, naked, empty, and very vulnerable."
Vance visited the Diaspora Museum in Tel Aviv and, as he viewed the exhibits, realized he knew little about his heritage. He was invited to visit a kabbalist rabbi
and was struck by the rabbi's kindness and perception. Vance visited the rabbi
several more times before leaving the country. He calls that trip the beginning of
his long road to Jewish observance. Back in the United States, Vance again got
wrapped up in the entertainment world as the music director for the NBC program *Saturday Night Live.* Still, he began to read books on Judaism, especially Jewish ethics and values, that he had been given in Israel. He was provoked by pas-
sages such as: "You learn three things from a train, a telephone, and a telegram.
From a train you learn what's here in one second can be gone in the next. From a
telephone you learn that what you say over here can be heard over there. And from
a telegram you learn that all words are counted and charged."

In 1984, Vance went to Crown Heights to hear Rabbi Simon Jacobson, a fol-
lower of the Lubavitcher Rebbe Menachem Mendel Schneerson. The rabbi's
words nourished Vance's soul. Vance found relevance in the rabbi's teachings,
and began wearing tefillin, praying daily, and attending Shabbat services. It gave
him strength and direction. "The word ritual is in the word spiritual," he explains of his observance. Throughout the eighties, Vance worked on films such
as *Streets of Fire, Eddie and the Cruisers,* and *Hairspray,* and also played small roles in
a series of films, including Woody Allen's *Crimes and Misdemeanors.* In 1989, he
made his first solo album in fourteen years. Titled *Short Vacation,* it included his
renditions of classic rock songs such as "Wonderful World," and "Heartbreak

*Kenny Vance takes time to daven. (Photo © r studio photopainting robin harvey.)*

Hotel," as well as originals. The album was produced by Peter Himmelman, and the inside cover included the Hebrew inscription "Tzafanath Paaneach" (Revealer of Secrets), the biblical description of Joseph. He worked to incorporate his deep faith into his music, not by performing Jewish songs, but by "infusing the songs with a soul."

In 1992, Vance reunited the Planotones, the vocal group he had created for the film *American Hot Wax*, and began touring the country, performing the unvarnished street corner doo-wop that thrilled him during his teenage years. In 1994, The Planotones released their debut CD, *Teenage Jazz*, and followed it in 1998 with *Looking for an Echo*, which also served as the soundtrack for the 1999 Armand Assante film of the same name. The inside cover of the CD included the inscription in Hebrew, "Yigdal Elohim Chai" (Living an Exalted King), a line from a morning prayer that struck Vance. In 2000, the Planotones released another record, *Live and Out of the World*. Vance believes that the durability and strength of his voice is linked to his deep Jewish spirituality. "My devotion does have something to do with my voice [staying in shape]. It comes from that place, and manifests itself in my body in a physical way," he says. Ironically, Jay Black, still performing into the new millennium, believes a divine power is responsible for his strong voice, though he stopped davening decades ago. The resiliency of his voice is one of the reasons he believes there just may be a God. "I'm very confused about God," Black says. "I want to understand more. I'm looking for answers and explanations. What's a soul? Where do you go after you die? These things torture me, but my voice has to come from God."

# Barry Mann and Cynthia Weil

Songwriters. Composers. Producers. Born Barrett Martin Imberman, February 9, 1939, Brooklyn, New York. Born Cynthia Weil, October 18, 1940, New York City. One of the most prolific songwriting teams of the rock era. Their hits include: "He's Sure the Boy That I Love" and "Uptown" by the Crystals, "On Broadway" by the Drifters, "Only in America" by Jay and the Americans, "We've Gotta Get Out of this Place" by the Animals, "Kicks" and "Hungry" by Paul Revere and the Raiders, "Here You Come Again" by Dolly Parton, "I Just Can't Help Believin'" by B. J. Thomas, "Just Once" by James Ingram, "Somewhere Out There" by Linda Ronstadt and James Ingram, "Don't Know Much" by Linda Ronstadt and Aaron Neville, and the Righteous Brothers' "(You're My) Soul and Inspiration" and "You've Lost that Lovin' Feelin." The latter was the most frequently played song on radio in the twentieth century. The couple was inducted into the Songwriters Hall of Fame in 1987.

*Barry Mann and Cynthia Weil early in their career, and marriage,*
*circa 1964. (Photo courtesy Barry Mann and Cynthia Weil.)*

In 1986, when Cynthia Weil was shown the script for the animated feature film, *An American Tail*, she was moved by what she thought was an adorable, charming story, but wondered how producer Steven Spielberg could think the world wanted to see "a movie about a Jewish mouse." At the same time, she was glad that Spielberg had approached her and her husband Barry Mann to write for the film. She identified with the film's Jewish immigrant story line, even if it was about a mouse. The couple, one of the most respected songwriting teams in popular music, had four weeks to write four songs with composer James Horner, but felt no pressure to come up with a radio-friendly hit. In fact, they didn't think they had written a hit. However, when Spielberg heard "Somewhere Out There," he was elated that the legendary Mann-Weil writing team and Horner had delivered what he thought was a hit song. It was decided to feature the song in the movie by getting established stars to sing it (Linda Ronstadt and James Ingram) and by showcasing it at the end of the film. Mann and Weil were surprised Spielberg had such faith in the song, for it sounded nothing like the tunes being played on radio at the time. They had given little thought to the commercial potential of the song, or the film, for that matter, as the Disney-led renaissance in feature-length cartoons was still several years away. *An American Tail*, of course, was a hit. "Somewhere Out There" sold more than one million copies, won Grammy Awards for Song of the Year and Best Song Written for a Motion Picture or Television, and was nominated for an Academy Award and a Golden Globe Award. By then the duo had amassed twenty-five years of hit songs and writing awards (as a team and writing with others). But for Mann and Weil, "Somewhere Out There," inspired by a Jewish theme, was a little sweeter because some of their grandparents had immigrant tales of their own.

Cynthia Weil's mother, Dorothy Mendez, traced her family's roots back to Sephardic Jews of Portugal, some of whom may have even fled the Inquisition. The Mendez family settled in Brooklyn and was very observant, to the point of having their neighbors turn on the lights for them on Shabbat. Cynthia's father, Morris Weil, who owned a pair of furniture stores, was the son of Orthodox Polish immigrants. His father was a professor at Yeshiva University in New York. Dorothy and Morris married in 1929 and lived in Manhattan where Cynthia was born. She remembers a kosher home with big Shabbat dinners and celebrating holidays at a Conservative synagogue. (Ironically, Weil had a German nanny through age six to whom her mother spoke Yiddish when she didn't want Cynthia to know what she was saying.) When Weil was eight, much of the family's Jewish observance began to erode with the death of her father. She did attend Sunday school, though she was not at all enamored of it, and was confirmed. But she vowed that no child of hers would ever have to go through the same.

Though her parents weren't musically inclined, music, dance, and theater were emphasized and appreciated. Cynthia and her brother both studied classical piano, and every Saturday Cynthia tuned into Martin Block's *Make-Believe Ballroom* radio show to hear the hits of the day by Patti Page and Perry Como. By high school she was a fan of Woody Guthrie and Pete Seeger, but her greatest influence was the Broadway musical. She harbored dreams of being a dancer on Broadway. (Her aunt, Toni Mendez, had been a member of the celebrated Rockettes at Radio City Music Hall.) But Weil injured her back at seventeen and had to shelve her dream of being a dancer. The theater still moved her; she saw it as a vehicle for releasing emotions and for self-expression, and as a place where she felt safe and secure. She studied theater at Sarah Lawrence, but decided she wasn't cut out to act or direct. She tried her hand at songwriting, initially adding lyrics to Harold Arlen and Cole Porter songs as exercises in playing with words. She also auditioned to sing in clubs. "I had more guts than talent. I was terrible," she says. While her singing didn't win her many friends, her song lyrics did. She had been encouraged as a child to be a writer, but she didn't like the isolation of writing. Songwriting, however, was another matter. It didn't have to be so solitary. She was twenty when legendary film and Broadway songwriter Frank Loesser (*Guys and Dolls, How to Succeed in Business Without Really Trying*) told her she had talent and invited her to work with the writers at his publishing company.

In 1961, Weil was writing songs with singer-songwriter Teddy Randazzo when another aspiring singer-songwriter by the name of Barry Mann dropped in to pitch some songs. "I thought he was so cute," says Weil. When she found out that Mann also was writing for the legendary Aldon Music publishing company, run by Al Nevins and Don Kirshner, she arranged to pitch songs to Kirshner in hopes of running into Mann again.

Barry Mann grew up in Brooklyn, the son of Sidney and Emma Imberman. His father was an accountant; his mother served as president of his school's PTA. Most of Barry's Jewish education and identity was gleaned from his paternal grandfather, David Imberman. Grandpa Imberman ran four-hour Passover seders, all in Hebrew, where Barry looked forward to reciting the *Fier Kashas*, or Four Questions. The family attended Conservative shuls, Barry went to Hebrew school and became a bar mitzvah. Though he remembers that the cantors at the neighborhood synagogues "were unbelievable," he found synagogue boring and felt much of Hebrew school was simply memorizing without comprehending. "My religious connection to Judaism is not good," he says, though his Jewish pride and identity run deep. His connection to music was much stronger. His mother and older brother, a podiatrist, played piano; they often gathered with several cousins who played string instruments to play classical music in their homes. The soulful minor key music that Mann heard in synagogue, coupled with the drama of the classical music he heard at home, influenced what Mann describes as a very emotional songwriting style. As a child, Mann often sat at the piano not knowing how to play much more than "Chopsticks." He began music lessons around age ten after watching a friend receive "thunderous applause" at a talent show. He found the lessons tedious, however. Around age thirteen, he learned to play the ukulele and began writing songs after seeing the same childhood friend pen his own tunes.

After graduating from high school, Mann enrolled at Pratt Institute in Brooklyn to study architecture but left after a year. He had sung in talent shows in the Catskills while working summer jobs to earn money for college and had met a music publisher. At eighteen, he took the money he had saved for college, recorded some of his original songs, and went to see the publisher. And that's where Mann's writing career began. "I guess I was destined to do this because of all the music in my family," Mann says. "It was there in the house, and my mother encouraged us."

Mann began peddling his songs and writing with others. By early 1959, at age twenty, he had his first hit as a songwriter, "She Say (Oom Dooby Doom)," recorded by a Canadian group called the Diamonds. About a year later, he joined Aldon Music and in 1961, aspiring to become a recording act and thinking his Jewish-sounding name a deterrent to stardom, Barry Imberman became Barry Mann. In September of 1961, the novelty song "Who Put the Bomp (in the Bomp, Bomp, Bomp)," co-written with another fledgling hit songwriter, Gerry Goffin, reached No. 7 on the *Billboard* charts. It was Mann's first and only Top Forty hit as a singer. The year is probably more notable for his meeting and marrying Cynthia Weil and beginning one of the most fruitful and enduring songwriting partnerships in history. "Barry introduced me to rock 'n' roll," Weil says. "Sometimes, I wish he'd gone my way" (the Broadway musical).

The couple was one of a stable of soon-to-be famous songwriting teams under contract to Nevins and Kirshner. These teams developed a style that came to be called Brill Building pop, named after one of several office buildings on the 1600 block of Broadway that housed record and publishing companies. (Ironically, the Aldon Music office wasn't in the actual Brill Building.) For the first half of the sixties, Mann and Weil were part of a songwriting atelier that included the teams of Gerry Goffin and Carole King ("Up on the Roof," "Will You Still Love Me Tomorrow") and Neil Sedaka and Howard Greenfield ("Calendar Girl," "Breaking Up Is Hard to Do"). The songwriting teams of Jeff Barry and Ellie Greenwich (Be My Baby," "River Deep, Mountain High") and Doc Pomus and Mort Shuman ("This Magic Moment," "Save the Last Dance For Me") were contemporaries, but they worked for other publishers. All were Jewish. The man responsible for hiring the musicians for the recording sessions that turned these songs into records was a Jewish sax, flute, and piccolo player named Artie Kaplan. One of the premier arrangers on many of those sessions, pianist Artie Butler, was a "Member of the Tribe," too.

That just about everyone at Aldon Music was Jewish meant little in the competitive atmosphere that Nevins and Kirshner created. Mann described Aldon Music as a pressure-filled school for songwriters. "We learned from each other, but it was also a big, dysfunctional, extended family, led by mother-father figure Don Kirshner. All we wanted to do was please Don Kirshner. We were filled with competitiveness." Pleasing Don Kirshner meant your song would be recorded by a hit-making act like the Crystals, the Drifters, the Ronettes, or the Righteous Brothers. With Mann writing most of the music, and Weil providing most of the lyrics, the duo, sometimes in collaboration with producer Phil Spector or writers Jerry Leiber and Mike Stoller, was nearly unstoppable. Their first collaborative hit was a song called "Bless You," which was recorded by Tony Orlando and reached No. 15 on the charts in 1961. The floodgates opened and for the next five years the hits flowed. Among them, "Uptown" and "He's Sure the Boy That I Love" by the Crystals, "On Broadway" by the Drifters, "Blame it on the Bossa Nova" by Eydie Gorme, "My Dad" by Paul Peterson, "Only in America" by Jay and the Americans, "I'm Gonna Be Strong" by Gene Pitney, "Walking in the Rain" by the Ronettes, "You've Lost that Lovin' Feelin'" and "Soul and Inspiration" by the Righteous Brothers, "We Gotta Get Out of This Place" by the Animals, and "Kicks" and "Hungry" by Paul Revere and the Raiders.

Mann and Weil were among the first pop songwriters to take on social issues.

"Uptown" was about a black man in a dead-end job told through the eyes of his girlfriend. "We Gotta Get Out of This Place" addressed class differences, and "Kicks" took on drug addiction. Of those songs, Weil says, "I always had a strong sense of justice. I wanted to write something ballsy that had something to say." When Don Kirshner heard "Uptown," he told Weil he didn't understand the song but encouraged her to write more songs like it. Says Mann: "Social protest songs were ingrained in us. I always felt really proud and connected to songs with messages." Still, it was a song about fading love that remains the commercial crown of their extensive catalog. "You've Lost That Lovin' Feelin'," co-wrriten with Phil Spector, became a No. 1 hit for the Righteous Brothers in late 1964. In 1969, Dionne Warwick took the song to No. 16. In 1980, Hall and Oates reached No. 12 with their version. In 1999, Broadcast Music International (BMI), the song licensing and performing rights agency, named "Feelin'" No. 1 on its list of "Top 100 Songs of the Century." BMI estimated the song had been played on radio and TV more than eight million times, far more than any other pop song in its library. Ironically, the song outperformed Mann-Weil's "(You're My) Soul and Inspiration," a huge hit for the Righteous Brothers in 1966 that stayed at No. 1 longer, and sold more copies, than "Feelin'."

With the Beatles and many of the other "British Invasion" bands writing their own songs, and influencing many American acts to do the same, Mann and Weil had fewer writing outlets. Still, the hits kept coming. In 1968, Bobby Vinton scored with Mann's "I Love How You Love Me." In 1969, Jay and the Americans turned "Walking in the Rain" into a hit for the second time, and Mama Cass Elliot took the Mann-Weill songs "Make Your Own Kind of Music" and "It's Getting Better" into the Top Forty. In 1970, "I Just Can't Help Believing" was a Top Ten hit for B. J. Thomas.

In 1973, the couple moved to Los Angeles to be closer to Mann's family and many of their music industry contacts. In 1977, they penned one of their biggest hits, "Here You Come Again." The record sold more than half a million copies, topped the country and pop charts, and turned country singer Dolly Parton into a pop star. Mann also hit the charts with, "Sometimes When We Touch," co-written with Dan Hill.

Though Mann and Weil co-wrote James Ingram's 1981 hit "Just Once," during the first half of the eighties the couple often worked apart, collaborating with other writers. This was partly due to a separation between 1983–1985. Between

1980 and 1986, Weil co-wrote the Pointer Sisters' "He's So Shy," Peabo Bryson's "If Ever You're in My Arms Again," and Lionel Richie's "Running with the Night" and "Love Will Conquer All." Shortly after the couple reunited, they struck gold with "Somewhere Out There" from *An American Tail*.

In 1989, Mann and Weil closed out the decade proving they still had their fingers on the commercial pulse of the public, when Linda Ronstadt and Aaron Neville reached No. 2 with "Don't Know Much." The couple stayed busy throughout the nineties producing and writing songs for films, including contributing a half dozen songs to *Muppet Treasure Island* in 1995. They were on the *Billboard* charts again in 1997, having collaborated with teenage sibling rockers Hanson on the group's hit "I Will Come to You." Weil also added a country hit to her co-writing credits, when Martina McBride topped the country charts with "Wrong Again," and she co-wrote a song called "Circle" that appeared on Barbra Streisand's *Higher Ground* album. (The album included Streisand's interpretation of "Avinu Malkeinu.") In 2001, the couple was working on a pair of shows for Broadway. One of the works in progress is based on their catalog of hits; the other is an original musical based on the film *The Mask*.

The mid-nineties through the new millennium was also a time Mann and Weil renewed and strengthened their connection to Judaism. In 1994, Mann took a Jewish history course at the University of Judaism in Los Angeles. Though he had been bar mitzvahed, he realized he knew little Jewish history. (Mann thought the Jews had only been kicked out of Spain, for example, not realizing they'd been expelled from just about every country in Europe at one time or another. He was shocked to learn that Jews number only about fifteen million worldwide.) "At this point, I'm very proud of being Jewish though I'm not really religious," he says. He can't watch any kind of program about the Holocaust without becoming angry. "I think about what the offspring would have added and contributed to the world. I think these are my people who were slaughtered. I still worry about Israel because Jews have been hated throughout history, and I don't know what is going to change that."

Weil was deeply moved by a book called, *I Have Lived a Thousand Years: Growing Up in the Holocaust*, by Livia Bitton-Jackson, about a thirteen-year-old Hungarian girl's experience in the Auschwitz death camp. "I suddenly felt so Jewish reading that book. I realized that it could have been me," Weil says. Even before reading the book, Weil, and Mann, made an important career decision based on being

Jewish. The couple declined to write songs for the 1996 film *Grace of My Heart*, a fictional account of the Brill Building era because they didn't think the script gave proper credit to the Jews who wrote and produced so many of those celebrated songs. "Most of the stuff that came out of there was by Jews, Italians, and blacks, and that was omitted from the movie, and that really bothered me," Weil says. "I don't usually get on my high horse about Judaism, but this was very important sociologically, so at least tell it truthfully." Another much happier event also heightened the couple's Jewish awareness. In 2000, the child Cynthia Weil swore would never have to endure Sunday school and confirmation classes, daughter Jennifer, married a nice Jewish boy who had lived on a kibbutz in Israel and was fluent in Hebrew. The date on the wedding invitations read 5761 as well as 2000. The newlyweds have created a Jewish atmosphere in their home and light candles on Shabbat. The hit songwriting team of Mom and Dad has an open invitation.

# Peter Yarrow

Singer. Songwriter. Political and social activist. Born May 31, 1938, New York City. Best known as one-third of the internationally acclaimed group Peter, Paul and Mary, which brought folk and protest music into the mainstream in the early sixties with songs such as "If I Had a Hammer," and "Blowin' in the Wind" and also took the John Denver–penned "Leaving on a Jet Plane" to No. 1. Yarrow co-wrote the classic "Puff, the Magic Dragon," and the Hanukkah standard, "Light One Candle."

*Peter Yarrow includes synagogues on his performing itinerary. (Photo courtesy Peter Yarrow.)*

In 1983, when Peter Yarrow's group mates, Paul Stookey, and Mary Travers, asked him to write a Hanukkah song for a Christmas concert at New York's Carnegie Hall (the two holidays fell during the same week that year), he wasn't sure he was qualified to do it. He had spent much of his childhood raised in a non-observant Jewish household and hadn't paid much attention to the rituals of Judaism or spoken publicly of his Jewish heritage. He did have a lot of Jewish friends in high places, however, and sought their counsel. Alexander Shindler, president of Reform Judaism's Union of American Hebrew Congregations, and David Saperstein, director of the Religious Action Center of Reform Judaism, were among those who convinced Yarrow that the healing music Peter, Paul and Mary had been playing for twenty years qualified him to write a Hanukkah song. The resulting song was "Light One Candle," which eventually was included on the 1986 Peter, Paul and Mary album, *No Easy Walk to Freedom*. The opening line, "Light one candle for the Maccabee children," left no doubt about the subject of the song. Anthemic in its energy and insight, it included the prescient lyric, "Light one candle for the strength that we need to never become our own foe." It also asked the timeless, provocative question, "What is the meaning we value so highly that we keep alive in that flame?" Yarrow calls the song "an exposition of what I think is my own Jewishness." If "Light One Candle" was energizing for Jews, it also was liberating for Yarrow. It was his way of announcing not only that he was a Jew, but how he was a Jew. The idea of *tikkun olam*, or repairing the world, had resonated with him at least since 1961 when Peter, Paul and Mary formed and began singing about justice and freedom. He had discovered the concept of tikkun olam when Jewish organizations such as the Mitzvah Corps, based at Jewish summer camps, began to embrace the group's music and civil rights activism. "To be Jewish is to me to be tikkun olam," says Yarrow. "If that piece is lost, then the essence of being Jewish is in jeopardy. That worries me."

Peter Yarrow was born into an intellectual family in New York in 1938. His father Bernard Yarrowsevich, had emigrated from the Ukraine when he was about seventeen. His mother, Vera Burt (Burtakoff), also from the Ukraine, arrived in the United States at age three. Both families initially settled in a community of Russian Jewish immigrants in Providence, Rhode Island. Peter's father was a member of the OSS (Office of Strategic Services) during World War II, helped devise Radio Free Europe, and eventually joined the U.S. diplomatic corps. His mother, the youngest of seven children from a poor family, began work in a factory, educated herself, and eventually became a speech, drama, and English teacher at Julia Richmond High School in New York. (Her eldest brother, the first Jew to attend Brown University on a full scholarship, became fluent in seven languages, finished college in three years, and taught at the Bronx High School of Science.)

Peter's parents, however, divorced when he was five. His father, according to his mother, became a practicing Protestant. His mother, who believed organized religion was the root of more harm than good, raised Peter and his sister with no religious observance but did not deny the family's Jewish identity, and she certainly promulgated Jewish values of doing good deeds and pursuing justice. His mother was a member of the teachers union and Planned Parenthood, when membership in such groups was considered radical. "My mother was an idealist who believed there should be greater economic fairness in the world. I grew up with that value system," Yarrow says. He eventually studied Judaism and was confirmed when his mother remarried. His stepfather, Harold Wisebrode, the executive director of Central Synagogue in New York, convinced him he should have some religious training. Confirmation class, however, was "an unpleasant experience." He found the other students insensitive to him and uninterested in the material. Turned off by religious school, he asked his teacher, Rabbi Seligson, if he could still be a good Jew if he eschewed Jewish ritual and just lived by the tenets of Judaism. After some reflection, the rabbi answered yes.

Throughout the rest of his life, while Yarrow kept quiet about his Jewish roots, he remained concerned about Jewish issues. "When Jewish events, or issues of Jewish continuity, took place, I was aware of them," Yarrow says, "and I was concerned about human rights and Refusenicks the same way I was concerned about victims of apartheid in South Africa." Like many Jewish homes, Yarrow's mother also placed an emphasis on learning, art and music appreciation, and intellectual pursuit. As a child, Peter began recorder, violin, and art lessons, and concentrated in art at New York's High School of Music and Art intending to become a painter. While still in high school, Yarrow switched to playing guitar after seeing folk acts such as Josh White perform during after-school programs at the 92nd Street YMHA. Performances by Pete Seeger and the Weavers also deeply affected him. "Pete Seeger inspired me to music," Yarrow explains. "He lived what he sang, and promulgated the cause of social justice and human rights with great spirit, fun, and humanity. He was my role model."

Though folk music was taking hold, Yarrow graduated from high school with the second highest academic average among all male seniors, won the school's physics prize, and was accepted to Cornell University as a physics major, which he soon changed to psychology. (This academic penchant continues to run in the family. Yarrow's daughter, Bethany, graduated summa cum laude from Yale.) It took two scholarships, jobs waiting tables and washing dishes, and help from his mother to pay his way through Cornell. Yarrrow, labeled "a turkey and a nerd" by classmates, perceived Cornell as an institution that was too hierarchical, had little regard for women, and was blind to dramatic societal changes that would sweep across the country in the late fifties and early sixties. During his senior year, however, he got an undergraduate instructorship for an elective English course that required being able to play guitar and sing folk songs, and he made an incredible discovery. When he played and the students sang, their demeanors and attitudes changed. "They sang their hearts out and their souls shined through," Yarrow recalls. "I thought they were yearning to feel the sense of connection folk music allows." More and more students began attending the course until all two hundred seats in the lecture hall were filled and more students lined the walls and outside hallway. Yarrow began leading student singalongs on Saturday mornings and recalls that "the sound was thrilling." He believed the world was about to change, and folk music was going to be a part of it.

After graduating from Cornell, Yarrow began performing in clubs, and in 1960 appeared on a CBS TV special called *Folk Sound USA* and performed at the Newport Folk Festival that summer. Impresario Albert Grossman, who ran the folk festival, suggested Yarrow try working with Noel Paul Stookey, a Greenwich Village singer and comedian, and Mary Travers, who had sung in an array of folk groups and done some work in Broadway musicals. The trio signed a management contract with Grossman, rehearsed for much of 1961, and after a showcase concert for record company executives, signed a record deal with Warner Brothers. Both earnest and entertaining, the trio was an immediate success. Their self-titled debut album released in 1962 contained the hit singles "Lemon Tree" and the Pete Seeger–Lee Hays classic, "If I Had a Hammer," which reached No. 10 on the pop charts and made protest music a force to be reckoned with. The album sold two million copies and reached No. 1. With its follow-up album, *Moving*, in 1963, the trio established its musical immortality when Yarrow's now-classic children's song "Puff, the Magic Dragon" reached No. 2, despite of being banned by some radio stations that incorrectly believed the song promoted drug use. Later in the year, the trio became the first of many acts to record and have a hit with a Bob Dylan song, taking "Blowin' in the Wind," and "Don't Think Twice," into the Top Ten. With those hits, from *In the Wind*, Peter, Paul and Mary put Dylan forever in the American consciousness.

At one point, all three of the trio's albums were on the record charts simultaneously. Before taking a break in 1970, the trio would score another five hits throughout the sixties, including "I Dig Rock and Roll Music," Gordon Lightfoot's "For Lovin' Me," Dylan's "Too Much of Nothing," John Denver's "Leaving on a Jet Plane," and Yarrow's "Day is Done." The trio reunited in 1978, resulting in the *Reunion* album, and they continue to regroup for tours into the new millennium. (Their recording legacy includes ten Grammy nominations and five Grammy Awards.) Yarrow's solo output include recording four albums, producing a film (*You Are What You Eat*), three children's TV specials, and co-writing and producing the pop song "Torn Between Two Lovers," a No. 1 hit for Mary MacGregor in late 1976. He also co-founded the annual Kerrville (Texas) Folk Festival in the mid- seventies to showcase, nurture, and pass the torch to up-and-coming singer-songwriters.

Since the beginning of their collective career, Peter, Paul and Mary practiced what they preached. They marched with Dr. Martin Luther King, Jr., in support of civil rights legislation and were present in Washington, D.C., for King's galvanizing "I Have a Dream" speech in 1963. In 1968 Yarrow, Stookey, and Travers, along with family members and friends, were arrested in front of the Embassy of South Africa in Washington, D.C., during a protest of that country's policy of apartheid. (A photo of the arrest was included on the cover of the 1986 album *No Easy Walk to Freedom*.) In 1969, Yarrow was among the organizers of the March on Washington that called for an end to the war in Vietnam. In 1978, Yarrow organized Survival Sunday at the Hollywood Bowl, a rally for the "No Nukes" movement. Throughout his career, with and without Stookey and Travers, Yarrow organized benefits for the hungry and homeless, and brought attention to issues from environmental disregard at home to human rights abuses in Latin America. A 1986 Peter, Paul and Mary PBS twenty-fifth anniversary special was turned into a benefit for the New York Coalition for the Homeless. In 1987, after touring the Middle East during what became known as the Intifada, Yarrow, from a stance of what he calls "loyal opposition," criticized some of Israel's policies in dealing with Palestinian rioters. Israel, he believed, lost its moral authority when it responded by arresting people without charging them with a crime, demolishing homes, and closing Palestinian schools. "I felt as if my own family was doing these things," Yarrow explains.

If any one song encompasses Yarrow's motivations, it is "Light One Candle." Every cause he has championed, every government policy he has questioned, is based on the pursuit of justice commanded in the Torah and the Talmud. In 1995, the Jewish Federation of Greater Miami honored Yarrow with its Tikkun Olam Award for his work in helping to repair the world. To remind Jewish communities across the United States of the importance of tikkun olam, Yarrow has been performing in synagogues with his daughter Bethany. They call their family concert appearances "The Legacy of Activism," the title a reminder of the Jewish people's role and responsibility in pursuing justice. Among Yarrow's latest projects is a character- and esteem-building program for schoolchildren called "Don't Laugh at Me." The program, in thousands of schools across the country, derives its name from a song of the same name on the 1999 Peter, Paul and Mary album *Songs of Conscience and Concern*. Co-written by Steve Seskin (who often performs it at his northern California synagogue) and Allen Shamblin, the chorus of "Don't Laugh at Me" includes the lines, "Don't laugh at me / Don't call me names / Don't get your pleasure from my pain / In God's eyes we're all the same." The program incorporates the Jewish notion of *lashon hara*, "the wicked tongue," and the idea that mean-spirited words can be more hurtful, and cause deeper wounds than sticks or stones.

Explaining the motivation behind his inexhaustible activism, Yarrow says, "My sensibility was not only from my mother, but from her ethical Jewishness. Her alliance was with those who were suffering, poor, disenfranchised. Music was going to be, for me, the rallying point for illuminating the world. I believe that's my task, my gift, my opportunity. There is nothing more glorious than being a part of healing."

# Bob Dylan

**Songwriter. Guitar player. Singer. Born Robert Allen Zimmerman,
May 24, 1941, Duluth, Minnesota. Best known for one of the most widely
respected and influential catalog of songs in rock 'n' roll, including classics
such as "Blowin' in the Wind," "Masters of War," "The Times They Are
A-Changin'," "With God on Our Side," "Like a Rolling Stone," "Positively
Fourth Street," "Rainy Day Woman #12 & 35," "Just Like a Woman,"
"I Shall Be Released," "Knockin' on Heaven's Door," "Forever Young,"
and "Tangled Up in Blue." His writing style, subject matter, and marriage
of folk to rock revolutionized popular music. He was inducted into the
Rock and Roll Hall of Fame in 1988. In 2000, the *Jerusalem Post* named
Dylan one of the "Fifty Jews Who Moved the Century."**

*Bob Dylan at the bar mitzvah of his son Jesse at the Western
Wall in Jerusalem in September 1983. (AP/Wide World Photos.)*

From 1979 through 1981, Bob Dylan released what is considered a trio of "Born Again" albums, *Slow Train Coming*, *Saved*, and *Shot Full of Love*. The song, "Gotta Serve Somebody," from *Slow Train Coming*, became a Top Forty hit and won Dylan a Grammy Award for Best Male Rock Vocal Performance. All three albums praised Jesus and fortified Dylan's 1978 declaration that he was now a believer in Jesus as the son of God. Dylan reportedly had a "mystical" experience in late 1977 during which he felt he was in the presence of Jesus. That led to Dylan spending time with a Southern California born-again Christian group called the Vineyard Fellowship and eventually accepting Jesus. After the 1981 release of *Shot Full of Love*, however, the lauded singer-songwriter and cultural icon released *Infidels*, an album that includes a song defending Israel, "Neighborhood Bully." He also visited the Jewish state and prayed at the Western Wall, and participated in numerous Jewish life cycle events involving his family, including the 1983 bar mitzvah of his oldest son, Jesse, in Jerusalem. He performed "Hava Nagillah" at a 1989 benefit for Chabad Lubavitch in Los Angeles, and, in 1995, made time in the midst of the Florida leg of a concert tour to attend Yom Kippur services in West Palm Beach. Still, people continue to ask, "Is Bob Dylan Jewish this week?" as if he swaps religions like baseball cards.

Dylan must find it amusing that, after decades filled with "Jewish" acts and activities, compared with his relatively brief exploration of Christianity, the public continues to speculate about his faith. Aside from 1978–1981, the Torah, not the New Testament, appears to have been a primary influence on Dylan's social and political perspective and worldview. If Dylan is one of popular music's most discussed and analyzed stars, his Jewishness is one of his most debated and analyzed characteristics. Numerous books, articles, and Web sites (*Tangled Up in Jews* is among the best known) devoted to Dylan have debated and discussed his moves and music for their Jewish content. Many of Dylan's references to Judaism and the Torah are well known.

A notable example is "With God on Our Side," from his 1963 album *The Times They Are A-Changin'*, with the following verse in which he alludes to the Holocaust. "When the Second World War / Came to an end / We forgave the Germans / and we were friends / Though they murdered six million / In the ovens they fried / The Germans now too / Have God on their side." The title song from Dylan's 1965 album *Highway 61 Revisited* opens with a tale straight from the Torah, the binding of Isaac. "Oh God said to Abraham, 'Kill me a son / Abe says, 'Man, you must be puttin' me on' / God say 'No.' Abe say, 'What?' / God say, 'You can do what you want Abe, but / The next time you see me comin' you better run / 'Well,' Abe says, 'Where do you want this killin' done?' God says, 'Out on Highway 61.'" The case can be made that the song "Forever Young," from the 1974 album *Planet Waves* (which includes Hebrew lettering on the album's sleeve) is based on the parents' Blessing of the Children on Shabbat. The blessing begins, "May the Lord bless you and keep you . . ." Dylan's song opens with, "May God bless you and keep you always / May your wishes all come true / May you always do for others / And let others do for you . . ."

If the three main pillars of Judaism are God, Torah, and Israel, then it appears Dylan found his way back to the tribe via all three routes. In 1983, he began spending time with Lubavitch rabbis in Brooklyn. His album *Infidels* includes "Neighborhood Bully," what can only be an impassioned, almost angry, eleven-verse defense of the Jewish homeland. Dylan used the song to illustrate how Israel (never named in the song, but quite obvious), vastly outnumbered and surrounded by a hostile world, still is tagged as the region's "neighborhood bully" for the mere act of surviving. (Casting Israel as "neighborhood bully" is exactly what the Palestinians managed to do at the end of 2000 and well into 2001 during "Intifada II," nearly twenty years after Dylan wrote the song. Painting the prey as predator in the eyes of the international community helped the Palestinians wage an effective propaganda war for a while.) The song's second verse sounded like an analysis of the world's biased view toward the Jewish state. "The Neighborhood Bully just lives to survive / He's criticized for just being alive / He's not supposed to fight back / he's supposed to have thick skin / He's supposed to lay down and die when his door is kicked in / He's the neighborhood bully."

Dylan has illustrated his "Jewishness" in life as well as on record. One of the least publicized instances occurred in January 1988 at the third annual Rock and Roll Hall of Fame Induction Ceremony at the Waldorf-Astoria Hotel in New York City. Dylan saved the ceremony from a growing tension and anxiety that threatened to cast a pall over what is supposed to be an annual celebration of a musical form that finally had a history. Dylan didn't use stardom, fame, or showmanship; he used humility, modesty, and an olive branch to uplift the evening. It was an auspicious year for the young Hall of Fame, featuring the induction of Dylan, the Beatles, the Beach Boys, the Supremes, and the Drifters, along with "early influences" such as Woody Guthrie. Unfortunately, it also was a year when Paul Mc-

Cartney of the Beatles and Diana Ross of the Supremes were embroiled in feuds with former group members, and were no-shows at the Waldorf. Beach Boys frontman Mike Love used his moment in the spotlight to criticize McCartney and Ross, which only added to an atmosphere of divisiveness and gloom. When a perceptive Bob Dylan approached the podium a few minutes later, after being inducted by Bruce Springsteen, he showed his depth of compassion. Instead of focusing on the honor he had just received, he addressed Mike Love's angry, critical remarks and the well-publicized feuds between members of the two legendary groups. Like a rabbi on a bima, Dylan leaned into the podium, gazed into the crowd of rock stars and music business movers-and-shakers, and reminded everyone that finger pointing and name-calling had no redeeming value or healing power. What was needed, Dylan said, was forgiveness. His conciliatory words changed the mood in the room. To Jewish ears, Dylan's remarks addressed the destructive power of *lashon hara*, the evil tongue, or the spreading of gossip, and called for a more constructive, spiritual resolution. It was an unexpected, unscripted moment unrecorded by television cameras. Dylan didn't speak up to get media attention; he did so out of an ethical obligation. Perhaps Dylan's words could have come from someone of any denomination, but coming from a Jew concerned about right and wrong all his life made it a profoundly Jewish moment. For a man many people continue to think shrugged off Judaism decades ago, Dylan has had many Jewish moments.

Dylan may have been born again in 1978, but he was born a Jew on May 24, 1941, in Duluth, Minnesota. His parents, Abraham and Beatrice (Edelstein) Zimmerman, moved the family north to much smaller Hibbing when their son, Robert Allen Zimmerman, was six. He attended a Jewish summer camp as a child and became a bar mitzvah. He began playing guitar by age fourteen, became enamored of rock 'n' roll, played in high school rock bands, and in 1959 while a freshman at the University of Minnesota, transformed himself into the folk troubadour, Bob Dylan. He moved to New York and in 1961 began performing in Greenwich Village coffeehouses; he was signed to a recording contract that year, and in 1962 released his debut album on Columbia Records. He also legally changed his name to Bob Dylan that year. By 1963, with the release of his second album, *The Freewheelin' Bob Dylan*, and with Peter, Paul and Mary turning his song "Blowin' in the Wind" into a hit single as well as a civil rights anthem, Dylan became a star. During the rest of the sixties, Dylan turned popular music on its head. He bent and broke songwriting rules, contemplated God, morality and justice in song as few others had done, inspired, if not invented, the musical form of folk-rock, recorded folk, blues, country, rock, and contemporary Christian albums at his own discretion, defying those who would label him, and irritated fans by rendering his classic songs unrecognizable in concert. Through it all, he never looked back. He did it all with a singing voice that could charitably be described as unconventional. His catalog of songs became one of the most recorded in the rock era, with acts such as the Byrds, Manfred Mann, Joan Baez, Judy Collins, the Band, and Richie Havens, among others, frequently relying on Dylan for material.

In 1991, the National Association for the Recording Arts and Sciences (NARAS) honored Dylan with a Lifetime Achievement Grammy. The following year, Columbia Records celebrated Dylan's thirtieth anniversary with the record label with a televised, star-studded celebration at Madison Square Garden in New York. In 1994, Dylan appeared at the Woodstock twenty-fifth anniversary concert, performing to a new generation of rock fans. In 1997, he was laid low by a life-threatening viral infection but made a quick recovery, returned to performing and also recording *Time Out of Mind*, heralded as his best album of new material in years. The album won three Grammy Awards, including Album of the Year. The kudos and awards kept coming. In 1998 he, along with actress Lauren Bacall, opera singer Jessye Norman, and actor Charlton Heston, was a Kennedy Center honors recipient for achievement in the performing arts. In 2000, reviewing the past one hundred years, the *Jerusalem Post* named Dylan one of the "Fifty Jews Who Moved the Century." In 2001, he won the Academy Award for Best Song for "Things Have Changed" from the film *Wonderboys*, and released another acclaimed album, *Love and Theft*. Not one to rest on his laurels, he stayed busy on what was dubbed "The Never-Ending Tour." In fact, he performed his Oscar-nominated song and delivered his award acceptance speech via satellite from a tour stop in Australia.

As he turned sixty that year, Dylan was the patriarch of a small but growing family musical dynasty. His son Jakob showed staying power with his band the Wallflowers; son-in-law Peter Himmelman remained a force as a concert performer; and nephew Seth Zimmerman got into the act in 1999 as leader of a country-rock band called Tangletown. (Unlike Dylan's son and son-in-law, however, Zimmerman has no Jewish identity and reportedly is married to a minister's daughter.) But to confine Dylan's patriarchy of a musical dynasty to his family is narrow-minded. Many of those profiled in this book have become songwriters and performers because of him. And to continue to question Dylan's Jewish identity is to create an issue where there is none.

According to Dylan biographer Robert Shelton, during a 1971 visit to a Jerusalem yeshiva, several American students asked Dylan why he "shied away" from talking pointedly about his Jewish identity and beliefs. Shelton reported that Dylan answered, "I'm a Jew. It touches my poetry, my life, in ways I can't describe. Why should I declare something that should be so obvious?" Dylan's identity as a Jew should still be obvious, even after his late-seventies born-again declarations. Consider those few years as Dylan's moment of *Yisrael*, of "wrestling with God." That period should be viewed as one of a maverick making sure he was not following Judaism just because he was born into it, but because, after deep exploration, it truly made sense. A clue to Dylan's change of heart can be found in "Every Grain of Sand," the last song on his final "born again" album, *Shot of Love.* When he sings, "In the fury of the moment I can see the Master's hand / In every leaf that trembles, in every grain of sand," Dylan is not praising Jesus, he is declaring his rediscovered awe of one almighty God.

# David Grisman

**Mandolin player. Composer. Producer. Born March 23, 1945, Hackensack, New Jersey. The respected, versatile, and prolific Grisman is best known for revolutionizing the role of the mandolin in popular music and for his unique hybrid jazz-folk-classical-bluegrass sound dubbed "Dawg music" played by his David Grisman Quintet. He is also known for his collaborations with the late Grateful Dead guitarist Jerry Garcia and for his contributions to albums by many popular acts. In 1995, he and clarinet and mandolin player Andy Statman released an acclaimed record of traditional Jewish music, *Songs of Our Fathers*.**

*Raised on bluegrass music, David Grisman has referred to his eclectic style as "Jewgrass" music. (Photo courtesy of Jay Blakesberg.)*

David Grisman's hybrid mandolin playing and composition style may be known as "Dawg music" to fans, musicians, and the media (the term is a nickname given by Grateful Dead guitarist Jerry Garcia), but Grisman often thinks of his style as "Jewgrass music." Grisman's influences include traditional Jewish and gypsy melodies, as well as the "black cloud" that has hung over Jews throughout history. The result: Grisman writes much of his music in minor keys and infuses it with a sense of the blues, and of revelry in spite of despair. The pull of Jewish music was so strong that, in 1994, after thirty years of playing a variety of American roots music, and developing an international reputation, Grisman invited his friend and former mandolin student Andy Statman to record an album of traditional Jewish music together. Statman, an Orthodox Jew, was a noted clarinet and mandolin player who had the rare distinction of having founded both bluegrass and klezmer bands. The pair dedicated the resulting record, the poignant and beautiful *Songs of Our Fathers*, to their mothers, Gladys Statman and Fanya Grisman. The record, released on Grisman's own Acoustic Disc label in 1995, contains reverent interpretations of songs such as "Shalom Aleichem," "Adir Hu," "Dovid Melach Yisrael," and "Adon Olam," among others. An accompanying booklet includes striking photos of Jewish life in early twentieth-century eastern Europe, an essay on the role of Jewish music, song explanations, and titles and opening-line lyrics in Hebrew. Ironically, the idea for the record came from a musician who had built his reputation playing in bluegrass bands and contributing his soulful mandolin licks to hit rock and pop albums. "I'm not very observant of anything; I'm agnostic," says Grisman, "but I have strong Jewish feelings, and a Jewish heart on a cultural level."

Grisman, an only child, grew up in Passaic, New Jersey, in a Jewish home that he describes as "Conservative, not kosher, middle of the road." The family celebrated all the major Jewish holidays, and David attended Hebrew school five days a week from age four until his bar mitzvah. "I wasn't passionate about it, but I didn't hate it," Grisman says. (He always took a cab to a Hebrew school downtown, and remembers the traumatic experience at age four of feeling abandoned after being dropped off at school only to discover it was closed in observance of a Jewish holiday. Nevertheless, he got home.) Grisman's father, Samson, ran a series of small businesses, but he had been a professional trombone player before David was born. At his father's urging, David began piano lessons at age seven, but because of a lack of interest wasn't a good student. He stopped taking lessons at age ten when his father died. His father's death was a shattering event that, he says, "cast a pall on my childhood."

For his bar mitzvah in 1958, Grisman received a gift that opened up the fledgling world of rock 'n' roll to him: an LP record player. His love affair with the music of Chuck Berry, Buddy Holly, and Elvis Presley was short-lived as his heroes died (Holly), went to jail (Berry) or into the army (Presley). His mother, an art teacher, was relieved; she wanted her son to be a doctor or lawyer. She didn't realize she already had helped start his music career by introducing him to one of her art students, Jewish neighbor Ralph Rinzler. Rinzler would go on to play mandolin in an early urban bluegrass band, the Greenbriar Boys, and, in the early sixties, introduce Grisman to the music of Bill Monroe, the mandolin-picking "father of bluegrass." Grisman also discovered two other older "kindred spirits, both Jewish" who influenced his musical direction, the folk singer Oscar Brand and record company founder Moses Asch. Brand hosted a popular acoustic music radio program on WNYC, The Folksong Festival, that Grisman tuned into, and Asch, along with Marion Distler, founded the Folkways record label that popularized the music of Leadbelly, Woody Guthrie, and Pete Seeger, among others. But it was a Folkways record, Mountain Music Bluegrass Style, produced by Mike Seeger and featuring "White House Blues" by Earl Taylor and the Stoney Mountain Boys, with incredibly fast and nimble banjo picking, that caused young Grisman to "flip out." After hearing that, and Bill Monroe and his Blue Grass Boys (the genre name "bluegrass music" comes from the name of Monroe's band) Grisman was hooked on the mandolin. By age sixteen, after incessant practicing—and no formal lessons—he had become a formidable player.

In 1963, while a freshman English major at NYU, Grisman joined a group called the Even Dozen Jug Band. The Jug Band performed at Carnegie Hall twice and appeared on the Hootenanny television program while Grisman was still in college. During that same year, he produced his first recording session for Folkways, featuring Red Allen and Frank Wakefield and the Kentuckians. In 1964, he began his lifelong friendship with Jerry Garcia, then a banjo player, after meeting him at a bluegrass show. After college, Grisman formed Earth Opera with his friend Peter Rowan, who had been playing guitar with Bill Monroe. Originally intended as a bluegrass band, Earth Opera quickly evolved into a rock band that released a pair of albums on Elktra Records in 1968 and 1969. The title song of the latter album, The Great American Eagle Tragedy, a harrowing criticism of the

Vietnam War, became a staple of underground FM radio stations and an anthem of the antiwar movement, and it remains the group's best known work. During this time, Grisman began studying jazz after what he refers to as a failed attempt to learn the alto saxophone. In 1970, Jerry Garcia invited Grisman to San Francisco to play on the Grateful Dead's acoustic rock record *American Beauty*. Grisman contributed stellar mandolin runs to classic Dead songs such as "Friend of the Devil" and "Ripple." His playing on that record raised his profile and created a heavy demand for his talent. During the seventies, Grisman played on albums such as, *Whales and Nightingales* by Judy Collins, *Maria Muldaur* and *Waitress in a Donut Shop* by Maria Muldaur, *That's a Plenty* by the Pointer Sisters, *Tarzana Kid* by John Sebastain, *Prisoner in Disguise* by Linda Ronstadt, *Gorilla* and *In the Pocket* by James Taylor, *Sweet Forgiveness* by Bonnie Raitt, and Dolly Parton's *The Hits of Dolly Parton*.

He also found time to form his own groups and record. In 1973, Grisman joined Jerry Garcia in Old and In the Way, a short-lived, but prolific bluegrass band (Garcia played banjo), that also included guitarist Peter Rowan, fiddler Vassar Clements, and bass player John Kahn. The group performed for only nine months and released one album, but it broadened the audience for bluegrass in the process. In the mid-seventies Grisman also composed three film scores: *Big Bad Mama* (1974), *Capone* (1975), and *Eat My Dust* (1976).

In 1976, Grisman formed the groundbreaking David Grisman Quintet. Its self-titled debut album the following year signaled the arrival of a new sound and an original voice. In 1978, hired to write the score for the film *King of the Gypsies*, he collaborated with his friend Andy Statman and jazz violinist Stephane Grappelli. In 1979, working with Grappelli again, Grisman released the critically acclaimed jazz-accented album, *Hot Dawg*, which put him on the map as a frontman and solo performer. An eclectic collaboration with Statman in 1983 titled *Mandolin Abstractions* also was hailed by critics.

During the 1980s Grisman remained busy as a session player and producer, contributing to numerous albums, and releasing at least an album a year. His musical daring and experimentation influenced a new generation of musicians, inspiring the likes of banjo player Bela Fleck, dobro picker Jerry Douglas, and fiddle player (and former DGQ member) Mark O'Connor to take traditional bluegrass instruments well beyond the genre's borders. In 1990, Grisman formed his own record company, Acoustic Disc, "100% handmade music," to have more control over his career, and provide a forum for others whose music he believed needed to be heard. The label has released more than fifty albums by an array of acoustic artists since its inception. Among them are half a dozen projects with Jerry Garcia, recorded at some forty sessions between 1990 and 1995.

In 1994, eager to record with Statman again, Grisman invited the New Yorker to Northern California to make an album of Jewish music. Statman, equally at home with bluegrass or klezmer music and respected and admired in both fields, selected the songs; Grisman picked the musicians, including celebrated rock drummer Hal Blaine (born Chaim Zalman Belsky in 1929). The music struck Grisman deep in his soul, and he found himself crying during some of the recording sessions, especially when playing "Shalom Aleichem." Blaine also was moved to tears. "I found myself crying half the night," Blaine recalls. "Playing that music goes right through me." The answer to why may lie in the record's liner notes: "The music on this recording is all part of a living tradition. The songs express love of God and compassion for all creatures, devotion to the teachings of Judaism, and joy in simply being a Jew. Despite centuries of persecution and suffering, the Jewish people and their music are still flourishing."

Since the release of *Songs of Our Fathers*, Grisman continued to revisit his Jewish roots. In 1997, he played on the Andy Statman Quartet's *Between Heaven & Earth: Music of the Jewish Mystics.* He also compiled an anthology of the late virtuoso mandolin player David Apollon. Apollon was a Jew from Kiev who immigrated to the United States and became a vaudeville and cabaret star, and in the process inspired bluegrass and jazz mandolin players such as Jethro Burns, also a friend and collaborator of Grisman's. The fifty-one song collection, *The Man with the Mandolin*, features music Apollon recorded between 1930 and 1956, including traditional Eastern European melodies and American evergreens such as "Stardust." Grisman has exposed his roots in concert, too. Despite a voluminous repertoire, he occasionally finds a place in his shows for "Shalom Aleichem," or "For the Sake of My Brothers and Friends," from *Songs of Our Fathers*, and introduces the tunes with affection. "This is a beautiful Jewish melody," he tells his audiences.

# Genya Ravan

**Singer. Producer. Songwriter. Harmonica player. Born Genya Zelkowitz, Lodz, Poland, April 19, 1945. Best known as lead vocalist for the trailblazing Goldie and the Gingerbreads, considered the first all-girl rock band; and as lead singer for the jazz-rock band Ten Wheel Drive. Ravan also has the distinction of being the first female producer hired by a major record label.**

*For Genya Ravan, singing is davening. (Photo courtesy Genya Ravan.)*

For Genya Ravan, singing in rock bands had little to do with stardom or money, and everything to do with survival. Songs were prayers; singing was praying. "If you listen to some of my songs with Goldie and the Gingerbreads, and songs like "The Sweetest One," and "Shadowboxing" from *Urban Desire*, [a solo album from 1978], you'll hear me *davening*. My religion definitely had a lot to do with my singing, and it still does," says Ravan. The singer-producer has spent much of her life coming to grips with being the child of Holocaust survivors and dealing with the family dynamic that that horror created. Her father lost eight brothers; her mother lost four sisters, including a twin.

And Genya, born in the basement of a building in Lodz, Poland, where her parents and sister were hiding at war's end, lost two brothers she'd never known. It is believed her parents, and perhaps her sister, survived a forced labor camp for Jews in Poland called Skarzysko Kamienna where prisoners slaved in a munitions factory making bullets, were put to work in a local power plant, or used to lay track for a nearby railway. Records indicate that as many as 23,000 Jews died there from 1942 through 1944. Her parents wouldn't talk about their wartime ordeal. Her father died in 1974, her mother in 1995. "My parents were very damaged. I could never ask anything because they would fall apart. It was a terrible way to be brought up. I always say if it wasn't for my singing, I probably would have been nuts," Ravan explains, adding that hers was a life of no aunts, uncles, cousins or grandparents. Genya and a sister are the only remaining family members.

Genya arrived in the United States in 1948, at the age of three, with her parents, Natan and Yadja, and her older sister, Halucia. As part of the family's Americanization, everyone got new first names: Nathan, Yetta, Helen and Goldie. Her father, who had run an ice cream shop in Poland, opened a luncheonette and candy store on Manhattan's Lower East Side. The Zelkowitz family kept a kosher home and observed Shabbat. (Sister Helen still does.) Initially, the family spoke only Polish and Yiddish, languages Ravan still can navigate. As she grew older, Ravan taught herself English, in part, by listening to gospel and R&B records. LaVern Baker and Ray Charles were particular favorites.

The Zelkowitzes, shaken from the war, ran a strict household and kept their daughters on a short leash for fear something dire might happen to them. Ravan recounts the time she asked her mother for roller skates so she could play with the neighborhood kids. Her mother bought her a pair, but allowed her to use only one skate.

Goldie began to rebel, not just against her family, but against Judaism, too.

She played hooky from Hebrew school, purposely brought bacon into the house and ate it, and only dated non-Jewish boys. "My parents had a whole persecution thing happening, and put such a horror into me that the last thing I wanted to do was be Jewish. I have only just begun to love my Judaism," Ravan says.

Ravan does credit her parents for pushing her toward entertainment. Yetta Zelkowitz was a real stage mother. She encouraged her daughter's singing, bought her toe shoes, signed her up for dancing lessons, and entered her in beauty contests. ("Goldie" never won.) Her father played harmonica and spoons as a hobby, and encouraged his daughter as well. (She eventually taught herself harmonica, drums and alto saxophone.) Even so, at sixteen, she dropped out of high school. To make money she began doing "cheesecake modeling," posing nude for publications such as *Nugget* magazine. By seventeen, she says, she was living in a Brooklyn apartment with a girlfriend, and earning a hundred dollars an hour for nude photo shoots. "Believe it or not, " Ravan says, "I was not promiscuous."

One evening, a little bit drunk, she jumped on stage at the Lollipop Lounge in Brooklyn and began singing along with the house band, the Escorts, led by future hit record producer Richard Perry. That night, Goldie Zelkowitz discovered her voice and became the band's lead singer for awhile, recording with them as Goldie and the Escorts. Their version of the song "Somewhere" from the musical *West Side Story* became a regional hit in the Detroit area. Because she was underage, she began lying about how old she was. That, Ravan says, is why reference books list her date of birth as anywhere from 1940 to 1943. In 1963, at 18, though she was claiming to be older, Goldie Zelkowitz became the lead singer of Goldie and the Gingerbreads.

With Goldie singing lead, Carol McDonald on guitar, Margo Crocitto on keyboards, and Ginger Panebianco on drums, Goldie and the Gingerbreads debuted at New York's Peppermint Lounge in 1963. In 1964, the band signed a recording contract with Atlantic Records. While performing at the Lounge, members of the British blues-rock band the Animals, impressed by the female quartet's musicianship and potential, invited them to London to record. The Gingerbreads arrived in England in late 1964. By early 1965, Goldie and the Gingerbreads had reached No. 25 on the British record charts with "Can't You Hear My Heartbeat," produced by Animals keyboard player Alan Price. Ironically, the English band Herman's Hermits was first to release the song in the United States, taking it all the way to No. 2.

Goldie and the Gingerbreads toured with England's rock royalty: the Animals, the Yardbirds, the Rolling Stones, the Kinks, the Who, and Manfred Mann. When touring the States, members of the Animals and Moody Blues, among others, would drop in on Goldie's mother for home-cooked meals. Two subsequent singles failed to chart, however. In the sixties, as the first all-female band on a major record label who could play as well as sing, Goldie and the Gingerbreads couldn't shake the perception of being a novelty. But Ravan is proud of the groundbreaking role she played in rock 'n' roll, paving the way for women musicians and female bands to be taken more seriously. "We did the fighting. We were an all-women band during the height of chauvinism. Being first is wonderful, but it's a fight to be the first." She adds, "No one knows Goldie and the Gingerbreads in Flatbush, but we're big in England."

In 1969, not long after the demise of Goldie and the Gingerbreads, Genya joined the horn-charged, jazz-rock army Ten Wheel Drive (which at one point included noted Jewish flute and sax player Dave Leibman). Genya contributed lead vocals and harmonica and co-wrote songs for three of the band's albums, *Construction #1* (1969), *Brief Replies* (1970), and *Peculiar Friends* (1971). When a member of the band suggested she call herself Raven because she sounded black when she sang, Goldie Zelkowitz adopted the stage name Genya Ravan (pronounced raven). Genya appreciated the Jewish sense of humor of Ten Wheel Drive's creative duo, guitarist Aram Schefrin and keyboard player Michael Zager, but became frustrated with the size of the band. It was tough to make a living with ten people in the group. Ravan also felt too musically confined by having to stick close to the band's horn charts. "I quit too early," she says in hindsight. "I think one more album and we would have been huge." Ravan, however, decided to go solo. She released a string of five albums between 1972 and 1979, including one in 1974 titled *Goldie Zelkowitz* in honor of her father, Nathan Zelkowitz, who died during the making of the record. "I wanted his name to go on," she says, adding that it was so emotionally painful to make, she cannot listen to it.

In 1975, RCA Records hired Ravan to produce an album by Gretchen Cryer and Nancy Ford, best known for writing the musical *I'm Getting My Act Together and Taking It on the Road.* That made Ravan the first woman producer ever hired by a major record company. (Joan Baez and Joni Mitchell had produced their own records, but no woman had ever called the shots for another major label act.) Throughout the rest of the seventies, and into the eighties, Ravan did it all. She made her own records; produced records for others, including punk rockers the

Dead Boys and former Ronettes lead singer Ronnie Spector, and played the role of session singer. She lent her voice to Lou Reed's *Street Hassle* album, Blue Oyster Cult's *Mirrors* LP, and the soundtrack album to the film *The Warriors*, among others.

1991 was a turning point in Ravan's life. She was diagnosed with lung cancer. Years of smoking, drinking, and drugs had finally caught up with her. Ravan vowed to beat the disease. The parallel between her parents' surviving the Holocaust and her own survival from cancer has not escaped her. "I can't put it in words, but I come from a family of winners," she says. "That was my parents' curse, that they won and nobody else [in their families] did. I was not ready to die. I refused to die. I was thinking about how bad my sister was going to feel." Ravan quit smoking, joined Alcoholics Anonymous, and swore off even going into smoky bars and clubs.

Along with producing records, Ravan found another way to spend her time. She began volunteering at New York's Memorial Sloan-Kettering Hospital, the hospital she credits with saving her life. She visited cancer patients. "For me to just show up and say, 'Hi, I'm a lung cancer survivor. I went through the [chemotherapy], the operation,' I'm the light at the end of their tunnel." She promised herself she'd do volunteer work if she survived because when she had the disease, she wanted to see survivors. But there were not many from whom to draw strength. "I thought," says Ravan, "if I live I'm going to be one of those."

Survival also triggered a Jewish renaissance within Ravan. She put a mezuzah on her doorpost, joined the Actors Temple in the Hell's Kitchen section of New York, and began re-learning some of the rituals she rebelled against as a youth. "I'm starting to understand my religion," Ravan says. "I happen to love being Jewish now. I get a nice, warm feeling from it now. I'm very tight with God."

In 1995, Polygram Records released *The Best of Ten Wheel Drive*. In 1997, Goldie and the Gingerbreads were featured in *The Rolling Stone Book of Women in Rock* and reunited for a live performance for the first time in thirty years. The following year the band was honored for its trailblazing role at the Second Annual Women in Music Touchstone Awards ceremony in New York. Ravan has reduced her role as a singer but remains active as a record producer. From 1997 through 1999, she served as head of production for CBGB Records, the independent record label of the legendary New York rock club CBGB.

# Manfred Mann

Keyboard player. Arranger. Producer. Composer. Born Manfred Lubowitz,
October 21, 1940, Johannesburg, South Africa. Co-founder of the British
bands Manfred Mann and Manfred Mann's Chapter Three, and founder of
Manfred Mann's Earth Band. Best known for the Top Ten American hits
"Doo Wah Diddy Diddy," "Mighty Quinn (Quinn the Eskimo)," and
"Blinded by the Light," and British hits "If You Gotta Go, Go Now,"
"Just Like a Woman," "Semi-Detached Suburban Mr. James," "Fox on
the Run," and "Davy's on the Road Again." Mann is one of the most
prolific and creative recording artists of the rock era, though unheralded
in America because he has made few U.S. concert appearances
since the British Invasion of the mid-sixties.

*Record sleeve for the 1964 Manfred Mann hit single "Sha La La," which reached No. 12 in the
United States. From left, drummer Mike Hugg, singer Paul Jones, keyboard player Manfred
Mann, guitarist Mike Vickers and bass player Tom McGuinness. (Photo courtesy EMI Records.)*

By the age of twelve Manfred Lubowitz was hard-pressed to believe that "an all-knowing, merciful God" really existed. Though he'd gone to Jewish summer camps, called *habonim* camps, and regularly attended a Reform synagogue in Johannesburg with his family, it all seemed so hypocritical to him while living in a police state that separated and subjugated blacks as part of the official government policy called apartheid. Manfred was puzzled, then angry at the South African Jewish community's silence and lack of outrage at the government's treatment of blacks. Many of the country's Jews had come to South Africa to escape persecution in Europe, and they had tasted their own form of "apartheid." Though Jews eventually became outspoken and influential leaders of the anti-apartheid movement, Manfred didn't believe his family or community did enough soon enough. "I grew up in a society where people were very careful not to eat bacon, pork, or shellfish, but didn't understand the difference between right and wrong. The defense was 'What could we do?'" Manfred says decades later. "Let me quote [author and concentration camp survivor] Primo Levi: 'We can refuse to give our consent.'" Young Manfred also wondered how God could allow such oppression of any people made in His image. Manfred only went through with his bar mitzvah at thirteen so he wouldn't break his grandmother's heart. His Torah portion, Abraham's near sacrifice of Isaac, further alienated Manfred from the spiritual aspects of Judaism. "I've never changed from the idea that that story is deeply immoral. The story has no redeeming value—do what you're told even though it seems wrong," Manfred says of his interpretation of the biblical tale. "I'm glad my father wasn't Abraham."

Manfred's father, David Lubowitz, a successful printer, and his mother Alma Cohen, a pianist, were South African natives. Their families had immigrated there in the late 1890s, "classic refugees from Eastern Europe." Manfred's mother taught him to play "Three Blind Mice" on the family's grand piano when he was a child. By age six he was regularly "fiddling about" on the instrument. Manfred's parents divorced when he was six, and he was raised for the most part by his maternal grandmother. He initially tried learning to read music but lacked the patience, as he already had become a pretty fair boogie-woogie player on his own. In his early teens, he also became transfixed by the improvisational inventiveness of bebop jazz giants Miles Davis, John Coltrane, and Dave Brubeck, and began performing at dances and coffeehouses in Johannesburg. Later, he took private music theory lessons from a professor at Witwatersrand University in

Johannesburg, while he worked for his father as a printer. Though his grand-parents had hoped Manfred would eventually take over their bacon factory (a business that they initially kept secret from other family members), Manfred had other ideas. In 1961, he moved to England hoping to make a living as a jazz mu-sician. He, like many of his South African friends, could not tolerate living in what he considered a fascist state. "I had a burning hatred for it," Mann recalls. He also feared that when the time came to have children, raising them in such an environment could easily lead to their becoming racists.

Shortly after his arrival in London, he adopted the stage name of Mann be-cause he didn't think Lubowitz sounded right for a jazz player, though he never legally changed his name. "There are two of me," he says. "I think of myself as Lubowitz. I'm only Mann on stage." In 1962, he met a kindred spirit, a jazz-and-blues-loving drummer and vibes player named Mike Hugg. They formed the Mann-Hugg Blues Brothers, an eight-man jazz and blues conglomeration com-plete with a horn section. They quickly discovered there was little demand for jazz groups, so they paired down to a quintet, changed the group's name to Man-fred Mann at the suggestion of a manager, against Mann's wishes, and took aim at the exploding pop market. "When I first got involved with pop music, it was purely a cynical means of earning a living," Mann says. His cynicism evaporated when he discovered songwriters such as Barry Mann and Cynthia Weil and Bob Dylan while seeking material for the group.

The band's first two attempts at a hit single failed to chart. Its third effort, however, the frenetic "5–4–3–2–1," reached No. 5 on the British singles charts. The song was adopted as the theme for the popular English TV program, *Ready, Steady, Go*, which showcased the hot acts of the day. The song became the first of sixteen British hit singles the group enjoyed from 1964 through 1969 (only four of which made the American Top 40). The band went through several lineup changes during that time, but always featured Mann, Hugg, and bass player Tom McGuinness at its core. The group distinguished itself from most other British Invasion bands of the time with impressive musicianship, thought-ful arrangements accenting keyboard and harmonica over guitar, and an ability to blend jazz and R&B elements into its pop songs. Though Mann, the group's reluctant namesake, was neither the lead singer nor primary songwriter, he was the group's quiet visionary as well as a gifted keyboard player. He recognized talented musicians who would work well together and had a knack for choosing songs (and singers) that best served the group's sound. Mann could hear new ways of presenting previously recorded songs, rearrange them, and turn them into hits for the group. In some cases Mann's arrangements and production became the definitive, or most commercially successful, version of a song. Mann's song selection and arranging talents were crucial to the band's success as neither he nor the other members could pen hit songs consistently, though he, Hugg, and lead singer Paul Jones co-wrote "5−4−3−2−1."

Mann didn't let pop star ego get in the band's way. "I looked around and saw the Rolling Stones, the Who, the Beatles, and figured we can't write as well as these guys. Writing is a gift. You can't write if you haven't got the gift. From that day on I decided we would cover songs [written by others]," Mann says, adding, "One of my biggest struggles in life has been finding material." The band's first U.S. hit, "Do Wah Diddy Diddy," which reached No. 1 in 1964, came from the American writing team of Jeff Barry and Ellie Greenwich. The band scored a British hit the following year with the Barry Mann−Cynthia Weil tune "Oh No, Not My Baby."

Tired of the pop star grind, and looking to expand musically, Mann and Hugg disolved the band and re-formed as the jazz-driven rock band Manfred Mann's Chapter Three. The band issued a pair of critically acclaimed albums, *Chapter Three*, and *Chapter Three Vol. 2*, that alienated Mann's pop fans and ended up as commercial disappointments. In 1971, Mann, minus longtime colleague Hugg, formed Manfred Mann's Earth Band, a harder rocking band than its sixties' pop predecessor. Mann reclaimed a spot on the British charts with the Earth Band in 1973 with a song called "Joybringer," and in 1976 was back on top of the U.S. charts with a stunning version of Bruce Springsteen's "Blinded by the Light." The group grazed the Top Forty six months later in 1977 with Springsteen's "Spirit in the Night." Mann had even greater success recording the songs of Bob Dylan, as did many American acts such as Peter, Paul and Mary, the Byrds, and the Turtles. Throughout the sixties and seventies, Mann selected the obscure as well as the classic from Dylan's catalog, and mined it more often than most. Mann scored substantial hits with Dylan's "If You Gotta Go, Go Now," "Just Like a Woman," and "Mighty Quinn (Quinn the Eskimo)." He also included Dylan's "With God on Our Side," "It's All Over Now, Baby Blue," "Please Mrs. Henry,"

"Father of Day, Father of Night," You Angel You," "Quit Your Low Down Ways," and "Don't Kill it, Carol," on Manfred Mann and Manfred Mann's Earth Band albums. (In 1972, he also produced *Lo and Behold*, a critically acclaimed album of unreleased Dylan songs performed by a short-lived English band called Coulson, Dean, McGuinness, Flint. McGuinness was Manfred Mann bassist Tom McGuinness.) One of the reasons Mann had such success with Dylan's work was that he was unafraid to radically alter the songs. "We never tried to do Dylan's songs in his style or in that sort of way, and we would change things if we didn't like them," Mann told Greg Russo, author of *Mannerisms: The Five Faces of Manfred Mann*. The Earth Band's last appearance on the American charts was in 1984 when "The Runner," a single from *Somewhere in Afrika*, a concept album about South Africa's apartheid system that blended rock, electronic music, and indigenous native chanting and instrumentation, reached No. 22. The album also was a substantial hit in Germany, where Mann's popularity has rarely waned. In 1991, Mann continued to spark his creativity and move beyond making strictly pop music by recording *Plains Music*, an album influenced by songs and chants of Plains Indians of the United States. The album reached No. 1 in South Africa.

Since the early 1990s, record companies have released numerous Manfred Mann and Earth Band retrospectives and compilations in Europe and the United States. Because of the volume of material that exists, it's been nearly impossible to produce a "definitive" collection. A Manfred Mann European reunion tour was organized to promote a 1992 compilation called *Ages of Mann*. Mann himself, however, declined to participate, so the band, which featured key members of the sixties' lineups, toured successfully as the Manfreds, in 1993 and 1994. In the meantime, an Earth Band compilation released in 1993 sold 300,000 copies in Germany alone. Since then, Mann has regularly toured Europe with his Earth Band, recorded new work (that has not been released in the U.S.), and watched record companies release more Manfred Mann compilation records. A hefty fifty-three song collection, *Manfred Mann: All Manner of Menn, 1965–1969* was released in 2000. A pair of CDs, totaling forty-five songs from four Manfred Mann albums was released in 2001. Mann, however, was looking forward, working on a new album between concert tours.

Years after Mann reluctantly became a bar mitzvah, he reread the Torah "with an open mind" to see if his atheist views had changed. They were only reaffirmed. He knows that marks him as a poor role model for Jews seeking a spiritual renaissance, but Mann does grant that he has deep Jewish roots and finds value in Jewish traditions. He simply can't come to grips with the existence of God and is adamant that religious zealots, including ultraorthodox Jews, should never gain too much power. "Once people feel they have God on their side—there's Dylan again—it's disastrous," he says.

# Zal Yanovsky
## of the Lovin' Spoonful

Guitar player. Singer. Born Zalman Yanovsky December 19, 1944, Toronto, Canada. Died December 13, 2002, outside Kingston, Ontario, Canada. Co-founder and lead guitar player of the Lovin' Spoonful, whose hits included "Do You Believe in Magic," "Summer in the City," "Daydream," and "You Didn't Have to Be So Nice." The band was inducted into the Rock and Roll Hall of Fame in 2000.

*The Lovin' Spoonful 1966–1967. From left, bassist Steve Boone, guitarist Zal Yanovsky, drummer Joe Butler and singer John Sebastian. (Photo by Henry Diltz.)*

Zal Yanovsky discovered his musical chops playing folk music on the streets of Yafo (Jaffa) and Tel Aviv in 1961 at age sixteen. He had gone to Israel for an extended visit with his uncle, also named Zalman Yanovsky. Uncle Zal, a fervent Zionist, had emigrated from Canada to Palestine in 1931 and become a member of the Degania Bet kibbutz, just south of the Sea of Gallilee, at its founding in 1932. For ten months, young Zal studied half a day and worked half a day six days a week. In his spare time, he'd "busk" (perform) on coastal city streets. Earning "a few shekels playing Pete Seeger songs" in Israel encouraged Yanovsky to pursue a music career when he returned to Toronto. Yanovsky's moment in the spotlight with the Lovin' Spoonful was just a few years away.

Yanovsky grew up in a liberal, left-wing, secular Jewish household. His Ukraine-born father, Avrom, drew political cartoons for a weekly Yiddish newspaper, the *Wochenblat*, and a Canadian communist publication called the *Tribune*, and also worked as a leather cutter. Zal's mother, Nachama, came to Canada as a child from Poland along with five sisters and a brother and became a Yiddish teacher. Both sides of Yanovsky's family initially settled in Winnipeg and moved to Toronto in the 1920s. Yiddish was the first language in the Yanovsky house; Zal didn't speak English until he was four. Through the seventh grade, every day after public school, he studied a variety of subjects in Yiddish at the Morris Vinchefsky School where his mother taught. His mother also was a member of Toronto's Yiddish Folk Choir. His father was active in the city's Yiddish theater as a set builder and actor. The Yanovskys filled the house with Yiddish music and with the songs of Woody Guthrie, Pete Seeger, the Weavers, and Paul Robeson. When Zal was about eleven, his parents gave him a guitar and encouraged him to learn folk music.

Toronto had a large Jewish community and many of its members visited the Yanovsky's home. "Theater people" dropped in, as well as "communists, socialists, religious Jews, nonreligious Jews," Yanovsky recalls. The result was a left-wing background and a susceptibility to folk music. "I remember picketing the U.S. embassy in Toronto before they fried the Rosenbergs," says Yanovsky, who was eight at the time. (Julius and Ethel Rosenberg were accused of passing nuclear weapons secrets to the Soviet Union and were executed for espionage in 1953 after one of the most controversial trials in U.S. history.) While Zal didn't follow in his father's footsteps as cartoonist or actor, he did start taking the guitar more seriously. He listened to, and studied, the playing of rockers like Chuck

Berry and country pickers Chet Atkins, Amos Garrett, and Don Rich of Buck Owens's band. And while "treading the boards" was not in the cards, Zal must have picked up something from his family's theatrical activity because he was quite an extrovert. His flashy smile and high-stepping antics during perform-ances helped him stick out from the crowd and led to his becoming the visual focus of the Lovin' Spoonful.

When he returned to Toronto from Israel in 1962, Yanovsky found a blossom-ing Canadian folk scene led by the likes of Ian and Sylvia, who released their debut album that year and in 1964 would make waves with their second album, *Four Strong Winds* and its title song. In 1963, Yanovsky, who "somehow got better on guitar," joined fellow Canadian Dennis Doherty in a folk group called the Halifax Three. With the addition of Cass Elliot (born Ellen Naomi Cohen), the group evolved into Cass Elliot and the Big Three, and eventually into the Mug-wumps, which also included singer-songwriter John Sebastian. By 1965, how-ever, the group was defunct. Doherty and Elliot eventually joined what would become the Mamas and the Papas, a California-based group. Yanovsky and Se-bastian formed the Lovin' Spoonful with drummer Joe Butler and bass player Steve Boone in New York. Both groups would have short life spans in their orig-inal incarnations but would leave a lasting impact on popular music. The two bands were among America's great hopes during the British Invasion of the mid-sixties, vying with the Beatles and a barrage of other bands from across "the pond" for airplay on American radio stations. A favorite saying of Yanovsky's at the time was, "Dress British, think Yiddish."

The Lovin' Spoonful's eclectic mix of jug band, folk, blues and rock influ-ences, coupled with solid musicianship and Sebastian's concise songwriting (none of the Spoonful's hits was longer than three minutes), was an immediate success. The band's first single, "Do You Believe in Magic," a breezy, exhilarating paean to "the magic of music that can set you free" (with its distinctive autoharp introduction) reached No. 9 and stayed on the charts for two months. The song was nothing short of two minutes and four seconds of adolescent wonder and euphoria over the emotional power of music, all kinds of music, with a beat you could dance to. It remains Yanovsky's favorite Spoonful recording. During the next two years the band was a hit-making machine. Few bands could match the diversity of the songs Sebastian wrote for the Spoonful. The sweet ballad "You Didn't Have to Be So Nice" (No. 2), the gritty rocker "Summer in the City"

(No. 1), with its automobile horn and jackhammer accompaniment, and the jug band joy of "Nashville Cats" (No. 8) came from the same quartet. (The latter hit would inspire the novelty song "Noshville Katz" by the Lovin' Cohens in 1967.) In the space of two years, the eclectic quartet scored seven consecutive Top Ten hits. The band also wrote and recorded the music for Francis Ford Coppola's *You're a Big Boy Now* and Woody Allen's *What's Up, Tiger Lily?*

The Lovin' Spoonful's run at the top, however, was over almost as fast as it had begun. The band's demise was precipitated by a 1966 drug bust of Yanovsky and Boone for marijuana possession. Yanovsky was only twenty-two. A bigger reason for the band's slide was the infamous "creative differences." Yanovsky liked to rock and wanted to do more club concerts. Sebastian's songwriting, however, was becoming more gentle and personal, and he had less inclination to tour. Yanovsky also thought the band had become too big and had lost control of its destiny. He criticized Sebastian's songwriting and the band's direction until the other three members fired him in the summer of 1967. The band replaced Yanovsky with guitarist Jerry Yester, and scored its final hit, "She Is Still a Mystery," in late 1967. But the band's chemistry was gone. So was the feel-good atmosphere generated by Yanovsky's smile and zany stage presence, not to mention his deft guitar playing, which was underrated at the time but was a perfect fit for the musically adventurous band. Sebastian departed in 1968. Under Butler, the group soldiered on for another album, *Revelation: Revolution '69*, and occasional tours, but by then, with its founders gone, the Spoonful was on life support, and off the charts. (The band reunited in 1980 to perform in Paul Simon's film, *One Trick Pony*.)

In 1968, Yanovsky released his lone solo effort, *Alive and Well in Argentina* on Buddha Records. It was a wacky, bizarre, hodge-podge of an album that included covers of George Jones's "From Brown to Blue" and Floyd Cramer's "Last Date," and, perhaps most telling, Ivory Joe Hunter's "I Almost Lost My Mind." The album title could be interpreted as Yanovsky's way of signaling that he was doing just fine in his exile from the band. The record flopped commercially, however. Yanovsky returned to Canada and worked in television, producing a program called *Magistrate's Court*, a forerunner of the many *Judge Judy*–style television shows that have become a staple of American TV during the past thirty years. He then returned to the music business, producing albums for singer Pat Boone and folk singer Tim Buckley and touring with Kris Kristofferson in 1969 and

1970. In 1974, he joined the touring company of *National Lampoon's Lemmings*, starring John Belushi and Chevy Chase. After that, he says, "the phone wasn't ringing off the hook." In 1979, Yanovsky went into the restaurant business, opening the Kingston, Ontario, eatery Chez Piggy, which he describes as "haimish" and "rather successful." In 1994, he and his wife Rose also opened a bakery, called Pan Chancho.

Before his untimely death, he hadn't completely given up music. He had repaired the rift with Sebastian years ago, remained close with him, and occasionally joined him for concerts and short tours, including a 1997 jaunt through Norway. In 2000, the Lovin' Spoonful was inducted into the Rock and Roll Hall of Fame. The original foursome reunited to perform a pair of songs at the induction ceremony. With only a one-hour rehearsal, however, they were less than impressive. "I'd say we'll never get together again. Perhaps in the next life," Yanovsky said of any possible reunions. One thing that was much more certain was his annual visit to Israel. Since 1988, Yanovsky made yearly trips to see his uncle Zal's family. (He had remained conversant in Hebrew and Yiddish.) Of his secular Jewish identity, he said, "Yiddishkeit is Yiddishkeit," and he had plenty of it. And, he believed, if another power ever pursues and persecutes the Jews again, whether Orthodox or atheist, "we'll all sit in the same oven."

# P. F. Sloan

**Singer. Songwriter. Guitarist. Keyboard player. Born Philip "Flip" Gary Schlein, September 18, 1945, New York City. Best known for writing the hits "Eve of Destruction" and "Secret Agent Man," as well as "A Must to Avoid" by Herman's Hermits, "You Baby" and "Let Me Be" by the Turtles, "Where Were You When I Needed You" by the Grass Roots, and "I Found a Girl" by Jan and Dean. He is the subject of the Jimmy Webb song "P. F. Sloan."**

*The P. F. Sloan–penned No. 1 hit "Eve of Destruction" was inspired by the Jewish concept of tikkun olam, or repairing the world. (Photo courtesy of David A. Stein/All the Best Records.)*

In 1964, P. F. Sloan was just a year out of high school and depressed by the Kennedy assassination, the country's racial turmoil, and the growing conflict in Vietnam when he wrote the controversial folk-rock protest song "Eve of Destruction." The song became a No. 1 hit for singer Barry McGuire in the summer of 1965. Sloan, who had considered becoming a rabbi before his music career took off in his late teens, wrote the song as a prayer about repairing the world. "The writing of 'Eve of Destruction' was a major experience. I felt in contact with the Divine," Sloan says. An "inner voice" awakened Sloan one night in mid–1964, telling him to take five sheets of paper and write a song title on each: "Sins of a Family," "Take Me for What I'm Worth," "This Mornin'," "Ain't No Way I'm Gonna Change My Mind," and "Eve of Destruction." He wrote the five songs in one night, wrestling with the voice he heard, especially on "Eve of Destruction." He'd write one lyric, and the voice would tell him to change it. "Think of all the hate there is in Red China," was originally written as "Red Russia," for example. Driven by McGuire's coarse, bluesy voice, the song opened like a newscast filled with fiery headlines: "The Eastern world, it is explodin' / Violence flarin', bullets loadin'." It continued with an in-your-face litany of injustices and hypocrisies that needed righting: "You're old enough to kill, but not for votin' . . . Marches alone can't bring integration, when human respect is disintegratin' . . . Think of all the hate there is in Red China, then take a look around to Selma, Alabama . . . Hate your next-door neighbor, but don't forget to say grace." Sloan's list of the nation's problems became a rallying cry for many and a favorite of radio stations and TV variety shows, but was totally misunderstood and blasted by others. Social critics called Sloan an anarchist and communist for daring to say such things, while some music critics slammed him as a second-rate Bob Dylan for his lack of subtlety and satire. McGuire's singing career was derailed, and Sloan had to lie low. "The song was about making simple repairs; yes, it was as simple as *tikkun olam*, but society, as shallow as it was, couldn't grasp that," Sloan recalls. "To cure an ill, you need to know what is sick," Sloan once explained. As late as 1991, the song was still taking critical hits in the press. "Eve of Destruction" was listed No. 3 among "The Top Ten Worst Dylanesque Songwriting Ripoffs" in the book, *The Worst Rock 'n' Roll Records of All Time*, by Jimmy Gutterman and Owen O'Donell. Despite the backlash, Sloan's prayer ("Eve" originally began with the words "Dear God"), has held up well, and many of its observations remain valid.

Sloan was born Philip Gary Schlein on September 18, 1945, in New York City. His paternal grandparents emigrated to the United States from Russia in 1914. His maternal grandparents, named Petranou, were Romanian Jews who never emigrated. Philip's American-born father, Harry, was a pharmacist; his Romanian-born mother, Clairitsa (known as Claire), was a housewife who taught herself to read, write, and speak English. His older sister, Lynn, gave him the nickname of "Flip" and eventually introduced him to the music of the Platters, Chuck Berry, and Elvis Presley. The Schlein family initially lived in an Italian neighborhood in the Bronx, then moved to a predominantly Christian neighborhood in Hempstead, Long Island. The family celebrated and observed most of the major Jewish holidays, but in a major concession to fitting in with the neighbors, also celebrated Christmas. It may have been comforting to feel like one of the crowd and may have helped young Phil better understand other religions, but it did not prevent him from being called "Christ killer" when he was six, or from being accosted in elementary school.

Around 1956 the family moved to the West Coast, settling in the heavily Jewish Fairfax section of Hollywood, California. Harry Schlein attended pharmacy school for a year to validate his New York pharmacist's license. While completing the course, he applied for a liquor license for a "sundries" store he was running, but was repeatedly denied a license. He decided to reapply under the name Harry Sloan, taken from the American painter John Sloan, and was granted the license. At the age of twelve, Philip Schlein legally became Phil Sloan. The family attended Temple Beth-El, a Conservative congregation in Hollywood. Philip was especially moved by the somber melody of the *Kol Nidre* each Yom Kippur. He attended Hebrew school from age eleven through fifteen, and he enjoyed studying for his bar mitzvah and learning the meanings of all the prayers and his Haftorah. His rabbi was so impressed with Phil's passion for learning and singing, he encouraged his student to pursue a career as a cantor. Sloan, however, was interested in becoming a rabbi to get closer to God. As a teenager, he developed an interest in kabbalah and its accompanying *Zohar* text.

At thirteen, Sloan's father bought him a guitar, though he hoped his son would follow in his footsteps as a pharmacist or doctor. Philip took the guitar to a music store to learn how to tune it and ran into Elvis Presley, who was having a guitar repaired. According to Sloan, Presley taught him several chords, thus giving Sloan his first guitar lesson. Sloan is mostly self-taught, influenced by guitar heroes such as Chuck Berry, Scotty Moore, Duane Eddy, and Dick Dale. In 1959, before his fourteenth birthday, Sloan got an audition at Aladdin Records, an R&B label in Los Angeles. He sang Little Richard's "Good Golly Miss Molly" and Elvis Presley's "I Don't Care If the Sun Don't Shine" and was sent home with a recording contract and the instruction to start writing songs. He returned with four songs; the company recorded two—"All I Live for Is Loving" and "Little Girl up in a Cabin"—and released them under the name of Flip Sloan in 1959. "Flip" was fourteen. The record went nowhere. The following year, pursuing music only casually while trying to get through high school, he released a single called "She's My Girl." The B-side was called "If You Believe in Me." Neither song made much of a ripple. At fifteen, Sloan, already struggling with the usual insecurities of a high school student, had to deal with classmates who ridiculed him for failing to generate a hit song. "One day you're handing out records in the hall to schoolmates, the next day you're a has-been because the record didn't make it," Sloan recalls. Still, Sloan put a band together to play in school talent shows and on one occasion earned a passing grade from a Spanish teacher by singing "La Bamba" to the class. While still in high school he got a job as a staff writer at Screen Gems Music for ten dollars a week. That led to a contract as a writer and recording artist with Dunhill Records from 1964 through 1967. It was an incredibly productive and successful period that showcased Sloan's multiple talents as a writer, singer, musician, arranger, and producer—not only on his own records, but for a wide variety of acts. It's all the more amazing when considering that by the time his four-year run at Dunhill ended, Sloan was only twenty-two.

During that time, Sloan, often with co-writer and musician Steve Barri (born Steve Lipkin), had a hand in hits for Jan and Dean, Johnny Rivers, the Turtles, Herman's Hermits, the Searchers, Freddie and the Dreamers, the Mamas and the Papas, and, of course, Barry McGuire. McGuire was looking to start a solo career after having had success as a member of the New Christy Minstrels. (He was the lead singer on the hit "Green, Green.") McGuire was looking for songs for his debut solo album when he decided to record a handful of Sloan's songs, including "Eve of Destruction." No one at the record company believed in the song. Sloan's musical collaborator, Steve Barri, didn't even like the song. It was too political, too serious, too Dylan, too controversial, and too different. Radio wouldn't play it; people wouldn't buy it. Even McGuire recorded it almost as an afterthought as time was running out in the studio. "Eve" was to be the flip side of a song he was much more excited about called, "What's the Matter With Me."

McGuire sang "Eve" cold, reading the scribbled lyrics from a piece of paper for the first time. Fate intervened. They were right about the song being different, but wrong about its appeal. Somewhere in radio land, a disc jockey played the B-side of McGuire's record, and a No. 1 hit was born.

Aside from "Eve of Destruction," Sloan is also celebrated for "Secret Agent Man," originally written as the musical introduction for the television show of the same name. Sloan was asked to add verses and complete the song. The result was a No. 3 hit for Johnny Rivers in 1966. The Ventures, Hank Williams, Jr., Devo, and Blues Traveler also have recorded the song, and just about every garage band in America included it on its set list. During the sixties, the Association, Kenny Rogers and the First Edition, Paul Revere and the Raiders, Tommy Roe, and Gary Lewis and the Playboys, among others, included Sloan-Barri songs on their albums. While writing and playing on recording sessions for many of these acts, Sloan and Barri found the time to make their own records under a long list of pseudonyms. Bands that were, for the most part, Sloan and Barri studio creations included the Fantastic Baggys, the Imaginations, the Lifeguards, the Rally Packs, the Street Cleaners, and Willis and the Wheels. Much of what the duo wrote was sixties' teenage surf-rock, which is why they meshed so well in the studio with Jan and Dean. As Sloan matured, however, he began to blend folk, blues, and rock 'n' roll.

The most successful band that began as a Sloan-Barri recording vehicle, however, was the Grass Roots. As the Grass Roots, Sloan and Barri scored a hit on their first try with "Where Were You When I Needed You," which reached No. 28 on the singles charts. The problem was there was no real band to undertake a tour to promote the record. While Sloan saw this as his opportunity to finally become a full-time performer, the powers-that-be at Dunhill who had him under contract believed Sloan was worth more as a writer churning out hits for others than as a performer. An area bar band called the Thirteenth Floor was pressed into service as the Grass Roots. Sloan continued to contribute to the Grass Roots in the studio, singing and playing guitar on the 1967 Top Ten hit "Let's Live for Today," which became an anthem for U.S. troops in Vietnam. He and Barri wrote another hit for the group that year, "Things I Should Have Said." The Grass Roots, without Sloan, went on to record a string of hits, including "Midnight Confessions," "I'd Wait a Million Years," and "Temptation Eyes." The Dunhill philosophy of keeping Sloan in the studio writing songs for other acts took its toll on him. Sloan did release a pair of solo albums: *Songs of Our Times* in 1965, featuring his rendition of "Eve of Destruction," and "Sins of a Family," which reached No. 87 on the *Billboard* Hot 100, and *Twelve More Times*, released in 1966. But neither album was a priority for the record company and, though critically praised, they failed to sell. In 1967, at odds with Dunhill Records, Sloan not only left the company, he left California, moving to New York to try his luck as a singer-songwriter in Greenwich Village. In 1968 he released the album *Measure of Pleasure*. In 1970, singer-songwriter Jimmy Webb ("By the Time I Get to Phoenix," "Witchita Lineman," "Up, Up and Away") wrote "P. F. Sloan," a tribute to his peer, and included it on his *Words and Music* album. Uncomfortable in New York, Sloan returned to California, and in 1972 released *Raised on Records*. Critics hailed both albums, but the records generated little commercial success.

Disenchanted, and physically and emotionally exhausted, P. F. Sloan dropped out of the music business. For nearly twenty years he halfheartedly worked a variety of nine-to-five jobs. In 1990, the National Academy of Songwriters honored Sloan and that year he wrote "(Still on the) Eve of Destruction," updating the 1965 classic for McGuire. In 1991, Sloan was introduced to Rabbi Shlomo Carlebach, who was in Los Angeles to perform several concerts. At one show, Carlebach invited Sloan to perform with him onstage. Of that experience Sloan says, "I hadn't felt the power of Jewish lament and joy for quite a while. I felt transported into a world much higher than the usual state I occupy." At Carlebach's suggestion, Sloan also made his first trip to Israel. In 1992, Bruce Jay Paskow, one of two Jewish members of the neo-folk trio the Washington Squares, coaxed Sloan into a recording studio in Seattle. The result was a ten-song CD that included "(Still on the) Eve of Destruction" and a wonderfully rough, revved up rendition of "Secret Agent Man," on which Sloan is backed by young Seattle musicians. The record was released in Japan in 1993 as *Serenade of the Seven Sisters*, which was finally released in the United States in 1997 on the All The Best Records label. In 1995, Sloan returned to writing songs on a regular basis with a new collaborator, Steve Kalinich, and performing in small clubs and participating in benefit concerts. In the spring of 2001, the record label Varese Sarabande released *P. F. Sloan, Child of Our Times*, a collection of songs Sloan wrote and recorded from 1963 through 1965.

A student of Hinduism for many years (he has traveled to India several times), Sloan also reads Torah daily and studies the teachings of the Baal Shem Tov, the founder of Hasidism. Studying Hinduism, Sloan says, "has helped me get closer to the meaning of God, and my Judaism."

# Michael Bloomfield

**Guitar player. Songwriter. Born July 28, 1943, Chicago, Illinois.
Died February 15, 1981, San Francisco, California. Influential electric
blues guitarist best known for his work with Bob Dylan, the
Paul Butterfield Blues Band, and the Electric Flag.**

*Michael Bloomfield performing in 1980. (Photo courtesy of the estate of Michael Bloomfield.)*

Few Jewish musicians as prominent as Michael Bloomfield have ever been as openly proud of being Jewish as he was. That may have been because Bloomfield cared strictly about making music and not about carefully cultivating an image to help him attain stardom.

In 1969, Bloomfield collaborated with his good friend Barry Goldberg on the album 2 *Jews Blues* against the advice and wishes of Columbia Records, the company that had him under contract. Label executives weren't able to keep Bloomfield from playing on the album, but they were successful in keeping his name and photo off the cover. The four songs he appears on are credited to "The Great." Bloomfield, who also used aliases Mikal Blumfeld and Fast Fingers Finkelstein when making guest appearances on others' records without informing his record company, wouldn't be credited by name on 2 *Jews Blues* until the album was re-released on CD in 1993, twelve years after his death.

In the mid-seventies during a period when Bloomfield was appearing solo in clubs as an "unplugged" act, no one could stop him from including his song "I'm Glad I'm Jewish" in his sets. It is unvarnished "Jewish blues," humorous on the surface, with grim reality lurking just below. On an unreleased recording of "I'm Glad I'm Jewish" made in San Francisco around 1975, one can hear that the song is not only driven by Bloomfield's silky slide guitar and earnest finger picking, but by a knowing, joyful vocal. The song begins: "I'm glad I'm Jewish. / I'm glad I'm Jewish. / Hebrew to the bone, Lord, Lord. / I'm glad I'm Jewish, / Hebrew to the bone. / You know the Christian girls / just can't leave them Jew boys alone." It ends, however, with the sobering lines, "I'm glad I'm Jewish, / Hebrew to the bone. / It kept me strong all my life. / There ain't nobody / leave the Jew boy alone."

Bloomfield had little respect for anyone who would deny his heritage. "He found that despicable," says his older brother Allen. "What you were born into should never in any way be denigrated; it was significant."

Judaism, directly and indirectly, played a significant role in Michael Bloomfield's musical development. As children he and his brother spent hours at their maternal grandfather Max Klein's pawn shop. Grandpa Max was a religious man who would discuss the Torah with his grandsons while they attempted to play the concertinas, guitars, and harmonicas that could be found throughout the store. It was Grandpa Max who took them to High Holiday services at an Orthodox synagogue on occasion instead of to North Shore Congregation Israel, the Reform synagogue where the family had a membership. The Orthodox services

*Michael Bloomfield on his bar mitzvah day with Rabbi Edgar Siskin at North Shore Congregation Israel in Glencoe, Illinois, in 1956. (Photo courtesy of the estate of Michael Bloomfield.)*

were too long, but Michael was smitten by the music. And the music would draw Michael back to synagogue, any synagogue, again and again for the High Holidays. "One of the things that influenced us to go to synagogue on Rosh Hashanah and Yom Kippur was the music,—"Avinu Malcanu," "Kol Nidre"—a seed was planted there," says Allen. "Michael always talked about the similarities of black music, Hebraic music, and gypsy music. He saw the expression in sound of a people's soul. In synagogue he'd hear that almost biblical cry, that depiction of sorrow and compassion."

Michael Bloomfield was an empathetic soul, a champion of the underdog. The music he heard in synagogue (and the blues he heard in Chicago's black clubs) only heightened his desire, his brother says, "to put the salve on. He thought blacks got a real short stick." Years later, he would use his fame and celebrity to get concert promoters to use acts such as B. B. King and Muddy Waters to open his shows, thus introducing pioneer black bluesmen to white audiences, dramatically expanding their fan base.

Ironically, Bloomfield was born into a wealthy family. His father, Harold, owned Bloomfield Industries, which made stainless steel. During World War II, the company manufactured bomb hoists, food trays, oxygen masks, K-ration can openers and other supplies for the military. After the war, Beatrice Foods bought the company. Though Harold was a piano player and a fan of Broadway musicals, he wanted Michael to join the family business, and Michael's decision to stick with the blues resulted in a difficult father-son relationship.

Michael's mother, Dorothy, had studied acting at Chicago's Goodman Theater, in the same class as Karl Malden, Geraldine Page, and Sam Wannemaker. She would go on to lend her voice to radio soap operas such as "Little Orphan Annie," "Backstage Wife," and "Life Can Be Beautiful." Dorothy encouraged her son to follow his heart. "You can't stop a creative person from being creative," she says.

The family celebrated the major Jewish holidays, sent the kids to a Jewish preschool, and attended a Conservative synagogue until moving to the suburb of Glencoe, where the Bloomfields joined the reform North Shore Congregation Israel. Michael went to Hebrew school, apparently enjoying it, and was bar mitzvahed there with Rabbi Edgar Siskin officiating. Siskin would play more than the role of spiritual leader in Michael's life. A jazz fan, Siskin was a friend of Columbia Records executive John Hammond, Sr., the man who had signed Bob

Dylan, among others, to a recording contract. Siskin kept Hammond apprised of Bloomfield's progress. Hammond eventually would sign Bloomfield to Columbia Records in 1964.

Among Bloomfield's bar mitzvah gifts were a Les Paul sunburst electric guitar and an amplifier, but it was the transistor radio Michael got that may have been even more influential to the precocious kid who would grow up to be one of the world's premier electric blues guitar players. While listening to that radio in bed each night (black stations exclusively after a while), Bloomfield discovered the blues. And fell in love with the musical style.

By fifteen he was playing in bands at temple dances and high school sock hops. By sixteen, to his parents' chagrin, he had moved from the well-to-do North Shore section of Chicago to the predominantly black south side of the city to be closer to the area's clubs so he could soak up the blues and learn from the masters. Bloomfield and his friend keyboard player Barry Goldberg were nervy enough as teens, not to mention as white boys, to ask to sit in with Muddy Waters, Howlin' Wolf, and B. B. King. By his late teens, Bloomfield was managing a folk club called the Fickle Pickle, had instituted a blues night on Tuesdays, and had begun bringing in black acts to play for the white patrons.

Bloomfield spent so much more time on his music and hanging out in clubs, than on his school studies that he was eventually kicked out, or dropped out, of New Trier High School (his mother is no longer sure which). He and friends Nick Gravenites and Barry Goldberg, also in academic trouble, finished their senior year of high school at the local YMCA. "He never concentrated on his studies," his mother says. "He was very bright, but he was bored. The music was number one. He practiced and played and listened to music for hours and hours. He played every type of music. He played Indian Ravi Shankar–type music. He played Israeli music, every culture he tried to play, but blues was his big thing. It moved him the most, though he always said there was a correlation in [all those types of music], a sad story."

Bloomfield may not have been interested in school work, but he loved to read. To help pass the time while practicing, he often read novels. He also studied and worked for hours with B. B. King and Muddy Waters to the point that, his mother says, "B. B. and Muddy were like his fathers." In 1964, Bloomfield's hard work paid off with a recording contract with Columbia Records, but Columbia not quite knowing how to promote Bloomfield's first effort, didn't release the album. Bloomfield also recorded with the Paul Butterfield Blues Band, but that record, *The Original Lost Elektra Sessions*, wouldn't see daylight until much later.

Though Bloomfield shunned the limelight, his work in 1965 would cement his reputation and, whether he liked it or not, launch a legend. Fans were captivated by his passion for the blues as well as by his musical precision, phrasing, and note-bending technique. He finally clicked with the Paul Butterfield Blues Band, recording a pair of acclaimed albums, *The Paul Butterfield Blues Band* and *East-West* (released in 1966), which featured the Bloomfield-composed, Indian raga–influenced, title tune. In between those two records, Bloomfield served as guitarist on Bob Dylan's classic *Highway 61 Revisited* and, with the Butterfield Blues Band, backed Dylan during the folkie's newsmaking, I'm-going-electric appearance at the Newport Folk Festival. But he declined an invitation to join Dylan's touring band, remaining with Butterfield.

In 1967, Bloomfield left Butterfield to pursue his vision for an "American music band." With a pumping, funky horn section, Bloomfield's blazing guitar, Barry Goldberg's soulful organ runs, Buddy Miles's muscular drumming, Nick Gravenites's pop songwriting sensibilities and vocals, and with Harvey Brooks anchoring on bass, the resulting Electric Flag was a band to be reckoned with. The short-lived group made an auspicious debut. *A Long Time Comin'*, the group's first and only album recorded with the original lineup (not counting a film soundtrack record), remains an influential recording, preceding horn-driven rock and pop bands such as Blood, Sweat and Tears and Chicago. The San Francisco–based band's first live appearance was at the Monterey International Pop Festival. Bassist Brooks recalls that during band rehearsals the exacting Bloomfield often would utter, "It's *farshemel!*" when the music didn't sound right. Drug problems and clashing egos derailed what might have been one of the country's seminal rock bands.

The following year, Bloomfield continued his run of acclaimed projects by joining Al Kooper and Stephen Stills for *Super Session*. The record, which also featured longtime Bloomfield and Kooper friends and musical associates Barry Goldberg and Harvey Brooks, was also a commercial success, adding fuel to Bloomfield's growing reputation as a guitar god equal to Eric Clapton. Through it all, Bloomfield struggled with a form of chronic insomnia that prevented him from undertaking long concert tours and finishing recording projects. He began using drugs to deal with that and other demons, though he never performed while high. "He knew it wouldn't sound good," his brother Allen says. Michael managed to continue making provocative music, though somewhat erratically. *Live at Bill Graham's Fillmore West* in 1969 and *Triumvirate*, a 1973 collaboration with John Hammond, Jr., and Dr. John, are among the keepers.

In 1976, he was convinced to take a shot at stardom one more time with the group KGB, which included Barry Goldberg, bassist Rick Grech, and drummer Carmine Appice. The record flopped. But in 1977, Bloomfield's instructional solo record, *If You Love These Blues, Play 'Em as You Please* was nominated for a Grammy Award. Throughout the seventies and up to his death in 1981 Bloomfield also wrote film scores and continued to perform solo or in ever-changing lineups as Michael Bloomfield and Friends. His music continues to be re-released in various packages and included on blues compilations.

Besides the blues, another constant in his life was his connection to Judaism, his Jewish pride, and his giving personality. "Though he didn't exclude anyone," his brother says, "his closest friends were all Jewish. He wanted to share the commonality of growing up Jewish and being Jewish." Adds his friend Barry Goldberg, who gave the eulogy at his funeral: "We were Jewish soul brothers. It was a bond we all shared and respected in one another."

Michael Bloomfield was found dead in his car on February 15, 1981. The circumstances of what is officially listed as a drug overdose remain a mystery. Goldberg recounted to *Vintage Guitar* Magazine that at the funeral he told the mourners, "Michael was a true hero not just to the Jewish people, not to just musicians, but to the world. Michael was about bridging gaps and tearing down barriers, and he used his music to do that. Michael just wanted life to go on, and for people to be happy."

# Barry Goldberg

**Keyboard player. Songwriter. Composer. Singer. Born December 25, 1942, Chicago, Illinois. Best known for playing organ in Bob Dylan's backup band at the 1965 Newport Folk Festival and on Mitch Ryder and the Detroit Wheels' Top Ten hits, "Devil with the Blue Dress On" and "Sock It to Me Baby!" and as a founding member of the Electric Flag.**

*Barry Goldberg performing during an Electric Flag reunion concert at San Diego State University in 1975. (Photo courtesy Barry Goldberg.)*

In 1969, Barry Goldberg recorded an electric blues album on the Buddah Records label called 2 *Jews Blues: Barry Goldberg and . . .* It was supposed to be called 2 *Jews Blues: Barry Goldberg and Michael Bloomfield*, but Bloomfield's record company, Columbia, would not allow his name or photo to be used on the cover. In fact, Columbia didn't want Bloomfield to have anything to do with the record and was legally able to block the stellar blues guitarist's participation. Bloomfield, who had known Goldberg since high school—the pair used to sneak into black blues clubs on the south side of Chicago together as teens—played on four of the album's nine tunes using the pseudonym "The Great." Bloomfield's real name didn't appear on 2 *Jews Blues* until the album was re-released on compact disc in 1993. The record almost didn't come out at all; many Jews in the music industry pressured Goldberg to change its title, but he would not. Goldberg had some clout. He was an A-list musician, having played at the Newport Folk Festival with Bob Dylan and the Monterey Pop Festival with the Electric Flag, and he had performed on hit records by Mitch Ryder and the Detroit Wheels and on *Super Session* with Bloomfield, Stephen Stills, and Al Kooper. He also was fiercely proud of his Jewish heritage and wasn't afraid to show it. "People told us not to title it that," says Goldberg. His response was: "But that's what the record is, that's what we are, and if Jews don't have the blues after what we've been through, well that's what we are, and this record lets everybody know it!"

When 2 *Jews Blues* finally was released, Goldberg was unaware that the other Jew pictured on the album cover with him was, instead of Bloomfield, Jesus Christ. Goldberg was not amused, but he could do nothing about it.*

Goldberg was one of the few Jewish rock performers in the sixties with a distinctly Jewish name who did not change it, even though he says it probably hurt his career as a recording artist. Though it was never suggested he change his name, he and Bloomfield decided that if asked to do so, they wouldn't. "Bloomfield and I were emphatic about keeping our real names. We were really into our

*One Jewish guitar player who was credited for playing on two songs on the album was Harvey Mandel, who frequently appeared on Goldberg's records. Mandel was born in Detroit on March 11, 1945, and, though not as celebrated as his contemporaries Bloomfield, Steve Miller, and Carlos Santana, was just as inventive. He is best known for playing in the "Woodstock" line up of the blues-rock band Canned Heat, 1969–1970; joining John Mayall's Bluesbreakers for a pair of albums in 1970 and 1971, and being on the short list of guitarists who auditioned to replace Mick Taylor in the Rolling Stones in 1975. "His was the most innovative, original style I ever heard," Goldberg says of Mandel.

heritage, and tradition, and proud of our names, and if people didn't like [our names], tough shit," Goldberg says. The self-described "Jewish soul brothers," also had a prominent Jewish role model to emulate. One of Barry's uncles was Arthur Goldberg, Secretary of Labor in the Kennedy administration, Supreme Court Justice from 1962 to 1965, U.S. Ambassador to the United Nations in the Johnson administration from 1965 to 1968, and, later, president of the American Jewish Committee. "I just thought of my Uncle Arthur and how he just blazed through politics and the legal system and faced a lot of adversity. It made me proud," Barry says. "When Kennedy wanted some advice, he called my uncle. Every time [my uncle] met with Lyndon Johnson, he went in there like a hero. I admired him for that." If the family name was good enough for Uncle Arthur, it was good enough for nephew Barry.

Barry Goldberg grew up in a fairly observant family proud of its Jewish heritage. His paternal great-grandfather was a rabbi in Kiev. His grandfather Joseph, who had emigrated to Chicago from Kiev, was a fruit and vegetable pedlar who became president of the city's Fourteenth Street Synagogue and later served as president of the Orthodox synagogue Agudas Achim, where Barry would become a bar mitzvah. Barry's parents, Frank and Nettie, were co-founders of Chicago's Park Synagogue, a Conservative congregation. Nettie had been a child star in the Yiddish theater from the age of five through seventeen and had toured the United States and Canada. After leaving the theater, she went to work as an operator for Western Union, where she met Frank. Barry was an only child in a home where Shabbat was kept, all the Jewish holidays were celebrated, and a profound sense of *Yiddishkeit* permeated the home. According to his mother, Barry was musically inclined as early as eleven months of age, waving his hands in time to the music he heard from his crib, as if conducting. Much of the music floating through the house included the songs of Yiddish singer Moishe Oisher and cantorial records by Yossele Rosenblatt.

By age two, Barry was trying to play the piano alongside his mother. By four, they were duetting on "Be Mir Bist du Shoen," and by seven, he could barely be pried from the piano, unless it was to play another instrument. (An aunt had bought Barry a full drum kit for his fifth birthday, and he and his mother would perform klezmer music for friends and family.) His mother also enrolled him in a piano class when he was seven, but after only three lessons, the teacher told Mrs. Goldberg to save her money. Her son was simply memorizing the pieces, then playing them "his way." Barry's mother encouraged his musical improvisation and curiosity. "He was always at the piano, always at the phonograph, always in music," his mother says. "He got better, and better, and better all by himself without lessons." By age ten, having discovered local piano legend Meade "Lux" Lewis, Barry was playing boogie-woogie music. A couple of years later, he discovered gospel music and blues radio stations, compliments of a black housekeeper. "We were all into rock music," says Barry, "but we had discovered this other music. Our parents didn't understand rock, but blues was like voodoo to them. They would hear Howlin' Wolf coming out of my bedroom and the walls would start to shake."

Around the time of his bar mitzvah, which with the death of his father three weeks earlier, was not the festive occasion it would have been, Barry met Michael Bloomfield. The two began sneaking out of their houses and together visited the black blues clubs on the south side of Chicago. (His mother says she wasn't worried.) The Jewish soul brothers would beg, plead, and pester the likes of Muddy Waters, Howlin' Wolf, and B. B. King to allow them to sit in. Sometimes they'd just jump onstage and join in without waiting for an answer. It worked. Goldberg and Bloomfield learned blues music from the masters. Goldberg kicked around in a variety of bands before joining a popular local act called Robbie and the Troubadours in 1962. The Troubadours was a show band, complete with sharkskin suits, black Beatle boots, and colored hair, and played hits by the likes of Chubby Checker and James Brown. The band was a fixture on Chicago's club-filled Rush Street, played parties at Hugh Hefner's Playboy mansion, and also was "the Mob's little band; we played all their parties," Goldberg says. Michael Bloomfield helped catapult Goldberg out of Chicago.

It was Bloomfield who, as a member of the Paul Butterfield Blues Band, invited Goldberg to sit in with the group at the Newport Folk Festival in 1965. Instead, Goldberg ended up on stage with the Butterfield Band and Al Kooper supporting Bob Dylan. It was the beginning of Goldberg's long and fruitful rock 'n' roll career. He returned to Chicago and formed the Goldberg-Miller Blues Band with guitarist Steve Miller. The band recorded one album that received little attention before Miller left for San Francisco. (Miller would become an FM radio favorite in the late sixties and a commercial blockbuster in the seventies with songs such as "Living in the U.S.A.," "Gangster of Love," "Space Cowboy," "The Joker," and "Fly Like an Eagle.")

In 1966, Goldberg returned to New York to work as a studio musician on recording sessions. Early jobs included session work for Jimi Hendrix and playing organ on the frenetic, soul-rock gems by Mitch Ryder and the Detroit Wheels, "Devil with the Blue Dress On," which reached No. 4 in late 1966 and "Sock It to Me-Baby!," which peaked at No. 6 in early 1967. If playing with Dylan at Newport had made him something of a celebrity, these recording sessions cemented his reputation as a musician. His playing was nothing short of impassioned, helping to propel the songs at a breathtaking pace. Michael Bloomfield approached him shortly afterward with an idea for "an American music band," a rock 'n' roll band with a horn section that would play everything: blues, soul, country. The band, dubbed the Electric Flag, was based in Mill Valley, California, and included Bloomfield, Goldberg, bassist and longtime acquaintance Harvey Brooks (born Goldstein), drummer Buddy Miles, and horn players Peter Strazza, Herbie Rich, and Marcus Doubleday. The band had an auspicious debut at the legendary Monterey International Pop Festival in June of 1967 and released its debut album, *A Long Time Comin'*, in early 1968. Though it didn't spawn any hit singles, it did reach No. 40 on the *Billboard* album chart, and was a portent of things to come, influencing groups such as Chicago Transit Authority (later renamed Chicago) and Blood, Sweat and Tears. Filled with stellar playing and ear-grabbing songs like "Killing Floor," "Groovin' is Easy," and "She Should Have Just," the album's status as a classic is ensured. The band, however, was short-lived, a casualty of egos, drug abuse, and all those diverse musical styles wrapped in one package. The band released one more album before disintegrating. "It was a wild ride at a chaotic and crazy time," Goldberg says of the band, and the era in which it lived. "We were like guinea pigs for chemists and drug dealers. A lot of people never survived it. I came through in one piece with a brain and mind fairly intact." In late 1968, Goldberg and Brooks served as backup musicians on the acclaimed *Super Session* LP that showcased musical collaborations between Bloomfield, Al Kooper, and Stephen Stills. The controversial Goldberg-Bloomfield project *2 Jews Blues* was released the following year.

Throughout the seventies, Goldberg released a series of albums as a solo artist and as the leader of the Barry Goldberg Reunion. He also played on numerous recording sessions and began a long and somewhat fruitful collaboration with songwriter Gerry Goffin (born February 11, 1939, in Queens, New York). Goffin, whose Jewish identity centered around his love of Israel, had become a songwriting legend, having written, with former wife Carole King, pop classics such as "Up On the Roof, "Will You Love Me Tomorrow," "The Loco-Motion," and many others. In 1973–1974, Gladys Knight and the Pips scored a No. 1 rhythm and blues hit and reached No. 4 on the pop charts with Goffin-Goldberg's "I've Got to Use My Imagination." The pair ended up at the recording sessions in Muscle Shoals, Alabama, during the High Holy Days polishing songs for Knight's *Imagination* album. Goldberg and Goffin found a social center converted into a synagogue for the holidays in the nearby town of Sheffield. Services were officiated by a circuit rabbi who came through town. "It's a heavy thing, a beautiful thing when Jews see someone else is Jewish, more so in smaller communities," Goldberg says of the welcome they received from the congregation. The following year, singer Rod Stewart recorded a Goffin-Goldberg composition, "It's Not the Spotlight," for his *Atlantic Crossing* album.

In 1975, Goldberg also took part in a brief Electric Flag reunion, then formed

*A 1967 promotional photo of the original Electric Flag lineup: From left, horn player Peter Strazza, singer Nick Gravenites, horn player Marcus Doubleday, keyboard player Barry Goldberg, bassist Harvey Brooks, guitarist Michael Bloomfield, and drummer Buddy Miles. (Photo courtesy Barry Goldberg.)*

"someone else's idea of a supergroup" with singer Ray Kennedy, Michael Bloom-field, bassist Rick Grech, and drummer Carmine Appice called KGB. The band, which Goldberg calls "a disaster," lasted for one forgettable album. In 1976, he moved from San Francisco to Los Angeles, not just for the work, but because he could get better chicken soup, chopped liver, and corned beef sandwiches. He added TV and film music supervisor, and composer, to his résumé. His music appeared in TV programs, such as the sit-com *Murphy Brown*, and in films such as *Dirty Dancing* and the 1992 Keifer Sutherland–Dennis Hopper film *Flashback*, which included Goldberg's production of Bob Dylan performing the soul classic, "People Get Ready." He also wrote music for the 1999 Kevin Bacon film, *Stir of Echoes*, and that year he was music supervisor for a star-studded, PBS–televised tribute to Muddy Waters at the Kennedy Center in Washington, D.C. In 2000, he was busy producing an array of up-and-coming acts as well as scoring the pilot for an animated series on VH1 called *Animal Tracs*.

Of his numerous projects throughout the nineties and into the new millennium, producing and playing on Percy Sledge's *Blue Night* album in 1994 was among the most memorable and gratifying. Soul singer Sledge became immortalized in pop culture for his 1966 No. 1 hit, "When a Man Loves a Woman." *Blue Night* was Sledge's first album of new material in twenty years, and it was nominated for a Grammy Award. "There's a certain affinity I have for black artists," Goldberg says. "I don't know if it's because we're both minorities, or were both enslaved, but my best, most soulful work is when I did Percy Sledge's record. When I met him I wanted to *kvell* [gush with pride]. It was the same with Gladys Knight, there's a connection, a feeling. It's a connection of suffering, unfortunately, and then you rejoice from the suffering."

# Harvey Brooks

**Bass player. Producer. Born Harvey Goldstein, New York City, July 4, 1944. Best known as a member of the groundbreaking band the Electric Flag and as one of the most in-demand bass players of the sixties and seventies. He played on Bob Dylan's *Highway 61 Revisited*, Eric Andersen's *'Bout Changes and Things*, Electric Flag's *A Long Time Comin'*, Miles Davis's *Bitches Brew*, the Doors' *Soft Parade*, Paul Kantner and Jefferson Starship's *Blows Against the Empire*, Seals and Crofts' *Summer Breeze*.**

*Bass player Harvey Brooks was a mischief-maker in Hebrew school. (Photo courtesy of BoHa Productions.)*

In 1963 outside the Pier 500, a rock club in Wyandot, Michigan, nineteen-year-old bass player Harvey Goldstein had his name beaten right out of him. Goldstein was in the backing band for a singer named Chico Holiday, and he was just starting to carve a career in music. Just before finishing his set, Holiday introduced the musicians by name. When Goldstein went outside to get some air, he was met by three club patrons for whom the name Goldstein triggered incomprehensible hatred. Goldstein, who gave as good as he got, refers to the incident in which fists and elbows flew as "a Jewboy scenario." It was a scenario that caused him to revert to using a stage name. His first stage name, Dane Harvey, which he used to get his cabaret card in 1961, was strictly a show business move, and he didn't always use it. The switch to the stage name Harvey Brooks after being attacked in Michigan was as much for self-preservation as it was for show business. "I never denied being Goldstein; it was no secret," he says. However, when performing or looking for work, Goldstein wanted a name that had no connotation and drew no attention. While working at Grossinger's Hotel in the Catskills, he saw a billboard with the name "Nat Brooks Orchestra," liked the sound of it, and dubbed himself Harvey Brooks. "That was the thing you did then," says Brooks, "you got a stage name. In those days, the saying was, it was easier to blend in than fight your way in."

Whether his name change had anything to do with it or not, Brooks's phone rarely stopped ringing throughout the second half of the sixties, the seventies, and beyond. He was in demand as a versatile recording session pro as well as concert performer. Acts who called on Brooks to back them on stage, or on record, included blues guitarists B. B. King and Lonnie Mack, jazz innovator Miles Davis; rock bands the Doors and Jefferson Starship, folk singers Judy Collins and Tom Rush, and pop acts Mama Cass Elliott, and Seals and Crofts. During much of the eighties, he toured with Bruce Springsteen foil and saxman Clarence Clemons. During the early nineties, Brooks was a member of Donald Fagen's New York Rock and Soul Revue and through much of the decade was a member of Al Kooper's band, the Rekooperators, before moving to Tucson, Arizona, in 1998 with his wife Bonnie and stepdaughter Julie. (He has two other stepdaughters, Celia, and Laurie, who is Orthodox and lives in Israel.)

Harvey Goldstein was born in Manhattan and grew up in a kosher home in the borough of Queens. In the early fifties, his family was part of the Jewish migration to Long Island, where the Goldsteins settled in a war veterans' housing development of two-family garden apartments. His mother, Faye, lit Shabbos candles every week, as did his paternal and maternal grandmothers, Rebecca and Sara. Most Jewish holidays were celebrated, with Passover an especially big family gathering. He had six aunts and uncles on his father's side, and seven on his mother's. In preparation for his bar mitzvah, Goldstein attended Hebrew school in a makeshift classroom in one of the development's storage rooms. The family was part of a new Conservative synagogue that was housed in a storefront. Unfortunately, according to Goldstein, his Hebrew lessons coincided with his Jewish juvenile delinquency. Keeping in fashion, he slicked back his hair and wore heavy black motorcycle boots to class. He hid a pair of squirt guns in his boots, and when the rabbi wasn't looking, drew them and fired at the blackboard. Brooks rebelled against Judaism's mountain of rules and commands, believing that 613 mitzvot were too much to ask of a mortal. Even so, "my personal Judaism has continued to be an essential part of my life and family," Brooks says.

Brooks's storefront synagogue not only had an ark but a pool table, which, on the day of his bar mitzvah, was used as seating. "I remember wondering if we could get up a game afterwards," Brooks recalls. Mischievous as he was, he also was moved by the music he heard in synagogue. "The sound of the scales, and the urgency and soulfulness of the music touched my heart," Brooks says. "It continues to resonate through my soul."

When young Harvey began to show an interest in music, his parents encouraged him. His father, Samuel, and two uncles, drove trucks for their father, Frank Goldstein, who had emigrated from the Russian-Polish border and settled on the Lower East Side of Manhattan around 1900. Frank began by driving horse and wagon teams, progressing to Model Ts. Hauling freight was an arduous business, and Samuel Goldstein wanted his sons Harvey and Gary to be anything but truck drivers, and he took his sons on the road to give them a taste of the grueling job. Music was always being played in the house, which at the time meant Teresa Brewer, Nat King Cole, Don Cornell, and Johnny Mathis records. Harvey's older sister, Roberta, however, turned him on to doo-wop music, and in junior high school a friend brought an acoustic guitar to French class one day and showed him some chords.

That opened up for Harvey the idea and possibility of playing music, and he began learning guitar. Two weeks after his first guitar lessons, knowing all of three chords, he earned fifty cents performing with some friends at a church dance. Then, around age fifteen, an even greater life-changing event occurred. Harvey Goldstein won a dance contest at his synagogue. First prize was an album by B. B. King called *The Blues*, a collection of previously released singles. Harvey had never heard anything like the electric blues before. That led to saving up to buy an electric guitar and attending the day-long rock 'n' roll revues promoted by legendary disc jockey Alan Freed, which featured twelve to fifteen acts backed up by Sam "The Man" Taylor's Orchestra. The music moved him in a new creative direction. He felt a soothing, spiritual connection to the R&B and soul music tumbling from the stage and blaring from his B. B. King album. He had heard those same musical scales and that soulful passion before, in synagogue.

He joined a dance band called the Citations. The band, two guitarists, a drummer, and a sax player, performed Duane Eddy tunes, Isley Brothers' songs, and jazz standards at bar mitzvahs, church and synagogue dances, and backyard parties. Suddenly, the chubby, lazy-eyed Goldstein felt special. "I got into music to be popular," he says. Music was never a career decision. Nor was playing the bass. Lacking a bassist, the Citations' manager, Sid Davidoff (who later became New York Mayor John Lindsey's righthand man), appointed Goldstein the new bass player. Goldstein studied bass players he liked, especially jazz musicians Paul Chambers, Ron Carter, Scott Lafaro, Dave Meyers, and Motown Records' in-house bass master, James Jamerson. By age seventeen, Goldstein was playing at bungalow colonies in the Catskills. Later he was a lounge musician at the famous Grossinger's resort. By nineteen, he was a road warrior, traveling the country as a backup musician and had been introduced to the world of anti-Semitism on that life-changing day in Michigan.

In 1964, Goldstein, going by the stage name of Brooks more frequently, landed a job performing at the New York World's Fair and invited his friend Al Kooper to form a band for the occasion that they dubbed the Clubmen. The Clubmen played at Carousel Park alternating sets with a musical carousel. Other early musical experiences included apartment-hopping in Greenwich Village to rehearse, jam and work-out songs with New York folk singers such as Eric Andersen, Judy Collins, Tom Rush, and Phil Ochs.

In the summer of 1965, Brooks was performing at a small Manhattan club when he got a call from Kooper asking if he was available to play on a recording session. A young singer-songwriter named Bob Dylan needed a bass player to finish recording an album. Brooks didn't know who Dylan was, but was happy for the work. The opportunity, however, proved to be greater than he ever imagined. The result of the sessions was Dylan's *Highway 61 Revisited*, which featured the groundbreaking rock song "Like a Rolling Stone," as well as "Ballad of a Thin Man" and "Desolation Row." According to Brooks, the recording sessions for the album (during which he happened to use his real name) "created a career in pop music for me, with all its ups and downs, and I loved every minute of it."

Though he didn't join Dylan for his legendary Newport Folk Festival performance on July 25, 1965, while *Highway 61* was still being completed, Brooks was invited to join Dylan's touring band for subsequent concerts. (Dylan would call upon Brooks again in 1970 to play on his *New Morning* album.) In 1966, Brooks played bass on Eric Andersen's acclaimed *'Bout Changes and Things*, which included the folk standards "Violets of Dawn" and "Thirsty Boots." He also contributed to singer-songwriter David Blue's (born David Stuart Cohen) self-titled solo album. The following year, he contributed to folk singer Richie Havens's *Mixed Bag* album, arranging the music with Havens. Later in the year, his friend guitarist Michael Bloomfield, who he had met during the *Highway 61 Revisited* recording sessions, invited him to be a part of a new band he was forming. It would marry an electric blues band with a powerhouse horn section to play a variety of what Bloomfield termed "American music." The Mill Valley, California–based band dubbed the Electric Flag was a super group of sorts that also included keyboard player Barry Goldberg, drummer Buddy Miles, and singer Nick Gravenites. Brooks recalls that while there was no talk of Judaism or celebration of Jewish holidays among the Jewish band members, he, Goldberg, and Bloomfield were not shy about joking, complaining, and cursing in Yiddish during band rehearsals. "In those days we had those Jewish stereotypes we were trying to escape from, yet at the same time those stereotypes created a comfort zone," he says.

The Electric Flag's first recorded effort was actually a soundtrack album for the 1967 film *The Trip*. One the band's first live performances was on June 17, 1967, at the Monterey International Pop Festival. The band was so new that early publicity for the festival referred to the group as "The Mike Bloomfield Thing." Bloomfield, Goldberg, and Brooks already had growing reputations for their work with Bob Dylan, among others, so there was great anticipation to hear what Bloomfield and company had cooked up. The band did not disappoint. Guitarist Steve Miller is quoted as saying, "The Electric Flag played so hard it hurt!" In 1968, the band released its debut album, *A Long Time Comin'*, to much acclaim, but the Flag was already fraying. Egos, drugs, and divergent musical interests splintered the group, though another album would follow in 1969. Ironically, later in 1968, Goldberg and Brooks would join Bloomfield, Al Kooper, and guitarist Stephen Stills for the acclaimed album, *Super Session*. Brooks also found time to contribute to Mama Cass Elliot's (born Ellen Naiomi Cohen) solo album *Dream a Little Dream*, which included the hit of the same name. He also co-produced the self-titled debut of the popular San Francisco band, Quicksilver Messenger Service. In 1969, Brooks contributed to another in a line of influential albums, jazz trumpeter Miles Davis's *Bitches Brew*. The album is considered a landmark in melding improvisational jazz with rock rhythms, and in the process giving birth to the musical genre known as jazz-rock fusion. The same year, Brooks also recorded tracks for the Doors' album, *Soft Parade*, playing on one of the band's biggest hits, "Touch Me." In 1970, Brooks was on bass when Jefferson Airplane co-founder Paul Kantner recorded *Blows Against the Empire*, an album that signaled the demise of the Airplane and the rise of Jefferson Starship and included the FM radio favorite "Have You Seen the Stars Tonight?" In 1972, Brooks's bass lines permeated another hit album, Seals and Crofts' *Summer Breeze*, which featured the Top Ten hit of the same name as well as the classic, "Hummingbird." In the early seventies, Brooks also became a staff producer for Columbia Records. He joined Kooper again in 1975 for one of Kooper's strongest solo albums, *Al's Big Deal (Unclaimed Freight)*. Brooks was also in an unheralded band in the first half of the seventies based in Woodstock, New York, called the Fabulous Rhinestones. In 1976, he moved to Atlanta to manage a recording studio. Brooks spent much of the eighties touring with Clarence Clemons and his Red Bank Rockers and the Paul Butterfield Blues Band, and he also formed a band with Lester Chambers of the Chambers Brothers ("People Get Ready," "Time"). In the nineties, Brooks performed with Donald Fagen's New York Rock and Soul Revue, and with Al Kooper and the Rekooperators. In 1995, he recorded with blues-rockers the Fabulous Thunderbirds on their *Roll of the Dice* album, and with gospel singer Fontella Bass on her *No Ways Tired* album. He joined Kooper for a series of fiftieth-birthday concerts in New York that were recorded for a live, two-CD Kooper set, and he also participated in a tribute to legendary guitarist and Fleetwood Mac founder Peter Green, called *Rattlesnake Guitar: The Music of Peter Green*. He also collaborated with songwriter-guitarist Danny Kortchmar on a project called Slo Leak, which was nominated for a Grammy Award, and performed at President Bill Clinton's second inauguration.

In 1999, Brooks legally changed his name to Harvey Goldstein Brooks. In the late nineties and into the new millennium, Brooks was playing with his own trio in Tucson, Arizona, and also recording with a new band of prominent song-writers and musicians called Raisins in the Sun. The group's self-titled album was released by Rounder Records in early 2001. Reflecting on how things have changed for Jewish performers since the sixties, Brooks has noticed an increase in Jewish pride in a more tolerant but far from perfect society. "Though anti-Semitism still exists, modern Jews have learned to stand toe-to-toe with their adversaries," Brooks says. And what about that name change all those years ago? "If I had to do it again," he says, "I wouldn't."

# The Blues Project
# Blood, Sweat and Tears
# Seatrain

**The Blues Project was formed in New York City in 1965. Danny Kalb, guitar player, born September 19, 1942, Brooklyn, New York. Steve Katz, guitar player, songwriter, singer, born May 9, 1945, New York City. Andy Kulberg, bassist, flute player, composer, born April 30, 1944, Buffalo, New York; died January 28, 2002, in California. Roy Blumenfeld, drummer, born May 11, 1944, Bronx, New York. Al Kooper, keyboard player, singer, songwriter, arranger, born Alan Peter Kuperschmidt, February 5, 1944, Brooklyn, New York. Groundbreaking band best known for blending folk, jazz and country with electric blues, and for exposing white audiences to the music of Muddy Waters, Willie Dixon, Jimmy Reed, and other black voices.**

*The Blues Project circa 1965. From left, guitarist and singer Steve Katz, keyboard player and singer Al Kooper, drummer Roy Blumenfeld, bass and flute player Andy Kulberg, and lead guitarist Danny Kalb. (Photo from the collection of David Spero.)*

Shortly after the release of its acclaimed album, *Projections*, in 1966, a writer referred to the Blues Project as "the Jewish Beatles." *Projections* had come out after the Beatles' *Rubber Soul* album and, similar to the Fab Four classic, was engaging and stylistically diverse. As likable, eclectic and adventurous as the band was, history has proved that though the band's music endures, the Blues Project was not another Beatles. But all the members were Jewish. While drummer Roy Blumenfeld calls the band's Jewishness "a comfort," the conscious connection between band mates had much more to do with music. Five Jewish guys in a rock band, however, was a big deal to the fans in their hometown of New York and other heavily Jewish cities and college campuses. It didn't matter that no one in the group was very religious or observant. This was about peoplehood. These guys were brothers. Sure there was Bob Dylan, and vocal groups such as Jay and the Americans, but there had never been a bunch of instrument-wielding rockers named Katz, Kulberg, and Blumenfeld confidently jamming together on one stage. So what if the Blues Project never had a Top Forty hit? The band was good; it was cool, and all the members were Jewish. Actually, the original lead singer, Tommy Flanders, who left after recording the band's debut album, *Live at the Café au Go Go*, was not Jewish. Once he left, however, the Blues Project equaled half a minyan.

Guitarist Danny Kalb and drummer Roy Blumenfeld knew each other growing up in Mount Vernon, New York. As a teenager, Kalb, the son of a lawyer, had studied guitar under and played with popular folk singer and blues man Dave Van Ronk, and he had recorded with Judy Collins. Blumenfeld had grown up in a musical household in which both parents played the piano and encouraged their children to try a variety of instruments. Blumenfeld had played clarinet in his high school band. His father was an orthopedic surgeon and his mother was the director of the Shalom Aleichem Folk Shul No. 38 at the Mount Vernon Jewish Community Center where Roy and his siblings studied Jewish history, holidays, literature, Yiddish, and Israeli dancing. Kalb and Blumenfeld moved to Manhattan and began to put together a band that would play traditional acoustic folk and blues on electric instruments. Guitarist Steve Katz, a member of the Even Dozen Jug Band and a Van Ronk associate, traveled in the same circles as Kalb. Katz was invited into the band when guitar picker Artie Traum, also Jewish, left during the band's formative stage.

Blumenfeld ran into Andy Kulberg in a dormitory at New York University where both were students for a short time. Kulberg was schlepping his upright bass down the hall, and Blumenfeld invited him to a rehearsal. Kulberg's Austrian-born father, Siegfried, escaped the Nazis in 1939, fleeing to Canada along with his sister, then to Buffalo, New York. Their parents perished in the Holocaust. Though Andy's mother, Lenore, was president of the Amherst, New York, League of Women Voters, as Jews, the Kulbergs kept a low profile in Buffalo. Much of that stemmed from his father's Holocaust experience. "My father told me to always keep about five thousand dollars in cash in a safe deposit box," Kulberg recalls. While Kulberg attended a Jewish summer camp in Maine, which he credits with nurturing his desire to play and perform music, he had little interest in "being Jewish." Kulberg buried himself in music early. By nine he was playing flute in a band. He enjoyed classical music and jazz, played in a calypso band for a while, and eventually was a member of his high school marching band. By his freshman year of college he was playing bass in the Boston University band. During his sophomore year, he transferred to NYU, where he met Blumenfeld. The final puzzle piece, session musician Al Kooper, was asked by Columbia Records producer Tom Wilson to play keyboards during a recording session for a Blues Project demonstration tape, and, in the process, was invited to join the band. The band members came from such disparate musical backgrounds that, at first glance, it's a wonder they were able to make music together. Kalb was a blues purist; Katz was a folkie with leanings toward pop ballads. Kulberg loved jazz and classical music. Blumenfeld's taste was eclectic, but he had developed a passion for African and Caribbean music, compliments of the interracial summer camp in the Catskill Mountains he had attended as an adolescent. Kooper already had experienced success in the music business as co-writer of the No. 1 hit, "This Diamond Ring" and as the organist on the Bob Dylan classic, "Like a Rolling Stone." He was a rocker who was weaned on his father's jazz and blues record collection, loved gospel music, and had penchant for writing Tin Pan Alley–style songs and arrangements.

Somehow, all these influences converged and connected. It is not a leap of faith to say that the members' common bond of being Jewish created a subconscious foundation of trust from which to work, and that may have been a primary reason for Flanders's departure. In his autobiography *Backstage Passes and Backstabbing Bastards*, Kooper refers to the band as "New York Jews for Electric Blues." The Blues Project took traditional blues, stood it on its ear, infused it with electrifying energy, and was unafraid to include pace-changing folk- and jazz-flavored tunes in the mix. Revamped Chuck Berry songs such as "I Want to Be Your Driver," and Wille Dixon's "Spoonful," were played next to folk singer Eric Andersen's "Violets of Dawn" (the band's first single) and Donovan's "Catch the Wind." In fact, one of the band's earliest jobs was backing Chuck Berry at New York's Town Hall in 1965. As the Blues Project gained confidence, Al Kooper originals such as "Wake Me, Shake Me," "Flute Thing," and "No Time Like the Right Time," became more prominent in the band's repertoire. The band became a fixture at the Café Au Go Go in New York's Greenwich Village, playing night after night for fifteen dollars per man, honing its act and gaining a following. "We slowly, doggedly stayed there," explains Blumenfeld, " and grew in popularity. "We had to do what we did. We didn't have day jobs, we just played music." When the band was ready, a deal was struck with Verve/Forecast Records to record a week's worth of shows at the club and release a live record. *Live at the Café Au-Go-Go*, released in mid 1966, was an impressive debut, serving notice that there was a new band on the block to be reckoned with. The band wasted little time in recording a follow-up, and six months later it released *Projections*, its finest record and the only studio album that includes the classic "Jewish Beatles" lineup. Produced by Tom Wilson, the record captured the energy and excitement of a band full of confidence and pride, playing with a sense of purpose. Not bad for a bunch of twenty-two-year-old kids.

Unfortunately, that magic didn't last. Kooper, ever adventurous and creative, lobbied his bandmates to add a horn section. His newest songs cried out for brass arrangements. With the band divided over its direction, Kooper left to follow his muse. Katz soon departed, joining Kooper in what became Blood, Sweat and Tears.

The original Blood, Sweat and Tears lineup was predominantly Jewish. Aside from Katz, Kooper added drummer Bobby Colomby, trumpeters Randy Brecker and Jerry Weiss, and sax and piano player and arranger Fred Lipsius, all members of the tribe. The band also included bassist Jim Fielder and trombonist Dick Halligan. (Eight of the dozen-person string ensemble that played throughout the band's record, *Child Is Father to the Man*, also were Jewish.) *Child Is Father to the Man* included "I Can't Quit Her," "My Days Are Numbered," and "I Love You More Than You'll Ever Know," three of the best songs Kooper ever wrote. His choice of material by other writers was inspired, and included folk singer Tim

Buckley's "Morning Glory," one of Randy Newman's unheralded gems "Just One Smile," Harry Nilsson's "Without Her," and "So Much in Love" by Gerry Goffin and Carole King.

The album opened in daring fashion with an orchestral overture and segued into horn- and string-complemented folk, rock, jazz, and blues. It may be Kooper's masterpiece, but it didn't live up to sales expectations. When Kooper was pressured to come up with a more commercial sound, which included replacing him as the primary singer, he gracefully bowed out. He joined Columbia Records as a staff producer, and many of his arrangements were used on the follow up BS&T album, though he was no longer a part of the band. The second album, simply titled *Blood, Sweat and Tears* and featuring Canadian singer David Clayton-Thomas, was a blockbuster. The record included three hit singles that all reached No. 2 on the pop charts: "You Made Me So Very Happy," "Spinning Wheel," and "And When I Die." But it also was a double-edged sword. Incredibly radio-friendly, it made lots of money, but it diluted the musical daring of Kooper's original concept and alienated the band's initial fans. Critics labeled the safe ersatz R&B–inflected pop of subsequent records "wishy-washy bar mitzvah soul," according to Lilian Roxon's *Rock Encyclopedia*. The band savored a few more Top Forty hits, then became a revolving door for journeymen musicians backing Clayton-Thomas.

While Kooper was launching Blood, Sweat and Tears, the Blues Project, with several new members, released the aptly titled *Planned Obsolescence*, supposedly to fulfill a contractual obligation. Kulberg and Blumenfeld then moved to the West Coast and formed a new band called Seatrain. The group's self-titled 1969 debut was a dandy, and for some reason, generally ignored by critics and radio. The band went through numerous personnel changes, including the departure of Blumenfeld, before releasing its second album, also titled *Seatrain*, in 1970. In addition to Kulberg, the group included violinist Richard Greene, keyboard player Lloyd Baskin (both Jewish), drummer Larry Atamanuik, guitar player Peter Rowan, and lyricist Jim Roberts. The album was a wonderful mix of country, bluegrass, rock, and folk, and included what may be the definitive version of Lowell George's country-rock evergreen "I'm Willin'," and "13 Questions," a modest hit by Kulberg and Roberts.

More interesting, perhaps, were a pair of tunes that indicated the band members' religious bent, or at least interest in the Old Testament—"Song of Job," by

Kulberg and Roberts and "Elijah," written by the deeply Protestant Rowan. "Song of Job" began as a lark, a comedy, but evolved into something more serious. "We liked the idea of God and the devil making a bet," says Kulberg of the song's genesis. "We wrote it as a total goof, the Bible as satire." But as the band rehearsed it, "Song of Job" turned into a more serious testament to the power of faith. "It was one of our most satisfying songs," Kulberg says. The American Bible Institute was impressed enough to use the band's photo in an advertisement headlined: "Look Who's Reading the Bible." The song also may have been partly responsible for Kulberg's reassessing his outlook on his Jewish heritage, something he had ignored most of his life. "There are great things that I really love and appreciate about Judaism now, though I don't practice," Kulberg says. He delved deeper into the Old Testament, finding in its stories, the Garden of Eden, Cain and Abel, Noah and the Flood, and the Tower of Babel a mother lode of songwriting inspiration.

Aside from delivering a dynamic record, Seatrain also was an engaging, high-energy concert attraction. This lineup released another album, *Marblehead Messenger* in 1971, but it, too, was greeted with a yawn. With the subsequent departure of Greene and Rowan, Seatrain was all but sunk. A new Kulberg-led lineup recorded one more album but it lacked the fire of its predecessors.

While Seatrain and Blood, Sweat and Tears chugged along, Danny Kalb made several attempts at resurrecting the Blues Project, but without the original (Jewish?) chemistry little came of it. After the breakup of Seatrain, and the hit-filled days of Blood, Sweat and Tears, the original members of the Blues Project gathered for occasional reunions. For a band that lacked a major hit song, plenty of fan demand remained. A 1973 reunion resulted in the album *Reunion in Central Park* (even though many of the tracks were from a concert in Washington, D.C.). In 1994, Kooper reassembled the band, and members of BS&T as well, for a series of concerts at the Bottom Line in New York to celebrate his fiftieth birthday and record a live album. *Soul of a Man: Al Kooper Live*, a two-CD set, was released the following year. In the summer of 2000 a concert promoter offered the Project members $100,000 each to regroup and join the Rascals and the Lovin' Spoonful for a twenty-city U.S. tour, but acrimony between some of the members prevented that reunion.

Since the disbanding of the original Blues Project, Blood, Sweat and Tears, and Seatrain, Kooper has been the most visible in the music world. After leaving

BS&T, Steve Katz turned to producing records, including several by Lou Reed (whose father Sidney changed the family name from Rabinowitz before Lou was born) and joined Danny Kalb to play New York clubs as a blues duo. Kalb also gave guitar lessons. Kulberg had success as a session musician for David Soul (born Solberg), mandolin master David Grisman, and Rolling Stones bassist Bill Wyman. He also composed music for theater, film and TV, most notably the seventies cop show *Starsky and Hutch*. Blumenfeld plays in bands in the San Francisco Bay area, including one composed of former members of Country Joe and The Fish, Quicksilver Messenger Service, the Youngbloods, and Big Brother and Holding Company.

Looking back, Blumenfeld believes that if the Blues Project had done more of Kooper's songs and allowed him to add a brass section, the Blues Project might have recorded *Child Is Father to the Man*, or something similar. "If the band had been open," he says, "we would have had a very long career, like an East Coast Grateful Dead." And though Kulberg initially disliked the media referring to the Blues Project as the Jewish Beatles, and initially believed that being Jewish had little to do with the band's brief but sparkling accomplishments, he changed that tune long before he died. "I realize the magnitude of all the Blues Project being Jewish, the role model and pride thing," he said. He added an even more startling note: "We were much more of a band when we were all Jewish."

# Country Joe and the Fish

Formed in San Francisco, California, in 1965. Joseph Allen McDonald, singer, songwriter, guitar player, born January 1, 1942, Washington, D.C. Barry Melton, singer, guitar player, born June 14, 1947, Brooklyn, New York. David Bennett Cohen, keyboard and guitar player, born August 4, 1942, Brooklyn, New York. Gary "Chicken" Hirsh, drummer, born March 9, 1940, Chicago, Illinois. Bruce Barthol, bass, born November 11, 1947, Berkeley, California. Best known as a leading force in the sixties antiwar movement. The band's "I Feel Like I'm Fixin' to Die Rag" was an anti–Vietnam War anthem. One of a handful of acts to perform at both the seminal Monterey International Pop Festival in 1967 and Woodstock Music and Art Fair in 1969.

*Country Joe and the Fish in New York in late 1968. From left, drummer Gary "Chicken" Hirsh, keyboard player David Cohen, guitarist Barry Melton, guitarist Joe McDonald, and bass player Bruce Barthol. (Photo courtesy Vanguard Records.)*

"I always thought of the band as being a Jewish band," says Fish drummer Gary "Chicken" Hirsh. "People called us a rock band, but I always said 'No, we're just a bunch of Jewish kids trying to play rock 'n' roll.'" Their efforts resulted in three well-regarded albums released between 1967 and 1968 that blended folk and jug band music, Dixieland jazz, rock 'n' roll and psychedelic jamming: *Electric Music for the Mind and Body, I Feel Like I'm Fixin' to Die,* and *Together.* But the band established its place in rock history with one song, the jaunty, satirical, but pointed "I Feel Like I'm Fixin' to Die Rag" (And it's one, two, three, what are we fighting for? Don't ask me I don't give a damn. Next stop is Vietnam . . .), with its sincere, vocal opposition to the Vietnam War. The band's appearance at the fabled Woodstock Music and Art Fair cemented its legacy, especially when McDonald's solo performance of an expletive version of the band's "Fish Cheer," ("Give me an F . . ."), with several hundred thousand people singing along, was featured in the documentary film of the festival.

Country Joe and the Fish was founded by guitarists Joe McDonald and Barry Melton. Both were the children of left-wing Jewish mothers from the East Coast and non-Jewish communist fathers from Oklahoma and Texas. McDonald's maternal grandparents Harry Plotnick and Bella Voronoff arrived in the United States from Russia in the early 1900s, met and married in Washington, D.C., and opened a tailoring, cleaning, and pressing shop. Harry was a Zionist; Bella was a member of the Communist party in America. McDonald's mother, Florence, accompanied Bella to Communist party meetings as a child and became involved in workers' rights groups. Though Florence married Oklahoman Worden McDonald, the son of a Presbyterian minister, and both parents were atheists, Joe attended a Jewish day school for a brief time. "I learned the "Dreidel Song" there, and sang it publicly. That was probably my first performance singing!" McDonald says. He also picked up some Yiddish listening to his mother and grandparents, who spoke it frequently. Grandpa Harry taught McDonald about Hanukkah and the Maccabees, and would give his grandson Hanukkah gelt to recount the Hanukkah story. Joe's parents, on the other hand, put up a Christmas tree. When McDonald was ten, his mother taught him about the Holocaust. He remembers her saying, "When the pogroms come, they will find you." His parents instilled in him a respect for working people and their right to a fair wage and a safe workplace. "Both of my parents were very moral, honest, and proud of their hard-working ethics, but were not religious at all," McDonald says. "My mother used to make fun of her grandfather who reportedly spent the whole day reading the Torah while the rest of his family worked . . . My mother, especially, believed in agitating for your rights, and pushing for worker and human rights at all times." It is not surprising that folk singers such as Woody Guthrie, Pete Seeger, the Weavers, and later, Bob Dylan, would become McDonald's musical inspirations.

Barry Melton's maternal grandparents arrived in the United States from the Russian port city of Odessa in 1914 and settled in Brooklyn. His mother, Taube "Tillie," later Anglicized to Terry, Kuchuck, married Texan James Melton, who worked for the National Maritime Union. Like McDonald's parents, they too were atheists and outspoken supporters of workers' rights. His mother often sang union songs in the house, while his grandmother sang Yiddish folk songs. Melton grew up with a strong Jewish identity, but little, if any religious education. His Jewish identity was so strong that during the sixties when the vehicle of choice for hippies and flower children was the German-built VW Microbus, Melton refused to drive one. "Culturally, Judaism was very important; religiously it was not. My parents thought religion was the opiate of the masses, but the minute someone was oppressed you stood up for him," Melton says.

Melton's non-Jewish father enjoyed Jewish tradition, values, music, and food. "My Dad became culturally Jewish—with a Texas accent— because he was surrounded by my mother's family," Melton says. "On Sundays, he walked to the deli and bought bagels and lox." In what could be called a Jewish twist, Melton wanted to be a lawyer, but his parents encouraged him to become a musician. They bought him a guitar, paid for lessons, and had him learn protest songs. Like Joe McDonald, Melton also played songs by the Weavers and Woody Guthrie. The Meltons moved to the West Coast in the mid-fifties to avoid the glare and fallout from the McCarthy investigations.

The band's classic lineup began to coalesce in the San Francisco Bay area in late 1965. It evolved out of the acoustic, politically oriented, Instant Action Jug Band of which Melton and McDonald, now a U.S. Navy veteran and editor of a local music magazine called *Rag Baby*, were members. Some of the band's earliest performances were at antiwar demonstrations.

By late 1966, the band's most heralded lineup was set, and it also had switched to electric instruments. Keyboard player David Cohen, who describes his paternal grandparents as anarchists, grew up in a culturally Jewish, but agnostic household. Drummer Gary Hirsh was born and raised in Chicago where he grew up in a non-observant home, but often accompanied his pious grandfather to synagogue. "My Judaism has always been tied to tradition, food, family, and the way I was raised, more secular than religious," Hirsh says. He believes that the band's music unconsciously embodied Jewish values of truth and justice. Bass player Bruce Barthol's Jewish maternal great-grandparents were from Poland. His grandmother, Rebecca Cohen, married an Irishman. His mother, Esther, was raised Presbyterian, and also married an Irishman. "I was raised agnostic, I suppose," Barthol says. Even so, he adds, "I'm not, not Jewish."

Melton believes the band members' Jewish roots enabled them to speak out against the war early and loudly. "The Jewish experience is unique in that you're able to engage in social commentary because you don't have a country. You're always ready to move. I wouldn't be here if some people hadn't been smart enough to move . . . A reason Jews have been hated through history is because they maintained their culture. They remained in places they could be critical of and not necessarily buy into the power structure.

"We're only one popular movement away from being on the outs again," Melton adds. "We never allow ourselves to be so comfortable that we're not ready to move. I tell my kids that. I used to say to Joe, 'If worse comes to worst, we just move.' A Jew can say that and we understand." Thus the Fish were unafraid to sing out against government policies they thought unfair and against a war they believed was unjustified. Melton also observed that Judaism and rock music shared an important characteristic: both absorbed new influences and adapted to their environment.

In June of 1967, Country Joe and the Fish performed at the Monterey International Pop Festival, considered more important musically and culturally than the better-known Woodstock Music and Art Fair of 1969. Organized by Jewish producer, songwriter, and impresario Lou Adler, and John Phillips of the Mamas and the Papas, the three-day Monterey festival was a social as well as musical wake-up call to the country, a statement that the times were truly changing. Blacks and whites were going to perform not only on the same stage, but also in the same bands. And rock music was becoming more inventive, louder, and heavier. Two years later, Country and the Fish (with only McDonald and Melton remaining from the original lineup) were immortalized on film performing at Woodstock, a festival celebrated for its "three days of peace and music" among a gathering estimated in the hundreds of thousands. (Four Jews organized the Woodstock festival: Michael Lang, Artie Kornfeld, John Roberts, and Joel Rosenman.)

The film unfortunately pigeonholed the band, freezing McDonald in time chanting a vulgarity. In 2001, McDonald told *Discoveries* magazine, "I always hoped that I'd be remembered as a sensitive poet. Instead, I'm remembered as the guy who led half a million people yelling 'F - - - .' Which is OK with me. It's good to be remembered for something." Commenting on the rioting during the thirtieth anniversary version of Woodstock (in which Country Joe and the Fish did not participate), Melton jokes, "That wouldn't have happened if they had had *nosh* pits instead of mosh pits."

In 1970, Country Joe and the Fish formally disbanded, though occasional reunions occurred over the years. McDonald has kept the highest musical profile, releasing numerous solo albums and becoming active supporting a number of social and political causes, especially veterans' rights. He continues to perform as a solo act. In 1982, Melton reached his childhood goal of becoming a lawyer, and he now serves as a public defender in northern California. "I defend the oppressed just like I did as a rocker," he says. He performs occasionally in a band called the Dinosaurs, which includes former members of Big Brother and Holding Company and the Blues Project. Cohen has toured and recorded with a variety of folk, blues, and rock acts, written instructional music books, and teaches music. He and his wife became practicing Buddhists in 1985. Hirsh runs a screen printing business in Oregon, and Barthol is the in-house composer for the San Francisco Mime Troupe, a theater group that performs political satire. In 1981, Rhino Records parodied the band's name, releasing (in the shape of a blue and white Star of David) a four-song EP by Gefilte Joe and the Fish, "The world's only Jewish senior citizen rock band." Songs included "Walk on the Kosher Side," "Matzo, Matzo Man" and "Hanukkah Rocks."

Of the band's legacy, Melton says, "The reason why it hasn't carried forward as much as it might have is because it invokes a painful time in American history. We were so identified with the antiwar movement, and people would just as soon forget the war, so [the music] doesn't get the play. On the other hand, it's an historic document. The kids don't remember it, but anyone my age does."

No matter who remembers the band's contribution, McDonald believes similar cultural backgrounds, especially a Jewish sense of humor, helped the group bond. Keyboard player Cohen exhibits some of that humor, adding, "By Jewish sense of humor, I think [Joe] means we all cut our teeth on the Marx brothers, including, of course, Karl."

# Pete Brown

**Songwriter. Poet. Percussionist. Born December 25, 1940, Surrey, Ashtead, England. Best known for co-writing the classic Cream songs "Sunshine of Your Love," "White Room," "I Feel Free," "Politician," and "SWLABR," as well as "Theme for an Imaginary Western," popularized by Jack Bruce and the trio West, Bruce and Laing.**

*Pete Brown, third from left, at a 1997 BMI Awards dinner in London. His friend, legendary guitarist and Fleetwood Mac founder Peter Green is at far left with his manager Michelle Reynolds. Christian Ulf-Hansen, Senior Director BMI Writer/Publisher Relations UK, is far right. (Courtesy of BMI and Pete Brown.)*

Pete Brown used to start food fights at his Jewish day school in London as a form of rebellion against the tyrannical rabbis who taught there. But he loved studying Hebrew and enjoyed the music he heard in synagogue. Songs such as "Avinu Malcanu" reminded him of the blues. But, he recalls, "the religious side of things was banged into you quite brutally. The school had corporal punishment, and I didn't take kindly to that." Brown believes much of that strictness was borne from postwar shock and a sense of urgency to make sure Judaism didn't die, a concept he was too young to understand at the time.

Brown and his close circle of classmates, he says, were "mischief makers and budding surrealists." Still, intense study of Hebrew, Greek, and Latin, and exposure to Jewish liturgical music helped instill in Brown a love of language, a passion for poetry, and the desire to become a musician. He would go on to form one of rock's most successful songwriting teams with bassist-singer-songwriter Jack Bruce. The pair wrote "White Room," "I Feel Free," "Politician," "SWLABR (She Was Like A Bearded Rainbow)," "As You Said," "Deserted Cities of the Heart," "Wrapping Paper," "Doing That Scrapyard Thing," and, with Eric Clapton, "Sunshine of Your Love," for the British power trio Cream.

Cream, comprising Bruce, guitarist-vocalist Clapton, and drummer Ginger Baker, was one of the rock era's most groundbreaking bands, blending blues, high volume but melodic psychedelic rock, jazz-like improvisation, and superb musicianship. The short-lived band (1966–1968) was inducted into the Rock and Roll Hall of Fame in 1993. Though not an official member of Cream, Brown played much the same role Keith Reid did with Procol Harum, providing the lion's share of the often surreal, impressionist lyrics that served the band's music so well. Brown co-wrote what might be considered the band's three biggest songs, the classic Top Ten American hits "White Room" (No. 6) and "Sunshine of Your Love" (No. 5), and "I Feel Free," which reached No. 11 in the United Kingdom.

Pete Brown was born in the south of England in an area British musicians call the Surrey Delta because so many famous English blues musicians grew up there, Clapton among them. Brown's family had been evacuated there from London during the Blitz after a bomb blew up the family house and shoe shop. Brown's mother's family (her maiden name was Koniarski, which was shortened to Cohen in England), left Poland around 1870 so the men in the family wouldn't be drafted to fight in the Franco-Prussian War. The family eventually settled in London around 1900. Brown's father, who came from Lithuania and whose original family name was either Labovitch or Liebowitz, arrived in London around the same time. Most everyone, Brown says, ended up in the *shmata* (clothing) trade in the East End of London. Family lore has it that Brown's father was in line for a manager's job at a shoe store, but was told that no one named Liebowitz (or Labovitch) was going to be promoted to manager. So he changed the family name to Brown. When Hitler began bombing London, the family moved to Surrey where Pete was born. The Browns were the only Jewish family in a small rural village where Pete remembers feeling like a curiosity. "People would come and look at you much as they looked at the first black troops who arrived during the war," Brown recalls. "Black troops were asked where their tails were. It wasn't so much prejudice as it was ignorance." When he was old enough, his parents drove him to a nearby town to attend Sunday school and learn Hebrew. Eventually they decided their only son needed to be in a more Jewish environment and moved back to London, settling in what Brown describes as "the Jewish suburb of Golders Green, the big Jewish ghetto." It was in a London Jewish grammar school that Brown came to the conclusion that being "racially" Jewish was cool, as were the moral lessons of the Torah. "I'm proud of a lot of the aspects of my racial identity, especially the kind of Jewish, socialist, pacifist identity that seems to go with some of the territory," he says. He also concluded, however, that organized religion was not for him. "I didn't like the amount of time that one had to spend in appeasing one's God in various devotional activities, which never seemed to get many results."

Brown was turned off by what he viewed as hypocrisy. Taught on the one hand that Shabbat was the most important Jewish holiday, he watched his parents work on Saturday, their most profitable day of the week, and only attend shul a couple of times a year. After his bar mitzvah, Brown rebelled. He became increasingly troublesome until he was thrown out of grammar school. He briefly enrolled in college and studied journalism, but quit. One thing he had excelled at in school and enjoyed, however, was English. He began reading Dylan Thomas and beat writers such as Allen Ginsberg, whose Jewish pride was a positive influence on Brown. Brown tried his hand at writing poetry and derived satisfaction from it. He sold his first poem in 1958 to an American publication called the *Evergreen Review.* He was eighteen. It beat the menial jobs he'd been doing to pay the rent.

In 1960, he met a magazine publisher and poet named Mike Horowitz, and together they co-founded the New Departures Group, which produced poetry shows that often included musical accompaniment. The shows became very popular, and they often were attended by up-and-coming blues and jazz musicians, who came not only to watch but also to perform. In 1961, drummer Ginger Baker, then a member of the Alexis Koerner Blues Band, performed with the New Departures. In 1965, after Brown gained attention reading his poetry at the Royal Albert Hall on the same bill with Ginsberg and Lawrence Ferlinghetti, he got a call from old acquaintance Ginger Baker. Baker had formed a new group called Cream with bassist-vocalist Jack Bruce and guitar player Eric Clapton. The band needed material, and Baker invited Brown to collaborate on songs with the trio.

Brown was eager to give it a try. He saw this as his entrée into the music world. Brown had always wanted to be a musician first and writer second. But after working with so many great jazz musicians in the New Departures, he had become intimidated. (It would take his substantial success as a songwriter to give him the confidence to later try his hand at performing and singing.) Brown had dabbled with playing trumpet as a teen and had developed a passion for jazz by listening to records by Gerry Mulligan, Chet Baker, and Sidney Bechet. As it turned out, when the songwriting sessions for Cream began, "The magic happened between me and Jack (Bruce)," Brown says. Brown's surreal lyrical style meshed with Bruce's inventive, sometimes complex musical ideas.

"I thought of Cream as an opportunity to get further into music," Brown explains, "and it did give me money and confidence to start my own band and make my own records. I had no idea Cream would generate [multi-million selling] albums." The terrific collaborative chemistry between Brown and Bruce was partly due to "racial minorities recognizing other racial minorities," Brown says. Bruce was born and raised in Scotland, a tiny country with little or no prejudice toward Jews. More importantly, with the middle name of Asher, Bruce suspected he had some Jewish ancestry, and enjoyed Brown's company and friendship. At least two Brown-Bruce songs incorporate some Jewish influence, opaque as it may be. The Cream song "As You Said," is a post-Job song containing a bit of "old-style Jewish resignation about the inevitability of things turning out pretty bad quite often," Brown says. And "Theme for an Imaginary Western," which equates Britain's rhythm and blues pioneers with cowboys, "is also about minorities in general and has got gypsy and Jewish characters in there somewhere," Brown says. But generally, it was Brown's love of language and fascination with the sound of words that agreed with the classically trained, musically inventive Bruce. Notable lines such as "I wait in this place where the shadows run from themselves" and "It's getting near dawn when lights close their tired eyes," not only meshed with the music, but suited Bruce's dramatic voice. Brown's lyrics rarely contained an obvious message. That was for listeners to figure out for themselves, as he was reluctant to play interpreter. The lyrics had to feel and sound right, and create atmosphere more than propose a point of view, or tell an obvious tale.

The Brown-Bruce collaboration continued long after the dissolution of Cream. Brown contributed to Bruce's first solo album, *Songs for a Tailor*, released in 1969, which included "Theme for an Imaginary Western." He also co-wrote for *How's Tricks*, released in 1977, and *A Question of Time*, out in 1989. Brown formed a series of bands throughout the sixties and seventies, including Battered Ornaments, which released the weirdly titled album, *A Meal You Can Shake Hands with in the Dark*. The tongue-twisting Piblokto came up with two albums, including one called *Things May Come and Things May Go but the Art School Dance Goes on Forever*. Bond and Brown, his 1972 collaboration with musical mentor Graham Bond, produced *Two Heads Are Better Than One*. A pair of bands, Flying Tigers and Back to the Front took Brown into the late seventies. Turned off by the punk music trend, Brown quit performing and recording until 1983, when a Back to the Front album recorded in 1977 finally was released. He also began writing television scripts and film screenplays.

Brown was more prolific in the nineties, wearing the hat of record producer as well as songwriter and performer. In the early nineties, he released a pair of soul- and blues-influenced albums, *Ardours of the Lost Rake* and *Coals to Jerusalem*. Though Brown's singing was erratic, and some of the songs bordered on silly, or at least the titles did—"They Call Me the Blob," "Don't Take Your Fish to the Swimming Pool"—most of the music, co-written with another longtime collaborator, Phil Ryan, was sublime, hook-filled, R&B-drenched pop. In 1996 an American record label, Viceroy Vintage, released a fifteen-song CD compilation of the two records called *The Land That Cream Forgot*. Unfortunately, Viceroy folded before the album had much of a chance in the U.S. market. Another project released in '96 that didn't get its due when Viceroy closed was an all-star tribute to Fleetwood Mac founder Peter Green called *Rattlesnake Guitar: The Music of Peter Green*, which Brown co-produced. The twenty-nine-song, two-CD set was a labor of love that featured Savoy Brown, Rory Gallagher, Harvey Mandel, Ian Anderson, Mick Abrahams, Billy Sheehan, Southside Johnny, and others. Not only did it serve as a reminder of Peter Green's substantial contribution to rock music, it opened the door for a long-dormant Green to pursue a comeback. In 1998, Brown produced *Destiny Road*, Green's first studio album of new material in eighteen years. (In 1996, Green had released *The Robert Johnson Songbook*, acoustic covers of Robert Johnson tunes.)

In the late nineties, Brown began studying music theory and also began performing with yet another collection of friends playing R&B music in a band called the Interoceters. In February 2000, another in a long line of Cream compilation albums, *20th Century Masters: The Millennium Collection—The Best of Cream*, was released. The eleven-song collection included four Brown-Bruce compositions. In 2001, Brown produced, sang, and played percussion on British sax player Dick Hextall-Smith's album, *Blues and Beyond*.

Because of Brown's international success with Cream, he spent a lot of time in the United States writing and producing. His experiences in the U.S. played an important role in his Jewish identity. "America contributed enormously to my Jewishness because Americans are much less afraid of being Jewish; they hide it less," Brown says. "By spending lots of time in America, I became more defined as a Jew."

# Janis Ian

**Singer. Songwriter. Guitar and piano player. Born Janis Eddy Fink, April 7, 1951, Bronx, New York, but raised in New Jersey. Best known for the hits "Society's Child" and "At Seventeen," and for writing the Roberta Flack hit "Jesse." She is a nine-time Grammy Award nominee and two-time winner, whose songs have appeared in numerous films and television programs and have been recorded by dozens of acts. She also has been a columnist for *Performing Songwriter* magazine, and *The Advocate* and a regular guest on Howard Stern's syndicated radio program.**

Janis Ian: *"Being Jewish means everything to me."* (Photo by John Scarpati.)

Throughout a career that spans five decades, one of the foundations of Janis Ian's songwriting has been based on her Jewish upbringing and perspective. Rabbi Hillel's famous Judaism-defining one-liner, "What is hateful unto you, do not do unto your neighbor," permeates Ian's writing, as does her perspective of the outsider trying to find a peaceful place in society. Even her choice of profession, wandering minstrel, stems from her Jewish roots. "We come from a culture forced to use our brains," she says. "People who could carry their profession with them were the ones who survived. The arts in America from the twenties through the forties were one of the few places Jews could go. Wall Street firms were closed, but the arts were open . . . because artists were outsiders from the start." Artists also were bold tell-it-like-it-is bearers of truth, thoughtful voices that did not follow blindly. From "Society's Child," Ian's electrifying folk song about an interracial relationship that put her in the spotlight in 1966, to "God and the FBI," the title song of her 2000 release, Ian has been a poignant and poetic voice for tolerance, fairness, and social justice. Ian is not without a sense of humor or a romantic side, however. She has written her share of beautiful ballads, and in concert she conjures up laughter as well as hope, concern, and outrage.

Ian has a distinct talent for wrapping dark and somber stories in beautiful, quiet melodies and enabling audiences to reflect on tales that few others care to tell, stories of how unkind people can be to one another, of how ruinous institutions can be to individuals. "God and the FBI" is based on the agency's secret surveillance of Ian's parents in the fifties and is about the damaging effect government paranoia has on innocent people, and how power corrupts. The song includes the lines: "Every politician is a sewer of ambition. / Hide me, hide you, better hide the baby, too. / We demand an interview. / How long have you been a Jew? / We can make you testify. / Freedom is no alibi." The album, which a friend wanted Ian to title *The Artist Formerly Known As Princess*, also includes "Murdering Stravinsky," a cautionary tale about the consequences of forgetting the past, which Jews are obligated to remember. Ian's preceding album, *Hunger*, released in 1997, included, "Black and White," about the deterioration of race relations, especially between blacks and Jews, since the heady civil rights movement of the sixties. "Hidden bigotry is something both blacks and Jews grew up dealing with," Ian recalls. Another album cut, "Honor Them All," is a sparkling up-tempo number that seems inspired by the Fifth Commandment, but wasn't a conscious influence. The chorus goes: "Honor your father, / Honor your mother. / Honor yourself above all. / Honor the gifts / You bring one another, / Each time you rise or you fall. / Honor them all." Honoring one's parents, Ian noted in the song, was another way of keeping the past alive. "I just wanted to write something nice about my family," she says of the song. "When you grow up with that strong a background, the concepts of *landsman* and *haimish* are comfort levels in life, and things you look for." The album's title song includes words from the Bible, a book she occasionally turns to for lyrical ideas and inspiration.

Ian's Grammy-nominated album *Breaking Silence*, released in 1993, included provocative songs about battered women ("His Hands") and incest ("Breaking Silence") which have been adopted by therapists to help heal victims, and Ian's wonderful we-shall-overcome declaration of hope and triumph, "This Train Still Runs." The album also included, "Tattoo," Ian's effort at explaining or at least responding to the Holocaust. Ian wanted to write a song about the Holocaust for years. She first learned about the horror at age ten when she came across a book in her home that contained photographs of bodies on carts with arms and legs dangling, and asked her parents about the pictures. (She got her first dose of anti-Semitism a year or two later when a neighborhood bully called her "Christ killer.") Years later, Ian grappled with how to handle such an overwhelming subject in song. In 1992, at a Nashville songwriters' showcase, she heard a song about a girl trying to escape from the Nazis and was embarrassed that she hadn't written it. She went home determined to write about the subject. It took her three months. Stumped on the last verse, Ian called a rabbi for advice. The rabbi's response held the key to completion: "[Holocaust] survivors never completely recovered. What they lost could never be found again." "Tattoo" has been used in textbooks and Holocaust exhibits. The Dutch government used the song for World War II anniversary events. Ian was invited to meet the Queen of the Netherlands when the country adopted the song as a reminder of the Shoah. "That's what you hope for," Ian says, "that your work will be used."

Though born in the Bronx, Janis Eddy Fink grew up in New Jersey. Her parents ran a chicken farm, and later, a summer camp for black and white children. They also were active in the civil rights movement and other social and political causes, which resulted in surveillance by the FBI beginning in 1950. Requesting a copy of her parents' FBI file in 1990, and finally receiving one in 1999, Ian learned that the agency had begun surveillance on her family after her father had attended a meeting about the price of eggs. Her father, Victor Fink, eventually returned to college, got a teaching degree, and became a teacher. The file solves the mystery of why he never received tenure at any of the schools at which he taught: the FBI paid a visit to each of those schools and cast doubt on his character.

Both sets of grandparents (from Kiev and Tashkent in the former Soviet Union, and Poland) arrived in the United States via England around 1918 and lived nearby in the New York–New Jersey area. Ian enjoyed the family's closeness and the contact, as it gave her a sense of the shtetl and the old country and instilled in her an acceptance of foreign accents, actions, and customs she otherwise may not have had. Her grandparents and parents were atheists, but the family celebrated Hanukkah, Passover, and Purim and attended synagogue on the High Holy Days. "My mother used to say, 'God doesn't care if I'm an atheist,'" says Ian, who is a firm believer in God. The family had a membership to the local Jewish community center for a short time, and Janis attended Hebrew school for perhaps a year. Much of her Jewish education and awareness came from reading the numerous books in her parents' library and from frequent family discussions at home. "There was a huge extended family, lots of cousins, and a lot of Jewish awareness," Ian recalls of her childhood. Her mother, Pearl, had been an actress in the Yiddish theater. She also had a record collection that included Debussy as well as jazz greats John Coltrane, Oscar Peterson, and Billie Holiday. Ian's father played guitar and piano. Janis lobbied for piano lessons as early as age three and studied piano through age ten, when she switched to guitar and taught herself to play. Father and daughter often played songs together. By 1963, at age twelve, Ian was performing original songs, and the folk magazine *Broadside* had published the lyrics to her song "Hair of Spun Gold." Her mother supported Janis's desire for a career in music, but suggested she learn how to type in case her dream of a music career crumbled. At twelve, Janis Fink changed her name to Janis Ian, her brother's middle name, because she wanted to establish her own identity and legacy, and performed her first concert for pay at a New Jersey club, earning thirty-six dollars. A year later, she was a regular at New York folk clubs. At age fifteen, while a student at Manhattan's High School of Music and Art, Ian wrote and recorded the future classic, "Society's Child." Radio stations ignored the song because of its taboo theme of interracial romance, but the national press, including *Time*, *Newsweek*, and the *New York Times*, interviewed Ian. The song was re-released in 1966 and was again ignored until conductor Leonard Bernstein featured Ian performing the song on his CBS TV special, *Inside Pop: The Rock Revolu-*

*tion*. The song took off, and Ian's self-titled debut album, which had been recorded a year earlier, was finally released in early 1967. (Jewish arranger and piano player Artie Butler played the distinctive harpsichord parts on "Society's Child" as well as the staccato organ riff that punctuates the song's finale.) By June of 1967 the controversial song reached No. 14 on the *Billboard* singles chart. The album was nominated for a Best Folk Album Grammy Award. In 1969, Ian, all of eighteen years old, was assigned to score her first film, *Four Rode Out*, starring Leslie Nielson, Pernell Roberts and Sue Roberts. She also performed as a headliner at the Newport Folk Festival. Between 1967 and 1974, Ian recorded a series of albums that commercially failed to equal her debut. In 1974, however, Ian released *Stars*, containing her song "Jesse," which had been a hit for Roberta Flack in late 1973. Ian followed *Stars* with her album *Between the Lines*, a commercial and artistic triumph. It included the song "At Seventeen," Ian's anthem for "those of us with ravaged faces, lacking in the social graces," which reached No. 3 on the *Billboard* singles chart in the summer of 1975. That year, Ian was the first musical guest on the premiere of the NBC comedy program *Saturday Night Live*. The million-selling *Between the Lines* was nominated for five Grammy Awards, winning Best Pop Vocal Performance Female, and Best Engineered Recording (Non-classical). Ian followed up with the critically acclaimed *Aftertones*, which spawned a No. 1 hit in Japan with "Love is Blind." Her 1979 album *Night Rains* included the disco number "Fly Too High," which was used in the 1980 Jodie Foster film *Foxes* and became a hit in Europe, Australia, and parts of Africa. Another song from the album, "Here Comes the Night," was used as the theme song for the Julie Harris film, *The Bell Jar*, and the tune "The Other Side of the Sun" was a hit in the United Kingdom. In 1981, Ian received another Grammy nomination, this time in a jazz category for a duet with Mel Torme on the song "Silly Habits." The following year she contributed to *In Harmony 2*, which won her a Grammy Award in the children's music category. Around this time, Ian's six-year marriage ended and she began a ten-year recording hiatus, moving to Los Angeles to study acting under the esteemed acting coach Stella Adler.

In 1993, Ian, now based in Nashville, released *Breaking Silence*, her first album in a decade. It was a quietly fearless work full of haunting tunes about the traumas people endure and fight to overcome, and it was nominated for a Best Contemporary Folk Album Grammy Award. (Ironically, Nanci Griffith's album, *Other Voices, Other Rooms*, which included Ian's song, "This Old Town," won that category.) In 1994, Ian, who had publicly begun discussing that she was gay, began writing a humor column for *The Advocate*, a newsmagazine for gay men and women. In 1995 she released her fifteenth studio album, *Revenge*, which included the AIDS anthem, "When Angels Cry," and which she performed on the TV soap opera *General Hospital*. Ian contributed all proceeds from the song to Elton John's Pediatric AIDS Foundation. Polygram Records released a forty-two-song career retrospective that year, *Society's Child: The Anthology*. Ian also began writing a column for the magazine *Performing Songwriter*. In 1997, she released *Hunger*, which showcased her impressive but unheralded guitar playing, especially on the bluesy "Acousticville." Along with guitar players Mark Knopfler, Larry Carlton, Travis Tritt and Clint Black, Ian was among the guitarists selected to salute guitar legend Chet Atkins at an all-star gala that year.

In 1998, Ian put her Internet savvy to use by holding the eight-week-long Janis Ian Online Auction, which raised $70,000 to establish four permanent scholarships at Goddard College in Vermont, her mother's alma mater. In 1999, Ian established the Pearl Foundation, named for her mother, to create and fund more scholarships at more institutions. She also kept a busy concert schedule, which included a Zero Population Growth benefit at Madison Square Garden in New York where she headlined with singers Jewel and Paula Cole. In 2000, Ian released her seventeenth studio album, *God and the FBI*. In 2001, Ian's projects included a drama/musical about the concentration camp Terezin (Theresienstadt), in Czechoslovakia, where many prominent Jewish artists, writers, and musicians from Germany, Austria, and Czechoslovakia were interred and died. Asked on one occasion what being Jewish meant to her, Ian replied, "Being Jewish means everything to me. It's one of the few things I feel strongly enough about to really dig my heels in over in a life or death situation."

# Chuck E. Weiss

**Drummer. Singer. Songwriter. Born Charles Edward Weiss, Denver, Colorado, March 18, 1945. Drummer for blues legend Lightnin' Hopkins, recorded with Willie Dixon; leader of the Los Angeles club band Chuck E. Weiss and the G-d Damn Liars, best known as the subject of the Rickie Lee Jones 1979 hit "Chuck E's in Love."**

*Chuck E. Weiss, left, with blues legend Muddy Waters, right, with Chuck Morris in background. (Photo courtesy Chuck E. Weiss archives.)*

Press materials that accompanied the release of Chuck E. Weiss's album, *Extremely Cool*, in early 1999, included the quote, "I always wanted to sing like a 'black man' and do business like a 'Jew', instead I sing like a 'Jew' and do business like a 'black man.'" Two songs on *Extremely Cool* include Yiddish or Hebrew words such as *meshuggenah* and *Shabbos*. A third song, "Rocking in the Kibbitz Room," is a tribute to Canter's Deli in Los Angeles and the "hep cat Jews" who hang out there. "Have a matzah ball if you want to / Or maybe some cabbage soup. / You be sittin' 'round diggin' all that rock 'n' roll music, / and hanging with the hep cat Jews. / All you little posers better come on over, / and try to beat the Tuesday blues," Weiss sings. Weiss spent so much time in the deli's Kibbitz Room, the owners named a booth after him. The song, simply about having a good time rocking and rolling, is Weiss's way of declaring that the words "Jew" and "hip" aren't mutually exclusive. "I always thought there was a stigma that Jews can't be cool because they are Jews," Weiss explains. One of the hippest fixtures on the Los Angeles music scene since 1975, Weiss stopped being reticent about proclaiming his Jewish heritage or worrying about being an uncool Jew long ago. (Neither is he afraid to be critical of Jews behaving badly, as in the song "Bad Jew from Malibu.")

Growing up in Denver in the fifties and sixties, Weiss realized early that the best defense was a good offense. That lesson came compliments of area anti-Semites who threw beer cans and rocks at the bus that, two days a week, took Weiss from public school to Hebrew school at Congregation Beth HaMedrosh HaGadol (better known as BMH) on the east side of the city. "It was frightening," he says, adding that he also witnessed Ku Klux Klan marches and heard anti-Semitic hate-mongers on Denver radio. The experience that scarred him most deeply, however, occurred during Christmas when his first-grade teacher asked if there were any Jews in the class. Weiss slowly raised his hand and turned beet red. The teacher asked him to explain "Cha-nooka" to the class. "I felt ashamed because of the way she said it," Weiss recalls. From that moment, he resolved no one would make him feel that way again.

As he grew up, Weiss made it clear to his schoolmates that he was one Jew who would not tolerate anti-Jewish behavior. "I was too crazy for kids to mess with me," Weiss says. "I'd take the biggest, toughest *goyim* in school and ask him to go for a ride with me on my bike. I'd put him on the handlebars, go down the steepest hill, then jump off the bike." His answer to those who might ask, "Why

did you kill our Lord?" was "Because he was there." Weiss pulled stunts in synagogue, too. During services, he wasn't beyond knotting together the tallis *tzitzis*
[fringes] of congregants sitting in front of him.

Weiss grew up in a Conservative Jewish household. The family lit candles on
Shabbat and attended High Holiday services. Chuck went to Hebrew school and
was bar mitzvahed. His mother, Jeannette, designed hats, ran a millinery store,
and played an active role at Congregation BMH. His father, Leo, ran a salvage
business and also was an inventor who, Weiss says, is credited with the wind-
shield ice scraper and automobile window tinting. While his mother performed
classical music on piano and played lots of Yiddish records by the likes of Mickey
Katz, Al Jolson, and Sophie Tucker, it was Chuck's father who instilled in him a
love of boogie-woogie and R&B music via the radio. "He knew what radio stations the cool stuff was on, and would play it for me before I could talk," Weiss
says. He even heard Khatchaturian's "Saber Dance," which Weiss says used to
put him in a frenzy. Throughout Chuck's childhood, his father also gave him all
kinds of records acquired through the salvage business. At age six or seven, a local
trash man also gave Chuck a huge collection of 78 rpm blues records. As a six-
and seven-year-old, Chuck also took the stage at the Wilhurst Country Club (really a speakeasy, Weiss says), and while the family awaited dinner, sang "Chata-
nooga Shoeshine Boy." At age nine or ten, his parents bought him a drum kit to
help him channel his musical energy. He admittedly drove the neighbors nuts,
but a career in music was born. He had natural time-keeping talent.

By high school he was playing in a surf music band and began earning money
playing clubs, bar mitzvahs and weddings. He'd spend his money on records and
became obsessed with learning about the sidemen and songwriters on every
song. He also searched second-hand clothing stores to buy the kind of clothes
worn by old blues men and swing musicians. While still in high school, Weiss got
a job as the house drummer at a Denver club called Ebbett's Field. That proved to
be his "big" break. Revered blues musicians like Willie Dixon, Lightnin' Hopkins, and Muddy Waters performed at the club, and Weiss backed and befriended
them all. He eventually recorded with Dixon and toured with Hopkins. During
the first half of the 1970s, he also had a radio show in Denver and taught a music
history class at the University of Colorado. In 1972, singer-songwriter Tom
Waits played the club, and the two struck up a lasting friendship. Three years

later, Weiss moved to Los Angeles to write and record songs with Waits. Singer Rickie Lee Jones was part of their circle of co-writers and friends. In 1979, Jones struck gold with the Top Five hit, "Chuck E's in Love." The song became more of a curse than a blessing for both singer and subject, as it was all anyone wanted to talk about. In 1981, Select Records released Weiss's debut album, *The Other Side of Town*. But not in the way he had anticipated. Upset with the company for releasing the seven-song demonstration tape in its raw, unfinished form, he did no promotion for the record and it barely made a ripple. Instead of trying to make a proper followup record, Weiss formed the eclectic Chuck E. Weiss and the G-d Damn Liars, which became the house band at the popular Los Angeles nightclub the Central (later renamed the Viper Room) for the next twelve years. He purposely left the "o" out of the band's name to show respect for his Jewish roots, and simultaneously got a mischievous kick from spelling out Damn. Weiss and the Liars became part of the musical fabric of the city, a must-see for locals and visitors alike. The band was therapy for Weiss. "I have to play out at least twice a week to keep life sane," he says. Occasional visits to temple also helped his equilibrium. (He does remember one less than positive experience, however, at a Chabad-sponsored Passover seder. He recalls that "it took us eight hours just to wash our hands, man. We washed our hands two or three times. I left and went to Burger King. I was starving.")

Prodded and encouraged by Waits, who also served as executive producer, Weiss returned to the studio. Slow River/Rykodisc Records released *Extremely Cool* in February 1999, eighteen years after his first effort. *Cool* received universally rave reviews. It was a playful, unpretentious, daring, and unpredictable musical stew incorporating all those diverse musical influences from his childhood onward. Slide guitar–drenched blues, zydeco, unvarnished rock 'n' roll, and groove-filled R&B were in the mix. The record also included the witty wordplay of "Do You Know What I Idi Amin." Subject matter ranged from the perverse "Deeply Sorry" to a conspiracy theory history of boxer Sonny Liston in "Sonny Could Lick All Them Cats," and that tribute to the performance space in Canter's Deli, "Rocking in the Kibbitz Room." And there was Weiss's voice, which one critic described as "a born-loser, jive-talk, torn sandpaper, howl-and-purr." *Cool* was weird, wonderful, and alive. It was unlike anything being played on mainstream radio, so mainstream radio didn't play it. That didn't deter Weiss. Encouraged by the critical acclaim and by acceptance at alternative and college radio stations, and with the record company's blessing, Weiss returned to the studio to ready another album. *Old Souls and Wolf Tickets* was released in February 2002. Like its predecessor, the album included Jewish-influenced songs that were a bit twisted. "The [Jewish] songs just come," Weiss says, adding, "I think it's so cool to be Jewish."

# Jerry Kasenetz and Jeffry Katz
## The Kasenetz–Katz Singing Orchestral Circus

**Jerry Kasenetz, producer, born May 5, 1943, Brooklyn, New York.
Jeffry Katz, producer, Born May 20, 1943, Brooklyn, New York. Also,
Joey Levine, singer, songwriter, born May 29, 1947, New York City.
Kasenetz and Katz are best known for creating the pop genre known as
bubblegum music via bands such as Ohio Express and 1910 Fruitgum
Company. Levine was the voice and author of many of the genre's hits.**

*Record producers Jerry Kasenetz (bottom) and Jeffry Katz, who put "bubblegum music"
on the map, on the phones 1969–1970. (Photo courtesy Michael White.)*

Jerry Kasenetz and Jeff Katz created the concept of bubblegum music, unleash-
ing upon the world between 1967 and 1969 such sugary pop confections as,
"Beg, Borrow and Steal," "Yummy, Yummy, Yummy," "Chewy, Chewy," "Simon
Says," "1, 2, 3, Red Light," "Goody, Goody Gumdrops," "Indian Giver," and
"Gimme Gimme Good Lovin.'" The case could be made, however, that were it
not for the duo's Orthodox grandfathers, bubblegum music might never have
been unwrapped.

Kasenetz picked up his interest in music, and probably some business acumen
as well, from his maternal grandfather, Jacob Cohen, who was always playing
Yiddish music in his home and office. More importantly, Cohen owned the
Deauville and Eden Roc hotels in Miami Beach and booked star attractions such
as the Supremes and James Brown at his resorts. Kasenetz was impressed with
the autographed photos lining his grandpa's office walls. Katz's maternal grandfather, Benjamin Lepofsky, a tailor, financed the boys' leap into the record business around 1966, loaning them twelve hundred dollars. They used the money
to record six songs to peddle to record companies under their new company
moniker, Super K Productions. Among the songs was the tune "A Little Bit of
Soul" by the Music Explosion. The song became a huge hit and garage band favorite in 1967.

Kasenetz and Katz met at the University of Arizona in Tucson in the early
sixties. Katz, a six-foot, two-inch, two-hundred-fifty-pound defensive tackle at
Thomas Jefferson High School in New York, had been awarded a football scholarship to Arizona. Kasenetz was the team's student manager. The pair formed a
fast friendship when they discovered they were both from New York and were
only two of three Jews involved with the football team. On Jewish holidays,
they'd often head for the local Jewish community center to be with other Jewish
kids. "We met because we were both Jews," Katz says. "There was a spark between us."

Kasenetz had an interest in business and music. His father, William, was a
successful real estate developer who made Jerry work construction jobs during
the summer to teach him what it was like to labor—that you learn from the bottom up and that things don't come easy. Katz had a background in art and was a
theater major. Both came from fairly observant Jewish families. Katz's father,
Nathan, however, had loosened the reins of his own strict religious upbringing
and encouraged Jeff to play high school football to build self-confidence and to

get into shape after a childhood of health problems. Still, shul attendance and Shabbat dinners at "bubbe" and "zeyde's" house were frequent for Jeff as well as Jerry, who grew up in an Orthodox home. While at Arizona, the two college students' entrepreneurial spirit became evident. They created a discount card for students to save money at local stores, selling the cards for ten dollars each. (Katz did this using Kasenetz's name so he wouldn't lose his scholarship.) Kasenetz also hustled selling advertising for the university newspaper.

The pair left school just before their senior year. Kasenetz wanted to go into the music business. Katz was disillusioned after being told that without connections in the theater world, his degree in theater wouldn't open many doors. Kasenetz asked Katz to form a music company with him. Their first joint venture was as concert promoters bringing one of the most popular British Invasion bands, the Dave Clark Five, to the University of Arizona. The pair then set their sights on record production. They moved back to New York and opened a tiny office on Broadway, bluffing and hustling their way to the top. Unable to afford their own telephone, they had a pay phone installed under a desk where no one could see it. They never made calls while a songwriter, singer, or band member was in their office, but could answer an extension phone on top of the desk if the phone rang. "People are always interested in people who are successful," explains Katz. "We didn't want people to know we had a pay phone." The pair spent hours at publishing companies and meeting with songwriters searching for just the right songs. "We knew in our heads what we wanted," says Katz. "We knew the sounds, the melodies, the lyrical type, up-tempo stuff you could dance to. We did anything we thought could be made into a hit." Both partners had to agree on a song and the group to record it before anything happened. They looked for songs that would appeal to kids aged five through fifteen. That was the age group, they recalled, that had been most interested in getting autographs from Arizona football players. It was the age group that, in 1966, appeared unserved by the pop music market. "All our ideas through college had been geared for kids," Katz says. "We thought there must be a niche for young kids five through fifteen. That's when we started getting into the idea of kids chewing gum and blowing bubbles." It was Buddah Records chief Neil Bogart who, when confronted with this teeny bop pop, asked the duo to come up with a marketing name for it. When they described the sound as "bubblegum," Bogart ran with it and promoted the genre as bubblegum music.

The pair's first successful records, however, were not what would be considered "bubblegum." Their first production was with a singer named Christine Cooper who managed a minor hit with "S.O.S. Heart in Distress" in late 1966. In 1966, Katz and Kasenetz also began working with an Ohio band called the Music Explosion that had scraped up enough money to get to New York and audition for the fledgling producers. The pair asked the band to learn a song called "A Little Bit of Soul." Originally written as a folk song, band and producers added some grit and the now-famous da-da-da-da, da-da-da-da opening riff, and recorded it. The song was dying at radio when Kasenetz got in his car and drove across the country promoting it. Stations in Los Angeles and Phoenix began playing it, and by July of 1967, the song had reached No. 2 on the charts, selling a million copies. Kasenetz and Katz were now music industry players, and bubblegum music was about to burst upon the land.

Kasenetz and Katz needed a band to put its name on a single called "Beg, Borrow and Steal," that had been recorded the previous year by the Rare Breed but failed to chart. Members of the Music Explosion recommended another Ohio band. Renamed the Ohio Express, their version of the song sneaked into the Top Thirty in late 1967. The young producers turned to a songwriter named Joey Levine to provide a followup song for the Ohio Express.

Levine had grown up in a musical household in Queens. His mother, Marion Steinberg, had sung professionally as Marion Kingsley. Her sister had performed in vaudeville. Levine's father, Eli, played the piano, and an uncle, Alan Stanton, was a record producer. By the time Joey was in high school, he had a band called Joey Vine and the Grapes, but he preferred songwriting to performing. In 1966, Levine was in a band called Third Rail that had a modest hit with a song called "Run, Run, Run," a commentary on the futility of the rat race. He had begun co-writing with another band member, Artie Resnick, who had scored big co-writing the Rascals' classic "Good Lovin'," and the Drifters' "Under the Boardwalk." Levine and Resnick had penned a saccharine song called "Yummy, Yummy, Yummy," that Kasenetz and Katz wanted Ohio Express to record. The song, which was built around the line "Yummy, yummy, yummy, I've got love in my tummy," reached No. 4, with Levine's practice vocals still on it. He thus became the band's lead singer on recordings, and also wrote the group's subsequent hits, "Down at Lulu's," "Chewy, Chewy," and "Mercy."

During the same period that Ohio Express was sprinkling tunes with preteen appeal on the pop charts, Kasenetz and Katz were having a field day with the 1910 Fruitgum Company, and a series of hits based on children's games and sayings. (While they came up with the band's name, it was Katz's father who "discovered" the group while sitting next to the band members in a New Jersey diner.) The 1910 Fruitgum Company put five songs in the Top Forty in the space of a year and a half: "Simon Says," "1, 2, 3, Red Light," "Goody Goody Gumdrops," "Indian Giver," and "Special Delivery." At a time when the Vietnam War was raging and political and social unrest dominated the headlines, bubblegum music provided a bit of a breather.

Kasenetz and Katz were so busy creating groups, or at least renaming them and producing records, that at their peak in 1968 the pair was using as many as four recording studios a day. To grab attention, they began anointing acts with more outlandish names. Among them were the Flying Giraffe, the Queen's Nectarine Machine, Fat Man's Music Festival, Captain Groovy and His Bubblegum Army, the 1989 Musical Marching Zoo, Lt. Garcia's Magic Music Box, and the St. Louis Invisible Marching Band. "We just wanted to come up with the weirdest, craziest names to make the kids go 'Wow,'" Katz explains. In late 1968, to promote many of their young acts, the duo created an umbrella group called the Kasenetz-Katz Singing Orchestral Circus. It included the Music Explosion, Ohio Express, 1910 Fruitgum Company, and half a dozen other acts the duo hoped to break nationally. The duo had arranged for the Singing Orchestral Circus and all its sub-groups to kick off a national tour with an extravaganza at Carnegie Hall followed two nights later by an appearance on *The Ed Sullivan Show*. They banked on the publicity from these appearances to sell tickets across the country. However, on June fifth, the night before the Carnegie Hall concert, presidential candidate Robert F. Kennedy was assassinated in Los Angeles. The show went on at Carnegie Hall, but the appearance on *Sullivan* was canceled, and so was the Circus's national tour. Still, the group released a song written and sung by Joey Levine called "Quick Joey Small (Run Joey Run)," which reached No. 25 on the charts in early November of 1968.

By 1970, bubblegum music, however, had run its course. It had been destined for a short shelf life. "Bubblegum" groups went through numerous personnel changes, as after a while musicians simply felt silly or embarrassed performing the material and left. "A lot of people shrug it off as nonsense," says Katz. "That's unfortunate because it had a place." Kasenetz and Katz also had a diffi-

*The cover of the 1969 Kasenetz-Katz Singing Orchestral Circus album
was shot in a New Jersey junkyard. (Photo courtesy Michael White.)*

cult time shaking the bubblegum image, even when they issued records that were decidedly not of that genre. In mid–1969, for example, the duo struck gold with a group called Crazy Elephant, which reached No. 12 on the charts with "Gimme Gimme Good Lovin'." The song was more mature than most of the previous Super K productions but still pegged as bubblegum. Not surprisingly, the song was written and sung by Joey Levine, who, along with former members of the Music Explosion, served as Crazy Elephant. The ubiquitous Levine reached the charts again (No. 8) in 1974 as lead singer of a one-hit wonder studio band called Reunion, with a song he co-wrote called "Life is a Rock (But the Radio Rolled Me)." Levine soon shifted to writing and singing commercial jingles, eventually opened his own business, and over the years has penned jingles for Diet Coke, Chevrolet, Revlon, Sears, 7-Up, and J.C. Penney.

In 1977, Kasenetz and Katz produced another Top Twenty hit, "Black Betty," by a group called Ram Jam. "Black Betty" was an old folk song written by the legendary Leadbelly. Guitarist Bill Bartlett, a former member of the Lemon Pipers (best known for the No. 1 hit, "Green Tambourine"), had rearranged it as a rockabilly song when he brought it to Super K. The duo turned it into a rock song and it took off. Kasenetz and Katz were quiet throughout most of the eighties, but when a bubblegum resurgence of sorts took hold in Europe, the duo began producing dance records there. In 1990, a reissued version of "Black Betty" by Ram Jam hit the charts in several European countries. Throughout the nineties, American as well as European record companies began releasing bubblegum retrospectives and sixties music compilations. Katz reportedly has collected nearly 200 CDs, each of which included songs the duo had produced more than thirty years earlier. "Bubblegum didn't die," Katz says, "the term died because people didn't want to be pigeonholed." In 2000, the duo compiled a career retrospective. The two-CD set, *Kasenetz-Katz: S.O.C., The Compilation*, was released in 2001.

Jerry Kasenetz summed up their career like this: "We were two guys who worked hard, knew what we wanted, and weren't afraid to go after it. And, we complemented each other." Of his Jewish roots, he explained, "I'm proud of being Jewish. I'm extremely religious, but I believe God is good to me because I'm good to others, not because I'm Jewish."

# Keith Reid
## of Procol Harum

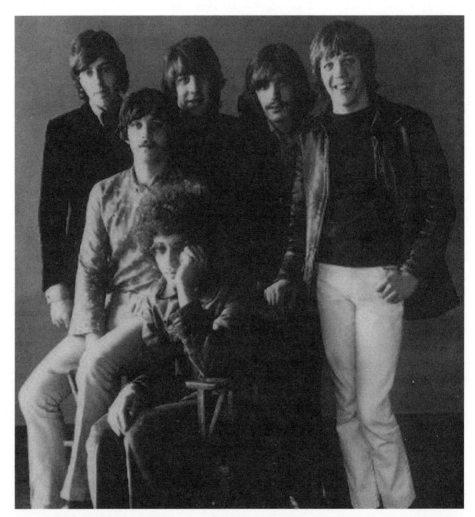

**Songwriter. Born Oct. 19, 1946, near London, England. Best known as nonperforming member of English classical-rock band Procol Harum. Co-wrote "A Whiter Shade of Pale," as well as the hits "Conquistador" and "Homburg."**

*A&M Records promotional photo for Procol Harum's 1969 album, A Salty Dog. Clockwise from foreground: Keith Reid, pianist Gary Brooker, bass player David Knights, drummer B. J. Wilson, organist Matthew Fisher, and guitarist Robin Trower. (Courtesy of A&M Records.)*

Keith Reid didn't realize the profound impact being Jewish had on his music until well after English classical-rock band Procol Harum's ten-year run from 1967 through 1977. "I was not aware of it at the time. At twenty-one, I was just happy to be able to write and luckily have some success," Reid says, "but the tone of my work is very dark, and I think it's probably from my background in some subconscious way." Reid is the son of a Holocaust survivor and grandson of Holocaust victims.

His father, a Viennese lawyer fluent in a half a dozen languages, was one of 6,547 Jews arrested in Vienna during Kristallnacht, November 9–10, 1938. Kristallnacht "Night of broken glass" in English, was Nazi government–sanctioned violence against Jews during which two hundred synagogues in Germany and Austria were vandalized and set ablaze, Jewish-owned stores looted, and shop windows smashed. Jews were beaten, raped and arrested, more than ninety were murdered, and some thirty thousand imprisoned in camps. The majority of Viennese Jews were sent to Dachau, a prototype Nazi concentration camp near Munich, Germany, then released three to four months later after promising to leave the country. Reid's father, Irwin, fled to England with a younger brother. The paternal grandparents Keith never knew vanished, victims of Hitler's Final Solution. Their fate was never determined.

The family name, Reiter, was changed to Reid after arriving in England. Unable to practice law, Reid's father got a job as a typesetter, eventually becoming a translator, primarily of business documents.

Reid's mother, born in England of Polish parents, maintained a Jewish home. She lit candles on Shabbat and made sure holidays were observed and that Keith and his older brother, Michael, had bar mitzvahs. Young Reid, however, had heard enough Holocaust stories and suffered enough anti-Semitism at Ben Johnson Primary School (where he was one of only four Jewish students) that a bar mitzvah was about the last thing he wanted. He saw it as one more ritual that set him apart. "The last thing you wanted to do as a kid was stick out, but I just stuck out," Reid says. Judaism, he adds, "only has negative associations for me. It only meant unhappiness and suffering. It goes back to my dad and what happened to him and the events of those times." He regrets, however, not asking his mother more about the family's history. He rebelled so strongly against his heritage of victimization during his youth that, as an adult, his knowledge of much of his family's past is shaky.

Being Jewish wasn't the only thing that set Keith apart. His mother taught him to read at an early age, making him the first reader in his kindergarten and first-grade classes. Like his younger sister, he also took piano lessons, and he had such a good ear that by age ten he had become a Junior Exhibitioner at London's Trinity College of Music. "I played quite well, but turned my back on it as it involved lots of practice and singled me out from everyone else. It was too much like school," Reid recalls. And Reid had no time for school. He "totally rebelled," paying no attention in class, just "killing time" until he could legally leave school at age fifteen.

But he did have one passion: reading. "I read a lot and it made me stick out from all the other kids. It marked me as being different. I loved to read prodigiously. I would go to the library all the time, the kids', and the grownups', library, as well. I literally went to the library and grabbed anything that looked interesting."

He also had fallen in love with popular music by age nine and had an inkling he would "do something in the arts." After leaving school, he took drama classes. Then, in 1965, he heard Bob Dylan. "When I heard Bob Dylan, I thought [songwriting] could be a career," Reid says. "I had no desire to perform. Once I heard Dylan, who I loved, I thought I could do that." He was much more impressed with Dylan than he was with the four fellow Englishmen in the Beatles, the hottest band in the world at the time. "For some reason the Beatles were less literary. Dylan's songs were simple musically, but quite sophisticated lyrically. The Beatles were so sophisticated musically, it was hard to imagine being able to do that. Dylan's surreal kind of imagery really influenced me."

Reid, as much poet as lyricist, was looking for a writing partner when he was introduced to pianist and singer Gary Brooker at the end of 1965. Brooker was playing rhythm and blues and soul music in a cover band called the Paramounts and was looking to do something original. The pair began collaborating, initially by mail, about a year later. Throughout their decade-long Procol Harum collaboration (the misspelled moniker is based on the name of a friend's cat, Procol Harun, which roughly translates from Latin as "beyond these things") Reid was always credited with "words" and never referred to as a lyricist. "I never felt like I was a lyricist," Reid explains. "Part of the reason is that for virtually the first ten years of Procol Harum I wrote the words first and Gary set them to music. Now I'm very happy to describe myself as a lyricist." (The band, in fact, was formed as a vehicle to perform the duo's songs.) Call them words or lyrics, the results were dramatic. Reid's literate but cryptic poetry, filled with surrealist imagery (and a fascination with sailors, ships, and the sea) fit Brooker's plaintive voice, classical melodies, and orchestral arrangements.

The pair hit their commercial pinnacle right out of the box in the summer of 1967 with the international hit "A Whiter Shade of Pale" (No. 5 in the United States, No. 1 in the U.K.). They followed with "Homburg" (No. 34, 1967) and "Conquistador" (No. 16, 1972, recorded with the Edmonton Symphony Orchestra) as well as oft-played FM radio tracks such as the title cut of 1969's *A Salty Dog*. But Procol Harum would never have as huge a hit again.

The band's lineup changed frequently, but for the first three albums included organist Matthew Fisher, guitarist Robin Trower, drummer B. J. Wilson and bass player David Knights. Not counting a "Best of" compilation, Procol Harum recorded ten albums in ten years. By 1977, tastes had changed. Punk and disco were in and Procol Harum's ethereal piano- and organ-drenched sound, introspective themes and mind-bending poetry were passé. Procol Harum played a farewell concert on May 15, 1977, ten years to the day of the release of "A Whiter Shade of Pale."

Reid turned to collaborating with a variety of songwriters and spent more time managing Bluebeard Music, the publishing company he co-founded in 1970. Over the years, his songs have been recorded by the Box Tops, Jack Bruce of Cream, Felix Cavliere of the Rascals, Annie Lennox of the Eurythmics, and twelve-string guitar wizard Leo Kottke.

In 1991, feeling the spirit of Procol Harum stirring, Reid and Brooker teamed again to write an album's worth of songs. Former band mates, organist Matthew Fisher and guitarist Robin Trower, joined the recording sessions. The result was *The Prodigal Stranger*, the first Procol Harum studio album in fourteen years, and a subsequent concert tour. With more concise, pop-oriented songs such as "Man on a Mission" and "A Dream in Ev'ry Home," the album's mood sounded deceptively brighter than previous records. But Reid was still preoccupied with lives, loves, and promises unfulfilled.

Still, nothing Procol Harum did ever struck the public like "A Whiter Shade of Pale." That song, which draws its musical influence from Bach, has been recorded by numerous acts and has appeared on film soundtracks. It resurfaced in 1998 on the fifteenth anniversary re-release of the soundtrack to the hit film

*The Big Chill*. It remains a staple of American classic rock radio stations, and it has been kept alive throughout the 1990s and into the new millennium by Brooker, performing the song to enthusiastic audiences as an occasional member of Ringo Starr's All Starr Band.

With its images of light fandangos, flying ceilings, and vestal virgins, "A Whiter Shade of Pale" is probably one of the most analyzed songs, its meaning among the most debated of all songs, in the canon of rock music. Reid has explained the title's genesis in interviews from time to time: He heard the phrase "You've gone a whiter shade of pale" spoken by a man to a woman at a party. And it stuck with him. He doesn't understand why the rest of the song is so mysterious, and he declines to reveal much more about it. "It's a story, a journey, as seen from the point of view from a man character," he told the London paper the *Independent* in 1994.

While Reid will be forever celebrated for "Pale," it is not the song that he most relates to, or that most defines him. Though he rarely analyzes or explains his writing, Reid offers that a song from the album *A Salty Dog*, "with the not very Jewish title 'Crucifiction Lane'" (co-written with Procol Harum guitarist Robin Trower), is his most autobiographical. The song, as grim as any in his catalog, is his response to the scarring torment wrought by anti-Semitism. In it, he declares that "my life is unimportant; what I've done I did through fear." It's not only about someone deathly afraid, it appears to be about someone who doesn't matter or deserve to exist. "I always felt it was kind of like writing my own obituary," Reid says. "I felt that at the time, and I still feel it."

# Randy Newman

**Songwriter. Film Scorer. Arranger. Pianist. Vocalist. Born Randall Stuart Newman, November 28, 1943, Los Angeles, California. Best known for the 1977 Top Five hit, "Short People," as well as "I Love L.A.," used as the theme song for the 1984 Olympic Games held in Los Angeles. He is a multiple Academy Award nominee for his songwriting and scoring work on films such as *Ragtime*, *The Natural*, *Parenthood*, *Avalon*, *A Bug's Life*, *Meet the Parents*, and *Toy Story*, which includes the modern children's classic, "You've Got a Friend in Me."**

*Randy Newman wrote about his family's assimilation. (Photo by Pamela Springsteen.)*

In 1988, Randy Newman released what is considered his most autobiographical album, *Land of Dreams*. It included a song called "Dixie Flyer," most likely the only rock song ever written about American Jews assimilating into the dominant culture. The song included the lines: "Her brothers and sisters drove down from Jackson, Mississippi. / In a great green Hudson driven by a gentile they knew. / Drinkin' rye whisky from a flask in the back seat. / Tryin' to do like the gentiles do. / Christ, they wanted to be gentiles, too. / Who wouldn't down there, wouldn't you? / An American Christian, God damn!"

Though Randy Newman didn't have much of a religious upbringing, and is a self-described atheist, his solo albums are the work of a deeply moral man. His songs sound as if they were written to carry out the Jewish commandment of *tikkun olam*, repairing the world. Since the early seventies, Newman has skewered, ridiculed, and illuminated the stupidity, folly, and absurdity of racism, bigotry, colonialism, corruption, and greed in some of the most biting, witty, and intelligent pop songs ever written. Whether he looks at it as fulfilling the Jewish commandment of repairing the world is another matter. (His songs also have questioned the value of organized religion and the purpose of God.)

Randy Newman was born in Los Angeles in 1943, but with his father, Irving, serving in Sicily as a doctor during World War II, his mother, Adele, took him on lengthy family visits to the South, especially to her hometown of New Orleans. Those visits continued well after Randy's father returned from Europe. Between his father's atheism and his mother's assimilation, Randy didn't have much of a Jewish education. Randy's three notable uncles, composers and film scorers Alfred, Lionel, and Emil Newman, weren't Jewish role models, either. They intermarried (as it seems was Hollywood tradition), played down their Jewish roots, and raised their children "in whatever faith they married into, Mormon, Episcopalian," Newman says. He recalls a few trips to temple on the High Holy Days, a couple of seders, and that's about it. "There was no spiritual Jewish environment in my home," Newman says, "though I think I probably had a very Jewish upbringing, culturally." As a child, he was practically unaware of what it meant to be a Jew. But then, he wasn't alone. The degree of assimilation he and some of his childhood friends experienced was deep. He tells one story of a Jewish friend who had been invited by a girl to attend a country club cotillion. The day of the ball, the girl's father called the boy and reportedly said, "My daughter had no right to invite you because no Jews are allowed." The boy responded with, "That's all right, sir," hung up the phone, and asked his father, "Hey Dad, what is a Jew?" By his teens, Randy already had decided he wasn't going to believe in any deity. Not everyone in the family assimilated, however. Randy's younger brother, Alan, a San Francisco doctor, provided his children with a Jewish education and bar mitzvah training. Randy attended but maintained his stance that God was a subject for song, not worship.

Newman's songs, many of which play like mini-dramas and tragicomedies, brim with satire, irony, and dry wit and are cast with thoughtless, selfish, ignorant, all-too-real oafs who see nothing wrong with their behavior or treatment of others. Collectively, Newman's catalog is one big plea for tolerance, brotherhood, and dignity. ("Treat a man like dirt / Give 'em no respect for who he is / Expect something dirty in return," he sings in "Can't Keep a Good Man Down.") Newman was raised to be aware of prejudice and not be a party to it. His father was an "angry, opinionated man, but he didn't have an ounce of prejudice in him," Newman says. Of his own code of moral and ethical behavior, Newman says it might be due to a Jewish gene, or more likely acquired "being a citizen of the world, and being cast on the outside."

If Newman's father wasn't keen on giving his son a Jewish education, the opposite was true when it came to music studies. Randy began taking piano lessons at age seven and spent a lot of his spare time watching nine-time Academy Award winner uncle Alfred at work. (Alfred Newman's credits include the scores to *Alexander's Ragtime Band*, *The Grapes of Wrath*, *All About Eve*, *How Green Was My Valley*, *Love Is a Many Splendored Thing*, *The Diary of Anne Frank*, *The Greatest Story Ever Told*, *How the West Was Won*, and *Airport*, as well as the Twentieth Century Fox theme music that introduced the studio's films.) By age fifteen, Randy was writing songs, occasionally collaborating with his father or brother. While still in high school, friends helped him get a job as a staff songwriter at a music publishing company, where he earned around a hundred dollars a month. His style incorporated his fondness for film scores; his influences included the Tin Pan Alley craft of Irving Berlin and George and Ira Gershwin, the New Orleans–flavored R&B of Fats Domino, and the southern-fried soul of Ray Charles. The subject matter would evolve from personal experiences of schoolmate taunting ("Four Eyes"), the puzzling segregation he witnessed during summers in the South ("New Orleans Wins the War"), and seemingly self-destructive and colonial foreign policy ("Political Science"). He would become fond (in the most ironic sense) of writing about American cities, states or regions, and pointing out their less-than-flattering characteristics in an almost beloved manner. "The Beehive State," "Old Kentucky Home," "Louisiana 1927," "Burn On" (about Cleveland and its flaming Cuyahoga River), "Birmingham," "Baltimore," "I Love L.A.," "Miami," "New Orleans Wins the War," and "Gainesville" not only illustrate Newman's interest in how people behaved in those places, but an interest in geography as well. Those songs and others illustrated his outlook on life, sharp powers of reasoning, and sparse but literate writing style.

Newman majored in music composition at UCLA before leaving to pursue a music career full time. In 1962, with Pat Boone producing, he released a single of his own, "Golden Gridiron Boy," which did little for his career as a recording artist. His affectionate, scratchy bray remains an acquired taste. It wasn't long, however, before acts began to record his songs, which in the early and mid-sixties, were often about unrequited love. That year the Fleetwoods were among the first acts to record a Newman song, cutting "They Tell Me It's Summer." In 1962, he also composed music for TV's *The Adventures of Dobie Gillis*. From 1964 through 1966, Newman stayed busy composing music for TV programs such as *Peyton Place*, *Voyage to the Bottom of the Sea*, *Lost in Space*, and *Judd for the Defense*. He also wrote a song with the wacky title of "Galaxy a Go-Go!" for the James Coburn film *Our Man Flint*, a take-off on James Bond movies. By 1967, he was a staff writer at Warner Brothers. While there, the Beau Brummels, Harper's Bizarre, and Ricky Nelson were among those who recorded his songs. He also collaborated with his uncle, Lionel, on a song for the *Daniel Boone* TV show. In 1968, he launched his solo recording career with *Randy Newman*, which included the oft-covered song, "I Think It's Going to Rain Today."

Few people realize Newman is one of the most "covered" songwriters in contemporary music. He is in the same league as Bob Dylan when it comes to the number and diverse array of acts that have recorded his songs. The best known is Three Dog Night's version of "Mama Told Me Not to Come," which reached No. 1 in 1970. Singer Harry Nilsson recorded a complete album of Newman's songs, *Nilsson Sings Newman*, the same year, and Barbra Streisand included Newman's "Let Me Go," on her *Stoney End* album. Since the mid-sixties, at least a dozen acts, including Gene Pitney, the Tokens, and Blood, Sweat and Tears, have recorded his song, "Just One Smile." Rock acts such as Joe Cocker, the Box Tops, Bonnie Raitt and Linda Ronstadt covered Newman's songs. Country swing act

Asleep at the Wheel, New Age pianist George Winston, jazz singer Ella Fitzgerald, blues belter Etta James, pop singer Neil Diamond, and reggae act Third World included Newman songs on their albums, truly illustrating the excellent craftsmanship and universal appeal of Newman's writing. British acts were especially partial to Newman's songs with Cilla Black, Dusty Springfield, Manfred Mann, ex-Animals Eric Burdon and Alan Price (separately), Petula Clark, Ringo Starr, Sheena Easton, and UB40, recording his compositions. Newman also kept busy as a session musician and string arranger on rock and pop albums by Don Henley, Joe Cocker, Ricki Lee Jones and Peggy Lee.

While Newman has done it all as a musician—composing, conducting, scoring, arranging, backing up others in the studio—he is not as prolific a recording artist as it might seem. That's because of a painstaking writing process and an increasing emphasis on film work. From the release of his self-titled debut album in 1968 through 1988's *Land of Dreams*, he released eight solo albums.

It is one of contemporary music's most impressive song catalogs, filled with insightful, provocative social commentaries on how supposedly civilized people treat one another. It is also one of the most misinterpreted collections of songs as well, and Newman one of music's most misunderstood writers. He is a perfectionist who refuses to state the obvious, who sucks in listeners with those bizarre characters making outrageous (but what they think are rational) statements. He may have been right about his diehard fans when he said, "I always think my audiences recognized my people are wrong, and wrong-headed, and stupid, and ignorant, and self-absorbed." But the general public often confused the well-drawn characters in Newman's songs with Newman himself. His biggest and lone Top 40 hit, "Short People," is a perfect example. The wildly misunderstood commentary on the absurdity of prejudice happened to use the "vertically challenged" as an example: "Short people got no reason to live. They got little hands, and little eyes. And they walk around telling great big lies . . ." Lines like that caused a public uproar and helped propel the song to No. 2 on the pop charts. The bigger the song became, the worse things got, because, says Newman, the song, "reached people to whom irony is not clear." He described the song as the worst hit he could have had because it caused people to boycott his concerts and resulted in death threats. All because he was trying to show how ridiculous it is to dislike someone because they have "little hands and little eyes." An earlier song, "Rednecks," from the 1974 album, *Good Ole Boys*, caught almost as much flak as "Short People." It opens with the lines, "Last night I saw Lester Maddox on a TV show with some smart-assed New York Jew," and glides into, "We talk real funny down here. / We drink too much, we laugh too loud. / We're too dumb / to make it in no northern town. We're keeping the niggers down / . . . We're rednecks, we're rednecks / We don't know our ass from a hole in the ground. / We're keeping the niggers down . . ." The song goes on to criticize similar racist behavior across the country and chastises the nation, not just the deep South, for racist policies and behavior. What throws listeners off, Newman thinks, is that "the bad people in my songs make a case for their behavior."

Religion is also a favorite Newman topic. He refers to it as "the biggest hit in human history, an enormously successful idea that's had an enormous impact on everything." His songs question man's faith in God. "God's Song," from his 1972 album, Sail Away, opens with "Cain slew Abel, Seth knew not why / For if the children of Israel were to multiply / Why must any of the children die / So he asked the Lord, and the Lord said / Man means nothing / He means less to me / Than the lowliest cactus flower / Or the humblest yucca tree." Newman is amused that after all the calamity on earth, man still believes in a forgiving God. He fails to understand how the biblical Job continues to remain faithful. He believes that people should be able to develop morality without being threatened with punishment from a higher authority.

In 1982, Newman composed the soundtrack to the film Ragtime, which earned him a pair of Oscar nominations for Best Song and Best Score. He followed that with the score to The Natural in 1984 (for which he won a Grammy Award), Parenthood in 1989, and Avalon in 1990. Songs and scores for films have poured out of him since then: Awakenings, The Paper, Maverick, Toy Story, James and the Giant Peach, Toy Story 2, Pleasantville, A Bug's Life, and Meet the Parents. Amid the flurry of composing for film, Newman managed to record a pair of albums. In 1995 he released the star-studded rock opera Randy Newman's Faust, his take on the relationship between the Devil and God. In 1998, he released Bad Love, his first real solo record since 1988. The record found him in fine subtly scathing form, commenting on subjects such as lecherous old men, aging rock stars, and the deadly effects of European colonialism. Also that year, Rhino Records released Guilty: Thirty Years of Randy Newman, a four-CD, 105-song retrospective of Newman's career. In 2001 an episode of the popular TV program Ally McBeal featured the songs of Randy Newman, and Rhino Records released the twenty-one song compilation, *The Very Best of Randy Newman*. The end of the year saw the release of the computer-animated film *Monsters, Inc.*, for which Newman had composed the soundtrack. After more than a dozen Academy Award nominations, he finally won his first Oscar for "If I Didn't Have You," a song from the film.

Over time, the purpose of Newman's songs has remained the same, serving as a reflection of our behavior and urging us to improve our individual and collective character. "Am I trying to tell people to be nice to each other by pointing out what is not nice," Newman asks? "You could accuse me of that, and not be wrong."

# Randy California

**Singer. Songwriter. Guitarist. Born Randy Craig Wolfe, February 20, 1951, Los Angeles, California. Died January 2, 1997, Molokai, Hawaii. Founder and lead guitarist of the band Spirit and writer of the hit, "I've Got a Line on You."**

*Spirit in concert at the Scene, New York City, 1968. From left, John Locke, Mark Andes, Ed Cassidy, Randy California, Jay Ferguson. (Photo courtesy of Epic Records.)*

In the late sixties, when it was still considered unwise to shine a light on one's Jewishness, Randy California paid no heed and followed his heart. The result: Hiding in plain sight on Spirit's second album, *The Family That Plays Together*, is a song called "Jewish." Of course, it was overshadowed by the lead song, "I've Got a Line on You," which reached No. 25 on the *Billboard* charts in March of 1969.

"Line" may have been the hit, but "Jewish" more closely defined the band even though California was Spirit's only Jewish member. "Jewish" is really a rocking rendition of King David's Psalm 133, better known as "Hinei Ma' Tov," written around 1000 B.C.E. California's version adds walloping drums and soaring, sustained, psychedelic guitar, as well as melodic changes. (King David isn't credited, however. The song copyright reads: "Words Traditional. Music by Randy California.")

Odder still than putting such a song on a rock record is that California asked band co-vocalist Jay Ferguson, a self-described "Scotch-bred Baptist boy," to sing it in Hebrew. California phonetically taught Ferguson how to sing the song, which explains the mispronunciations on the track. Ferguson was flattered that California trusted him to sing the song, though why California wanted it on the record remains a mystery, "I don't think the rest of the band knew what to think of it," Ferguson says. "Here's Randy with this song, and it was incredibly Jewish, and it was about his faith, and it was in Yiddish or Hebrew, and so in deference to Randy, 'Sure, we'll do it.' Then he comes around and says, 'By the way, I want you to sing it!' And you could knock me over! I still to this day don't know why I'm singing 'Jewish.'" It was, possibly, California's way of sharing the song with his bandmates and giving that famous opening couplet deeper, more universal meaning: "Hi-nei ma'tov u-ma na-im/ sheh-vet a chim gam ya-chad." (Behold how good it is, and how pleasant, when we dwell together as brothers.) California lived by those words, even at seventeen, when he turned them into a rock song. His mother, Bernice Pearl, describes him as "an eclectic, worldly kind of person who believed in one world, one love, one God, that's all we got. Anything that had to do with war he was against."

The concepts of brotherhood, social justice and environmental stewardship, and the importance of spirituality in one's life permeate California's songs. The beautiful, heartfelt "Nature's Way" cautions against environmental ruin; the seething "1984," which was pulled from radio in late 1969 because of its tone and topic, is a wake-up call about allowing Orwellian powers to "run your life."

The sheet music to "Jewish," Randy California's psychedelic rock rendition of King David's Psalm 133 also known as "Hinei Ma Tov." (Words and music by Randy California. Copyright © 1968 Hollenbeck Music. Copyright renewed. All Rights Controlled and Administered by Irving Music, Inc. All Rights Reserved. Used by Permission.)

"Shake Your Ego Down," the opening track on *Cosmic Smile*, released posthumously in 2000, is a rocking plea for humility and kindness.

Randy California, born Randy Craig Wolfe, grew up with three sisters in a home that his mother, Bernice Pearl, describes as a Tent of Abraham. A fifth sibling died at age three. The house was pervaded by the Jewish ethic, "Do good, keep your door open, and offer shelter and food," Pearl says. "Our door was always open to musicians who needed a break. It was important that the kids learned by actions and deeds."

Randy attended Hebrew school for a short time but did not become a bar mitzvah. He was more interested in music and politics and school, where he excelled at math and languages, becoming fluent in French. He did, however, love singing Jewish songs during the family gatherings at Passover and Hanukkah, which often were attended by one or more of his four Orthodox uncles and their families. (One uncle lives on a kibbutz in Israel.) He heard lots of Yiddish as a child because his Russian-born maternal grandparents were more comfortable speaking it.

Music was even more prevalent than Yiddish. Musical instruments shared the house with the menorah on the mantel. Randy's mother, who taught guitar and piano, hung mandolins, banjos, and guitars on the walls and encouraged the children to experiment with them. By age three, Randy was sitting along side his mother on the piano bench bombarding her with questions such as "Why is one hand playing one thing and the other hand playing something else?" As he grew up, he taught himself to play all the instruments hanging on the walls of the house. In addition, Randy's uncle, Ed Pearl, owned the popular Los Angeles blues and folk club, the Ash Grove. When Uncle Ed visited the Wolfe home, he occasionally would bring blues men such as Sonny Terry and Brownie McGhee with him. Jam sessions often followed, with young Randy strumming an autoharp. On one occasion the blues duo gave Randy a child-size Spanish guitar.

By fifteen, Randy, though a very good student, dropped out of high school to play professionally. Around that time the family, which now included stepfather and future Spirit drummer Ed Cassidy, had moved to New York where Cassidy had work. There, while checking out guitars in a music store, Randy met Jimi Hendrix. Hendrix was using the name Jimi James and fronting a band called the Blue Flames. Hendrix invited Randy to play with the band at Café Wha. The one-night invite lasted three months.

It was Hendrix who gave Randy Wolfe the moniker Randy California to avoid confusion with another Randy in the Blue Flames who Hendrix dubbed Randy Texas. The name stuck. Hendrix also invited California to move with him to England to start a new band, but Randy's mother thought fifteen-year-old Randy was too young. One can only imagine what the Jimi Hendrix Experience might have sounded like with Randy California in the lineup.

Instead, California's family returned to Los Angeles. There he and stepfather Cassidy reunited with singer-songwriter Jay Ferguson and bass player Mark Andes, with whom they'd previously played in a band called the Red Roosters. With the addition of keyboard player John Locke, the band evolved into Spirits Rebellious, and by mid–1967, were making music under the name Spirit.

With its members coming from divergent musical backgrounds—Cassidy and Locke leaned to jazz, Ferguson and Andes to rock and pop and California to folk, blues, and country—the band's overall sound was dramatically different from southern California counterparts such as the Byrds and the Beach Boys. So were the topics the band tackled in song. "Fresh Garbage," for example, is a head-bopping observation of a strike by city sanitation workers. Spirit also challenged pop music convention with shifting tempos, jazzy arrangements, and songs that would surprisingly shift gears from gentle acoustic strumming or nimble piano runs to searing electric guitar riffs. California also enjoyed tinkering with special effects guitar sounds, especially echo and delay.

It all added up to one very engaging, provocative rock band with great expectations. In a three-year span Spirit released four highly acclaimed albums, *Spirit*, *The Family That Plays Together*, *Clear*, and *The Twelve Dreams of Dr. Sardonicus*. The band became a favorite of fledgling FM radio, with California's "I Got a Line on You," "Nature's Way," "1984," and "Prelude–Nothing to Hide," and Ferguson's "Animal Zoo" and "Fresh Garbage" becoming FM staples. To see only "Line" reach the Top 40 and watch bands that once opened for Spirit, such as Led Zeppelin and Traffic, go on to stardom, demoralized the band. Members began to leave for other music projects, returning over the years to perform or record as Spirit in various configurations with the California-Cassidy core, until California's drowning death (he was caught in a riptide) off the Hawaiian island of Molokai in 1997.

Randy California had survived rough going in the early 1970s, fracturing his skull in a fall from a horse, and later suffering a nervous breakdown. Through it all, he continued to make solo albums and record and tour with other acts, including filling in as lead guitarist for Deep Purple and contributing to B. B. King's *L.A. Midnight* album in 1972. Three years later, California began recording as Spirit again, frequently touring the United States as well as Europe, where his music probably was more appreciated. In 1989, he was invited to be part of Night of the Guitar, an all-star guitar player tour and recording project that included the Doors' Robby Krieger, Steve Howe of Yes, Leslie West of Mountain, and Alvin Lee of Ten Years After, among others.

Even so, California remains somewhat underrated. Jimi Hendrix, Led Zeppelin's Jimmy Page, and Eddie Van Halen, all appear to have been influenced by him. Friends, associates, and band members cite musical chapter and verse from California's canon, pointing out Zeppelin-like licks and Van Halenesque technique long before Page or Van Halen used them. They add that while California learned from Hendrix, Hendrix also picked up a bluesy idea or two from the teenage whiz kid.

According to California's mother, something else can be heard in her son's playing if you listen long enough: melodies and sounds that are centuries old. "I always felt Randy's solos sounded like what I remember from temple," Pearl says. "I told him that sometimes his guitar sounded like a cantor in synagogue. He would just smile a shy smile."

The year 2000 saw the release of *Cosmic Smile*, the first album in a proposed series mining California's huge catalog of unreleased music recorded up until his death. The title is a reference to God. The record's opening lyrics are the essence of California's spirit: "Cast off hatred. Shake my ego down . . . Cast off hatred, Lord . . . When it reaches zero I will walk in the light of the sun."

# Leslie West and Corky Laing

## of Mountain

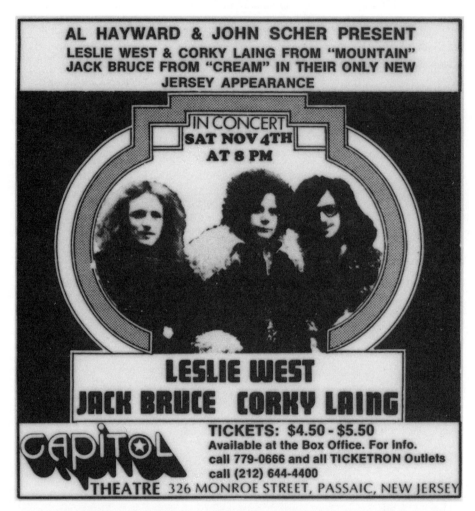

Leslie West, lead guitar and vocals. Born Leslie Weinstein, October 22, 1945, Queens, New York. Corky Laing, drums. Born Lawrence Gordon Laing, January 26, 1948, Montreal, Canada. Formed in 1969, Mountain was one of the pioneer bands in the hard rock/heavy metal genre and is best known for the hard rock classic "Mississippi Queen."

*Poster advertising a 1972 West, Bruce and Laing concert. Note the ticket prices. (Courtesy Robert Solberg.)*

In 1969, when guitarist Leslie West and bass player and producer Felix Pappalardi asked Corky Laing to be the new drummer in their volcanic metal band,
Mountain, Laing's one condition was that he would not play on the High Holy
Days. More than thirty years later, after many sibling-like ups and downs, West
and Laing still collaborate and even occasionally saddle up that rock 'n' roll war
horse known as Mountain. Laing has no doubt that the pair's common Jewish
roots helped sustain their relationship. "There's some sort of stock or fiber that
goes with a friendship, and we had the same sense of humor, and the same cynical attitude. On some level there's no question that [being Jewish] had to do with
it," says Laing. West, Laing, and Pappalardi, along with keyboard player Steve
Knight, forged one of rock 'n' roll's most ear-shattering, earthshaking sounds.
In the process, the band, whose heyday ran from 1970 through 1973, produced
one enduring rock anthem in "Mississippi Queen." The song, with its signature
cowbell introduction, monster guitar riff, avalanche of grating power chords,
gut-wrenching vocals, and pounding percussion, was a throbbing rafter rattler
that delighted teens, shook up parents, and provided garage bands everywhere
with a set-list staple. "Mississippi Queen" was a Laing-penned disco-pop song
before West got his heavy-metal mitts on it, rewrote some of the music, and
added that evergreen guitar riff that sounded like a carnivore choking on dinner.

Laing grew up in a close-knit, observant, Conservative Jewish household in a
lower-middle-class section of Montreal. He was the youngest of five siblings
that included a set of older triplet brothers. His father, Hyman, was a textile
salesman, but it was his maternal grandmother, Zelda "Sadie" Schachter, who
was the family's guiding spiritual influence. The family kept kosher, observed
Shabbat, and attended Shar Sh'Mayim Synagogue in Montreal, where, in 1958,
Corky's brothers became the first triplets to become b'nai mitzvah in the history
of the city. (Singer-songwriter Leonard Cohen also became a bar mitzvah at this
synagogue.) Passover at the Laing house was most memorable. Laing describes
the family seders as being "like *War and Peace*. They went on forever, but they were
amazing. There was the feeling of spring, the ice was melting, and there was
hope of a good summer." All the Laing children attended Hebrew school and,
according to Corky, "hated it." After the history-making b'nai mitzvah of his
brothers, Corky's bar mitzvah was a low-key affair. The most memorable thing
about it was receiving a set of bongos as a gift. Laing embraced the instrument.
He practiced until his hands were bruised from playing along with the Xavier

Cougat and Tito Puente records his mother, Sarah, frequently played in the house, along with the music of Duke Ellington, Art Blakey, and Ray Coniff. Sarah Laing used the music to teach all her children the cha-cha, meringue, and other dances so they would be at ease at parties. Corky also tuned into rock radio stations from Buffalo and Rochester and was smitten by the Everly Brothers and Roy Orbison, as well as Elvis Presley, who he saw on television.

The bongos became a security blanket that Corky took to parties and dances. He found that performing enhanced his popularity. By age fifteen, Laing was in his first band, the Starlites. Because his parents couldn't afford to buy him drums, he borrowed kits from friends in exchange for lessons. At seventeen, he bought his first drum set using college scholarship money. With music not yet considered a career possibility, Laing had enrolled at Sir George Williams University to study accounting, and he also had thoughts of becoming a history teacher. But Laing's college band, Bartholomew Plus III, became one of the hot local bands in Montreal. Laing began making a lot of money playing bar mitzvahs, sweet sixteen parties, and weddings. Through a series of industry connections, Laing's high school and college bands had the chance between 1964 and 1966 to spend summers recording and performing in New York. During that period Bartholomew Plus III changed its name to Energy, and performed at the same clubs in Westhampton, New York, where the Leslie West–led Vagrants and the Young Rascals played. Laing was struck by the Vagrant's bludgeoning, blues-based style. "The heaviness of the way Les played, the volume, was my first introduction to hard rock and heavy metal," Laing explains. "The drums sounded like playing corrugated roofs; they had a metallic sound them." The Laing-West friendship took root.

Leslie West, a self-described "non-Jew Jew," was born Leslie Weinstein in Queens in 1945. Though his father, Bill, had studied to be a cantor (but ended up in the family restaurant business), and a great grandfather was a rabbi at a Brooklyn yeshiva, Leslie and his younger brother Larry had little interest in Jewish ritual and observance. By age ten, Leslie's passions were evident: baseball and rock 'n' roll, in that order. Although Leslie dreamed of being a professional baseball player, it's easy to see why playing concerts won out over playing third base. Several members of his family were prominent in the entertainment business. A cousin, Barry Blitzer, was a writer for the *Gomer Pyle* and *Car 54, Where Are You?* TV programs, as well as the film *McHale's Navy*. Another cousin, Kenneth

Mars, was in the Mel Brooks film *The Producers*. But it was great uncle Will Glick-
man, a writer for *The Jackie Gleason Show*, among others, who unwittingly changed
Leslie's life when in 1955 he arranged for Leslie's family to attend a broadcast
of the show. Band leaders Jimmy and Tommy Dorsey were filling in as hosts
for Gleason and had a special musical guest that night, an up-and-comer
named Elvis Presley. Hearing Presley perform "Heartbreak Hotel" and "Blue
Suede Shoes," West says, made him want to play guitar. Too small to handle a
full-sized guitar, a relative gave Leslie a ukulele. His mother, seeing a budding
talent, "schlepped" her son to dance lessons and talent shows. He eventually
won a contest sponsored by a radio station by performing "Jailhouse Rock" on a
guitar with four strings. West recalls that his mother, Rita, "pushed me good, but
gently." At age twelve, Leslie's parents separated. Leslie did a very short stint at
Hebrew school and, in 1958, had an abbreviated bar mitzvah that consisted of
reciting a couple of *brachahs*. "I just wasn't interested," he says, especially when
all his friends were outside playing baseball. When Leslie's parents divorced
after his bar mitzvah, Rita Weinstein decided to start fresh with a new name and
gave Leslie and Larry the choice of recasting themselves as West or Winston.
Leslie chose West, he says, "because I didn't want to be named after a cigarette."
His truncated bar mitzvah netted him his first electric guitar, a Fender Strato-
caster. At Forest Hills High School in Queens, West formed the Vagrants, with
his brother Larry on bass guitar. By the mid-sixties, the Vagrants were one of the
most popular concert attractions in the New York–New Jersey area, vying with
neighboring groups like the Young Rascals for rock 'n' roll supremacy in the
northeast. Unlike the wildly successful Rascals, the Vagrants had a run of bad
timing and bad luck. The band's first single, for example, a crowd-inspiring version of Otis Redding's R&B sweat-inducing workout, "Respect," was released at
the same time a young singer named Aretha Franklin released her version of the
song. Franklin's version became a No. 1 hit while the Vagrants' version became a
rock 'n' roll footnote. By 1969, after releasing five commercially disappointing
singles, the Vagrants were history. West teamed with the band's producer, Felix
Pappalardi, to work on a solo album called *Leslie West—Mountain*. (The title was a
reference to West's size—the guitarist checked in at around 300 pounds at the
time.) Pappalardi was an Italian Catholic from the Bronx who, as a youth, attended Stissing Lake, a Jewish summer camp where his father was the doctor.
Pappalardi became fairly conversant in Yiddish, and later impressed his Jewish

colleagues with his ability to recite the Passover seder's Four Questions in Hebrew. Pappalardi had cemented his professional reputation a few years earlier
working as a producer and arranger for the British supergroup Cream, a blues-
based power trio, which featured Eric Clapton, one of West's guitar heroes.
West's solo record signaled the arrival of a new, innovative guitar hero on the
block, despite being criticized for sounding a bit too much like Cream. West and
Pappalardi decided to form a band called Mountain, adding keyboard player
Steve Knight to avoid more Cream comparisons and using drummer Norman
Smart, who had played on West's album. That lineup had only performed three
times when it played in front of an audience of several hundred thousand at the
fabled three-day Woodstock music festival in August, 1969. Before the year was
out, Smart was replaced by Laing.

The new lineup released three albums in quick succession: *Mountain Climbing*,
which sold half a million copies and included the hit single "Mississippi Queen,"
*Nantucket Sleighride*, which also sold half a million copies, and *Flowers of Evil*. Bassist
and songwriter Pappalardi, road weary and suffering hearing problems, left the
band in 1972. To maintain the band's momentum, a concert album, *Mountain
Live—The Road Goes on Forever*, was released after Pappalardi's departure, signaling the end of that chapter of the Mountain story. West and Laing quickly formed
West, Bruce and Laing, with former Cream bass player, singer, and songwriter
Jack Bruce. That trio released three albums before disbanding in 1974. From that
year West and Laing, and occasionally Pappalardi until his shooting death in
1983, worked together sporadically as Mountain and on various other musical
projects.

Both also worked separately on outside projects. In 1988, for example, West
was part of an all-star recording and touring lineup of celebrated guitarists that
released a pair of records, *Guitar Speaks* and *Night of the Guitars*. After working with
Laing on a retrospective Mountain compilation in 1995 and a new Mountain studio album in 1996, a substantially slimmer West released a critically acclaimed
solo album in 1999 called *As Phat As It Gets*. In 2001, West produced albums for a
young rock band called Clutch and the blues-rock guitarist Smokin' Joe Bona-
massa, contributing a song to the former, and vocals and guitar to the latter.

Laing also kept busy. From 1979 through 1981, he toured with Kinky Friedman
and the Texas Jewboys, laid down the musical foundation for Meat Loaf tours between 1987 and 1989, and was a talent scout for Polygram Records in Canada

from 1989 through 1995. In between music projects, he also worked for a music publishing company, since 1998 has worked for the Canadian branch of the American Federation of Musicians. In 1999, he teamed with former Spin Doctors' guitarist and songwriter Eric Shenkman in a band called Cork and released a well-received album of melodic hard rock called *Speed of Thought*. He also put the finishing touches on *The Secret Sessions*, an album featuring Ian Hunter, Mick Ronson, Leslie West, Todd Rundgren, John Sebastian, and others recorded in 1978 but never released. A portion of album proceeds were earmarked for Handgun Control.

In 2000, Laing and West performed several shows together to celebrate the release of a Mountain concert recorded in 1974. Laing also was working on another record to benefit Handgun Control. "My mother taught me that if you find enough *mazel* in your life, you've got to give it back," says Laing, who, since 1990, has added Buddhist chanting to his Judaism. As for West, for a "non-Jew Jew," he has been more than willing to remind the public of his Jewish background. On his album *As Phat As It Gets*, West, for a reason he doesn't yet understand, used his birth name Leslie Weinstein on the production credit. In a *King Biscuit Flower Hour* radio interview, he mentioned his Jewish roots without being asked. Again, in a *Rolling Stone* magazine article on guitars, West proudly stated that he bought a guitar with his bar mitzvah money. West, however, doesn't appear headed on a course toward becoming *baal t'shuva*. He worships in the temple of rock 'n' roll. "I keep waiting for that guy Elijah to show up on Pesach," West says with a cynical laugh. "He still hasn't shown up."

# 1970s-1980s

**"A soul sings at all times . . ."**
RABBI ABRAHAM ISAAC KOOK

# Lee Oskar
## of WAR

Harmonica player. Songwriter. Born Lee Oskar Levetin, March 28,
1948, Copenhagen, Denmark. A founding member of the
Latin-funk-pop-jazz band WAR, best known for co-writing hits such as
"Slippin' into Darkness," "The Cisco Kid," "The World Is a Ghetto,"
"Gypsy Man," "Why Can't We Be Friends," and "Low Rider."
Also designed a line of signature harmonicas.

*WAR's formative days, circa 1969. From left, harmonica player Lee Oskar, bassist B. B. Dickerson,
guitarist Howard Scott, sax player Charles Miller, percussionist Papa Dee Allen, drummer Harold Brown,
and keyboard player Lonnie Jordan. (Photo © Far Out Productions. Courtesy of Avenue Records.)*

When Lee Oskar walked on stage the first time WAR performed in Toronto, Canada, his mother, Rachel Becker Levetin, did what many proud, bold Jewish mothers might do. She rose from her seat, pointed to the kid with the harmonicas, and shouted, "That's my son!" Mama's unabashed kvelling that night in 1969, over a son who was in the infant stages of rock stardom, was a mother and child reunion. They hadn't seen each other in three years, when both still lived in Denmark.

Lee Oskar arrived in New York in 1966 from Denmark on a Polish ship called the *Batory*. He was looking to break into the music business and put some distance between himself and his family. His parents wanted him to be a doctor, engineer, anything that seemed more secure than playing music for a living. But having discovered the harmonica at age six and Ray Charles and Elvis Presley via Danish radio by age eleven, Oskar harbored dreams of becoming a musician. For a career in music, Oskar believed, the United States was the Promised Land.

He left home for another reason as well: he needed some emotional breathing room. His Lithuanian-born mother was a survivor of the Kovno Ghetto and Stutthof death camp in Poland, where her mother was murdered in a gas chamber. After the war, she learned that more than one hundred forty aunts, uncles, and cousins had been killed in Lithuania; she, along with a sister and brother, survived. Lee's father, Joseph, had served in the Danish underground, which helped save the country's Jews from the Nazis by ferrying more than seven thousand of them to neutral Sweden in October of 1943. Joseph, the son of Russian-born parents, was a first-generation Danish Jew, and a hat maker by trade. Having survived the war, the Levetins didn't take their Judaism for granted. The family attended synagogue (one of two in Copenhagen) and belonged to a Jewish social club where Lee and his younger brother, Ralph, were exposed to Yiddish music. The Levetins also maintained a kosher home, more out of family tradition than religious observance, and spoke Yiddish as well as Danish. Lee was sent to a Jewish day school called the Kavelineskolen. He had little interest in school, studying just enough to get by, but respected his teacher, Bent Melchior, who eventually became the chief rabbi of Copenhagen.

Lee's parents were very protective of him as he grew up. He was instructed that if anyone asked where he was going during his daily streetcar ride across town to school, to answer "religious school," not Jewish day school. Even in tolerant, accepting Copenhagen, there was a sense of paranoia in his home. "My parents felt very vulnerable. My mother was very nervous and intense," says Oskar, who admits to similar traits. Wherever he goes, he knows where the back door is. He is uncomfortable traveling in Germany, spending as little time there as possible. It was a long time before he confided to his fellow band members in WAR that he was Jewish, even though the group's managers and producers Jerry Goldstein and Steve Gold were Jewish, and Gold wore a Star of David around his neck. When Oskar finally told the other band members, who were black, Oskar says, "they related a lot because we shared a history of bigotry."

Oskar arrived in New York with little money and even less fluency in English. He gravitated to the Peppermint Lounge and began sitting in with the bands. Once, when a musician told him he played a "bad" harmonica, Oskar thought his music career was over before it had begun. He didn't understand that bad was slang for good. After about six months of barely getting by in New York, Oskar decided to try his luck in Los Angeles. By 1968 he was sitting in with bands at clubs such as the Experience and Whisky A Go Go. Oskar often jammed with Blues Image, frequent performers at the Experience, before Blues Image struck gold with the Top Five hit, "Ride Captain Ride," in 1970. British blues-rocker Eric Burdon, who had left the very popular and successful band the Animals ("House of the Rising Sun," "Don't Bring Me Down," "We Gotta Get Out of This Place") and was looking for a new project, also enjoyed sitting in with Blues Image. He and Oskar became fast friends, with Oskar often crashing on the couch in Burdon's Laurel Canyon house.

It was in a club called the Rag Doll, however, that Burdon and Oskar met the core of what would become WAR. Drummer Harold Brown, guitarist Howard Scott, keyboardist Lonnie Jordan, (Jewish) bass player Peter Rosen (soon replaced by B. B. Dickerson), sax player Charles Miller, and percussionist Papa Dee Allen were in a band called Night Shift. They served as the backup band for former Los Angeles Rams football star Deacon Jones, who was vainly trying to make it as a singer. Burdon and Oskar followed a recommendation to check out Night Shift. When Deacon Jones finished his set, Oskar jumped on stage and began jamming with the band. Something clicked.

There are several stories of how the band named itself WAR. Oskar's version is that while sitting around a swimming pool the following day, he remarked that "everyone walking around saying 'Peace,' was a joke, because no one is really at peace with themselves. Creativity is a part of us that's struggling. It's a war inside ourselves." That, says Oskar, is why he suggested war. "We never associated ourselves with war, it was the inner struggle, the war inside ourselves."

A unique sound began to develop. It was based on Burdon's blues-rock roots, Allen's jazz background and love of Latin music, the others' soul and R&B leanings, and twenty-year-old Oskar's ability to invent and weave percussive or melodic horn lines, often in tandem with Miller's sax, through anything the band tried. And the band was open to trying anything. "Eric would send me to rehearsals with Count Basie and Big Joe Turner records to jam with," Oskar recalls. "Nobody was sitting there trying to intellectualize and come up with a blueprint [for a sound]. There was no talk. We'd just jam and play and things took shape."

Initially, Oskar was nervous and insecure about his tenure in the band. He could not read music, and he had blustered and played his way through many jam sessions since he had arrived in the United States. He also had brazenly told Burdon he could arrange horn parts, omitting the fact that he could not write out the parts. It didn't matter. Burdon told him that soul and expressiveness, which Oskar possessed, were the most important requirements. Percussionist Papa Dee also advised him to "just play." Oskar relaxed, followed his heart, and found his place in WAR. "The guys in the band allowed me daily for so many years to really shape my expressions and emotions through my instrument," Oskar says. "It was a wonderful way to develop my musical skills."

The band's songwriting process was evolutionary. Someone would bring a lyric, melody, rhythm to the table and the band would start jamming around it until a song took shape. Songs often were created from editing tapes of long jam sessions into four-minute radio-friendly singles. Generally, everyone shared in the songwriting credits, even though some members were much more prolific than others. The songs, often brimming with social commentary, were conciliatory in nature: "The World Is a Ghetto," "Why Can't We Be Friends," "Peace Sign." The band's optimistic, upbeat nature combined with its funky grooves appealed to whites and blacks. Add to that the band's spontaneity and love of improvisation, and audiences were treated to concerts that were as inspiring and surprising to the band as they were to fans. "We still play that way," Oskar says. "It's all about the magic, the soul and the interaction. The only road map we had was the mood we were in."

Initially known as Eric Burdon and War, the band released its first album, *Eric*

*Burdon Declares War*, in 1970. The record included the hit single "Spill the Wine," which rose to No. 3 on the record charts. WAR quickly released a followup album, *The Black Man's Burdon*. A single from the album, "They Can't Take Away Our Music," reached only No. 50 on the charts, but the band was gaining momentum and set out on a European tour. In mid-September of 1970, WAR was performing at a club in London when Burdon's close friend Jimi Hendrix stopped by to jam. It was the last time the heralded guitarist would perform. The band was expecting him to sit in the following night, but Hendrix was found dead in his apartment the next morning. "Hendrix came in all messed up, gets up and sits in and plays with us," Oskar recalls. "At one point, he looked at me and asked, 'Am I playing OK?'" Surprised at the question, Oskar did not know what to say to the guitar legend. Shortly after Hendrix's death, Burdon abruptly quit the band without any explanation. With the tour getting rave reviews, the band decided to carry on without him.

The band proved more than capable without its superstar frontman, and it spent most of the seventies on the record charts. Songs such as "All Day Music, "Slippin' into Darkness," "The World Is a Ghetto," "The Cisco Kid," "Gypsy Man," "Why Can't We Be Friends?," "Low Rider," and "Summer" remain staples of classic rock radio. ("Why Can't We Be Friends" has the distinction of being the song NASA broadcast during the historic link in space of U.S. astronauts and Soviet cosmonauts in 1975.)

In the midst of WAR's popularity, Oskar began fashioning a side solo career. In 1976, he released his first record, *Lee Oskar*. Filled with funky jazz-fusion instrumentals, the album recapped Oskar's struggle as a Danish kid with a dream. Compositions included "I Remember Home (A Peasant's Symphony)," "The Journey," "The Immigrant," "The Promised Land," and "Blisters." Hearing it, his mother said, reminded her of the Yiddish melodies she used to sing as a child. The album helped earn Oskar Instrumental Artist of the Year in the music industry trade publications *Billboard*, *Cashbox*, and *Record World*. In 1978, Oskar released his second solo album, *Before the Rain*. His third record, *My Road Our Road*, released in 1981, featured songs about the effect World War II had on his mother and about his hopes for a brighter life for the world's children.

In 1983, he formed Lee Oskar Enterprises and launched his own line of signature harmonicas in conjunction with the Japanese instrument manufacturer

Tombo. "I want to do for the harmonica what Les Paul did for the guitar," Oskar explained when he began the company. Customers have included Chicago blues man Junior Wells and the Rolling Stones' Mick Jagger.

Oskar left WAR in 1993 but hasn't slowed down. His most recent record for the U.S. market, *So Much in Love*, was released in 1997. He travels the world giving master classes and concerts and attending musical instrument trade shows. He is especially popular as a solo artist in Japan and Korea, where he has recorded and performed with numerous Japanese and Korean acts. A *Best of Lee Oskar* CD, was set for release in Japan in 2001. Oskar also reunited in 2000 with three other founding members of WAR—Harold Brown, B. B. Dickerson, and Howard Scott—under the name of S.O.B. (Same Ole Band) to perform their old WAR repertoire. (Producer Jerry Goldstein controls the rights to the name WAR and declined to allow them to use it. He has his own touring version of WAR led by lone original member Lonnie Jordan.) Oskar, who lives in Washington state, has presented clinics at Paul Allen's Experience Camp at the Experience Museum in Seattle and participated in a school program called "Say Hello To Yourself," designed to develop self-esteem in children aged six through twelve. "It's not about the harmonica," says Oskar. "The harmonica is my tool. It's about finding the canvas on which to paint inside yourself."

While Oskar performs mitzvot, especially when it comes to helping children, it's been a long time since he was involved in organized Jewish life. He refers to himself as a "cardiac Jew, a Yid from the heart." He became disappointed long ago by how people were behaving in synagogue. "I'm proud of my heritage and what Judaism stands for," Oskar says. "Judaism to me is a very sacred, special idea of integrity and morality, which I try to honor in everyday life. It's not about going to shul to do it, not about having to put on airs and impress people." He adds that Judaism is not about "how life is treating me, it's about how I am treating life."

# Norman Greenbaum

**Singer. Songwriter. Guitar player. Born November 20, 1942,
Malden, Massachusetts. Best known for writing and performing
the international No. 1 hit "Spirit in the Sky."**

*Norman Greenbaum followed his 1970 smash, "Spirit in the
Sky," with "a song about traife." (Photo by Lloyd Johnson.)*

Is he or isn't he? That's the question Jewish kids were asking in the spring of 1970 as the upbeat "Spirit in the Sky," buoyed by churchy hand claps and psychedelic fuzztone-laced guitar, began blaring from radios and nightclub sound systems. Was Norman Greenbaum Jewish? The lyric "I got a friend in Jesus" threw everybody off. For most, a guy named Greenbaum singing about Jesus was an oxymoron. The song released as a followup to "Spirit" added to the mystery. It was titled "Canned Ham."

The question persists. Greenbaum gets at least a dozen e-mails a week from Jews and non-Jews alike from as far away as Japan asking the same question. It's become so tedious that, if he's in a mischievous mood, Greenbaum will get pretty creative with his response just to entertain himself. Few would care to know the answer if the song weren't so powerful and enduring, or so synonymous with his name. Mention one and the other follows. Norman Greenbaum and "Spirit in the Sky" are a team, forever linked, and in contention for the Biggest One-Hit Wonder award. No one would have known to ask "Is he or isn't he?" if Greenbaum had changed his name or recorded it under the name of the band he'd had some success with in the late sixties: Dr. West's Medicine Show and Junk Band. That group reached No. 52 on the charts in 1967 with (no kidding) "The Eggplant That Ate Chicago."

Is he or isn't he? The answer, of course, is a resounding "Yes." "I grew up kissing a mezuzah on the way into the house," Greenbaum says. And he still identifies as a Jew. He's not a Messianic Jew or a Born Again Christian. But he is extremely proud of that song. "Without bragging, 'Spirit' is a phenomenal song that transgresses cultures, and transmutes, and leaves itself open to all kinds of interpretation," he says. So why did a Jewish kid with Orthodox roots write a Hallelujah gospel-rocker praising Jesus? It was an artistic and commercial idea, not a profound religious epiphany. "[Horror writer] Stephen King doesn't eat flesh even though his characters do. That's the way I look at it," says Greenbaum.

Greenbaum's maternal grandparents emigrated from Russia to Massachusetts in the early 1900s. His paternal grandparents came from Poland via England (where his father was born in 1906) around the same time. Greenbaum grew up in a Jewish household that fell somewhere between Conservative and Orthodox. His mother lit Shabbat candles every Friday night. The family walked to Beth Israel synagogue in Malden every Saturday. Norman attended Hebrew school a couple days a week after public school and had Orthodox tutoring for his bar mitzvah. Like most other kids, he was relieved to get it over with, and proud to have gotten through it. The family kept a (nearly) kosher home. They used two sets of dishes, and separated meat and dairy, but didn't buy only kosher food. (While he has long since abandoned most Jewish practice and ritual, Greenbaum still won't drink milk with meat.) In 1960, when his father died, Norman wrapped tefillin every Shabbat to say kaddish.

Very little music was played in the Greenbaum house when Norman was growing up. His older sister, however, had crushes on Frank Sinatra and Eddie Fisher and bought their records. When she played them, Norman listened. Then he heard Elvis Presley, and he never heard music the same way again. "In reality, Elvis was doing southern blues, and he wasn't Pat Boone, and I realized that all these white singers were covering black music." Greenbaum became fascinated by what he calls southern country blues, and he especially loved the lyrics. The artists had a way with words filled with double entendres that went far beyond "Baby, I love you," or "Baby, it's over." Greenbaum cites Howlin' Wolf singing "I asked for water, she gave me gasoline," as an inspirational lyric that "really got my mind going in the mid-fifties." He also loved the humor of the Marx Brothers, especially Groucho's subtle wordplay. Greenbaum and a friend bought guitars, taught themselves some chords, and tried to write songs. While his friend quit, Greenbaum discovered a love and ability for writing lyrics. By junior high school he knew he wanted to be a musician. He spent most of his only year at Boston University frequenting the city's coffeehouses. He also began to drift away from Jewish observance at BU but did "hang out and play ping pong" at the school's Hillel House. By 1965 Greenbaum was living on the West Coast and playing in Dr. West's Medicine Show and Junk Band. It was essentially a psychedelic jug band, an acoustic outfit that played an odd assortment of instruments, including an aluminum trash can drum kit. The band members painted their faces in colorful masks and performed with a hallucinogenic-like light show. Double entendre-filled comedy shtick and a kazoo version of the Beatles' "Eleanor Rigby" also were part of the show. This modern version of vaudeville tasted success with the novelty hit "The Eggplant That Ate Chicago," but by 1967 the novelty had worn off and the band broke up.

In 1968, Greenbaum began working as a solo act and released his first album in the following year. The album's first single flopped. The second single, "Spirit in the Sky," wasn't faring much better. The record company wanted to give up on it. One independent record distributor with faith in the song was able to keep it playing on a Los Angeles radio station at the eleventh hour. He told the station's program director he had just bought fifteen thousand copies of the record, and asked him to play the song for one more week. Two weeks later the song was No. 1 in Los Angeles, and its popularity spread from there. "Spirit" sold two million copies and reached No. 3 on the *Billboard* charts. It also hit No. 1 in England.

Greenbaum had decided to try to write a religious rock song after watching country crooner Porter Wagoner on TV perform a song about a preacher. Greenbaum figured a gospel-flavored rock song mentioning Jesus would have great commercial potential. "Does the average American youth care about a Jewish character or Buddha? Who cares, right? It was a ten-second elimination," he says. Jesus won. He wrote the lyrics in ten minutes: "Going up to the spirit in the sky, that's where I'm gonna go when I die. When I die and they lay me to rest, I'm gonna go to the place that's the best . . ." Coming up with the right music took months. "I started writing the song in L.A., did some in Mill Valley, finished it in Petaluma and recorded it in San Francisco," Greenbaum says. Throughout the process, he adds, "It never entered my mind that I was Jewish, just that I was a songwriter." Greenbaum's mother wondered what her son was doing writing about Jesus, but she was ecstatic that her son had a hit song and was a working musician. After enduring watching her boy paint his face and sing about an eggplant a few years earlier, singing about Jesus wasn't really so bad. The most difficult part was to come. What do you do for an encore after your first hit song embeds itself in a nation's consciousness?

The record company demanded a follow up fast. "They wanted me to write 'Spirit in the Sky 2' and I couldn't. It wasn't possible, and it still isn't. It would be like [Led Zeppelin] trying to write another "Stairway to Heaven." Greenbaum did try, and wrote what he believed were solid, though not typical tunes. "Canned Ham" was inspired by a trip to the supermarket with his wife at the time. The couple in front of them at the checkout lane had purchased a canned ham, something Norman never realized was available in a can. His imagination began to roam. He ran home and in fifteen minutes wrote a love song that revolved around a canned ham. "Me in my infinite weirdo-ness, I come up with 'Canned Ham.' It's bad enough I'm singing about Jesus, now I'm singing about traife," Greenbaum recalls. The ditty bombed. So did another effort, "California Earthquake." Greenbaum tried to relieve the pressure with odd projects, such as a concept album about farm life called *Petaluma*. He frustrated his record company and producers in the process, making it nearly impossible for them to market his unconventional projects. He ignored their advice and followed his own weird muse. The music flopped. He took another stab at success with a song he says was influenced by his memories, real or imagined, of luring ten men for a morning minyan with a little schnapps. But again, for mass appeal, he transformed it into a song with the clever title of "The Day They Served Beer in Church (Everybody Came to Pray)." Record companies, believing southern Baptists would fail to see the song's humor, declined to release the song. In 1995, the song was included on a *Best of Norman Greenbaum* compilation CD.

While trying to repeat the success of "Spirit in the Sky," Greenbaum also ran a goat dairy farm, selling goat milk to northern California health food stores from 1970 through 1973. He joined a band called Crossfire in the mid-seventies and started a band management and concert production company. He then retreated from the music business, becoming a cook for ten years, and doing farm work. In 1986 he was thrust back in the spotlight when the British band Doctor and the Medics had a No. 1 hit in England with its version of "Spirit in the Sky." "Spirit" became the only song in British rock history to reach the top of the charts by two different acts. Greenbaum didn't like the Medics' million-selling version, but he appreciated the royalties. An English TV station filmed him for a special on Top Ten One-Hit Wonders. "Spirit" came in at number two. Since then, the song also has had new life in some dozen films, including *Miami Blues*, *Apollo 13*, *Wayne's World 2*, *Contact*, *Saving Grace*, and *Remember the Titans*. It also has been featured in TV shows such as *Beverly Hills 90210*, *The Drew Carey Show*, *Gideon's Crossing*, and *Arli$$* and it has been used in television commercials for Infiniti, HBO, and American Express.

"Spirit" of course remains a staple on classic rock radio stations. Garage bands still play it. A new generation of rock fans is writing to him about the song. Born-again Christians tell him they sing it around campfires at retreats. He even has been asked to perform "Spirit in the Sky" at funerals. He has had, as he puts it, more than his fifteen minutes of fame. "I'm a question on *Rock 'n' Roll Jeopardy* and *Trivial Pursuit*. I'm a piece of history." The song doesn't seem to be running out of steam. The original recording was re-released in early 2001 on the Varese Sarabande record label. The only negative effect from the song, Greenbaum says, is from the occasional narrow-minded person who "doesn't want to take it for what it is; a piece of art, like a book or a painting. A good piece of art is open to interpretation, and most people interpret it positively. It's a good thing for me, mentally, to know that I didn't just write a cruising tune."

# Marc Bolan

**Singer. Songwriter. Guitarist. Born Mark Feld, September 30, 1947, London, England. Died September 16, 1977, London, England. Best known in the United States for the Top Ten hit "Bang a Gong (Get It On)" and in England and Europe for the hits "Ride a White Swan," "Hot Love," "Jeepster," "Telegram Sam," "Teenage Dream," "Metal Guru," "20th Century Boy," "The Groover," and "I Love to Boogie."**

*Marc Bolan during his Tyrannosaurus Rex days in 1969. (Photo courtesy the Official Marc Bolan Fan Club.)*

Kaddish, the Jewish prayer for the dead, has been said for Marc Bolan at his burial site at the Golders Green Crematorium every year since 1997, the twentieth anniversary of his death. His cousin Caroline Feld has made sure of that. "I feel like Marc's pushing me. I feel like Marc's asking me to do it," Caroline says. For Bolan fans, September sixteenth, the day he died in a car crash not far from his London home, is a sacred day. Throughout the year, but especially every September sixteenth, several thousand fans bearing flowers, poems, placards, and photos have flocked to Bolan's burial site, marked by a white rose bush on the peaceful green tree-lined crematorium grounds. The site, with its white marble memorial plaque, is nothing less than a shrine. Though he had only one substantial hit in the United States, the Top Ten "Bang a Gong (Get It On)," Bolan was a superstar in England and Europe for much of the seventies, and his music endures. His albums still sell; his songs are still played on radio, performed by other acts, and used in films. He still has an active fan club, and numerous Web sites and fan 'zines are devoted to him. Bolan conventions are held throughout the year, and younger generations of fans continue to discover his music. Marc Bolan fans are as touched and moved by his musical legacy, and his legend, as much as Elvis Presley fans are affected by the King. Fans find Bolan's music uplifting and full of life, potent enough to pull them out of the doldrums, and take them even higher in good times. They also have connected personally with Bolan, enough not only to name their children after him, but after characters in his songs as well. "He's not just a rock idol, we look on him as a brother" says Barry Smith, co-operator of the Official Marc Bolan Fan Club and editor of its biannual fan magazine, *Electric Boogie.*

Marc Bolan was born Mark Feld on September 30, 1947. His father, Simeon, was Jewish, and had a variety of jobs, including working at the popular Bloom's Kosher Butchers and, later, driving a truck. Mark was named after an uncle who died at about age nineteen while in the army, beaten to death by a fellow soldier. Some family members believe it was an anti-Semitic act. Marc's mother, Phyllis, belonged to the Church of England, worked in a munitions factory until older brother Harry was born, and later ran a fruit stand at a market. Marc and Harry, older by two years, had no formal Jewish education, nor did the family observe Jewish ritual or celebrate Jewish holidays at home. The boys' mother read them the Bible for its moral rather than religious content. "We had a very moral upbringing, but it was left to us to sort out what religion we would take," Harry Feld explains. "I don't think Marc actually followed any religion." The Feld brothers grew up in the heavily Jewish Stamford Hill section of London. They were among the Jewish students who had permission to leave Northwold Road Infant and Primary School early every Friday to get home in time for Shabbat, even though the family didn't celebrate it.★ Most of what the Feld kids learned about Judaism came from attending family bar mitzvahs, weddings, and funerals. Even with no Jewish observance or schooling, and though he rarely, if ever, discussed Judaism, Marc identified culturally as a Jew. Growing up, his best friends were Jewish, he attended social events at Jewish youth clubs, and dated Jewish girls. And, according to his brother Harry, when in the company of friends, Marc often referred to himself as "a nice Jewish boy." But as he grew older and got caught up in the world of rock stardom, he rarely referred to his Jewish background and in 1971 married June Child, a non-Jew. "Marc had very little Jewish identity that I was aware of," says Tony Visconti, Bolan's record producer from 1968 through 1974, though Bolan did once refer to a shirt as a *shmata*, Visconti recalls. The non-Jewish Visconti had grown up in Brooklyn, gone to predominantly Jewish New Utrecht High School, and knew more Yiddish and Jewish custom than Bolan did. Bolan, however, was partial to his aunt's chopped liver and chicken soup and often made sure the Jewish soul food was waiting backstage after concerts.

Bolan knew as early as age nine that he wanted to be a rock star. By then, he had discovered Elvis Presley, thanks in part to his father, who brought his son American records he'd come across at the Petticoat Lane open air market where he sometimes worked. Bolan was even more taken with English pop star Cliff Richard, whom he tried to imitate. He began teaching himself guitar and frequenting the Hackney Empire, an old theater not far from his home that had been converted into a TV studio and concert hall. He pestered the staff until they allowed him backstage where he watched the music show *Oh Boy* being filmed, observed how rock stars such as Eddie Cochran and Cliff Richard carried themselves, and noted what transpired behind the scenes at rock concerts. By age fourteen, he was standing outside coffee shops in Stamford Hill playing guitar and singing folk standards like "Blowing in the Wind," using the stage name of

---

★One of Marc's older Jewish schoolmates, Helen Shapiro, would become a teenage singing sensation in England in the early sixties. On a tour of the United Kingdom in 1963, a young group called the Beatles was her opening act. In 1987, Shapiro became a Messianic Jew, and promoted her new religious views in song.

Toby Tyler, nicked from a Walt Disney film. His handsome looks also enabled him to get work as a model during his early teens. Between the modeling and the music he never had trouble getting dates. "He was a Mod, good looking, and always had girls flipping around him," his cousin Caroline says.

He signed his first recording contract with Decca Records in 1965. The company was not thrilled with the Toby Tyler moniker or his real name and wanted to release his first record under the name of Marc Bowland, a name he didn't like. To regain some control over his stage name, he dropped "w" and "d," and enjoyed the fact that the resulting Bolan closely resembled the name of his friend, actor James Bolam. (Another story is that he came up with Bolan by compressing the name Bob Dylan.) No matter his name, Bolan's first three singles were commercial disappointments but illustrated his interest in mythology and fantasy, and they were an introduction to the quivering, high-pitched voice that would soon dominate the airwaves in England. In 1967, he joined a band called John's Children, penning the group's best-known song, "Desdemona." That same year, he and percussionist Steve Peregrine Took formed Tyrannosaurus Rex. Originally conceived as a rock band, the group evolved into an acoustic guitar-and-bongos duo because they couldn't afford to buy or rent the necessary equipment. The duo released three albums between 1968 and 1970. The titles alone signaled Bolan's fascination with author J. R. R. Tolkien's fantasy world, mysticism, magic, and Summer-of-Love peace and happiness: *My People Were Fair and Had Sky in Their Hair But Now They're Content to Wear Stars on Their Brows*, *Prophets, Seers and Sages, The Angels of the Ages*, and *Unicorn*. While the albums yielded no major hit singles, they earned him a strong underground following. A fourth album, *Beard of Stars*, with Mickey Finn replacing Took, was a transitional record that included a switch to electric guitar and a budding penchant for Chuck Berry and Eddie Cochran guitar riffs. Shortly after that album's release, Bolan shortened the duo's name to T. Rex, as much for marketing reasons as anything else, and added a rhythm section for a fuller, more arena- and stadium-friendly sound. He then took aim at the teen market with the release of the album *T. Rex*. He also recorded the soft-rock tune, "Ride a White Swan," which soared to No. 2 in England and stayed on the charts for six months. It was the first of ten consecutive Top Five hits in England from 1970 through 1973. A master at self-promotion, he later appeared on the British TV program *Top of the Pops* wearing eyeliner and glitter on his cheeks. In the process, he jump-started the glam-rock movement, paving the way for the

likes of David Bowie and Gary Glitter. The result of his TV appearance was a No. 1 hit, "Hot Love," which stayed at the top of the charts for six weeks.

Bolan sometimes used his brother Harry as a reverse sounding board. "He'd ask me what I thought, and if I liked it, he'd put it in a cupboard. My liking it meant it wasn't commercial. We were loving brothers, but our tastes were completely different," Harry Feld says. Bolan's popularity peaked in 1972 with the international bestsellers *Electric Warrior* and *The Slider*. *Warrior* included Bolan's sole Top Forty U.S. hit "Bang a Gong (Get It On)." A throbbing beat, and sky-high background vocals by former Turtles members Mark Volman and Howard Kaylan, helped propel the song to No. 10 in the United States. Volman, who is often mistakenly identified as Jewish but is not, and Kaylan (born Kaplan), who is Jewish, provided the background vocals for many of Bolan's songs from 1971 through 1973. (In 1985, the Power Station, featuring singer Robert Palmer and members of Duran Duran, would take their version of the song to No. 9 on the U.S. charts.)

In 1972, the media also coined the term "T-Rextasy," to describe the Beatlemania-like frenzy of Bolan's fans and the magnitude of his popularity. His superstar status was cemented when he became the first rock act to sell out England's seventy-two-thousand-seat Wembley Stadium that year. Former Beatle Ringo Starr produced a Bolan documentary, *Born to Boogie*, in 1972, which included footage from the Wembley concerts. *The Slider*, while not as successful in the United States as *Electric Warrior*, included two British and European No. 1 hits. Aside from "Bang a Gong," American audiences didn't embrace Bolan with the same enthusiasm as European audiences did. Even Bolan's fascination with all things American, especially cars, about which he wrote several songs, couldn't make him a fixture on the U.S. charts. By the time America discovered glam-rock, Bolan already had dropped that image and moved on to experiment with soul music.

Though he would continue to put songs on the British charts through 1976, Bolan's career began sliding after a 1973 U.S. tour. In 1974, he divorced his wife, and began living with American soul singer Gloria Jones, who had been a backup singer on his U.S. tour. He reportedly put on weight and drank too much. In 1975, the couple had a son, Rolan. The resulting parental responsibilities seemed to revitalize Bolan. After several years out of the glare reserved for superstars, he seemed poised for a comeback with the 1977 album *Dandy in the Underworld*. But

Bolan, who often remarked that he didn't think he'd live past the age of thirty, was killed when the car Jones was driving crashed into a tree two weeks shy of his thirtieth birthday. The crash site, like his burial site, is now a shrine marked with a plaque, and is also regularly visited by fans from around the world.

Bolan's father wanted him to be buried in a Jewish cemetery (and supposedly Marc wanted a Jewish ceremony when he died), but there was concern that fans might dig up the body. So the rock star was cremated and his remains buried in Golders Green Crematorium. An aunt made sure a rabbi was present. His parents, who both died in 1991, also were cremated and their remains were placed

Cover of the Marc Bolan tribute record, Great Jewish Music: Marc Bolan, featuring interpretations of Bolan's songs by a variety of acts, released on John Zorn's Tzadik Records label in 1998. (Cover illustration Maruo Suehiro, courtesy Tzadik Records.)

under the rose bush next to their cherished son. For years, Bolan's parents mingled with fans visiting their rock 'n' roll hero's gravesite on the anniversary of his death. After the memorial services fans traditionally gather at the nearby Club Extreme to celebrate Bolan's music through concert videos and live performances until sunrise. All money raised goes to various charities.

Bolan's music has been especially prevalent throughout the nineties and into the new millennium, with reissues, compilations, and tributes. In 1998, John Zorn released *Great Jewish Music: Marc Bolan* on his Tzadik record label. It included an array of Jewish and non-Jewish jazz, rock, and avant garde acts such as Vernon Reid, Gary Lucas, Cake, Lloyd Cole, and Modeski, Martin and Wood, interpreting nineteen Bolan tunes in their own unique voices. (It was the third release in Tzadik's "Great Jewish Music" series, which also has included tributes to Burt Bacharach and Serge Gainsbourg.) In 2000, a French Canadian ensemble gave Bolan's songs a sixteenth-century feel on a record called *Beltane: A Musical Fantasy*. The record included the songs "Pavilions of Sun," "Sea Beasts," "Children of Rarn," and "Dragon's Ear" among others. A British act called Bus Stop also had a hit with Bolan's "Bang a Gong (Get It On)" in 2000. And the Official Marc Bolan Fan Club announced the 2001 release of *Live at the Boston Gliderdrome*, a tape of the 1972 concert that inspired the term "T-Rextasy." The inclusion of a half dozen Marc Bolan songs in the hit film *Billy Elliot* reignited interest in the rocker, creating a new generation of fans. In England, a number of CD compilations, books, and special events commemorated the twenty-fifth anniversary of his death in September 2002. Asked about how the late, great rocker might feel about what's happened since his death, Harry Feld replied, "He'd be thrilled to pieces. He was all about show business."

# Steve Goodman

**Contemporary folk singer. Songwriter. Guitar player. Born July 25, 1948,
Chicago, Illinois. Died September 20, 1984, Seattle, Washington.
Best known for writing the folk classic "City of New Orleans,"
a Top Twenty hit for Arlo Guthrie in 1972, and "You Never Even Call
Me by My Name," a Top Five country hit for David Allen Coe.**

*Steve Goodman, center, with Jethro Burns, left, and Jim Rothermel, right. (Photo courtesy of Red Pajamas Records.)*

God blessed Steve Goodman with a lot of talent, smarts, wit and humor, but a very short amount of time. Goodman used what God gave him and led an exemplary life for the thirty-six years he was allotted. The tributes from friends and colleagues described a rabbi more than a wandering minstrel. Johnny Cash called him "a man of great compassion." Emmylou Harris described him as "a man of extraordinary humor, but good humor. No matter how sharp his wit . . . he was never cruel." Jackson Browne viewed Goodman as "bounding with the good will and humor it takes to survive the blows of this world." And comedian Steve Martin noted that "Steve could change a hostile audience into a warm, loving one. They sensed his goodness and responded in kind."

For sixteen years, Goodman struggled with leukemia with indomitable public grace and dignity and a sense of humor. He referred to himself as Cool Hand Leuk. He used his illness and heightened sense of mortality as inspiration, combining it with his unyielding sense of humor to come up with songs that both laughed at and acknowledged death. The upbeat ragtime tempo of "You Better Get It While You Can," included the line, "From the cradle to the crypt, it's a mighty short trip, so you better get it while you can." Even "Watching Joey Glow" (a comedy about the advantages of radiation) and "A Dying Cub Fan's Last Request" harbored a wisdom in what, on first listen, sounded like novelty songs.

Not all his songs were laced with humor or played for a laugh. "You're the Girl That I Love," "Would You Like to Learn to Dance," and "Hand It to You" were drawn by a serious romantic. "Banana Republics," popularized by Jimmy Buffett, was a bittersweet observation about "the expatriate American." "My Old Man" was an autobiographical tearjerker about the passing of his father, and it remains universal in its parent-child observations. Goodman's masterpiece, "City of New Orleans," was a vivid portrait of a fading piece of Americana. The opening lines of the chorus, "Good morning America, How are you? Say, don't you know me I'm your native son?" are among the most familiar and recognizable in pop music, and remain a part of the fabric of American song. "City of New Orleans" was a career hit for Arlo Guthrie in 1972 and was also recorded by Willie Nelson, John Denver, and Judy Collins, among others. In the liner notes to the 1994 Goodman anthology No Big Surprise his wife Nancy wrote that Goodman's lyrics "do not muse on the meaning of life . . . he gleaned his truths from the philosophers among everyday people: taxi drivers, the porters on the City of New

Orleans, Cub fans." She also wrote that "Steve wanted to live as normal a life as possible, only he had to live it as fast as possible."

Goodman was a mensch long before he contracted leukemia at age twenty and realized he probably wouldn't make it to the biblical three score and ten years most people anticipate. Goodman grew up in a loving, middle-class Jewish home in the Chicago suburbs. His father, Joseph "Bud" Goodman, was an auto salesman who had piloted C-47s in the China-Burma-India theater during World War II. His mother, Minnette (maiden name Erenburg), was a housewife, and his younger brother David a talented photographer. Steve got his earliest musical training as a member of the children's choir at Reform congregation Beth Israel. Though no one else in his family was musical, Goodman's voice was impressive enough by age ten that he assisted the cantor during the High Holy Days and at weddings. He began his Jewish education at age five, attending Sunday school, then Hebrew school. He became a bar mitzvah and was confirmed, but the family had assimilated far enough into mainstream America to also stick gifts under a tree at Christmas. He began playing guitar at thirteen but didn't take it seriously until he was in high school. He honed his singing and performance skills in musicals at Main Township High School East (where he and Hillary Rodham Clinton were classmates). He was an avid reader, especially enjoying history, and was an excellent student who easily retained lessons and grasped concepts and ideas. His natural ability at academics translated to music, where he quickly became an admired guitar picker and developed into a respected songwriter without knowing how to read music. He enrolled at the University of Illinois to study political science but left a month before finishing his freshman year to join the booming folk scene in New York in the summer of 1967. After several months, he returned to Chicago and enrolled at Lake Forest College, paying his way through school by playing in area folk clubs. In 1968, he was diagnosed with leukemia. In 1969, he decided to make another run at a career in music, becoming a fixture at a club called the Earl of Old Town. The following year he met and married Nancy, a waitress at the club. Goodman looked forward to being married by his rabbi in the synagogue where he had sung in the choir and become a bar mitzvah. But because Nancy was not Jewish, the rabbi declined. Goodman had a Jewish wedding elsewhere, but his mother never forgave the rabbi. Steve and Nancy would go on to have three children.

*Steve Goodman on his bar mitzvah day. (Photo courtesy of Red Pajamas Records.)*

In 1971, singer-songwriter Kris Kristofferson recommended Goodman to his friend, pop singer Paul Anka. After seeing Goodman, Anka worked to get him a recording contract with his record company, Buddah Records. When Anka asked Goodman if he'd like to fly to New York to talk about a recording contract, Goodman reportedly answered, "Would you like to see a short, fat Jewish guy dive into a bowl of chicken soup?"

Goodman made two acclaimed albums for the company, *Steve Goodman* (1972) and *Somebody Else's Troubles* (1973). They failed to break out commercially, even though they included "City of New Orleans" and "You Never Even Call Me By My Name," which became hits for others. (Goodman's version of "City" stalled at No. 113 on the record charts.) Throughout his life, Goodman worked extensively with fellow singer-songwriter John Prine. They'd befriended each other playing the Chicago club circuit, and when Goodman was offered a record deal, he helped get Prine one as well. Goodman produced, co-wrote with Prine, and played on his albums. Jimmy Buffett was another frequent collaborator. Buffett recorded at least half a dozen Goodman songs between 1974 and 1985. Goodman contributed guitar as well as songs to many of Buffett's career-defining albums from the seventies, including *A-1-A*, *Havana Daydreaming*, *Changes in Latitudes, Changes in Attitudes*, and *Son of a Son of a Sailor*. Trisha Yearwood, Marty Stuart, Joan Baez, and the Nitty Gritty Dirt Band, with whom Goodman co-wrote, were among the many other acts that included his songs on their albums.

More than writing or recording, Goodman lived for the stage. Performing energized him. And while his albums didn't generate big sales, Goodman was an in-demand performer on the national club scene and at summer festivals. Ace mandolin player and fellow Chicagoan Jethro Burns often accompanied Goodman in concert. Singer-songwriter Wendy Waldman, who worked with Goodman for a short time, explains that "Steve Goodman viewed making music as a service and a joy." After being dropped from several record labels because of poor sales, Goodman borrowed a page from John Prine's business plan, and on a shoestring budget, with help from his managers, started his own record label, Red Pajamas Records. In 1983 the new label released a pair of acclaimed records, *Artistic Hair*—the title an allusion to the effects of chemotherapy—and *Affordable Art*. The following year, Goodman and company issued *Santa Ana Winds*. Goodman died in September of that year in a Seattle hospital from kidney and liver failure. Four months later, in January of 1985, a tribute concert was held at

McCormick Place, a Chicago theater, and recorded for commercial release. Later in the year, the two-record, nineteen-song *Tribute to Steve Goodman* was released on Red Pajamas. It featured performances by many of his friends including John Prine, Arlo Guthrie, Richie Havens, Bonnie Raitt, Jethro Burns, David Bromberg, and the Nitty Gritty Dirt Band. Red Pajamas continued to release posthumous Steve Goodman recordings well into the nineties, including a two-CD, forty-two-song anthology in 1994.

Goodman had lived as if the great sage Hillel was constantly by his side reminding him that the essence of Judaism was abiding by the golden rule, and the rest just commentary. Though he was forced to live with a fatal disease, he preferred to brighten others' lives rather than complain about his own. He could have complained about the lack of a cure for his body and of the lack of a hit for his career. Instead, he just kept singing, entertaining, and enlightening. Steve Goodman was a good man in the truest sense of the word. "I don't know that he advertised it," said his mother, "but he certainly was a Jew, there's no denying that."

# Kinky Friedman and the Texas Jewboys

**Singer. Songwriter. Satirist. Guitar player. Mystery novelist. Magazine columnist. Born Richard S. Friedman, November 1, 1944, Chicago, Illinois, but raised in Texas. Best known for combining country music with satire and sarcasm, resulting in humorous social commentary such as "They Ain't Making Jews Like Jesus Anymore."**

*Kinky Friedman took a lot of heat from Jewish groups, including bomb threats from the Jewish Defense League, for naming his band the Jewboys. (Photo by Don Imus.)*

Playing off the name of the legendary country swing band Bob Wills and the Texas Playboys, Kinky Friedman founded the Texas Jewboys as a source of Jewish pride and a force for ridiculing anti-Semitism and bigotry of all kinds. Friedman often was the only Jew in the group's shifting lineup, though other members went by monikers such as Little Jewford and "Snakebite" Jacobs. Jewish rights groups and anti-Semites alike misunderstood the Jewboys' in-your-face name as well as their music. The name symbolized the twin cultures of Texas cowboys and Jewish intellectuals from which Friedman had sprung as well as an attempt to defuse the volatile term "Jewboy." Kinky once noted that cowboys and Jews were the only two groups to wear their hats indoors and "attach a certain importance to it." He also saw a similar toughness and pioneer spirit in Texans

*The cover of Kinky Friedman's 1973 debut album,* Sold American. *(Courtesy Vanguard Records.)*

and Israelis; no wimps existed in either camp. Kinky frequently has made Jewish references, stating, for example, that when he writes his autobiography it will be from right to left. He's also had fun with Jewish stereotypes. When he ran for political office in his home of Kerrville, Texas, in 1986, his campaign slogan was "If you elect me your first Jewish justice of the peace, I'll reduce the speed limit to 54.95." (He lost.) He also proudly uses a guitar strap emblazoned with a yellow Star of David when he performs. Still, Kinky (a nickname bestowed upon him because of his curly hair) remained misunderstood by many. "Calling ourselves the Jewboys probably set the ADL [Anti-Defamation League] back in its work fifty years," Friedman says, reflecting on the origins of the band's name. "Hipper Jews rallied to us, but B'nai B'rith types didn't get it. They didn't bother to listen to the songs." The group's first two albums, *Sold American* (1973) and *Kinky Friedman* (1974) included "Ride 'em Jewboy," "We Reserve the Right to Refuse Service to You," "The Top Ten Commandments," and "They Ain't Making Jews Like Jesus Anymore," and they resulted in bomb threats from the Jewish Defense League. And some Jewish record store owners refused to stock the records. Jews thought Friedman was being irreverent and self-hating, while anti-Semites thought they had discovered a kindred spirit. A closer listen to the group's clever wordplay, twang-laden vocals, and resonating country harmonies would have revealed the truth. "They Ain't Makin' Jews . . ." was nothing short of a defiant warning disguised as a comic bar brawl. The chorus said it all: "No, they ain't making Jews like Jesus anymore. / We don't turn the other cheek / the way we done before. You could hear that honky holler / as he hit that hardwood floor. / No they ain't making Jews like Jesus anymore."

Though Friedman prefers the role of court jester to make a point, he can get serious in song. The title, "Ride 'em Jewboy," sounds funny and irreverent, but the ballad is a eulogy for the six million Jews murdered during Hitler's Final Solution. Friedman also puts aside the humor on "Shield of Abraham," a song encouraging the Jewish people to keep the faith, and have no fear because "We've got the shield, we've got the shield, we've got the shield of Abraham, little children." The poignant, bittersweet "Tramp on the Street," is a plea for compassion as well as a reminder that "Jesus was a Jewboy his self."

Jesus is a recurring character in Kinky's songs, admired by the songwriter as "The first Jewish troublemaker in history." Kinky tackled more than anti-Semitism and bigotry; anyone and anything was fair game for his cynical eye. In 1973 the

National Organization of Women (NOW), in another example of a group that
missed the point, gave Kinky Friedman and the Texas Jewboys its Male Chauvin-
ist Pig Award for the perceived anti–women's rights rant, "Get Your Biscuits in
the Oven and Your Buns in the Bed." Kinky was not raised to be a male chauvin-
ist pig.

Kinky was born Richard S. Friedman in Chicago on November 1, 1944, but was
whisked off to Houston, Texas a year later. His father, Tom, a navigator on a B-24
bomber during World War II, took a job in the community relations department
of a Jewish agency in Houston. His mother, Minnie, started the first speech therapy program in the Houston public school system. In the early fifties, Tom Friedman became a psychology professor at the University of Texas at Austin and
moved the family there. In 1953, Tom and Minnie started a summer camp for
Jewish children called Echo Hill Ranch. Richard, already writing poetry, began
writing parodies, and discovered a talent for entertaining his peers while a
camper at Echo Hill. He was eleven when he wrote "Old Ben Lucas" (Old Ben
Lucas / had a lot of mucus / coming right out of his nose), a song that would appear on record about twenty years later. Raised in a household that observed
most Jewish holidays, Richard also attended Sunday school and Hebrew school
and became a bar mitzvah. It wasn't until college at the University of Texas that
Friedman, a fan of Jimmy Rogers, Hank Williams, and Johnny Cash, began to
take musical parody and comedy more seriously. He formed his first band, King
Arthur and the Carrots, and in 1964 recorded his first song, "Schwinn 24," a
smirking surf-rock send-up about a bicycle, ("Pedal up, pedal down, pedal all
around town on my Schwinn 24").

In 1967, inspired by President Kennedy and the Jewish commandment to repair the world, Friedman joined the Peace Corps after graduating from college.
"I'm not remotely religious at all," Friedman says, "but I'm sure Jewish values
had something to do with [joining the Peace Corps]." Friedman spent two and a
half years in Borneo, an island nation south of the Philippines, where he says
with tongue firmly planted in cheek, his job was to "help people who had been
farming successfully for two thousand years improve their agricultural methods."
The isolation of the Borneo posting enabled Friedman to view America more
clearly from a distance and experience "a culture that moves more slowly and
more thoughtfully than ours." He began writing songs. Future Kinky classics

such as "Ride 'em Jewboy," "Sold American," and "The Ballad of Charles Whitman" were written in Borneo.

In 1971, a couple of years after Friedman's return from Borneo, he formed the group whose name and repertoire shocked, confounded, and enlightened so many for so long. The group released its first album, *Sold American*, in 1973. The record featured Eric Clapton playing dobro on two songs and Ringo Starr playing Jesus on one. The self-titled *Kinky Friedman* and *Lasso from El Passo* followed in 1974 and 1976, respectively. In 1976, the group joined Bob Dylan's Rolling Thunder Review tour. Even with Dylan and stars such as Willie Nelson and syndicated radio personality Don Imus singing the group's praises, the Jewboys were unable to develop more than a loyal cult following. Kinky dissolved the band in 1979, moved to New York, and performed solo at various clubs, becoming a fixture at the Lone Star Café in Manhattan. He released another album in 1983, *Under the Double Ego*, but it was a commercial disappointment.

Down and out and broke, Kinky tried another form of entertainment—writing detective novels. In 1986, the first of a series of humorous whodunits, *Greenwich Killing Time*, was published. It featured none other than the "Kinkster" himself as a country musician-turned-private eye. Since then, more than a dozen comic novels starring Kinky as a sleuth have been published with titles such as *Armadillos & Old Lace; Elvis, Jesus & Coca-Cola; A Case of Lone Star; The Love Song of J. Edgar Hoover; Blast from the Past;* and *The Mile High Club*. The books are more popular in the United Kingdom, Europe, and Australia than in the United States, though presidents Clinton and George W. Bush are reportedly fans. The success of the books renewed interest in Kinky's music. "Very few Jewish performers are openly Jewish in their work. Bob Dylan and Paul Simon are not. I was, and I think it cost me commercially," Kinky says. "I'm more popular now, and much of that is due to the books."

In 1992, Kinky released a twenty-one song "best of" compilation titled *Old Testaments and New Revelations* (on Fruit of the Tune Music). Primarily available through mail order, it sold more than a hundred thousand copies. He followed that in 1995 with *From One Good American to Another*. In 1999, the tribute album *Pearls in the Snow: The Songs of Kinky Friedman* was released on his own Kinkajou Records label. The seventeen-song collection, hailed by critics, featured notable country and roots-rock singers Willie Nelson, Tom Waits, Lyle Lovett, Dwight

Yoakam, and Delbert McClinton performing their interpretations of Kinky classics. (Imagine Nelson singing "Ride 'em Jewboy.") To publicize his books and
records, Kinky embarked on a two-and-half-month-long, forty-city tour of Europe with former Jewboy Little Jewford. Ironically, one of Kinky's biggest fan
bases is in Germany, over which his father flew thirty-five bombing missions
during World War II. Appreciative of German support but not completely forgiving of their history, Kinky has told his German audiences on more than one
occasion, "The Germans are my second favorite people. My first is everybody
else." An album chronicling the tour, *Classic Snatches from Europe*, which includes
new songs such as "First Jewish Justice of the Peace" and "Bob Dylan's Dream,"
was released in 2000.

In 2001, he teamed with Texas musician Billy Joe Shaver for "The Two Moving
Parts" tour of the Lone Star State. It appeared that audiences had finally caught
up to Kinky, or at least his rebellious, satirical musical catalog. "The songs are
thirty years old and most really are connecting today; they still have their spiritual legs," Kinky says. In April of 2001, Kinky began writing a column for *Texas
Monthly* magazine. In the fall, another detective novel was published, as well as
*Kinky Friedman's Guide to Texas Etiquette, or How to Get to Heaven or Hell without Going
through Dallas–Fort Worth*. Aside from writing, recording, and touring, he is co-
founder of the Utopia Animal Rescue Ranch, established in 1999, and credits
Jewish values as part of the reason he got involved in saving animals. As far as Judaism goes, Friedman quotes a recurring character from his novels named Ram-
bam: "If he's a practicing Jew, he needs more practice." Friedman adds that his
Jewish identity is based on the outsider looking in. "That's where my voice comes
from. It's an important Jewish angle on mankind, being outside the mainstream,
but having influence on the mainstream."

# Mike Garson

**Pianist. Composer. Born Brooklyn, New York, July 29, 1945. Best known for revolutionizing rock 'n' roll piano solos with his work on David Bowie's 1973 *Aladdin Sane* album. He has toured and recorded extensively with Bowie since then. During the nineties he added his unique touch to the music of Smashing Pumpkins, Nine Inch Nails, Seal, and No Doubt.**

*Michael Garson chose rock 'n' roll and jazz over the rabbinate. (Photo by Shannon Treglia, courtesy of Mike Garson.)*

On June 25, 2000, Mike Garson walked onstage at the Glastonbury Festival in Somerset, England, and started playing "Greensleeves" in front of a hundred thousand rock 'n' roll fans. Garson was nervous playing such a delicate song to such a wild crowd, but that's how his boss, David Bowie, wanted to start the set that would close the three-day, one hundred-band extravaganza. Few, if any, in the audience knew that Bowie's longtime keyboard player, the man who turned heads with his classical, avant garde, and jazz improvisations on Bowie staples such as "Aladdin Sane," had almost gone into the rabbinate instead of rock 'n' roll. The rabbinate's loss was David Bowie's gain. "It's pointless to talk about [Mike's] ability as an artist," Bowie says. "He is exceptional. However, there are very, very few musicians, let alone pianists, who naturally understand the movement and free thinking necessary to hurl themselves into experimental or traditional areas of music, sometimes, ironically, at the same time. Mike does this with such enthusiasm that it makes my heart glad just to be in the same room with him."

Up until the age of fifteen, Mike Garson had every intention of becoming a rabbi. He enjoyed attending Shabbat services every week at the Avenue N Temple off Ocean Parkway in Brooklyn with his maternal grandfather, Harry Horowitz. And he was the prize pupil of Morah Mandelbaum's Hebrew class. Mrs. Mandelbaum thought Garson had all the right ingredients to become a rabbi—a love of Hebrew and Torah study and, more important, compassion. Garson also was studying Hebrew in high school for his language requirement and was good enough to earn a scholarship to study in Tel Aviv at age fourteen. He loved Israel so much he almost didn't come home. (It was 1959 and Israel was only eleven years old.)

Garson also had been studying piano since he was seven. Everyone in the Garson house—his father, mother, and older sister, Barbara—played piano. Mike was the natural, with perfect pitch, and he had the benefit of an inspiring teacher. But he was not crazy about practicing. His mother often threatened to cancel his lessons to get him to practice. She also bribed him to practice, once offering him fifteen dollars if he could learn Liszt's "Hungarian Rhapsody No. 2." It was not an easy task for a twelve-year-old, but he did it. A short time later he discovered and developed a passion for jazz. At fourteen, Garson also had begun working summer jobs in the Catskills playing in bands backing up the likes of Jackie Mason and Mel Torme. Working for big name singers and comedians was marvelous training for learning to quickly sight read music for a different act each night. Later that year, a couple of neighborhood kids toting electric guitars invited themselves into Mike's house to jam. They wanted him to join their rock band, but Mike, while he enjoyed the boogie-woogie and blues jam session, wasn't interested in that music. By fifteen, Garson had cooled on being a rabbi. Morah Mandelbaum "was crushed" when Mike broke the news to her. The lure of a career in music was overpowering, though he did later enroll in Brooklyn College as a pre-med student. That was short-lived when a friend paid him three dollars for a piano lesson. Garson was seventeen when he began teaching piano regularly. He switched his major to music and education and while still in school got further training backing up jazz masters like Stanley Clarke, Elvin Jones, and Freddie Hubbard in New York clubs.

He was twenty-four before he dove into rock 'n' roll. In 1969 he replaced Dr. John (of "Right Place Wrong Time" fame) in a band called Brethren. The band had a recording contract with Scepter Records and a big time manager in Sid Bernstein, the man who brought the Beatles to America. Garson recorded a pair of albums with Brethren and the band toured as an opening act for Traffic, Joe Cocker, and Mountain, among others, but couldn't generate a hit song. The group dissolved around 1971. That same year, Garson got a job as music director and piano player for a Martha Reeves and the Vandellas oldies concert at Madison Square Garden in New York. His father, Bernard, was so delighted by his son's professional musical pursuits he thought his son was the next Gershwin. His mother, Sally, saw her hopes for Mike's becoming a doctor fading rapidly. And a stranger's phone call to her son in 1972 ruled out a career in medicine for good.

David Bowie, already heading toward superstardom in Great Britain, had arrived in New York for his first tour of the United States. Bowie was performing as Ziggy Stardust, his theatrical, glam-rock persona, and needed a piano player for an eight-week stint. Mike had no idea who Bowie was when, on the recommendation of a friend, the singer phoned and asked him to audition for the job at RCA Records in Manhattan. When he got the call, Garson had been performing in jazz clubs and was weary of the pittance he was earning despite years of diligent studying and practicing. He was ready for a change, and he thought this might be it. He accepted Bowie's invitation but was rather surprised when he walked into the studio and saw guys with hair in rainbow colors wearing clothing more befitting a circus. Despite the unusual ambiance, Garson quickly impressed his auditioners. "I played about twelve bars that took ten seconds and [lead guitarist] Mick Ronson said, 'You got the job,'" Garson recalls. Coincidentally, band leader Woody Herman called the same night offering Garson a job. But two weeks later, Garson was wearing platform shoes, a wild tuxedo, and playing Carnegie Hall with his "hair flowing like Beethoven." The eight-week job lasted two years. "I was in five bands with Bowie. I was the one constant. He was looking to stretch, and my musical abilities were pretty wide, plus I was stable. That means a lot in that world, especially during the seventies," says Garson.

During his tenure with Bowie, Garson was featured on a series of ground-breaking Bowie albums: *Aladdin Sane, Diamond Dogs, David Live, Pin-Ups,* and *Young Americans.* It was on the *Aladdin Sane* title track, however, that Garson laid down one of the most influential piano solos in rock music and made a name for himself in the process. By combining classical, jazz, and avant-garde styles, Garson gave Bowie the ear-grabbing atmosphere he wanted, not just on the title song, but throughout the album. Garson's playing on "Aladdin Sane," however, has influenced and inspired numerous bands ever since. "Not a week goes by that someone doesn't bring up that song," Garson says.

For the next twenty years, Garson would compose his own music and release solo records, contribute scores to television and film, continue to teach piano, and perform in various jazz combos. In 1980 he was invited to perform at a jazz festival in Jerusalem. Garson became an overnight sensation in Israel when he walked onstage and addressed the audience of ten thousand in Hebrew. He opened with Gershwin's "Rhapsody in Blue." The Israeli media swarmed all over him. He was offered a teaching job at Hebrew University in Jerusalem and was invited back to the festival in 1981 and 1982, at which time he became even more popular performing a jazz interpretation of the Hebrew song "Erev Shel Sho Shanim" ("Evening of Flowers"). Garson had family in Israel and thought seriously about moving there, but wasn't ready to uproot his wife and two children. And his Jewish connection wasn't what it had once been. Shortly after those performances, however, Garson began to rediscover the love of Judaism he had as a youth. "There were a lot of years I didn't appreciate the Judaism I grew up with," Garson says. "I think we tend to dismiss, for whatever reason, our roots. It's a crime. It's wonderful when we restore it. I realize now that [Judaism] is something to respect and cherish." (His next visit to Israel would be with Bowie in 1995 when the singer played to thirty thousand people in Tel Aviv.)

The Bowie-Garson connection was re-established in 1993 when the singer invited him to join the recording sessions for the album *Black Tie, White Noise*. Garson worked with Bowie through the rest of the decade and into the new millennium. His piano licks graced the Bowie albums *Outside* in 1995 and *Earthling* in 1997. He also toured with Bowie from 1995 through 1997 and again in 2000 and 2002. Between Bowie tours and albums, Garson composed and performed duets with jazz saxophonist Dave Liebman, composed music for the Pittsburgh Symphony Orchestra, and wrote a clarinet suite that was performed at the 1998 University of Ohio Clarinet Festival. He also performed all the piano work for the television movie *Liberace* and scored the music for several network features as well. He performed in and composed most of the music for Free Flight, a classical and jazz–fusion group. In 1998, he lent his talents to Seal's *Human Being* album, and to Nine Inch Nails' *Fragile* in 1999. In 2000, he contributed to Smashing Pumpkins' *MACHINA/The Machines of God* and No Doubt's album, *Return of Saturn*. He also hit the road with the Smashing Pumpkins for the band's 1998 "Adore" tour and again in 2000 for the Pumpkins' farewell concerts. Amidst that schedule, he developed "Now! Music," in which he improvises classical music and records it directly to computer disk, creating an ever-growing catalog of new music. Several concert pianists have debuted some of the resulting sonatas and nocturnes.

As Garson has grown older, his belief in God and his Jewish pride have grown stronger. Divine inspiration is the only reason he offers for having composed seven hundred classical and jazz pieces in four years. He also has added a jazzy version of "Hatikvah," the Israeli national anthem, to his repertoire. "I am convinced God is there, even if you think he's not. You just have to let him in," Garson says. Of his Judaism, he adds, "I'm very proud of who and what I am. I've been acknowledging it more now. I'm blessed." He's also convinced that if the definition of rabbi is teacher, then perhaps he has been one throughout much of his career. After all, he has taught nearly fifteen hundred piano students. And on concert tours he is so helpful to younger band members that David Bowie has dubbed him "Garson the Parson."

# Wendy Waldman

**Singer. Songwriter. Pianist. Guitar player. Producer. Born Wendy Steiner, November 29, 1950, Burbank, California. Best known for writing hit songs such as Vanessa Williams's "Save the Best for Last" and "The Sweetest Days," the Dirt Band's "Fishing in the Dark," and Don Johnson's "Heartbeat." Also among the first women to produce albums in the country music field.**

*Torah ethics and morality permeate Wendy Waldman's songs. (Photo by Eric Staudenmeir.)*

Judaism has been a bedrock influence on Wendy Waldman's song writing since her career began in the early seventies. Though Judaism itself is never specifically mentioned, the pillars of the religion—*tikkun olam*, *tzedakah*, carrying out *mitzvot*, observing the Golden Rule, as well as Talmud-like dilemmas—are frequent topics in her tunes, especially on her solo albums or in her work with the band Bryndle. For example, "Back by Fall" is about doing what one can, no matter how small, to repair the world; "Is He Coming at All?" is about the Messiah. "'Til the Storm Goes By" is a Noah's Ark–related tale that explores how good survives in an evil world; "Love Is the Only Goal" is about sacrifice and accepting that God's work is done in many ways. One of her newer songs, "My Time in the Desert," is about forty years of personal wandering. To Waldman, the act of songwriting is holy, and the resulting music more than entertainment. "While music can double as a commercial product bought and sold," she says, "It is a force from God. The vibrations of music have existed as long as the universe."

Most of Waldman's in-depth knowledge of Judaism, and passion for it, comes from informal but serious study at home. She and her older sister, Jillian, grew up in a musical family that was "extremely Jewish in consciousness" but did not belong to a synagogue, or any other Jewish institutions. The sisters did not have a formal Jewish education or become bat mitzvahs. Their father was not raised in an observant household; their Russian-born mother was raised in a strict, though not Orthodox Jewish environment, which she rebelled against to a degree. But, unlike many Jews in the film and television industries thirty or more years ago, Fred and Shirley Steiner made no secret of their faith. Both parents embraced Judaism and impressed upon their daughters the importance of understanding what it meant to be Jewish. "We had a profound sense of Jewishness, we had a Jewish identity, but were not raised in temple. Generally artists aren't really great joiners. They don't sit comfortably in a room full of believers," Waldman explains. "I learned from my mom that [Judaism] has a special history, and is a powerful thing." By the age of seven, Waldman says, she was aware of the Holocaust, the history of persecution, and what it meant to be a Jew in Europe, and she had developed a strong sense of Jewish pride. "It was clearly understood in our household we would not renounce our Judaism, and never walk away from our Jewishness. We could not forget the persecution, or the Diaspora. Whether we paid lip service to established Jewish society or not, we had to know what it meant to be a Jew."

Understanding and studying music was just as important. When it came to a career in music, Wendy was to the manor born. Her paternal grandfather was a Hungarian musician named George Steiner who immigrated to New York in the early 1900s. He played violin and viola in what Waldman describes as a "café orchestra" and also composed music for movies and radio, including episodes of *Laurel and Hardy*. Waldman's father, New York–born Fred Steiner, was one of the most prolific composers of television music in Hollywood history. His credits include the theme for *Perry Mason* as well as scoring numerous episodes of *Play-house 90*, *Gunsmoke*, *Have Gun Will Travel*, *The Twilight Zone*, and the majority of the original *Star Trek* episodes. He also tackled animated programs such as *Rocky and Bullwinkle*, and *Beanie and Cecil*. Waldman's mother, Shirley Lipkin, was a virtuoso violinist who by age fourteen was playing in the New Haven Symphony Orches-tra. Fred and Shirley met as teenagers at the Oberlin Conservatory of Music. They married after college in New York and moved to the West Coast around 1949 to get in on the ground floor of the television revolution.

By age seven, Wendy was studying piano and taking ballet lessons. Her sister was given classical guitar lessons. Music was playing in the house all the time, and it was not uncommon for legendary film scorers such as Elmer Bernstein and Jerry Goldsmith to drop in to play chamber music with Wendy's parents. To take a rest from Hollywood's breakneck pace, the Steiner family spent three years in Mexico City during Wendy's childhood. Wendy and Jillian attended Hebrew school there and went to temple on occasion, mostly for the social connection. In Mexico, Wendy also learned about Third World poverty. "We saw things about life that most kids never see; poverty and pain at a level that was an eye-opener," Wendy says.

Back in Los Angeles, she soaked up Ravel and DeBussy and Broadway musi-cals by the time she was thirteen, and loved them all. Then her sister introduced her to the guitar and to folk music. By sixteen, Wendy was a self-described "blues and jazz hound." In high school she began to write songs and play gigs with Peter Bernstein, Elmer's son, and Andrew Gold. Gold's father, Ernest, wrote the score for the film *Exodus* (which is probably why he is mistakenly listed as Jewish in many reference books) and his mother, Marni Nixon, was the singing voice for Natalie Wood in *West Side Story* and for Audrey Hepburn in *My Fair Lady*. Andrew would hit the pop charts in the late seventies with "Lonely Boy" and "Thank You for Being a Friend." Another high school friend, Karla Bonoff (her father condensed the name from Borodonoff) would have success as a songwriter with "Someone to Lay Down Beside Me," "Lose Again," "If He's Ever Near," and "All My Life," all recorded by Linda Ronstadt.

Wendy left her friends and went off to the University of California at Berkeley to study political science and philosophy. She was a good student, but the pull of the Los Angeles music scene was too strong. Her father was not pleased at her leaving school and less enamored of the blues, folk, and pop Wendy wanted to play. He did, however, encourage her to prove herself.

Around 1969, Wendy formed a band called Bryndle with Gold and Bonoff, and Kenny Edwards, who had been in the Stone Poneys with Linda Ronstadt. Bryndle recorded one unreleased album in 1970, then disbanded. The group's harmony-laden folk- and country-rock was just a few years ahead of its time. The friendships and working relationships endured. Waldman and Bonoff considered Gold and Edwards honorary Jews. They had *Yiddishkeit*. And while Bryndle didn't take off, it was the start of long careers in music for each of them. Over the years, all four would find a common denominator writing, recording and/or touring with Linda Ronstadt, as well as contributiong to each other's solo records.

In 1972, at age twenty-two, Waldman got her first real break. Singer Maria Muldaur recorded a pair of Wendy's songs, "Vaudeville Man," and "Mad, Mad, Me" on her self-titled debut album. The following year, Wendy had her first recording contract as a solo artist. Wendy's sweet, emotive voice sparkled on songs built on all her musical influences: classical, blues, lullabies, Mexican mariachi music, and more. Her musical inventiveness and engaging voice were critically applauded album after album. But, for some reason, throughout six solo albums from 1973 through 1982, the singer-songwriter failed to reach the charts.

She moved to Nashville where her talents as a songwriter and producer flourished. Her songs, many co-written with a variety of Nashville collaborators, were recorded by a "who's who" of country music. Reba McEntire, Patty Loveless, Kathy Mattea, Sweethearts of the Rodeo, Southern Pacific, Restless Heart, New Grass Revival, the Nitty Gritty Dirt Band, and Matraca Berg and Suzy Bogguss, whose albums Waldman also produced, selected her songs for their albums. Pop and rock acts such as Aaron Neville, Melissa Manchester, the Hooters, and Patti Austin also recorded her tunes. Vanessa Williams and Don Johnson had the most notable success with her songs. *Miami Vice* star Johnson took "Heartbeat" to No. 5 in 1986. Williams spent five weeks at No. 1 in 1992 with "Save the Best for

Last" and reached the Top 20 in 1994 with "The Sweetest Days." Waldman is also known for her precise harmony singing and has provided background vocals on countless records, including releases by Jimmy Buffett, Al Kooper, Clint Black, Wynonna Judd, Randy Newman, and Hank Williams, Jr.

In the early nineties, Waldman returned to Los Angeles and shortly afterwards reunited with Bonoff, Gold, and Edwards to make a second Bryndle record. The self-titled album, brimming with well-crafted songs and closecut harmonies was released in 1995 on the Music Masters boutique label. It received critical acclaim but modest airplay. It included the song "'Til the Storm Goes By." Of that song, Waldman says, "The subtext is very much Noah's Ark. How does good survive in an evil world? How do we survive and ensure our children get a chance?" The following year, Warner Brothers Records issued the eighteen-song career retrospective, *Love is the Only Goal: The Best of Wendy Waldman*. Her look at tikkun olam, the quiet, jazzy ballad, "Back By Fall," was among the eighteen chosen songs. In a plaintive voice Waldman sings: "There's crying in the city. / All the people are sad. / I heard it way up on the mountain / where I was living. / No food for the children, / and the times are so bad. / Well, what ever happened to giving? / Mama, mend the hole in my coat. / Take my guitar off the wall. / I've got to go see what I can do. / And I hope I'll be back by fall . . ." The song is, she says, "clearly about service" and doing whatever one can to ease the burdens of others.

In 2000, Waldman was busy working with Bonoff, Edwards, and Gold on another Bryndle album, recording a solo record, producing a disc for roots rocker John Cowan, and making sure her eleven-year-old son Abraham was getting proper bar mitzvah training. (Abe became a bar mitzvah in the summer of 2002.) Waldman also continues to consume books about Judaism. "I know I'm a Jew. I know no matter how much I might try to hide it, when the second Inquisition comes, they're going to know, so I want to understand what it really, really means to be a Jew," she says of her constant quest for Jewish knowledge. She adds that, for her, Judaism is much more than a subject to study. "Judaism is a gift, but it's also an obligation, and you fulfill that obligation in whatever way you can."

# Mickey Raphael
## of Willie Nelson and Family

Harmonica player. Born Michael Siegfried Raphael, Dallas, Texas,
November 7, 1951. A member of Willie Nelson and Family since 1973,
he has recorded more than thirty albums with Nelson, playing on hits
such as "Blue Eyes Cryin' in the Rain," "On the Road Again," and
"Always on My Mind." Raphael has played on dozens of records
by other acts ranging from John Denver to U2.

*Willie Nelson & Family in concert in 1980. From left, Bee Spears, Mickey Raphael,
Willie Nelson, and Jody Payne. (Photo from the archives of Mickey Raphael.)*

On September 17, 2000, harmonica player Mickey Raphael took his place on stage with Willie Nelson and the rest of Nelson's band to perform at Farm Aid, the nearly annual, star-studded, day-long benefit concert and lobbying effort on behalf of the American farmer. Nelson co-founded the event in 1985 with John Mellencamp and Neil Young, and Raphael had performed at all twelve benefits held since then. At each Farm Aid concert, usually held in the fall, Raphael couldn't help but think of the harvest holiday of Sukkot that took place around the same time of year. He remembered the sukkas, or booths, of his childhood that were decorated with fruit and greenery. How appropriate it was, he thought, to help raise money and awareness for beleaguered American farmers at the same time of year when Jews rejoice in the season's harvest and are commanded to share their good fortune with the hungry and needy. Raphael also was marking twenty-seven years as a member of Willie Nelson's backup band. When Nelson invited Raphael to hit the road in 1973, Nelson already was a respected country songwriter, having written the Patsy Cline hit "Crazy." But he was just beginning to gain national acclaim as a performer, and an atypical one at that, especially for a "country" act. Raphael, only twenty-one, had been touring with singer-songwriter B. W. Stevenson (whose biggest hit was "My Maria" in 1973).

Raphael was born and raised in Dallas. His mother Selma, was from New Orleans. His father, Arno, arrived alone in the United States from Manheim, Germany in 1936 at age seventeen, a few years after Hitler came to power. He spent time in Louisville, then moved to New Orleans where he met and married Selma. They moved to Dallas, where Arno's older brother Ralph had settled, and opened a furniture design and fabrication shop. (The Nazis had imprisoned Ralph for a while after he was overheard insulting Hitler's Brown Shirts, saying: "We Jews got through the Red Sea, we'll get through the Brown shit." He was able to flee Germany and get to America in 1935.) Though Arno and Ralph were born in Germany, family lore has it that their ancestors can be traced to Spain.

Selma, a housewife, loved writing poetry and playing the family piano, especially Gershwin's "Rhapsody in Blue." In Dallas, the Raphael family first joined Conservative synagogue Sherith Israel, then joined the Reform Temple Emanuel where Rabbi Levi Olan and Assistant Rabbi Gerald Klein were the spiritual leaders. Mickey attended Hebrew school and was confirmed there. He gravitated to music because he was not athletic and had little interest in sports. In fact, because his father was from Germany, Mickey had had little exposure to American

team sports such as baseball, basketball, and football. His father preferred sail-
ing, ice skating, and skiing. "I was the kid always chosen last, or not chosen at
all. I was not real popular growing up," Raphael says. A family friend gave him
his first harmonica at age thirteen, but aside from learning to play "Anchors
Aweigh" and "Oh, Susanna," he did little with it at the time. Ironically, the first
instrument he tried to play was a forty-five-pound tuba. He had volunteered to
carry the "metal monstrosity" in the Hillcrest High School marching band during his sophomore year in exchange for getting out of dreaded gym class. After
a few months of marching with a tuba, as well as playing in the school orchestra,
Raphael decided that there must be something lighter that he could drag around.
He switched to electric guitar but became frustrated with the instrument, and
quickly gave it up.

He became interested in the harmonica around age sixteen after getting a
few pointers from local legend Don Brooks. "He got me started," says Raphael.
"He was the first professional to actually show me some stuff on the harmonica." Raphael really became enthusiastic about the harmonica after attending a
Canned Heat concert in 1968. He went home and tried to imitate Al Wilson, the
band's harmonica player. "I played a lick that made sense," Raphael says. A self-
described loner as a teenager, Raphael buried himself in music and discovered a
natural affinity for the harmonica. He began listening to folk and blues musicians such as John Sebastian and Paul Butterfield as well as the Nitty Gritty Dirt
Band's Jimmie Faddon. After graduating from high school, Raphael enrolled in
El Centro Junior College and spent two years taking geology, philosophy, and
history classes, "because I knew I couldn't make a living playing the harp," he
says. He also became a regular at a Dallas coffeehouse called the Cellar, sitting in
with folk and blues performers. He began doing session work at a local recording studio as well. Cowboy singer-songwriters Michael Martin Murphey and
Jerry Jeff Walker were among the acts he jammed with at the coffeehouse. By
age twenty, Raphael had hooked up with B. W. Stevenson, and in 1972 recorded
a pair of albums with the singer-songwriter.

One of Raphael's early fans was University of Texas football coach Darrell
Royal, who'd seen Mickey play in clubs in Austin. One day, Royal invited Raphael
to his hotel and told him to bring his harmonica. When Mickey arrived at Royal's
suite, a circle of musicians were passing around a guitar and singing. Royal's
friends Willie Nelson and Charley Pride were among them. Raphael joined in,

only vaguely aware of who the other musicians were. Nelson liked Raphael's quiet, laid-back, melodic style and invited Mickey to sit in with him anytime. Through much of 1973, whenever Nelson's schedule brought him to the Dallas area, Raphael showed up if he could. "I'd sit in with him in clubs around Texas, and in dance halls and clubs that I was afraid to go into. I was like a hippie kid and these were redneck bars," Raphael says. One night after sitting in during a show, Nelson asked drummer and bandleader Paul English how much they were paying Raphael. The answer was "Nothing." "Well," Nelson responded, "double his salary." Raphael became an official member of Willie Nelson and Family, earning fifty dollars a show.

Adding a harmonica to the band was a bold, innovative move. Most country bands included a pedal steel guitar player or fiddle player to broaden or define their sound; Nelson supplanted those traditional instruments with Raphael's blues-based harp, and it became a distinctive part of Nelson's sound. (In 1997, for example, when the band was in Dublin, Ireland, Nelson and Raphael had dinner with the members of U2. The band's lead singer, Bono, had written a ballad for Nelson called "Slow Dancing," and Nelson and U2 recorded it that night with a nice Jewish boy from Dallas adding the harmonica licks. The song was released in Europe in 2000.) Experiences like that, and Nelson's desire to try practically anything, kept the music challenging and rewarding for Raphael. Nelson may be pigeonholed as a country music act, but he has done it all, including broadening the scope of country music by working with folkies, rockers and blues musicians. It is probably a primary reason Nelson hired Raphael. In fact, of the thirty-plus albums Raphael recorded with Nelson (the first being *Red-Headed Stranger* in 1975), Raphael's favorites are far from what is generally considered country music. Nelson's 1978 album *Stardust* was a tribute to Tin Pan Alley songwriters, and included Gershwin's "Blue Skies" and standards such as "Georgia on My Mind" and "Someone to Watch Over Me," as well as the title song. Fifteen years later, Nelson, joined by duet partners such as Paul Simon, Bob Dylan, Bonnie Raitt, and Sinead O'Connor, delivered another Raphael favorite, the critically acclaimed, *Across the Borderline*. Nelson put his imprint on Simon's "Graceland" and Peter Gabriel's "Don't Give Up," and encouraged Raphael to stretch.

Record producer Don Was, who has worked with Raphael on several occasions, calls Raphael "a modern-day klezmorim," and says that outside of blues musicians, few people can pull as much emotion out of a mouth harp. "Mickey isn't really playing the blues, and he's not really playing the harp," Was says. "It's more like he's playing the violin. He's the soulful counterpart to what Willie is playing." Raphael's visibility, versatility, and ability to conjure up a broad palette of sonic textures put him in demand as a session player. As prolific as Nelson is, Raphael still found time to contribute to albums by roots music acts including Emmylou Harris, Johnny Cash, Nanci Griffith, Pure Prairie League, Leon Russell, Jerry Jeff Walker, Tanya Tucker, Randy Travis, and Gregg Allman of the Allman Brothers. He also played on Vince Gill's 2000 release, *Let's Make Sure We Kiss Good-bye*. More surprising are his turns on albums by the Beach Boys, Elton John, jazz-rock flutist Tim Weisberg, actor Don Johnson's 1986 album *Heartbeat*, and the alternative rock band Supersuckers' 1997 album, *Must've Been High*. He wandered farthest afield, however, in 1985 when he played a solo on pop-metal band Motley Crue's Top Twenty hit, "Smokin' in the Boys' Room." In 2001, he was back in the studio recording another Willie Nelson album.

A lifetime of touring has provided its share of experiences as well. One of the most memorable occurred in 1991 at the Concorde Hotel in the Catskills. Raphael's fellow band members couldn't understand why they were prohibited from having milk with their steaks at the kosher resort. Raphael vainly attempted an explanation. Even Nelson made a wrong turn when he decided to end that night's show with the hymn "Amazing Grace," and received a collective cold shoulder from the predominantly Jewish audience. Many in the crowd, however, suspected Raphael was Jewish, including a Reform rabbi who befriended him and began sending him books on Judaism. Since Raphael joined Nelson, he has had his hands full dealing with band members and other Nelson associates ignorant of Judaism and Jewish custom. Besides trying to explain why they couldn't have milk with meat at a kosher hotel, he's tried to get them to understand that the Jews didn't kill Jesus, and that the phrase "Jew 'em down," is not a term of endearment. "If I were to punch someone every time they said that . . . ," says Raphael, who lets perpetrators know that he's Jewish and doesn't appreciate the remark. Nelson himself has understood these concepts from the beginning. (After all, Nelson was the first white country act to give a break to a young black singer named Charley Pride, taking him on tour as an opening act in the sixties.) Through it all, Raphael has never lost his sense of humor. Years ago, when Kinky Friedman, the singer-songwriter and crime novelist, asked Raphael what it was like being the only Jew in Willie Nelson's band, Raphael's response was classic. "Besides manipulating the press, and controlling world banking, I've really got my hands full."

On tour, Raphael spends much of his spare time reading about Jewish history. If Nelson has a concert on the High Holidays, Raphael won't miss the show, but he will seek out a temple and spend time in services. When he turned forty, his interest in learning more about Judaism and his Jewish heritage intensified. "Maybe it's because your mortality comes into focus, and you begin to look for some meaning in life," Raphael says. In 1999, he married Heidi Klostermann. She attended conversion classes and has dragged Mickey to Temple Micah in Nashville more times than he intended to go. Resolved to add more spirituality to their lives, Heidi has laid down the gauntlet with her husband: "If you don't take me to temple," she says, "I'll go to church."

# Billy Joel

**Singer. Songwriter. Composer. Piano man. Born William Martin Joel, May 9, 1949, Bronx, New York. One of the most popular concert attractions in rock 'n' roll, and writer and performer of more than thirty Top Forty hits. Those include the evergreen "Just the Way You Are" and the classic "Piano Man," as well as "The Entertainer," "Tell Her About It," "Keeping the Faith," "An Innocent Man," "We Didn't Start the Fire," and "River of Dreams." Non-charting fan favorites include "New York State of Mind" and "The Ballad of Billy the Kid." Joel received the Living Legend Grammy Award in 1990, and was inducted into the Songwriter's Hall of Fame in 1992 and the Rock and Roll Hall of Fame in 1999.**

*The Piano Man Billy Joel performing in Chicago in 1978. (Photo by Paul Natkin, Photo Reserve, Inc.)*

The first time Billy Joel wore a yarmulke he was forty-three years old and visiting the graves of his paternal grandparents in the Jewish cemetery in Nuremberg, Germany.* With practically no Jewish references in his songs, interviews or stage banter, it's no wonder few people realize Joel, one of the most consistent hit songwriters and exciting performers of the rock era, is Jewish. Most fans assume he's an Italian Catholic because more than one song includes such references. "And he's proud of his scars and the battles he's lost. / And struggles and bleeds as he hangs on his cross," from the 1976 song "Angry Young Man," sounds autobiographical when viewed through the lens of Joel's precarious youth. Even the song with the most overt Jewish reference, "River of Dreams," the title track from his 1993 album, sends conflicting signals with its gospel arrangements and references to being "baptized by fire," on one hand, and "wading into the river that runs to the promised land," on the other. Even more misleading is that during his childhood, Joel attended Mass with Catholic friends on occasion. He had little, if any, Jewish upbringing or education, though his parents, German-born Howard Joel and Brooklyn-born Rosalind Nyman, are Jewish.

Joel is a self-described atheist who believes in the spiritual world. He may be best known for romantic ballads such as "Just the Way You Are" and "She's Always a Woman," but spiritual overtones permeate much of his music. "Keeping the Faith," a hit in 1985, sums up the nature of his work in a song title. Joel has paid tribute to downtrodden, unemployed steelworkers in "Allentown," to forgotten and disparaged Vietnam veterans in "Goodnight Saigon," and to Long Island fisherman struggling to make a living in "The Downeaster Alexa," and, rejected, well-meaning suitors in "An Innocent Man," illuminating the pride, dignity, and resolve in each. That faith is also evident in more autobiographical songs such as "And So It Goes," and "Leningrad."

"The thing that fascinates me most as an artist is the human condition, the drama in life, not fiction, but reality," Joel stated in the souvenir program for his 1990 *Storm Front* concert tour. "What people go through in day-to-day living is really epic to me. Just to get through a day and come home and try to keep a family together and live a decent life and be a good person is probably one of the most difficult things in the world; there are so many temptations against it. It's been a theme that's probably gone through all my songs . . ."

*Steve Wick, "'I Can See the Ghosts': A Grandson's Search for Answers." In *Newsday*, April 18, 2000.

The factors that inspired (or forced) Joel to keep his musical and personal faith are, oddly enough, probably the same that contributed to his family's lack of religious observance and his later reluctance to keep his Jewish faith. Joel's paternal grandparents, Karl Joel and Meta Fleischmann, and his father, Howard, barely got out of Germany in 1939 before the Nazis implemented the Final Solution, the assembly-line plan to exterminate the Jews of Europe. The blows of losing their successful mail-order fabric business and Nuremberg home to the Nazis, being forced to flee, and spending three years as refugees in Cuba, may have caused the Joels to keep their Jewish roots under wraps when the family arrived in the United States in 1942. (Howard Joel, a classically trained pianist in Germany, met his future wife that year at City College of New York where both were involved in a theater group.) In one of life's great ironies, Howard was drafted in 1943, sent back to Europe, fought in Italy (Anzio, Monte Casino), and later was among the troops who liberated Dachau, the infamous Nazi concentration camp in southern Germany. "We went there and looked around and took pictures of the heaps . . . of the dead people. And then we moved on because we were a combat troop," Howard Joel told *Billboard*'s Timothy White in 1994. "I had relatives that were in concentration camps, although not Dachau, and some of them were put to death. But at Dauchau . . . it was terrible. We were too late to help." Howard Joel returned home a sullen man. In 1946, he married Rosalind Nyman and worked as an electrical engineer for General Electric; Billy was born in 1949. Unfortunately, members from opposite sides of the family did not get along, preventing large festive gatherings. His parents' divorce when he was eight also put a damper on Jewish celebrations, or any kind, for that matter. Joel wouldn't see his father for fifteen years, for Howard Joel moved to Austria, next door to the native land he and his family were forced to leave nearly twenty years earlier. There, he remarried.

That background instilled in Joel a streak of defiance, a toughness and a temper, He spent some time as an amateur boxer, and, as he says in song, ran with "the wild boys." He also developed a tenacious work ethic and determination to succeed. As he matured and became more successful, he developed humility, kindness, and a sometimes self-deprecating sense of humor, rare in stars of his stature, that he managed to keep despite bad business deals and failed marriages. "I'm probably happy with more than half the recordings," Joel told *Billboard* as he reviewed a career that spanned fifteen albums and included more than thirty hit songs and more than one hundred million records sold. "The writer,

I'm happy with; the singer, I'm never happy with. He always lets me down because my heroes were always black singers and I'm not black. I'm just a little Jewish kid from Levittown who's trying to sound black, but I'm not kidding me." He added, "I became a musician partially because of my physical limitations. I wasn't tall. I don't have Cary Grant looks. I had to transcend somehow."

Transcend he did. By age three, Joel was following in his father's footsteps, seriously dabbling at the family piano, taking formal lessons by age four, and writing songs by six. Joel also was a ravenous reader by the time he was seven. At home, his father played Chopin on piano, and his mother played music by Gilbert and Sullivan. When his parents divorced, Billy, his mother, and older sister Judith became pariahs in their Hicksville, Long Island, neighborhood, as divorcees were socially unacceptable in the 1950s. Joel not only lost contact with his father, he lost his musical hero. By his teens, Joel was playing in high school rock bands and attending as many Broadway musicals as possible. Like so many other fledgling teenage musicians at the time, Joel saw the Beatles on *The Ed Sullivan Show* in February 1964 and his course was set. (Joel also cites Ray Charles, Sam Cooke, Otis Redding, and the Rolling Stones as inspirations.) He joined a popular Long Island band called the Hassles in 1968. The group released a pair of albums that failed to sell. He formed another band called Attila, but that band also failed to take off. Joel was playing in a Los Angeles piano bar under an assumed name, Bill Martin, when Columbia Records offered him a recording contract in 1973. Album sales were initially slow, but by 1978, with hits such as "Piano Man," "The Entertainer," "She's Always a Woman," and the double Grammy-winning "Just the Way You Are" in his repertoire, Joel was on his way to becoming a superstar, and remaining one on his terms.

More Grammy Awards followed in 1979 and 1980 for the albums *52nd St.* and *Glass Houses*. In 1987, Joel became the first American rock star to perform U.S./Soviet government–sanctioned concerts in the USSR. In 1989, Joel performed at the Berlin Wall the day after it came down and Germany was reunited. He received the Living Legend Grammy Award in 1990. In 1994, he joined forces to tour with Elton John, the first of several such successful pairings of the piano men during the nineties and into the new millennium. In 1996, Joel traveled the college lecture circuit with a presentation titled "An Evening of Questions, Answers . . . and a Little Music." That year, he also established the Rosalind Joel Scholarship for the Performing Arts at his mother's alma mater, City College of

New York. The following year, Joel announced he was retiring from recording rock records to try his hand at classical composition. In 1999, he was inducted into the Rock and Roll Hall of Fame.

Aside from receiving musical honors and awards, Joel has been a generous philanthropist. He has performed numerous benefits, including the first Farm Aid concert and U.S.A. for Africa in 1985, the Concerts for the Bays and Baymen in 1990, and America: A Tribute to Heroes, to aid victims of the September 11, 2001, terrorist attacks on New York City and Washington, D.C. When an earthquake struck Kobe, Japan, while on tour there in 1995, Joel donated the proceeds of his show in Osaka to earthquake relief. He also has contributed to AIDS and cancer research. In 2002, Joel received the MusiCares Person of the Year award from the National Academy of Recording Arts and Science (NARAS) for his advocacy of music education and his philanthropy.

With such a stellar career, it's easy to forget that through much of the late seventies and eighties Joel often was pilloried by the rock press and slammed as a lightweight songwriter and pseudo rocker. During his shows, Joel often held up newspapers and mocked the criticism in front of the adoring audiences that filled arenas for his concerts. Joel may have become a completely assimilated Jew, but he wasn't one that was going to be pushed around. He ended his performances telling his fans to stand up for themselves, with the words, "Don't take shit from anybody!"

# Phoebe Snow

Singer. Songwriter. Guitar player. Born Phoebe Anne Laub, July 17, 1952,
New York City. Best known for the 1974 Top Five hit, "Poetry Man,"
the voice behind numerous television commercials during the eighties,
and as a member of Donald Fagen's New York Rock and Soul Revue
in the early nineties. She possesses one of the most soulful
and versatile voices in popular music.

*Phoebe Snow on the cover of the June 5, 1975 issue of Rolling Stone magazine.*
*(Photograph © 2002 by Annie Leibovitz/Contact Press Images, courtesy of the photographer.)*

Phoebe Snow's Jewish story is akin to that of the biblical Job. By age twenty-two, the once shy performer was soaring with a self-titled debut album that sold more than a half million copies, included the Top Five single "Poetry Man," and earned her a Best New Artist Grammy nomination. Just as thrilling for her was having esteemed jazz tenor sax player Zoot Sims and revered jazz pianist Teddy Wilson among the guest performers on her album. The critical praise was frosting on the cake. *Rolling Stone* magazine called Snow "one of the most gifted voices of our generation" and featured her on its cover on June 5, 1975. Her stunning, soul-drenched voice was a natural gift she nurtured and infused with an array of influences that leaned heavily toward black singers such as Aretha Franklin, blues legend Muddy Waters, and rock 'n' roll pioneer Little Richard, though Judy Garland also was an inspiration.

Snow's rise continued as she toured with Paul Simon, and her duet with him, "Gone at Last," from his album, *Still Crazy After All These Years*, reached No. 23 on the *Billboard* singles chart. Her followup studio album, *Second Childhood*, released in 1976, reached No. 13 on *Billboard*'s album chart and also sold more than 500,000 copies. She was named Best Female Jazz Singer in *Playboy* magazine's annual jazz poll that year, finishing ahead of Ella Fitzgerald (something Snow still finds "absurd"). During this period, Snow also was invited to lend her voice to Janis Ian's *Aftertones* album, Billy Joel's *The Stranger*, and David Sanborn's *Sanborn*. Bette Midler recorded the Snow composition, "I Don't Want the Night to End" on her album, *Songs for the New Depression*.

In late 1975, Snow's daughter, Valerie, was born with severe disabilities. Snow chose the Herculean task of caring for Valerie at home. The time, money, and energy that feat required, compounded by the shock and anger that consumed Snow, along with a divorce, sent the singer into a tailspin. To make matters even more unbearable, Snow's mother, Lili, was diagnosed with cancer. "I was in shock for twenty-three years. I walked around in a daze," Snow says. Handlers led her from one concert and recording session to another, and she compliantly followed record producers' instructions. "I was completely beaten. I lost my life force," Snow says. In 1990, she slowly began to pull herself together through counseling and prayer. By 2001, Snow confidently declared that she no longer carried a plank-sized chip on her shoulder. Though she was not a practicing Jew, one of the things that got Snow through each day was a card she carried in her wallet that bore this passage from Isaiah: "Fear not, for I have redeemed you. I have called you by name. You are mine." "For some reason I believed in that when I couldn't believe in anything . . . and I am most profoundly grateful," she says. Snow had a positive new outlook on life and was enthusiastically working on a new project.

Phoebe Anne Laub grew up outside Teaneck, New Jersey, not too far from the Lackawanna Railroad's northern line to Buffalo. By age seven, after hearing her first Little Richard record, she knew that music was her calling. She also decided that when she became famous she would change her name to Phoebe Snow, just like the name painted in tall white letters on the sides of the Lackawanna passenger train that passed not far from her home. "Laub wasn't a marquee name," Snow says. Though she was painfully shy, becoming an entertainer was not so far-fetched. Her grandfather, David Laub, was a burlesque comedian. Her father, Merrill Laub, who held a variety of jobs including that of English teacher, also dabbled in acting. And her mother, Lili (née Grossman), was a dancer who performed with Martha Graham and Merce Cunningham using the stage name of Lili Mann. Her parents spoke Yiddish when they didn't want Phoebe or her sister, Julie, to know what they were discussing.

Phoebe's Jewish education was cut short at age six, after she and most of the other children attending a practice seder at a local shul contracted measles. Her mother never let her go back. "My mother had a burst of Jewish pride for about ten seconds and sent us to shul classes. After that, we went to ethical culture classes," Snow recalls. She wasn't too upset with her mother's decision. Even as a child she didn't care much for Jewish studies or ritual; the only things she liked about Passover, the most important holiday to the family, was searching for the afikomen, and eating her mother's "slammin" matzo brie and chicken-and-matzo ball soup. Her noninterest in Judaism had more to do with the environment in which she and her sister grew up. "If I had been raised and nurtured more in certain aspects of life it might have been different. Now Judaism fascinates me more, as well as other religions," Snow says.

Music was the one thing in the house where everyone generally found common ground. A variety of music was being played all the time, and Phoebe let it all wash over her. Her father loved Dixieland jazz, Art Tatum, Benny Goodman, and Louis Armstrong. Her mother enjoyed Debussy and Gershwin, and was friendly with Woody Guthrie, Pete Seeger, and the Weavers. Both parents loved

Mickey Katz. When Phoebe tried to add Little Richard records to the family's musical mix around age seven, however, her father complained about her taste in music. That didn't stop Phoebe from embracing rock 'n' roll. "Four bars of Little Richard, and I knew what I wanted to do," Snow says. "Every cell in my body woke up and saluted." From ages four through twelve Phoebe took mandatory piano lessons but disliked her teachers, who she found too strict and demanding. She switched to guitar as soon as she could, and while in junior high school fell in love with the blues of Muddy Waters, Big Bill Broonzy, Bessie Smith, Ma Rainey, John Lee Hooker, and Howlin' Wolf. If that was love, then hearing Aretha Franklin testifying on "I Never Loved A Man (The Way I Love You)" in 1967 was complete adoration. Ironically, Snow was kicked out of the Teaneck High School choir twice for "kibbitzing," she says. As her home life became more tense during her teens, music became, and would always be, her lifeline and secret best friend. She immersed herself in it, and she unknowingly developed a dazzling, deeply expressive voice that could move hearts and motivate minds. Snow credits a boyfriend with convincing her to perform at amateur nights at Greenwich Village folk clubs in the early seventies. Initially she wanted to be a member of his band with the goal of becoming an "A-list" session guitar player. But he told her she was too good to be in his band. With his cajoling and encouragement, Snow began performing at clubs like the Gaslight and Bitter End. A confidence-boosting turning point occurred in late 1971 when Snow performed live on an all-night, listener- sponsored radio program on WBAI in New York. She felt secure performing at 4:00 a.m. because she thought no one would be listening. But the phone lines lit up requesting to hear more music from the unknown singer.

One night in 1972, Snow was outside the Gaslight crying because she had been unable to convince the MC to schedule her set before or after a young rocker named Bruce Springsteen. Legendary talent scout John Hammond was coming to see Springsteen, whose star was ascending, and Snow hoped she'd have the chance to perform for Hammond, too. Believing a golden opportunity had slipped away, Snow was in tears outside the club when Springsteen saw her and comforted her, saying, "You'll be discovered, too, don't worry." On another occasion at the Gaslight, Snow ended up in an unexpected jam session with blind blues harmonica player Sonny Terry. After their three-song session, Terry said, "I can't see you, and if I had just heard you play—without knowing you were a young girl—I would have thought you were an old black blues man from the Delta." Snow, who was about twenty at the time, calls that one of the greatest moments in her life.

Later that year, a Shelter Records executive dropped by the Bitter End on amateur night, happened to hear Snow, and offered her a recording contract on the spot. In 1973, she traveled to the company's headquarters in Tulsa, Oklahoma, to make the record. Released in the summer of 1974, *Phoebe Snow* included eight Snow-penned songs and heralded the arrival of a stunning new voice with few limitations. That album remains special to her. "It was my fledgling attempt on a shoestring budget and so much could have gone wrong. It was the little album that could," she says. She followed her debut with another bestseller, *Second Childhood*, in 1975. In spite of the immense challenge of having to care for her severely disabled child, Snow released her third highly praised album, *It Looks Like Snow*, in 1976. She released another four albums through the end of the decade, then, emotionally and physically exhausted from her overwhelming responsibilities as a single mother, virtually disappeared as a recording artist. She stayed busy singing commercial jingles for Bloomingdales, Stouffers, General Foods International Coffee (with its memorable "Celebrate the moments of your life" hook), Hallmark Cards, and Fruit 'n Cream breakfast cereal. She remained a sought-after session singer and appeared on albums by Billy Joel, Steve Goodman, Stephen Bishop, Bobby McFerrin, Laurie Anderson, and Dave Mason. Though she is not credited, she also participated in the star-studded "No Nukes" concert at Madison Square Garden in 1979, sitting in with acts such as Jackson Browne and Bonnie Raitt. She also performed solo concerts on occasion. "Music was the part of my life the trauma couldn't touch," she says. "When it was time to sing you never would have known there was a problem."

In 1989, Snow released *Something Real*, her first album in nearly ten years. (It was dedicated to her mother, who died in 1986.) In the early nineties, she hooked up with Donald Fagen's New York Rock and Soul Revue, touring and recording one album, *Live at the Beacon*, with an all-star ensemble that included Michael McDonald. She also toured as a solo artist. In 1997, Snow sang the title track on a Laura Nyro tribute album, *Time and Love: The Music of Laura Nyro*. Along with Dolly Parton, Lou Rawls, and others, Snow also sang on the gorgeous Ladysmith Black Mambazo album, *Heavenly*. Her lead vocals on the South African vocal group's version of the Curtis Mayfield classic "People Get Ready," is five minutes and fifty-four seconds of unparalleled singing that transports listeners out of this physical world. In 1998 Snow released *I Can't Complain*, her first album since *Something Real* nearly a decade earlier. It is an eclectic mix of folk, rock, and blues, on which Snow shines in performances of Janis Joplin's gritty blues-rocker "Piece of My Heart," as well as Joni Mitchell's torch song, "A Case of You." Snow also participated in the PBS-sponsored, *Kennedy Center Presents: A Tribute to Muddy Waters, King of the Blues*, appearing on a bill with Bo Diddley, Gregg Allman, Buddy Guy and Keb Mo', among others.

Something more profound occurred in 1998: Snow came out of her depression. "I prayed myself well," she says. The shock faded; the daze disappeared. "I'm not that fragile Phoebe anymore," she says.

For a time, Snow found herself renewing her interest in Judaism through its music and culture. She rediscovered the depth and passion of Jewish music (mostly through attending Jewish life cycle events) and in the process realized the origin of her own remarkable voice. While she appreciated Jewish music and tradition—and loved the food—a spiritual void remained.

"In retrospect, life never stopped being complex and stressful, and I always searched to find an effective means to deal with it by exploring many avenues of spirituality," Snow says. Her search appeared to end in early 2002 when she was introduced to Buddhist chanting. "Everything fell into place, and continues to fall into place, in my daily life," she says. "But more importantly, the peace, serenity, and clarity, that I've yearned for all my life now exists in my soul."

A year earlier, Sony/Legacy Records released *The Very Best of Phoebe Snow*, a sixteen-song retrospective illustrating why Phoebe Snow is a national treasure.

# Max Weinberg

**Drummer. Born Newark, N. J., April 13, 1951. Best known as "Mighty Max," the "rhythmic backbone" of Bruce Springsteen's E Street Band (1974–1989 and 1995–present), and leader of the Max Weinberg Seven, the house band for the hit NBC television program, *Late Night with Conan O'Brien* (1993–present).**

*Drummer Max Weinberg of Bruce Springsteen's E Street Band backs up "The Boss" during a Miami concert in 2002. (Photo by Tom Craig.)*

When Max Weinberg takes the stage to perform as a member of Bruce Springsteen's E Street Band or as leader of his own Max Weinberg Seven, house band for the hit NBC TV show *Late Night with Conan O'Brien*, he's thinking seder. That's right, seder. That's because much of his playing, he says, "is based on the whole concept of seder, of order. If you're a good drummer, you serve the music. That's the only thing that matters. You have to have some sense of order and organization to do that."

That philosophy has served him well since 1974, when he auditioned for Springsteen to replace the departed drummer in the E Street Band. At the time, he was twenty-three, living at home, attending Seton Hall University, providing the back beat for the Broadway production of *Godspell*, and looking for something more. Weinberg's disciplined, meat-and-potatoes playing style and musical philosophy clicked with Springsteen immediately. Dubbed Mighty Max by Springsteen, Weinberg's powerful, yet controlled playing was evident on Springsteen's albums *Born to Run*, *Darkness on the Edge of Town*, *The River*, and *Born in the USA*, as well as numerous concert tours, before the Boss sent the band on a long hiatus in 1989. Commenting on *Born in the USA*, Springsteen told *Musician* magazine that "Max was the best thing on the record." Weinberg's ability did not go unnoticed by the public or the media, winning Best Drummer in *Playboy* magazine's annual Pop and Jazz Music Poll in 1985 and *Rolling Stone* magazine's Critics' Poll in 1986.

During those glory days, Weinberg kept busy between Springsteen records and tours. He served up the big fat beat to Meat Loaf's classic 1977 release, *Bat out of Hell*. In 1983, he earned the rare distinction of drumming on hit singles that were No. 1 and No. 2 on the charts the same week, with Bonnie Tyler's "Total Eclipse of the Heart" and Air Supply's "Making Love Out of Nothing at All." He lent his formidable percussion skills to albums by fellow Jersey boys Southside Johnny and the Asbury Jukes, and by Ian Hunter, Gary U.S. Bonds, and Carole King.

Weinberg also authored with Robert Santelli *The Big Beat: Conversations with Rock's Great Drummers*, published in 1984. Writing the book allowed him to interview boyhood influences such as Elvis Presley, drummer D. J. Fontana, Ringo Starr of the Beatles and the Rolling Stones' Charlie Watts. (He calls meeting renowned Jewish drummer Bernard "Buddy" Rich and legendary Jewish horn player and band leader Artie Shaw (born Artie Jacob Arshawsky) inspiring moments.)

Max Weinberg had known he wanted to be a drummer since the age of five, when he saw Elvis Presley on television. While his three sisters were focused on the King, young Max couldn't take his eyes off Presley's drummer, J. D. Fontana. By age six, Max was taking lessons. He made his public debut a year later, sitting in with a bar mitzvah band playing "When the Saints Go Marching In." His mother, Ruth, had proudly told the bandleader that her son played the drums, asking if Max could join in for one song. Max was impressive, and the bandleader occasionally incorporated him into the act. Max's father Bertram, an attorney, proved just as proud and supportive, schlepping his son's gear to rehearsals and gigs for Max's high school band, the Epsilons.

The family belonged to Temple Sharey Tefilo-Israel in South Orange, N.J., which Max enjoyed attending. "I had a wonderful Jewish background, I believe because my main inspiration in that area was Rabbi Avraham Soltes, who was one of the most stirring, poetic men I've ever known," Weinberg told the *Jewish Bulletin of Northern California* in 1998. "I was fortunate. He married my wife [a Methodist] and [me], and he was really amazing because he made the study of Judaism come alive for his students and congregation."

One of the concessions Weinberg made as a "rock star" was cutting back on synagogue attendance. Marathon Springsteen tours often meant performances on Friday nights, and sometimes on the High Holidays. Still, he made an effort to get to synagogue whenever he could. "I love going to temple," he told the *Bulletin*. "I really do enjoy it . . . I like the repose I feel. And I love the music." Judaism continues to play an important role in his life.

He used that faith and the support of his family to maintain morale after Springsteen broke up the band. Married and with children, he returned to school to finish a degree in communications with the idea of remaking himself as a lawyer. He soon realized he wasn't cut out for it. He also worked for a record club and as a talent scout and producer for a record label. He hadn't been drumming for nearly four years and had begun to feel his ability slipping away. Fearful of losing his touch, he began sitting in with bar mitzvah and wedding bands to regain his form. In the summer of 1992, he was invited to fill in for the drummer in 10,000 Maniacs who had been in a car accident. After playing with the band for six weeks and "getting good again," he began to consider a return to performing.

A good administrator, he got involved with putting together a band dubbed the E Street Revue to do benefits for World Hunger Year in late 1992, as well as play the New York–New Jersey Ball celebrating President-elect Bill Clinton's inauguration in January 1993. The response to those shows was so strong, Weinberg says, "I began to feel I was missing the boat by not drumming. I was still rusty, but I had potential to be up there again." With his wife, Becky, urging him on, Weinberg set himself the goal of getting back to the big time.

In May of 1993, the couple was in New York celebrating his selection as second substitute drummer for the Broadway production of *The Who's Tommy*, when he spotted Conan O'Brien, who had just been named to replace *Late Night with David Letterman* on NBC. The two began talking about a band for the new show and, as he had with Bruce Springsteen nineteen years earlier, "hit it off in two minutes." Weinberg put together a band in a matter of days to audition for O'Brien and the show's producers, and got the gig. The show debuted on September 13, 1993, relying heavily on Weinberg, who, although he had no television experience, was the most seasoned performer in the cast by virtue of playing in one of the world's most acclaimed rock bands for fifteen years. The Max Weinberg Seven, playing everything from Gershwin to the Rolling Stones, took the pressure off the untested O'Brien. "I was appreciated as a stable force in the early years because I was older," says Weinberg. "A major thrust of the publicity for the first year was the fact that I was the band leader. People focused on the band as Conan took a lot of hits, and it gave the show a chance to grow." As the show evolved, so did Weinberg's role. He became involved in many of the show's comedy routines as well as serving as bandleader. (During the show's premier season, Rhino Records released *Max Weinberg Presents: Let There Be Drums!*, a three-CD collection of his favorite songs and drum performances from the fifties, sixties and seventies.)

Once the show found its legs Weinberg also hit the lecture circuit, delivering a talk titled *E Street to Late Night: Dreams Found, Lost and Found Again*. In 1995, he was the first guest lecturer to speak at the Rock and Roll Hall of Fame and Museum in Cleveland, giving a talk titled, "Why Teach Rock in Schools?"

Weinberg's defiant, booming "E Street" sound re-surfaced when Springsteen reconvened the band in 1995 to record new tunes for his *Greatest Hits* record, and again in 1999 when Springsteen summoned the band for an acclaimed world tour. (NBC approved Weinberg's extended hiatus in exchange for Springteen's appearance on the show.) In 2002, Springsteen again reassembled the E Streeters to record *The Rising*, Springsteen's cathartic response to the terrorist attacks on New York City and Washington, D.C., on September 11, 2001. It was his first new full-length record in seven years, and his first with the E Street Band since *Born in the USA* in 1984. A forty-six city tour followed the summer release of the album, which debuted at No. 1 on the record charts. During a pre-tour interview with ABC News' Ted Koppel, Springsteen described Weinberg as "The engine that drives the machine."

# Marcy Levy, a.k.a. Marcella Detroit

Singer. Songwriter. Guitarist. Born Marcella Levy, June 21, 1952, Detroit, Michigan. Best known as backup singer for Bob Seger, Leon Russell, and Eric Clapton, and as co-writer of the 1978 million-selling Clapton hit, "Lay Down Sally." Under the name of Marcella Detroit, she was half of the England-based duo Shakespear's Sister, and co-writer of Sister's 1992 Top Five hit, "Stay."

*Marcy Levy as her alter ego Marcella Detroit during a 1992 Shakespear's Sister concert at the Roxy in Los Angeles. (Photo by Markus Cuff.)*

You may never have heard of Marcy Levy, but it's likely you have *heard* Marcy Levy.
Since 1971, she has toured as a backup singer and/or recorded with Bob Seger,
Leon Russell, Eric Clapton, Quarterflash, George Duke, Stanley Clarke, Jeffrey
Osborne, Leo Sayer, Michael Bolton, Belinda Carlisle, Crosby, Stills and Nash,
Melissa Manchester, Aretha Franklin (her vocal idol), Don Henley of the Eagles,
the Charlie Daniels Band, Bette Midler, and Brian Setzer. Her songs have been re-
corded by Clapton, Manchester, Carlisle, Chaka Kahn, Philip Bailey, Al Jarreau,
Tom Jones, and country swing band Asleep at the Wheel. And though stardom
eluded her in the United States, she found it as singer Marcella Detroit in the English group Shakespear's Sister (misspelling and all). Though the group broke
up in 1993, Levy/Detroit has retained a sizable fan base in England, Europe, and
Japan as a solo act.

Between 1971 and 1991, despite a chaotic rock 'n' roll schedule, Levy did her
best to observe major Jewish holidays, fasting on Yom Kippur even if she had to
perform, and sending up a prayer to God asking forgiveness when she had to
work on the holiday. With the birth of her son, Maxwell, in 1991, Levy dug deeper
into her Jewish roots and wrote some Jewish-influenced and issue-oriented
songs. It may not be immediately evident from the lyrics, but her song "I Believe," a Top Ten Marcella Detroit hit in England in 1995, began as a song about
a relationship going sour and ended up as song about anti-Semitism and racism.
("Now everybody has a right to be living their lives, / but we're a long, long way, /
a long way from paradise. / If there is freedom, tell me / why everybody wants to
fight, / oh, 'cause we're a long, long way, / a long way from paradise . . . Give a
little bit of love / and you get it back. Give a little bit of pain / and you're caught
in a trap.") Since the arrival of Max, Levy and her husband Lance Aston, who is
not Jewish, have celebrated Jewish holidays, made every effort not to work on
Rosh Hashanah and Yom Kippur, and striven to raise their son as a Jew. Maxwell
is named after Levy's maternal grandfather, Max Berger, who, more than anyone, instilled a love of Judaism in her.

Levy grew up in what she describes as a very Reform household. Her father,
Milton, was a talented artist and illustrator who became a tool-and-die maker to
support the family. The family was on such a tight budget that he couldn't even
fulfill his daughter's request to register her for Hebrew school. Her father also
was "kind of an atheist," celebrating only the High Holy Days, so Marcy stayed at
grandpa Max Berger's house every Friday night to celebrate Shabbat. She at-

tended the Conservative synagogue Ahavas Achim with her grandfather, a house painter from Poland, every Saturday. When grandpa Max died, sixteen-year-old Marcy's religious upbringing withered as well. "He held it all together," Levy says. "After he died, we never had those holiday get-togethers. I learned a lot of love and caring and generosity from him." Levy's father, however, did have a strong enough Jewish identity to move the family to a more Jewish neighborhood when Marcy turned twelve in the hope she would begin to meet Jewish boys. He also wanted to get her away from the kids down the block who constantly asked her, "Why did you kill Jesus Christ?" The move backfired a bit as the Jewish kids in her new neighborhood "were cruel in another way," remaining cliquish and making fun of a front tooth she chipped during a gym class mishap.

Levy found comfort in music, something her parents loved as well. Bobby Darin's version of "Mack the Knife" and other pop hits of the day, as well as country music, often could be heard wafting from the family radio and hi-fi. Her parents also took her to classical music concerts. Levy's father played the ukulele, and from the time Marcy was five, father and daughter often would sing together. From kindergarten through high school Marcy sang in the school choir, performed in school plays, and entered talent shows. At eight she began taking violin lessons (discovering many years later that her paternal grandfather was a concert violinist). By eleven she was playing the accordion and harmonica. At twelve her father bought her an electric guitar and amplifier. (Marcy wanted to be in the Beatles.) She began writing songs and also discovered that she had inherited her father's talent for illustration—in her case fashion illustration, the profession she originally thought she'd pursue. She majored in art at nearby Oakland Community College but found herself enthralled by music, especially by Aretha Franklin, Stevie Wonder, and the rest of the Motown Records roster. The folk music and blues of Leadbelly, Fred Neil, Maria Muldaur, and Muddy Waters inspired Levy, too. When she left what she describes as an abusive relationship at the tender age of eighteen, music became her consolation. She sang and played guitar for hours at a time. She vowed that one day she would sing with another one of her musical heroes: Oklahoma-based singer, songwriter and multi-instrumentalist Leon Russell. Levy's parents tried to warn her that making it in the music business was a million-to-one long shot. Her response was, "Watch me!" She was confident in her ability, deeply connected to music, and determined to carve a career in rock or pop. At eighteen, Levy joined an Ypsilanti,

Michigan–based group called the Bad Luck and Trouble Blues Band. The following year she was a member of a popular Detroit band called Julia that mixed Beatles' songs with original tunes. In 1971, Bob Seger, who was beginning his climb
to superstardom with the Top Twenty hit "Ramblin', Gamblin' Man," hired Julia
as his backup band.

In 1972, Levy moved to Tulsa to join a band with members of Julia who had
decided to return to Oklahoma. Playing as Marcy Levy and Friends, the band
lasted about a year and a half, but Levy was in the right place at the right time.
Topflight musicians and songwriters such as J. J. Cale, bassist Carl Radle of the
Eric Clapton-led Derek and the Dominoes, and drummer Jamie Oldaker were
working out of the city. So was one of Levy's musical inspirations, Leon Russell,
who had grown up in the area and launched his own record company, Shelter
Records. In late 1973, Russell, whose song "Tight Rope" had reached No. 11 on
the pop charts the previous year, hired Levy to sing in his band. Soon after Levy
joined Russell, Clapton came to Tulsa looking for musicians for his next recording project. He offered Levy a spot in the lineup, but she kept a nine-month commitment to Russell, before joining Clapton in Jamaica for the recording of his
album *There's One in Every Crowd*. Three days into the recording session, Clapton
offered her a job with his touring band in tandem with the other backup singer
Yvonne Elliman (who would have a No. 1 hit as a solo artist in 1978 with "If I Can't
Have You" from the *Saturday Night Fever* soundtrack). From September of 1974
through October of 1977, Levy was not only a fixture in Clapton's studio group
and touring band, where Clapton gave her a moment in the spotlight during concerts, but a noticeable contributor as a songwriter. She had a hand in writing
songs for Clapton's seventies albums, *No Reason to Cry* ("Innocent Times," "Hungry"), *Slowhand* ("Lay Down Sally," "The Core"), and *Backless* ("Roll It"). Of those
songs, the jaunty, percolating "Lay Down Sally," became a million-selling U.S.
hit that reached No. 3 on the pop charts in early 1978. She also contributed the
title and a line or two to Clapton's Top Ten hit "Promises." Just before the release
of the *Backless* album, Levy found out through the grapevine that Clapton had
decided to revamp his band for his next album, *Just One Night*, and tour. The
twenty-five year old Levy was upset with the way she found out about Clapton's
decision to let her go, but remained grateful for the experience. "It was a whirl-
wind going from buses to Lear jets and playing to thousands and thousands of
people," she says. " It gave me more confidence in myself. He had never heard of

us when he hired us. He always gave me a feature, a solo, in the show. He was very generous that way. He never felt intimidated. He let everyone have their chance."

Between 1979 and 1985, the versatile Levy, who had relocated to Los Angeles, became a sought-after session singer. She provided soulful backup vocals on albums by jazz musicians Stanley Clarke and George Duke, country singer Johnny Lee (including his 1980 Top Five hit "Lookin' for Love"), soul queen Aretha Franklin, rockers Quarterflash ("Harden My Heart," "Find Another Fool"), former Eagle Randy Meisner, solo Eagle Don Henley, pop singer Melissa Manchester, R&B singer Jeffrey Osborne, and British singer-songwriter Al Stewart. In the early eighties the songwriting team of Burt Bacharach and Carole Bayer Sager hired Levy to sing on "demo" (demonstration) tapes filled with songs the writers pitched to record companies. In 1982, Levy found time to release her debut solo album, *Marcella*, but the record didn't find much of an audience. Levy also contributed vocals to the hit movie soundtrack *Footloose* (1984), and sang a song called "Help Me" with Bee Gee Robin Gibb for the film *Times Square*. In 1985, Clapton invited her to rejoin his band. She returned to record Clapton's *Behind the Sun* album, contributing the song "Tangled in Love," and also toured to support the record. Levy left after a year to pursue her solo career. In 1987, her voice could be heard backing Bill Medley and Jennifer Warnes on their No.1 hit "(I've Had) The Time of My Life," from the *Dirty Dancing* film sountrack.

That year, songwriter and producer Richard Feldman invited Levy to join songwriting sessions for British singer Siobhan Fahey. Fahey, a member of the female vocal trio Banarama (and wife of Eurythmics guitarist Dave Stewart), was preparing a solo record and was about to announce her departure from the very successful Banarama ("Cruel Summer," "I Heard a Rumour"). Levy co-wrote nine of the eleven songs on what would become the debut album of the Fahey-led group Shakespear's Sister. Levy also sang and played guitar and harmonica on the debut, *Sacred Heart*, released in 1989, and joined Fahey and band on tour. The critically acclaimed album of synthesizer- and guitar-driven Brit-pop included the British Top Ten hit, "You're History," co-written by Levy, who, at the suggestion of Fahey, had recast herself as Marcella Detroit to break away from her past as a backup singer. With the album's success, and the resultant performance and songwriting chemistry between Fahey, Levy, and producer Feldman, Levy was invited to share center stage with Fahey. Previously, Shakespear's Sister essentially had been Fahey backed by a band. Fahey and Levy collaborated on the 1991 followup record, Hormonally Yours, so titled because both women were pregnant during the making of the album. By 1992, "Stay," a single from the album, was a Top Five hit on both sides of the Atlantic, and in early 1993 the song won a Brit Award, the British equivalent of a Grammy, for Best Video. Later in the year, the duo won Britain's prestigious publishing prize, the Ivor Novello Award for Best Contemporary Collection of Songs (essentially a best album award). Ironically, during the awards ceremony, Levy was told that Fahey was dissolving the group. (That year Levy also recorded a song with Elton John for his Duets album.)

Surprised but undaunted, Levy stepped out on her own with the 1994 Marcella Detroit album Jewel, which included her plea for tolerance, "I Believe." The song was a Top Ten hit in Britain and Australia. The following year, she released the album Feeler, which included "Somebody's Mother," a song decrying war crimes in Bosnia. The album unexpectedly sold fifty thousand copies in Japan, and Levy (as Detroit) was the first singer to perform a concert for the fledgling MTV Japan. In 1995, she also wrote songs for, and made a guest appearance on, the popular BBC television sitcom, Absolutely Fabulous. In 2000, Levy worked on new Marcella Detroit songs, performed in England, collaborated with notable songwriters such as Chris Difford of the British pop-rock band Squeeze and with some highly touted young bands in England and the Netherlands. Back home in California, she joined celebrated keyboard player Barry Goldberg and ace guitarist Harvey Mandel for a series of concerts and sang the blues. In 2001, she released a Marcella Detroit solo album, Dancing Madly Sideways.

All the while, Levy planned her schedule to be home to celebrate Jewish holidays with her son in the hope that Jewish observance gives him what it has given her. "Being Jewish gives you a sense of who you are and where you came from," Levy says, adding, "I don't believe Judaism is just a religion. It goes deeper than that. It's a sense of brotherhood with other Jews who have been through so much. Judaism makes up a lot of who we are, and there's a sense of pride in having fought for who and what you are."

# Graham Gouldman
## of 10cc

**Singer. Songwriter. Multi-instrumentalist. Born Manchester, England, May 10, 1946. The band formed in 1972 in Manchester, England, and is best known for the U.S. Top Ten hits "I'm Not in Love" and "The Things We Do for Love." U.K. Top Ten hits include "Donna," "Rubber Bullets," "Life is a Minestrone," "Wall Street Shuffle," and "Art for Art's Sake." Gouldman also wrote the sixties hits "For Your Love," "Heart Full of Soul," "Look Through Any Window," "Bus Stop," "Listen People," and "No Milk Today."**

*English pop-rock quartet 10cc in 1975. From left, Kevin Godley, Eric Stewart, Lol Creme, and Graham Gouldman. (Photo coutesy Graham Gouldman.)*

In private, the members of the English pop-rock quartet 10cc endearingly referred to themselves as Three Yids and a Yok. The "Yids," Gouldman, singer-songwriter-drummer Kevin Godley (born Manchester, England, October 7, 1945), and songwriter–multi-instrumentalist Lawrence "Lol" Creme (born Manchester, England, September 19, 1947) grew up in Jewish neighborhoods on the north side of Manchester. The "Yok," singer–songwriter-multi-instrumentalist Eric Stewart (born Manchester, England, January 20, 1945), was from another part of town. The term yok, British slang for *goy*, or non-Jew, was used with affection in this case. The four, all accomplished multi-instrumentalists, began working together as session musicians at Strawberry Studios in the town of Stockport outside Manchester. The studio was partly owned by Stewart and Gouldman. Though they'd met earlier, Gouldman began playing and collaborating with Stewart in 1968 when the two were both members of the Mindbenders, best known for the hits "The Game of Love" and "A Groovy Kind of Love." Godley and Creme had gone to art school together, and eventually would go on to direct some of the most memorable rock videos of the eighties.

Gouldman already was a star of sorts, acclaimed as a songwriter who provided a number of British bands with some of their biggest hits between 1965 and 1967, during what became known in the United States as the British Invasion. Gouldman wrote the Yardbirds' first three hits "For Your Love," "Heart Full of Soul" (both Top Ten songs in the United States), and "Evil-Hearted You," which reached No. 3 in England. He was only nineteen. Gouldman also penned the Hollies' hits "Look Through Any Window" and "Bus Stop," as well as "Listen People," and "No Milk Today," hits for Herman's Hermits. Jeff Beck, Shirley Bassey, Chris Isaak and Richard Elliot were among those who later recorded Gouldman's songs. He viewed his early songwriting success as the best revenge toward anti-Semitic schoolmates who often referred to him as a "Jewish bastard," and toward teachers who told him he'd amount to nothing but "factory fodder" if he didn't do better in school.

Gouldman grew up in a kosher home and, up through his bar mitzvah, regularly attended Shabbat services with his father, Hymie, at Stenecourt Synagogue, an Orthodox shul in the north end of Manchester. He was moved by the confidence-building words of Rabbi Perlman, and even more so by the music he heard there. The beautiful melody of the Israeli national anthem, "Hatikvah," and the atmosphere-setting music of the Kol Nidre service on Yom Kippur were especially appealing. He found the minor-key music of Jewish prayer more soulful than what he calls "more Christian, white" major chords. Later, minor chord progressions would frequently find their way into Gouldman's pop songs. The A-minor chord, he says, "has been very good to me." His bar mitzvah also remains an important musical experience. "After my Haftorah," Gouldman says, "Rabbi Perlman kissed me and said I sang beautifully." Gouldman's mother, Betty, a homemaker, also was very supportive of her son's musical ambitions. Gouldman's greatest influence, however, was his father, who Graham describes as "a very literate man who should have been a professional writer." Instead, his father ran various businesses ("they were nonsense," Gouldman says) to support the family during difficult times just after World War II. On the side, Hymie Gouldman wrote award-winning Jewish-themed poems, essays, and columns for British publications such as the Jewish Telegraph and the Jewish Gazette. He also won awards for his locally produced plays, in which Betty often acted. Once Graham began writing songs on a regular basis, Hymie, known among 10cc band members as Hyme the Rhyme, became his son's sounding board. If Hymie couldn't be a professional writer, he was going to make sure his son had every chance to do so. It was Dad who came up with the title of one of Graham's hits, "No Milk Today," and who often wrote lyrics with his son. "When you're growing up in a literate house and can give your dad a lyric and he says, 'That's wrong,' or suggests changes, it's like having another songwriting partner. That was my foundation and influence," Gouldman says. Even when Gouldman began striking gold regularly, his father continued to encourage him to be original.

Gouldman had begun playing guitar at age eleven. He grew up listening to the Elvis Presley, Buddy Holly, and Eddie Cochran records that were making their way across the ocean in the late fifties and early sixties. He also was exposed to homegrown skiffle (folk) groups and rock bands such as Cliff Richard and the Shadows. Gouldman formed his first band in his mid-teens. Called the Whirlwinds, the group practiced in the evening at the Jewish Lads Brigade, a Manchester center for Jewish youth. He quit school at sixteen, where he admits he was " a bit of a dunce," and watched many of his classmates go off to college. During the day Graham worked in a men's clothing store. After two years of frequent tardiness due to late night rehearsals and gigs, he was fired.

By the mid-sixties, enamored of the Beatles and Burt Bacharach, he left the Whirlwinds ("too much like lounge music") to pursue songwriting full time. If the Beatles could do it, he thought, he could, too. "I loved rock 'n' roll," Gould-man says. "The first thing that struck me was Elvis Presley, the way he looked, sounded, and what he represented, but I wanted to be in the Beatles." Gouldman was in the right place to make music. Manchester was a university town with lots of clubs where musicians could hone their skills in front of teens who, feeling like second-class citizens, were beginning to assert themselves with rock 'n' roll as their sonic calling card. He formed another band called the Mockingbirds and enrolled in music school, but dropped out after two lessons when he realized the lessons couldn't teach him to be creative. He believed you either were creative, or you weren't. With the help of friend Harvey Lisberg, Gouldman's manager to this day, he began peddling his songs. Lisberg originally approached the Beatles with "For Your Love," but by then the Fab Four were recording only their own songs. That week, however, the Yardbirds were opening for the Beatles at the Hammersmith Odeon in London. And they were looking for songs. The rest, as they say, is a songwriter-band relationship that included three substantial hits and turned Gouldman into a music industry golden boy before he was twenty.

While the hits kept coming for him as a songwriter, his band the Mocking-birds, which included drummer Kevin Godley, had not taken off. He had better luck with a 1968 solo album called *The Graham Gouldman Thing*. His goal, however, was to be in a successful band; he wasn't interested in solo stardom. Gouldman spent six months touring with the Mindbenders (formerly Wayne Fontana and the Mindbenders), which also included Eric Stewart. The following year bubble-gum pop production kings Jeffry Katz and Jerry Kasenetz invited Gouldman to the states to work on songs for their acts. "I went over for a while. They were very charismatic, enthusiastic, and loved music," Gouldman recalls, "but it was a little bit like a factory." Uncomfortable there, he convinced the producers to allow him take the unfinished songs back to England and make demos at Straw-berry Studios in Manchester with Stewart, Godley, and Creme, who were the stu-dio house band at the time and collectively known as Hotlegs. Katz and Kasenetz agreed. "One could say," Gouldman offers, "that Kasenetz and Katz were the cata-lyst for 10cc."

Little came of the sessions for Kasenetz-Katz, but Hotlegs began having re-cording desires of its own. The trio scored a Top Forty hit in 1970 with "Nean-derthal Man." Shortly after the song became a hit, Gouldman joined Hotlegs as opening act for a Moody Blues concert tour. Though Hotlegs dissolved as a band, the foursome continued to do studio work. They even co-produced a pair of Neil Sedaka albums, *Solitaire* (1972) and *The Tra-La Days Are Over* (1973). The lads from Manchester also played guitar, bass, and drums, and sang backup vocals on those records. Stewart also served as engineer. The two albums, released only in England, ignited a Sedaka comeback in Great Britain that crossed the Atlantic, and (with the subsequent help of Elton John who offered Sedaka a U.S. record deal) put the pop singer back on top of the American record charts. In 1974, Sedaka reached No. 1 with "Laughter in the Rain."

During this time, Gouldman and company sent a song called "Donna," one of several they had recorded, to Jonathan King, head of U.K. Records. He signed the quartet to a recording contract and named them 10cc. (The name supposedly is a play on the nine centimeters of semen the average male ejaculates.) Released in 1972, "Donna" reached No. 2 on the British record charts. A satire of fifties' teen-idol pop, it was the first of a dozen Top Ten hits the band would score in Great Britain throughout the seventies. That success also took solid root in the United States with a trio of "Love" songs, the Top Five ballads "I'm Not in Love" and "The Things We Do for Love," as well as "People in Love."

The quartet succeeded with a combination of exacting musicianship and songwriting craft, wit, satire, and sentiment. 10cc was schizophrenic, bouncing back and forth from gorgeous love songs to wry, sly social commentary slightly hidden under shimmering harmonies, shifting tempos and endearing pop hooks. "Life Is a Minestrone," "I'm Mandy, Fly Me" (which reached No. 60 in the United States), "Wall Street Shuffle," and "Art for Art's Sake," the latter two, barbed criticisms about the greed in those two arenas, played better in Britain than the United States. The British also appreciated bizarrely titled tunes such as "The Second Sitting for the Last Supper," "The Worst Band in the World," "Marriage Bureau Rendezvous," and "Honeymoon with B Troop." The titles verged on the novel and comic, but smart word play, strong musicianship, and thoughtful production prevented such songs from falling into an abyss of utter silliness. "Kevin and Lol were more experimental than Eric and me and inspired us to be more witty," Gouldman explains. "No one in the band would take any middle-of-the-road crap. We all knew we had better come up with something good."

The original line up lasted through 1976 when Godley and Creme left to pursue other interests, including producing and directing music videos, and recording. Their 1978 album L included "Punchbag," a song about being bullied and taunted in school. The song included the lyrics, "And the laughs came, and the nerve went, and 'Dirty Jew' was written on the blackboard . . ." Godley and Creme entered the video production business just as MTV was being hatched and were on the cutting edge of a new art form. The duo are the creative minds behind videos such as Duran Duran's "Girls on Film," Herbie Hancock's "Rockit," and "Every Breath You Take" by the Police. They also scored a Top Twenty U.S. hit in 1985 with the song "Cry."

Gouldman and Stewart continued as 10cc, adding additional musicians for tours, and subsequently experienced one of their greatest successes with "The Things We Do for Love" and the No. 1 U.K. hit "Dreadlock Holiday." The band lasted into the early eighties, but the hits had stopped coming. Gouldman and Stewart went on to do production and session work for others; Gouldman for the Ramones and Gilbert O'Sullivan, and Stewart with Paul McCartney. In 1984, Gouldman joined forces with Andrew Gold and as a duo called Wax released three albums during the eighties. They had a U.S. hit in 1986 with "Right Between the Eyes" and a hit in Europe the following year with "Bridge to Your Heart." In 1992, Gouldman and Stewart reunited under the 10cc banner for the album *Meanwhile* and teamed again in 1995 to record an album called *Mirror, Mirror*.

In the fall of 2000, Gouldman released a solo album, *And Another Thing*, a play on the title of his first solo album, *The Graham Gouldman Thing*, released thirty-two years earlier. The album includes a song influenced by a trek in Israel's Negev Desert in 1997. Titled "Walking with Angels," the song was inspired by thoughts Gouldman had of his father, who died in 1991. During the trip, Gouldman remarked that it would be nice if his father could see him trekking through the Promised Land. A friend replied "He can," and the idea for a song was born.

Deserts, especially, the Negev, mean a lot to Gouldman. "I like the desert," he says. "You think it's empty, but it's not. It's harsh, but everything is provided. It's a metaphor for faith and trusting in God," adding "to walk in the desert, your own desert, is a remarkable, wonderful thing." Deserts and wilderness are also the places Gouldman goes to do his share of *tikkun olam*, or repairing the world. He is involved with the British charities Teenage Cancer Trust and One-to-One, an organization that helps children in crisis around the world. Gouldman raises money by getting sponsors to back him on treks in an array of countries around the globe, including Morocco, Nepal, and Peru as well as Israel, a country he has visited many times on charity treks and with his family as a tourist.

Gouldman is in the rare position of having four children, from two marriages, with different religious upbringings. The two children from his first marriage are observant Jews; the two younger children are non-Jews. All have been to Israel, however. And Gouldman talks enough about Judaism—and forbids pork products in the house—that his youngest child lobbied for a kosher home. "My dad used to say we all have different degrees of hypocrisy. We do what we feel is right," says Gouldman, who still belongs to a synagogue, but rarely attends. "I'm very proud of being Jewish, and the synagogue's there if I want to go."

# David Lee Roth

Singer. Songwriter. Born October 10, 1954, in Bloomington, Indiana. Lead vocalist of the hard rock/heavy metal band Van Halen. The band scored seven Top Forty hits, including "(Oh,) Pretty Woman," "Jump," "I'll Wait," and "Panama," during Roth's 1975–1985 tenure. As a solo act, Roth reached the Top Twenty with a remake of the Beach Boys' "California Girls," the medley "Just a Gigolo/I Ain't Got Nobody," "Yankee Rose," and "Just Like Paradise." Roth built a reputation as one of the most physical and flamboyant showmen in arena rock. His cocky, ringmaster style was a blueprint for many eighties' hard rock and metal bands that followed Van Halen.

*David Lee Roth struts his stuff during a 1978 Van Halen video shoot. (Photo by Torbjorn Calvero.)*

In his 1997 autobiography, *Crazy from the Heat*, David Lee Roth revealed the secret to his success as one of rock's most engaging and energetic performers: being Jewish. Roth spent a whole chapter, cleverly titled "The Engine Room," explaining how his Jewish identity propelled him onstage, providing the power source from which he draws his physical energy, bold personality, and "live life to the max" philosophy. To truly appreciate Roth's performances, it is best to understand how he views himself as a Jew. And in *Crazy from the Heat*, he tells you: his bar mitzvah speech focused on his dislike of the social alienation that came with being Jewish. As he became famous and was invited to speak to young congregants at his synagogue his "pep talk" counseled young Jews not to view themselves as white, and to remember that they'd probably have to work twice as hard to break even, or to be accepted. That being the case, he also counseled them to stand up for who they were. As difficult as being Jewish may have been for him, Roth never tried to conceal his roots. As one Jewish Roth fan observed: "David Lee Roth was proof that you neither had to hide your identity, bob your nose, change your name, nor sacrifice your Borscht Belt influences to indulge in all the forbidden pleasures of rock 'n' roll." In other words, Roth was one rock star who wasn't going to assimilate to join a club or increase his popularity. (Nor was he going to let Judaism stand in the way of a good time. He wasn't the most observant Jew, but he took pride in the peoplehood, its history, and culture.)

Roth had his own special way of shouting "Never again!" He did it through performance. In *Crazy from the Heat*, he wrote, "Every step I took on that stage was smashing some Jew-hating, lousy punk ever deeper into the deck. Every step. I jumped higher 'cause I knew there was going to be more impact when I hit those boards. And if you were even vaguely anti-Semitic, you were under my wheels . . . That's where the lyrics came from, that's where the body language came from, that's where the humor came from . . . All equally as important . . . What you get from repression, and what you get from hatred, is fury, and fury was one of the main trigger points for the great Van Halen." Roth added that when he left Van Halen, the band lost its drive. "What's missing is the passionate convicted commitment. And I got a lot of mine from my religious background . . . So y'all best stop imagining . . . some defenseless Hasidic Jew with a little yarmulke on his head, 'cause that ain't here for you." On the occasions he detected anti-Semitism from interviewers, Roth was known to smash a tape recorder, or halt the interview on the spot.

Roth learned more than pride and toughness from Judaism; he also learned the value of being educated. He is smarter than his comic book rock 'n' roll persona would lead you to believe. He may not have a Ph.D. in engineering, but he has been engaged in nonstop independent study his whole life. "I didn't study at the hand of a talmudic scholar. I did learn that learning is sacred, and reading is great," Roth says in his autobiography. Roth devoured books and every kind of magazine imaginable, not just to stay informed about the world, but to get a feel for what his fans were thinking and to "borrow" ideas for his act, an act that has Jewish origins. Roth may have a rock 'n' roll heart, but he's got a Jewish vaudeville soul. Strip away Roth's in-your-face, party-hardy, sexual innuendo–laden, often profane stage persona, and you'll find an old-fashioned song-and-dance man who knows how to sell his shtick to an audience. For Roth, early twentieth-century Jewish performing legends such as Harry Houdini, Al Jolson, and Eddie Cantor were as influential as Led Zeppelin's Robert Plant and the Who's Roger Daltrey, non-Jewish blond-maned rockers who preceded Roth by a decade. Roth's appreciation for vaudeville is evident in his 1985 revival of "Just a Gigolo" and "I Ain't Got Nobody," songs that were originally hits in 1931 and 1921, respectively. Roth's now-classic video for the two-song medley, which he conceived and directed and stuffed with a chorus of bikini-clad babes, may be rock 'n' roll to you, but your grandparents called it burlesque. (He also directed the popular Van Halen videos for "Jump" and "Hot for Teacher.") Call it what you will, Roth's charisma helped Van Halen (comprising Eddie and Alex Van Halen on guitar and drums and Michael Anthony on bass) launch an assault on the record charts and become an international concert attraction. Roth recalls hearing someone once say that the Van Halen brothers may play the music, but "the Jew sells it."

Roth simply updated vaudeville. He wrapped himself in Hollywood hype, plugged in, turned up the volume to eleven, and, *voila*, created "Diamond Dave," a hedonistic rock 'n' roll character for public consumption. He transformed himself into one of the most riveting frontmen in rock music using his quick wit, mischievous smile, and gymnastics-filled performances that were heavy on humor and light on pretense. (Behind the scenes, he may have been a party animal, but he also worked hard to stay in shape and improve his act.)

Roth was born in Bloomington, Indiana, but also spent several years in eastern Massachusetts before his father, an ophthalmologist, moved the family (which included a younger sister, Lisa) to Pasadena, California, in 1963. Throughout his childhood, Roth felt like a minority. Through about age five, he had to wear braces on his legs, separating him from others his age. As he grew older, he found himself caught between the jock and academic/artistic camps. He loved sports as well as reading and painting, but didn't feel accepted by either clique, so books and films became his best friends. On top of all that, Roth suffered the occasional barbs of anti-Semitism. He remembers swastikas painted on synagogue doors in Brookline, Massachusetts. Roth had a Jewish upbringing. His paternal grandmother, who he visited often, kept a kosher home. He attended Sunday school, Hebrew school, confirmation classes, went to a Jewish camp for a short time, and became a bar mitzvah. He had mixed feelings about his Jewish education and preparation to become a "son of the Commandments." He felt further alienated from the non-Jewish community, preferring to spend his time doing anything but learning Hebrew. On the other hand, he learned how to sing while studying for his bar mitzvah. And singing during Shabbat services gave him a feeling of belonging and strengthened his sense of self-worth. He had a sweet, versatile voice as a child. ("Now," Roth says in his autobiography, "I sound like four flat tires on a muddy road.") Other important influences Roth carried into adulthood were *Mad* and *Playboy* magazines. He learned how to deliver truth through satire and parody from the former, and learned the power of social and political commentary from the latter. Throughout his youth, Roth visited his Uncle Manny and Aunt Judy Roth in New York City. Uncle Manny owned the celebrated Café Wha? in Greenwich Village. Those visits to the big city taught Roth tolerance for all kinds of people, from prostitutes to poets. In southern California, Roth discovered the music of Little Anthony, Major Lance, Diana Ross, Marvin Gaye, and the Beatles. He was transfixed by the legendary disc jockey Wolfman Jack and the bold, fast-talking boxer Cassius Clay.

In elementary and junior high school Roth became class clown and court jester, and by age twelve he was taking karate lessons. In 1972, during his senior year at John Muir High School, Roth joined the Red Ball Jets, a rock band that played Chuck Berry and Rolling Stones songs at backyard parties. It was on the party circuit that he met the Van Halen brothers, who had a band called Mammoth. The two bands competed for jobs at parties, local parks, and youth centers. After high school, Roth and the Van Halens studied music theory and orchestration at Pasadena City College. Roth flunked out, but the lessons would serve him well later.

Roth and the Van Halen brothers joined forces in late 1974 and recruited a new bass player, Michael Anthony. Roth reportedly urged that the new band be called Van Halen (instead of the suggested Rat Salade). It wasn't long before Van Halen, spurred by Roth's showmanship and Eddie Van Halen's dazzling and inventive guitar playing, became one of the most popular rock acts on the southern California club scene. By 1977, the band's metal-meets-melody style, and hummable, head-banging original tunes, had drawn the interest of Kiss co-founder Gene Simmons, who tried to help the band get a recording contract. The band was signed to Warner Brothers Records in 1978, and *Van Halen*, the band's self-titled debut that year shook the rock world's rafters. On the strength of songs such as "Jamie's Cryin'," "Runnin' with the Devil," and a memorable rendition of the Kinks' "You Really Got Me," the album sold more than one million copies in its first year of release. In 1979, the band earned its first Top Twenty hit with "Dance the Night Away," from the album *Van Halen II*. The group's popularity increased on the strength of its raucous concerts featuring the one-two punch of Roth's high kicks and Eddie Van Halen's hot licks, backed by the propulsive drums and bass of Alex Van Halen and Michael Anthony. The band continued to release successful albums during the eighties—*Women and Children First*, *Fair Warning*, and *Diver Down*, peaking in 1984 with the album *1984*. The addition of warmer, fuller keyboard sounds to the band's stripped-down hard rock helped the album reach No. 2 on the charts and spin off three hit singles: the No. 1 "Jump," "I'll Wait," and "Panama," as well as the radio and video favorite "Hot for Teacher." On the strength of the playful videos Roth created for "Jump" and "Hot for Teacher," Van Halen became a staple of MTV. Tension within the band, however, caused a widening rift between Roth and Eddie Van Halen. Early in 1985, Roth released the four-song EP, *Crazy from the Heat*, with its hits, "California Girls" and "Just a Gigolo/I Ain't Got Nobody." In April, Roth left Van Halen after ten wildly successful years. (The band hired Sammy Hagar to replace him.)

Roth put together an impressive band to record his first full solo album in 1986. Guitairst Steve Vai, bassist Billy Shehan, and drummer Gregg Bissonette helped Roth's *Eat 'Em and Smile* album sell more than one million copies and spawn the hit single "Yankee Rose." Roth and company repeated the feat in 1988 with the album *Skyscraper*, and its Top Ten hit "Just Like Paradise." But band members began departing and subsequent albums, *A Little Ain't Enough* (1991) and *Your Filthy Little Mouth* (1994) fared less well. In 1995, for a series of Vegas shows, Roth also put together the Blues Bustin' Mambo Slammers. Roth and his fourteen-piece band, which included a horn section and keyboardist/saxophonist Edgar Winter, were met with mixed reviews. In 1996, rumors and reports of Roth rejoining Van Halen were rampant when it was discovered that he had recorded a pair of new songs for a band retrospective, *The Best of Van Halen Vol. 1*. What appeared to be a full-blown reunion never took off. In October 1997, Roth's insightful and hilarious autobiography, *Crazy from the Heat* (based on the title of his 1985 EP), was released. A week later, Rhino Records issued the twenty-song compilation, *David Lee Roth: The Best*. In 1998, Roth put together the hard rocking DRL Band, and released an album on his own Wawazat! record label.

In early 2000, Roth performed a mitzvah, recording a song for the charity organization *Songs of Love*, which provides children with personalized songs by their favorite artists to raise their spirits and help them in their struggle against life-threatening illnesses. During Hanukkah, when a reporter for the Web site Launch.com asked Roth what being Jewish meant to him, he replied, "I value my culture, and my traditions, and the food, and what amounts to a whole society gig, you know, way more than most people value their other religions."

# Stan Lynch

## of Tom Petty and the Heartbreakers

**Drummer. Songwriter. Producer. Born May 21, 1955, Cincinnati, Ohio. Co-founded the Heartbreakers in 1975 in Los Angeles, California. The band is best known for the hits "Breakdown," "Don't Do Me Like That," "Refugee," "The Waiting," "Stop Draggin' My Heart Around" (with Stevie Nicks), "You Got Lucky," "Mary Jane's Last Dance," and others. Lynch also co-wrote the Don Henley hit "The Last Worthless Evening" as well as the Henley songs "Drivin' with Your Eyes Closed," "You Don't Know Me at All," "Learn to Be Still" (for the Eagles reunion album); and he co-wrote and co-produced songs on Henley's album, _Inside Job_. Lynch also has done session work for Bob Dylan, the Byrds, Aretha Franklin, Stevie Nicks, Jackson Browne, the Mavericks, and Warren Zevon, among others.**

_During his nearly twenty years with Tom Petty & the Heartbreakers, Stan Lynch always packed a hanukkiah for winter concert tours and celebrated Hanukkah on the road. (With permission from Stan Lynch archives.)_

Whenever Tom Petty and the Heartbreakers hit the road for a long winter tour to deliver Top Forty hits such as "Refugee" or fan favorites such as "American Girl," drummer Stan Lynch made sure to pack a Hanukkah menorah (Hanukkiah) and candles. In his twenties and thirties, Hanukkah was Lynch's strongest connection to his Judaism. Alone and far from home, he turned the candle-lighting ceremony into a ritual of great personal significance. He recited the blessings and lit the first night's candle to honor his mother, and thought of her as the candle glowed. He honored his father, as well as his divorced parents as a couple, with the second night's candle. The third night's candle was dedicated to his sister, Jody, who he affectionately calls "the brains of the outfit." On the fourth night, he remembered all his grandparents. On night five, he thought of all his friends as the candles flickered. Candle number six represented Lynch's past. Candle seven was dedicated to his present ("I reflected on it and how fortunate I was to be having this moment," he explains). On the final night of Hanukkah, Lynch considered his future and what it might hold with the lighting of the eighth candle. The Shammas, the candle used to light all the others, represented Lynch. "I pretended it was me," he says "I would see that light and say that all those other candles are what I am and all I'll ever be, and we're giving each other light. I connected to those things. It was a life force between us." During the first few years with the Heartbreakers, Lynch loudly recited the blessings hoping his bandmates would be curious, but no one ever asked any questions. In fact, some band members joked about the nightly candle lighting. So Lynch withdrew a bit, and quietly celebrated Hanukkah in his own special way at the back of the tour bus, or in his hotel room, all over the world. "For years that's how I survived being on the road," Lynch says. "It was fun, and it reminded me of home where my dad used to sing Hanukkah songs."

Stanley Lynch II was born into a vibrant Jewish community in Cincinnati, Ohio. His father, Stanley, Sr. (both were named after the same deceased relative), was the son of Edward Youngerman, whose two brothers were rabbis. When Edward Youngerman died at age thirty-nine, his wife Mitzi remarried and took the name of her new husband, Nathan Lynch, also Jewish. That transformed Stanley Youngerman into Stanley Lynch. Stanley, Sr., was working for UPS in Ohio when he decided to reinvent himself by becoming a psychology teacher and moving the family, wife Sally, son Stan II and daughter Jody, to Gainesville, Florida. From about 1960 through 1966, the Lynch family moved back and forth from

Gainesville to Miami for a variety of teaching jobs before setting down roots in Gainesville. Stan II's mother, Sally, was a schoolteacher and librarian and, later, an aerobics instructor. Stan grew up in a Reform household that at one brief point included a Christmas tree as well as a Hanukkiah. The family also observed the High Holy Days. Lynch remembers his father studying the holidays as he taught them to his children. The family had neglected observance for a while, and was trying to reconnect. Passover often was spent at the Orthodox home of his great aunt and uncle, Rose and Lou Heines in Coral Gables, Florida. Stan's religious upbringing, however, was quite informal. He didn't attend Hebrew school or Sunday school, or officially become a bar mitzvah. But his father did convey to him that being a Jew was something special, and that as a Jew Stan was in good company.

Above all, he was taught it was paramount for Jews to look after fellow Jews, and that when it comes to struggle, Jews grit it out. "My dad's theme was the bittersweet human experience," Lynch says. Lynch knew two other Jewish kids his age in high school. One, Fran Berger, played trumpet in the Gainesville High School Band. The other, Marty Jourard, a sax and keyboard player, eventually became a member of the Los Angeles–based band, the Motels, which garnered Top Ten hits in the early eighties with "Only the Lonely" and "Suddenly Last Summer." Jourard's father was Sid Jourard, noted psychologist and author of *The Transparent Self*. "Jews were a big mystery in Gainesville," Lynch says. "When people found out I was Jewish they stood back in horror and delight. One guy wanted to shake my hand because he had never shaken a Jew's hand before." On the other hand, Lynch experienced more than one instance of anti-Semitism, which he rarely tolerated, and that sometimes meant fighting. After his parents divorced, Lynch, who was about fifteen, created his own mystique about Judaism and began his special Hanukkah candle-lighting ceremony. What he didn't know, he somehow figured out, or filled in with concepts that worked for him.

Music permeated his home throughout his childhood. Lynch's father played the trumpet; his mother played piano. The first record he remembers being smitten by was the theme from the film, *Exodus*. "I could listen to it all day," he says. Broadway show soundtracks, Ray Charles, Count Basie, Dean Martin, and Frank Sinatra also were often played on the family hi-fi. Stan took violin lessons in the first grade, switched to piano in the third grade, tried trumpet a year later, then, following his sister's lead, took guitar lessons. It appeared doubtful Stan would stick with an instrument long enough to become proficient, until about 1965 when he noticed the drummer on *The Tonight Show*, Ed Shaunessy. Soon after, he was exposed to renowned drummers such as Buddy Rich, Gene Krupa, and the Beatles' Ringo Starr. "I think the attraction to drums was visual. I couldn't take my eyes off the drummer," Lynch says.

He began drum lessons at age eleven while living in Miami and continued with a new teacher when the Lynches returned to Gainesville. His instructor used fascinating teaching techniques. In fact, it was two years into lessons before Stan actually touched any drums. He practiced playing on a rubber pad and spent a lot of time doing exercises to strengthen his wrists and improve his coordination. That included hanging tea bags from his fingers to learn how to keep them in the right position when playing. By fourteen he was in his first garage band, Styrofoam Soul. The popular regional show band, which included a horn section, even had the distinction of playing for inmates at the women's prison in Valdosta, Georgia. Lynch hadn't yet graduated from high school and he was earning a hundred dollars a week in Styrofoam Soul and saving money to buy a car. By seventeen, he was in another popular area band, Road Turkey, with his friend Marty Jourard. As his music career blossomed, Lynch became a bit of a troublemaker and attended three high schools in three years, but he graduated on time. He met Tom Petty and several other members of the future Heartbreakers in the early seventies, when Petty asked him to fill in for the drummer in his band, Mudcrutch, for a show in Tampa. Soon after, Mudcrutch relocated to Los Angeles. In 1973, Lynch also headed west to seek his fortune. He floundered in Los Angeles for a couple of years until running into former Gainesville guitarist Mike Campbell and keyboard player Benmont Tench, who had been in Mudcrutch. The three Floridians, along with bass player Ron Blair, joined forces. When Tom Petty reappeared in 1975 with a record deal in hand, the rockers formed Tom Petty and the Heartbreakers. Though the band appeared on the scene in the midst of a pop music trend labeled New Wave, the Heartbreakers found their inspiration in the folk-rock of Bob Dylan, the chiming guitars of the Byrds, and the belief that rock 'n' roll could save your soul. The band's songs, mostly penned by Petty, were flag-waving anthems of encouragement for social outcasts with lyrics like, "You don't have to live like a refugee," "Even the losers get lucky sometime." "I won't back down."

The band released its self-titled debut album in 1976. Though the album included future FM radio staples "Breakdown" and "American Girl," the record floundered until the band toured England, and the record hit the charts there. "Breakdown," released in the United States, became a hit in early 1978, more than a year after the album's initial release. Tom Petty and the Heartbreakers were on the rock 'n' roll map. While the band's second album, You're Gonna Get It!, released in 1978, didn't include any Top Forty hits, a pair of songs, "I Need To Know," and "Listen to Her Heart," were FM radio favorites, and solidified the band's reputation. It was the group's third album in 1979, Damn the Torpedoes, that catapulted Petty and company to stardom. The record included the hits "Don't Do Me Like That," and "Refugee," as well as concert favorites "Even the Losers," and "Here Comes My Girl."

Throughout the glory, the stardom and the tours, Stan Lynch proudly lit his Hanukkah candles. As a traveling musician, he embraced the idea of the Wandering Jew. "It felt much more ethnic to light the Hanukkah lights when traveling, much more right. It was almost strange to light the menorah at home," Lynch says. He also read books about Judaism while on the road, with Howard Fast's The Jews leaving its mark. The book's melancholy tone reminded him of his father's lessons about the Jews' history of struggle.

In 1986, the Heartbreakers embarked on a tour as Bob Dylan's backing band. The tour began in Israel, and Lynch's stay there had a profound effect on him. He was moved and sobered by his visit to Yad Vashem, the Holocaust museum in Jerusalem, and disturbed that none of his bandmates asked him about the museum visit, or what it felt like to be a Jew in the Promised Land. He appreciated and understood that inconveniences such as hotel blackouts and armed guards were for his protection; his bandmates didn't. He was humbled when he used the "I'm-a-rock-star" line to sweet talk some Israeli women only to discover they were pilots in the Israeli Defense Force. Lynch was embarrassed when Tom Petty threw a tantrum in the band's kosher hotel on Shabbat because the bandleader couldn't have bacon and eggs and Lynch was angered when he heard a member of the band's entourage shout from a hotel balcony that it was too bad there were so many Jews in a country as beautiful as Israel. "I was a Jew in Israel with a bunch of guys it didn't mean squat to, while it was sort of a pilgrimage for me," Lynch recalls. Israel's constant state of emergency and the effort made to safeguard all visitors also humbled him, and it made him realize "what a protected hothouse flower" he had been as a rock star.

After the tour, Lynch began looking to branch out. He did more songwriting and session work, something all the band members had become known for between touring and making their own records. Over the years, Lynch had played drums on albums by T-Bone Burnett, Stevie Nicks, Jackson Browne, Bob Dylan, the Eurythmics, and Aretha Franklin.

In 1989, Lynch rekindled a working relationship with a fellow Jew that endures. Danny Kortchmar, one of the music industry's most fabled songwriters, session guitarists, and producers, invited Lynch to work on Don Henley's solo album, *The End of the Innocence*. Lynch had worked with the pair a few years earlier, co-writing "Driving with Your Eyes Closed" for Henley's 1984 album, *Building the Perfect Beast*. This time, however, Lynch's role was dramatically increased to include writing, producing, and playing throughout the album. His contribution included co-writing the hit "The Last Worthless Evening." The following year, his song "Love That Never Dies" was one of four new songs recorded by the Byrds for the band's retrospective boxed set. He also played drums on Byrd Roger McGuinn's solo album *Back from Rio*. In 1991, the Heartbreakers released another record, *Into the Great Wide Open*, and followed that in 1993 with a "greatest hits" collection that included a pair of new songs.

Lynch said "Shalom" to Tom Petty and the Heartbreakers in 1994, leaving to pursue songwriting and record production. That year the Lynch-Henley–penned "Learn to Be Still" was one of four new songs recorded for the Eagles' reunion album, *Hell Freezes Over*. Since the early nineties, Lynch also has collaborated with Nashville acts and had his songs recorded by the Mavericks, Restless Heart, and Matraca Berg. He worked with rockers Meredith Brooks and Eddie Money, and in 1995 worked with Henley and Kortchmar again on a "greatest hits" collection that included a pair of new songs he co-wrote. In 2000, he co-wrote, co-produced, and played on the lion's share of Henley's album, *Inside Job*.

Looking back at his nearly twenty years on the road with the Heartbreakers, Lynch credited Judaism with helping to ground and mature him in the crucible of rock 'n' roll. "There are certainly some parallels in Jewish history that can help you understand your career in terms of patience, perseverance, discipline and graciousness," Lynch says. Around the time he left the Heartbreakers, Lynch, with the encouragement of his girlfriend Michelle Ganeles, began delving deeper into his Judaism. He even considered having a bar mitzvah and discussed it with a rabbi. The rabbi's response was heartwarming. "He answered that just by the

virtue of my asking, and 'living as you have, you are a bar mitzvah,'" Lynch recalls. Lynch didn't go through the ritual of a bar mitzvah, but he did join Temple
Bet Yam in St. Augustine, Florida. "It's always painful when I leave the synagogue," Lynch says, "because I feel if I did more, I'd know more. It's a mixed bag
of guilt and joy."

# Melissa Manchester

**Singer. Songwriter. Pianist. Actress. Born February 15, 1951, Bronx, New York. Best known for the Top Ten hits "Midnight Blue," "Don't Cry Out Loud," "You Should Hear How She Talks About You."**

*Melissa Manchester takes the Jewish concept of mitzvah to heart. (Photo by Randee St. Nicholas.)*

As a child Melissa Manchester used to lie in bed with the windows open during the High Holy Days and listen to the services next door at B'nai Jeshurun on West Eighty-Eighth Street in Manhattan. Her mother, Ruth Polsky, an Orthodox Jew whose family came to the United States from the Russian-Polish border in 1914, usually went to services alone. Her father, David Manchester, a bassoon player with the Metropolitan Opera, was an atheist. He disapproved of Melissa and her older sister, Claudia, accompanying their mother to synagogue. But he couldn't keep his daughters from watching their mother light candles and recite the blessings on Shabbat. That tradition remains a cherished memory for Manchester as an adult. Her mother also did all the cooking for the family seders, which Melissa describes as "very joyful, and not too serious, much to the chagrin of our more religious relatives." Manchester's parents did share a cultural Jewish pride, often remarking about the number of celebrated Jewish composers. Her parents' religious conflict turned out to be a positive experience for Manchester. "I'm much more Jewish than I ever was. Our home is more Jewish now because, as children, no one was rebelling against anything." Manchester calls Judaism "a gift," and, she says, "I hope my children see it as a gift."

Observing the religious dichotomy between her parents strengthened Manchester's belief that spirituality was vital to nourishing the human soul. That came after years of "searching" and studying comparative religions. "One thing I wonder is how people live without a sense of faith, without a spiritual belief," Manchester says. "The Old Testament is really hard, and filled with scoundrels, but it's also filled with poetry and the need for the spirit to rise above human impulses." And while Manchester believes all religions are "pretty much going to the same place," she appreciates the fact Judaism doesn't claim to be the only way to get there. More importantly, she says, "It was one of the first sparks of light spiritually, and that resonates very deeply with me."

Aside from her parents' contrary views on God, Manchester grew up in a house full of light and music. Her paternal grandmother was talented enough to sing at the Metropolitan Opera, but chose to raise children instead. One of those children, Melissa's father David, made his mother proud as the bassoon player at the Met for nearly thirty years. During World War II, Manchester's mother and her mother's two sisters sang in New York supper clubs and lounges. (Ruth Polsky Manchester would become one of the first women to run her own fashion design house and manufacturing plant.) Melissa even remembers her maternal grandparents, who had fallen on hard times after emigrating from Russia, always playing classical music in their "poor, sickly, sad house." Listening to her father practice and watching him make his own reeds ("he was the only man I knew who used pink nail polish," she says) was a major inspiration. So was the jazz and music from Broadway shows that filled the house.

Manchester's parents were a dramatic couple, "childlike in their joy," who threw glamorous parties where the kids met opera stars and musicians. They also created a nurturing, as well as musical, household for their children. Melissa and her sister were encouraged to pursue their interests and raised to believe they could reach any goals they set. "My mom's mantra was to find beauty, and if you can't find beauty, create it," Manchester recalls. Growing up in that environment and, as early as age five, being moved to tears by Ella Fitzgerald singing songs from George Gershwin's *Porgy and Bess*, Manchester's dream was to sing, or at least "be in the neighborhood of how and where you make that happen."

Manchester's singing and songwriting career reads like a map of faith and destiny. She is among just a handful of performers who have succeeded in every facet of the entertainment business. She has sung hit songs, written hit songs for herself and others, written and sung for film and television, acted in film and TV, won Grammy Awards and been nominated for Best Song Academy Awards. Stand-up comedy is about the only performance medium that has eluded her.

Manchester's résumé brims with Jewish mentors and colleagues, including Paul Simon; Bette Midler and Barry Manilow, who gave her one of her first big breaks as a backup singer; and Carole Bayer Sager, a longtime friend and songwriting partner. In 1999, Barbra Streisand recorded one of Manchester's songs, "Just One Lifetime" (co-written with Tom Snow), on her record, *A Love Like Ours*, released in honor of Streisand's marriage to actor James Brolin. There's a bond with fellow Jewish singers and songwriters that is "instant and immediate," she says of these connections that have touched her throughout her life. "There are commonalities, including neuroses, that you can share." She describes Midler and Streisand as fiercely determined, highly brilliant women whose instincts and abilities attract people who are supportive of the singers' artistic vision.

Manchester attended the High School of Performing Arts in New York, the school that inspired the 1980 hit film *Fame* and the spinoff TV series of the same name. More interested in the working world than school, Manchester spent more time earning money as a theater usher and car valet on Broadway than studying.

"I was a very dopey student," she says. "I just wanted to work." By fifteen, she was singing commercial jingles for Pepsi, McDonald's and United Airlines. By seventeen, she was a staff writer for the prominent publishing firm Chappell Music. Later, as a student at New York University's School of the Arts, she was one of nine students accepted into a songwriting class taught by Paul Simon. Still in her teens, she began performing as a singer-pianist in Manhattan clubs. In 1971, Barry Manilow, then Bette Midler's music director, hired twenty-year-old Manchester as a member of the Harlettes, Midler's trio of backup singers.

Six months later, Manchester had her own recording contract, and in 1973 released her first solo album, *Home to Myself*. Many of the songs on the album were co-written with Carole Bayer Sager, who had seen Manchester in concert with Midler the previous year. In 1975, Manchester co-wrote (with Sager) and recorded her first Top Ten hit, "Midnight Blue." Music industry trade publication *Billboard* named "Blue" Adult Contemporary Song of the Year.

Manchester was just getting started. In 1977, The Captain and Tenille used the Manchester-Sager composition "Come in from the Rain" as the title track for their new album. The following year Manchester scored a Top Five hit co-writing the Kenny Loggins' hit "Whenever I Call You Friend." Manchester scored another Top Ten hit, the Sager–Peter Allen-penned "Don't Cry Out Loud," in 1979. Two more Top Forty hits followed with "Pretty Girls" in 1979 and "Fire in the Morning" in 1980. The same year, Manchester became the first singer in the history of the Academy Awards to have been the voice of two movie theme songs nominated for Oscars. She also was the first to perform two songs during the awards show: "Through the Eyes of Love," the theme from *Ice Castles*, and "I'll Never Say Goodbye," from *The Promise*. Manchester's roll continued as she won the 1982 Grammy Award for Best Female Vocalist (after previous nominations in 1978 and 1979) for the Top Five hit, "You Should Hear How She Talks About You."

In 1984, Manchester made her acting debut on the TV series *Fame*, playing the role of a singer-turned-teacher and performing a pair of songs. She also co-wrote the script with her husband and manager Kevin DeRemer. While her acting career was just getting started, she remained in demand as the voice of movie theme songs, singing the themes for *Thief of Hearts*, *A Little Sex*, and *The Great Mouse Detective*. Acting credits also included starring roles in the Andrew Lloyd Webber musicals *Song and Dance* and *Music of the Night*, a recurring role in the TV series *Blossom*, and a co-starring role in the Bette Midler film, *For the Boys*.

In 1997, Arista Records released a nineteen-song Manchester retrospective CD titled *The Essence of Melissa Manchester*. In 1999, she co-starred with Kelsey Grammer (of *Frasier*) in a twentieth anniversary production of Stephen Sondheim's hit musical *Sweeney Todd* in Los Angeles. That year, Barbra Streisand not only recorded Manchester's "Just One Lifetime," but sang that song at her wedding. ("I found out about it in June and didn't stop screaming until August," Manchester says.) In 2000, Manchester finished composing and recording the film score for *Lady and the Tramp II: Scamp's Adventure*," a sequel to the animated Disney classic. Bette Midler also recorded a Manchester song for a forthcoming album.

Throughout the nineties, Manchester had become a regular on the Windham Hill record label's annual "Colors of Christmas" tour with Peabo Bryson, Sheena Easton, Roberta Flack, Philip Baily, Oleta Adams, and Jeffrey Osborne, among others. In 1997 she also recorded a Christmas album for Angel Records called *Joy*. The album was important to her because it came without the normal record industry pressure for radio play or a hit single. The eleven-song album, recorded in Nashville in ten days, included two tunes co-written by Manchester as well as other "Christmas" songs written by Jews—"White Christmas" and "I've Got My Love to Keep Me Warm" by Irving Berlin, and "The Christmas Song" co-written by Mel Torme.

Manchester admits it's "weird" to do Christmas tours and albums but adds that while "it's not my religious holiday, it is a lovely time of year, and a beautiful holiday." The Christmas projects have been pressure-free. "No one has asked me to convert," she says. "Everybody respects my Judaism, and we don't talk about the fact that Christ is Jewish. And, I get to sing very beautiful songs. If there was a Righteous Hanukkah Tour, I'd be there."

Manchester has been *there* in many other ways. In 1995, she lent her voice to *Liberation'95*, a celebration of Jewish survival marking the fiftieth anniversary of the end of the Holocaust, and a benefit for the Museum of Tolerance in Los Angeles. A decade earlier, she was one of the first singers to do a benefit to help raise money to find a cure for AIDS. More recently, on Mother's Day of 2000, Manchester participated in the Million Mom March urging Congress to pass laws requiring all gun owners to be registered and licensed and to take gun safety training courses. Manchester performed "A Mother's Prayer," written a year earlier in response to the shootings at Columbine High School in Littleton, Colorado. (Manchester heard about the shootings en route to a songwriting session in Nashville. After writing the song, with Karen Taylor-Good, on a Friday, she attended Shabbat services at Nashville's Temple Micha to mourn the tragedy and come to grips with her grief.) Country singer Collin Raye recorded a slightly revamped version of the song as a duet with Manchester called "A Mother and Father's Prayer," and included it on his album *Counting Sheep*.

Whether it's helping to find a cure for AIDS or playing a role to reduce gun violence, *tikkun olam*, repairing the world, is an important part of Manchester's life. The more she reads about *tikkun olam* and the qualities that create a good life, she says, "The more you start to live consciously. You don't just exist. You ask 'What's the gift I can give back?'" One gift that may have been "giving back" for years may be "Come in from the Rain," Manchester's most spiritual song. "It's about forgiveness, and about an open door, and empathy for someone who's struggled with something," Manchester says. "That to me is Jewish in its essence, leaving the door open."

# Trevor Rabin

**Singer. Songwriter. Guitarist. Composer. Born October 14, 1954, Johannesburg, South Africa. Best known as a member of progressive/art-rock band Yes from 1983 to 1995, and for writing the band's hits "Owner of a Lonely Heart," "Leave It," "Love Will Find a Way," and "Rhythm of Love."**

*Promotional photo of Trevor Rabin for his 1989 solo album, Can't Look Away. (Photo courtesy Trevor Rabin.)*

Trevor Rabin can trace his musical roots back to his paternal great-grandfather, a cantor from Lithuania. While his grandfather, Gershon Rabinowitz, was a kosher butcher who came to South Africa in the late nineteenth century, Trevor's father and two uncles all had musical talent. So did Trevor's mother. His father, Godfrey Rabin, put himself through law school playing violin in jazz combos and spent fourteen years as the leader of the Johannesburg Symphony Orchestra, while also running a law practice. Uncle Morrie Rabin was a piano teacher. Uncle Bertie, a bass singer, immigrated to England and changed his name to Raeburn to break into the opera world. Trevor's mother, Joy, a Jew by choice, was an accomplished pianist, ballet dancer, fine artist, and well-known actress in the theater. (Godfrey and Joy met in the entertainment unit of the South African army in the early forties.) Brother Derek, older by three years, was an award-winning violinist as a teenager until he broke a finger during a motorbike accident at age seventeen. Music, especially jazz and classical, was a fixture in the Rabin home.

So was morality. The Rabin household was more secular and culturally Jewish than religious, with seders viewed as opportunities for family gatherings, but it was a household in which the pursuit of justice, truth, and mitzvot was paramount. Aside from leading the Johannesburg orchestra, Trevor's father also was a prominent lawyer, and extremely anti-apartheid. Few Jews supported the oppressive apartheid regime that relegated blacks to squalid ghettos and deprived them of civil rights. Most South African Jews were members of the Progressive Party that supported one-man-one-vote legislation and worked for the civil rights of all. "My dad was such a moral guy," Rabin says. "He was always going on about the truth." A paternal first cousin, Sidney Kentridge, was the senior counsel representing the family of black activist Stephen Biko in its wrongful death lawsuit against the government. (Biko, the founder of the country's Black Consciousness Movement, became a martyr to the anti-apartheid cause in 1977 when he died while in the custody of South African police.) The journalist Donald Woods, who wrote the best-selling apartheid exposé, Biko, on which the 1987 film Cry Freedom was based, is a first cousin on Rabin's mother's side.

Bolstering all these crusading family members was the Rabin family's spiritual leader at Temple Israel in Johannesburg, Rabbi Super. "I learned compassion from him. He was a gentle, yet powerful man with incredible depth and foundation," Rabin says. The moral lessons learned from relatives and rabbi alike would guide Rabin throughout his rock 'n' roll career.

Rabin began studying piano at age six and bought his first electric guitar at twelve, having been introduced to rock 'n' roll by schoolmates. His earliest rock music influence was the British band Cliff Richard and the Shadows. Rabin even joined the band's official fan club. By thirteen, he also had become a fan and student of *mbaqanga* and *kwela* music, acoustic Zulu folk music. That year, he spent money he got for his bar mitzvah to upgrade his music equipment. (Of his bar mitzvah, he says, "I was actually looking forward to it, but I was concentrating so much on getting it right, I can't remember much about it.") By age fourteen, Rabin was in a band called the Conglomeration. By sixteen, he was proficient enough on the guitar to be earning "a good living" doing recording sessions for record producers. With the goal of becoming a conductor, he also took private lessons in orchestration and arranging. In 1971, the Conglomeration won a national "Battle of the Bands" contest, then broke up. Later that year, Rabin was drafted into the South African army and, like his parents before him, joined the entertainment unit, where he served for a year. The army was an eye-opening experience for Rabin, who had grown up in an affluent, isolated Jewish neighborhood. He learned more about his country's history and culture of apartheid, and he soldiered with rural Afrikaans farmers who had a completely different outlook on life than he and his family.

Upon his discharge he returned to working in Johannesburg recording studios. During that time he was asked by a local producer to join some other area musicians to record the Jethro Tull hit, "Locomotive Breath," under the band name Rabbitt. The song became a national hit, staying on the record charts for fourteen weeks. Rabin was eighteen. The band didn't become a serious project, however, until the teen idol–cute quartet began drawing overflow crowds at a Johannesburg club called the Take It Easy, where the group was able to develop its original songs. Rabin described the band's sound as pop tunes laced with John McLaughlin–influenced jazz-fusion guitar solos. Rabbitt released its debut album, *Boys Will Be Boys*, in 1976. The record won the equivalent of several Grammy Awards and catapulted Rabin and his bandmates to national stardom. The band's followup record, *A Croak and a Grunt in the Night*, proved even more successful and heightened what had become known as "Rabbitt-mania." Rabin's classically trained parents were completely supportive of the band; Trevor's father even played violin on the Rabbitt recordings.

Rabin, however, was an uncomfortable and unhappy star. He was becoming increasingly frustrated with the South African government's racist policies and decided to leave the country. "It was tough to leave," he recalled in a 1988 interview. "I was in a big band living in the lap of luxury. People didn't believe I would go. But I was upset about playing to segregated audiences." Rabin settled in England in 1978, hung out a shingle as a record producer, and ended up signing a recording contract with Chrysalis Records. In 1979, he married Shelley May, his high school sweetheart. From 1978 through 1981, he released three solo records he says he'd rather forget. The record company pressured Rabin to jump on the punk-rock craze seizing the U.K. at the time, but he refused. "Much of that was a social comment on conditions in England and I couldn't feel that in my bones," says Rabin who hadn't been in the country very long. Even worse, he recalls, was the record company trying to take advantage of his good looks, and billing him as the "Donnie Osmond of heavy metal."

In 1981, with his solo career stalled, Rabin took the advice of an American record company executive and relocated to the United States to work on his music. The following year, he began polishing the songs for what he intended to be his first American solo record. During that time, he was invited by former Yes members Steve Howe and Geoff Downe to join their new band, Asia. He practiced with the band but the chemistry wasn't right, and he declined, even though he needed the money. He also had been offered a job touring with Foreigner as a keyboard player but couldn't get the proper working papers in time. Shortly after declining to join Asia, and just before he was to sign a recording contract with RCA Records, former Yes bassist Chris Squire called looking for a guitarist. Yes had disbanded in 1980, and Squire was starting a new band called Cinema with former Yes drummer Alan White. Squire had heard a tape of Rabin's music and was impressed. Rabin joined Cinema, and so did former Yes man, keyboard player Tony Kaye. The foursome recorded an album using much of the music from what was to be Rabin's debut solo record, including Rabin's song, "Owner of a Lonely Heart." Squire asked Yes singer Jon Anderson to listen to the record, then invited him to sing on it. All were ecstatic at the result: polished yet powerful hook-laden pop with precise harmonies and musical edginess. With three original members (Squire, Anderson, Kaye) and one longtime member (White) of Yes now involved, Atlantic, the band's record company, suggested Cinema change its name to Yes.

Rabin was reluctant, even though Yes had a worldwide fan base and access to immediate airplay. He had written most of the songs before joining Cinema and

didn't want to "ride on the back of someone else's past glories." He finally relented. "Owner of a Lonely Heart" shot up the record charts, spent two weeks of
1984 at the top of the heap, and became the first and only Yes song to reach
No. 1. A followup single, "Leave It," reached No. 27, while the six-minute opus
"Changes" became a rock radio favorite.

The band released a followup album, *Big Generator*, in 1987. Rabin's role ex-
panded to include producing, engineering, arranging strings, playing guitar, and
singing as well as writing the hit single "Love Will Find a Way" (No. 30), and co-
writing six of the seven other songs. In 1989, between Yes albums and tours,
Rabin recorded his fourth and most acclaimed solo album, *Can't Look Away*. The
record integrated rock 'n' roll with the Zulu street music he loved as a child in
South Africa. The title song was a commentary on his native land, which he saw
as a "fool's paradise that could turn any minute." He considers it the most spiritual song he's ever written as "it talks about life and is an attempt to make sense
of what this all means."

Rabin served as producer, engineer, and guitarist on two more Yes studio albums, *Union* in 1991 and *Talk* in 1994, before leaving the band in 1995. While he
enjoyed performing, the record-making process, record company pressure to deliver another "Owner of a Lonely Heart," and band politics had become tedious.
"The graph was not going up, it was staying parallel to the ground. It got to the
point where I wanted to move on and embrace the unknown. It's much more exciting," says Rabin.

The unknown turned out to be composing music for films. He had always
found himself critiquing the music when watching movies, so he decided to see
if he could do better. While he played guitar on the soundtrack of the 1996 film
*Twister*, his real break came after giving actor Steven Segal guitar lessons. When
Segal asked if there was anything he could do for Rabin, Rabin wasn't shy,
and asked for film score work. Segal happened to have a film called *The Glimmer
Man* that needed music. That led to writing some of the music for the Arnold
Schwarzenegger film, *Eraser*, and to composing the score for the Nicolas Cage action film *Con Air*. In 1998, three films for which Rabin composed the music were
released, the small-scale, quaint *Homegrown*, the blockbuster doomsday flick *Ar-
mageddon*, and the holiday romance *Jack Frost* starring Michael Keaton and Kelly
Preston. He also began work on the music for *Enemy of the State*. In addition to all
that, his son Ryan became a bar mitzvah. In 1999, he composed the soundtrack

for *Deep Blue Sea* and began work on *Gone in 60 Seconds*, released in 2000. He also provided the soundtrack for the Denzel Washington film *Remember the Titans*, also released in 2000. Between film scores and soundtracks, he has played guitar on recording sessions for Michael Jackson, Manfred Mann, Tina Turner, and Rick Wakeman, among others.

Throughout Rabin's career, morality and integrity have been more important barometers than money or fame for making life-changing decisions. He left his homeland and a successful band because he couldn't abide by the country's apartheid policies. He refused to jump on the profitable punk-rock trend in England because it wouldn't have been morally or artistically honest. At a time when he really needed the money, he turned down membership in a super-group because he wasn't passionate about the music the band was making. He had to think long and hard whether changing the name of Cinema to Yes was an honest move. And of making records, he says, "You should only make an album because you have something to say, not because the last one sold nine million units."

# Johnny Clegg

**Singer. Songwriter. Guitar and concertina player. Born June 7, 1953,
Rochdale, Lancashire, England. Best known as the co-founder and leader
of South Africa's first multiracial band, Juluka, which had a series
of national hits, and later Savuka, which scored a No. 1
international hit with "Assimbonanga" in 1987.**

*Internationally acclaimed for fusing African rhythms with western song structure, Johnny Clegg spent
years coming to grips with his dual identity as an African and a Jew. (Photo courtesy Johnny Clegg.)*

Johnny Clegg was already an international pop star and a hero in the anti-apartheid movement when he went to see a rabbi in 1990 to help resolve the conflict inside him over his Jewish identity. He also had begun reading books on Judaism and Jewish history, such as Paul Johnson's *A History of the Jews*, to gain insight into his neglected heritage. Clegg began to reconnect; he was in his late thirties. One of the results of his re-examination of his roots and beliefs was the Grammy-nominated album *Heat, Dust and Dreams*. Released in 1993, it featured "The Crossing," a song about coming to terms with who he really was.

Until the nineties, Clegg was more knowledgeable of, and comfortable with, the Zulu culture he had embraced as a teenager than he was of the Jewish culture and religion he had been born into. He spoke Zulu but didn't know Hebrew. He learned to sing in Zulu, but not Hebrew. He had become an expert at the ritual Zulu stick dancing called *Inhlangwini*, but didn't know the *horah*. He had a better grasp of the Zulu concept of God than the Jewish one.

As an adolescent, Clegg rebelled against his heritage, going so far as to refuse to become a bar mitzvah or even associate with other Jewish kids at his school. Later, though he married a Jewish woman, he made sure they had a traditional Zulu wedding along with a Jewish ceremony officiated by a rabbi under a *chuppah*. And while his sons were circumcised, he viewed it as a forced entry into the covenant.

For years he had been trying to make peace with his dual identity as an African and a Jew, define what it really meant to be a Jew, and determine how he could incorporate that into his life. Part of the problem was that Zulu and Jewish cultures were contradictory. But much of his internal conflict, he believed, came from being overwhelmed by the Jews' history of persecution.

"I was exposed, like all my generation, to the fact of the Holocaust, and that I belonged, whether I liked it or not, to a minority which had been historically persecuted," he explains. "I sometimes think that my initial denial of my Jewish connection was related to the heavy weight and responsibility of this collective group memory and all the emotional and social burdens it implied."

On the other hand, the Jewish story made him empathetic, made him reel subconsciously from his country's policy of apartheid. "It certainly made me aware of the concept of an oppressed minority," he says. He adds, however, that his opposition to apartheid "evolved over a period of time from trying simply to be with my black friends and make music, which was forbidden by the laws of cultural and racial segregation of the time."

His identity crisis also had taken root in his mother's interfaith marriage, her frequent moves from country to country, and her shifting views of Judaism. His mother, Murial Braudo, was the daughter of observant Russian Jews (original surname Braslovsky) who immigrated to Rhodesia (now Zimbabwe), where they became farmers. Zimbabwe-born, Clegg's mother attended college in Johannesburg, got involved in the Zionist movement, and was a volunteer in Israel during its war of independence in 1948. But, unable or unwilling to relate to Jewish men, she married a non- Jewish Scotsman who was a pilot in the Royal Air Force. They moved to England where Johnny was born.

The marriage was doomed, and mother and son returned first to Rhodesia, then made *aliyah* to Israel. That lasted for less than a year, when his mother became disillusioned with the Zionism she had been so passionate about, and returned to Rhodesia.

In 1960 she moved to South Africa to pursue a singing career. ("She wanted to be Ella Fitzgerald," Clegg says.) Johnny was already seven and wouldn't have his first synagogue experience until he was nine. Concerned that Johnny was learning little if anything about Judaism, an uncle took him to a Shabbat synagogue service, but the experience did not resonate with him. He saw old people praying, while the kids were outside playing and having more fun.

Of his minimal Jewish education, Clegg told an interviewer in *Cutting Through the Mountain*, a book about Jews involved in the anti-apartheid movement, "I said to my mother, 'You know you never really gave me a Jewish upbringing.' She answered, 'Yes, but the important thing was that I never denied I was Jewish. All I said to you was, 'Study the Ten Commandments, and if you can get half of them right you're way ahead of everybody. That's all it is—You keep the Ten Commandments – don't worry about the rest.'"

Life became more confusing when his mother married a younger man who was, again, not Jewish. Johnny was seven. He was twelve when his sister was born. That marriage didn't last either. In an ironic twist, while his mother went on to become involved in Buddhism, his sister turned toward Orthodox Judaism, married an observant Jew, and eventually moved to Israel. ("She gets a lot of sustenance, and a lot of meaning and structure from her faith," Clegg said in *Cutting Through the Mountain*.)

If Clegg spent years confused about his identity, the opposite was true when it came to music. He had an unbridled passion for the *kwela* and *mbaqanga* music,

indiginous folk music he heard in the streets and black townships. He also became enamored of Zulu dance and the male dance competitions neighborhood
teams engaged in as masculine rituals.

Though it was against the law, the teenaged Clegg befriended black musicians
and dancers and studied under them. He was arrested countless times for visiting black neighborhoods and hostels where migrant laborers lived. But Clegg returned time after time, studied kwela and mbaqanga guitar techniques, learned
Zulu rhythms and song structure, and became an expert in ritual dancing.

Juluka took root in the mid-seventies when Clegg met farmer-turned-musician
Sipho Mchunu, who had heard about the white kid who could play like a Zulu and
challenged him to a guitar competition. They formed the duo Johnny and Sipho,
and though they were forbidden to play in public and often harassed by authorities, word of them spread; by 1976 they had a hit single with a song called "Woza
Friday (Come Friday)." Meanwhile, Clegg studied social anthropology at the
University of Witswatersrand in Johannesburg and became a lecturer there.

Musically, Clegg and Mchunu began experimenting with combining English
lyrics and Western melodies and electric instruments with Zulu rhythms, chanting, song structure, and social commentary. They put together a band and dubbed
it Juluka, the Zulu word for "sweat." The result was a sound that was powerful,
seductive and unlike anything ever heard in the country before. As the first integrated band in South Africa, it was also unlike anything ever *seen* before. Incorporating Zulu dance into their concerts was frosting on this colorful cake. (Juluka
was one of the inspirations behind Paul Simon's 1986 album, *Graceland*.)

"Juluka was never a political protest band, although political themes form a
considerable part of the repertoire," Clegg wrote in the liner notes of the 1996
compilation, *A Johnny Clegg and Juluka Collection*. "Juluka was more a band seeking
to find meeting points between modern and traditional society, rural and urban
experiences, exploring as many facets of the cultural reality of South Africa, trying to find commonalities and universal themes." The band, Clegg added, "was
more about trying to stand for something rather than protesting against a specific issue." Juluka was radical in the simplest of ways: A band of black and white
musicians playing a brand of music that blended "black" and "white" concepts
in a country whose official government policy was one of segregation.

The release of the albums *Universal Men* (1979) and *African Litany* (1981) propelled Juluka to stardom in South Africa and beyond. With the band's fame

spreading to Europe, Clegg left academia to devote all his energy to music. With the release of *Scatterlings* in late 1982, Juluka's popularity and influence was cemented in Africa and Europe and spread to the United States, where even without a hit single, the band was a hot concert attraction. In 1985, exhausted from touring and from the constant harassment of South African authorities, Mchunu decided to return to the family farm.

The following year, Clegg formed a new band called Savuka (Zulu for "we have awakened"). Leaning more toward Western rock and pop music, the band's 1987 debut, *Third World Child*, sold more than two million copies. A single from the album, "Assimbonanga," a veiled call for the release from prison of Nelson Mandela, was banned in South Africa but became a hit throughout Europe. The followup album, *Shadow Man*, earned the group opening act spots on a Steve Winwood tour of the US, and a George Michael tour of Canada in 1988. Clegg released two more acclaimed Savuka albums—*Cruel, Crazy, Beautiful World* in 1989 and *Heat, Dust and Dreams* in 1993—touring extensively. Ironically, Clegg sometimes found himself at odds with the international anti-apartheid movement, members of which felt the interracial band was making the government look good. If the South African government was racist, then what were these guys doing freely traveling about the globe? On one occasion, Savuka was denied permission to perform at a birthday concert for Nelson Mandela held at Wembley Stadium in England.

In 1996, Clegg reunited with Sipho Mchunu for a Juluka reunion album and a tour that included twenty-five shows in the United States. In the nineties, Clegg formed his own record company as well as a management company to develop and showcase other South African acts. In the summer of 2002, the South African national hero and pop star set up shop for a two-week run at the Johannesburg Civic Theatre to perform a career retrospective: "Johnny Clegg: A South African Story." Much of Clegg's repertoire included songs about defining himself as an African, but at least one alluded to discovering himself as a Jew.

*Sharon Katz campaigned for Nelson Mandela.*
*(Photo by Susan Bulkin.)*

In 1993, another Jewish singer-songwriter rose to prominence in South Africa. Sharon Katz, born September 18, 1955, grew up in Port Elizabeth where her Zionist parents helped found the Theodor Herzl Primary and High School. Katz became fluent in Hebrew and got involved in *Habonim*, the Jewish youth movement. "The Jewish youth movement taught me a lot about politics and helped me define who I was as a person and a Jew. The concept of *Or L'Goyim* (Light unto the Nations) was very much a part of my morality, and had a strong influence on me," Katz says. Katz began studying guitar at age eleven, and formed one of her earliest professional bands at fifteen, Shalom Bomb, which played a mix of American protest songs, Jewish folk songs and contemporary Israeli and African music. Like Clegg, she was fascinated by African music, befriended black musicians, and began sneaking into black townships to study and perform with them. In 1993, Katz became a household name after forming When Voices Meet, a 500-person integrated youth choir, whose landmark concerts in Durban were broadcast nationwide on radio and television. She solidified her reputation when she and her backup band the Peace Train campaigned, much of it at train stops, for Nelson Mandela in 1993 and 1994. In 1996, her song "Siyajabula (We Are Happy)," inspired by Mandela's presidential victory, became an anthem for the country's national soccer team. Clegg and Katz contributed songs to *Carnival!*, a benefit CD for pop star Sting's Rainforest Foundation, but the two musicians have met only once.

# Billy Steinberg

**Songwriter. Born February 26, 1950, Fresno, California.
Best known for co-writing five No. 1 hits including "Like a Virgin,"
"True Colors," and "So Emotional."**

*Billy Steinberg, center, during a 1989 songwriting session with Bangles singer and guitarist Susanna Hoffs
(the granddaughter of a rabbi) and co-writer Tom Kelly. (Photo by Bill Rubenstein, courtesy of Billy Steinberg.)*

Billy Steinberg still remembers when his Sunday school class at Temple Isaiah in Palm Springs, California, visited the temple sanctuary and learned about the "Ner Tamid," the Eternal Flame. The Eternal Flame made a lasting impression on the future hit songwriter.

"I remember they'd take us into this darkened, quiet synagogue and there was just this little red light bulb. They called it the eternal flame and I remember thinking, 'Wow, an eternal flame that never goes out!' It seemed like a very deep thought, like contemplating the stars in the sky. I filed it in the Wonderment File." Years later, he says, "It jumped out as a song title."

The ballad "Eternal Flame," co-written with longtime collaborator Tom Kelly and Bangles guitarist and singer Susanna Hoffs, became a No. 1 hit in 1989 for the Bangles, an all-female pop-rock quartet. (The Bangles previously had reached No. 1 in 1986 with "Walk Like an Egyptian.") By 1989, the Steinberg-Kelly song-writing team had turned writing number one hits into a habit. Their credits included Madonna's "Like a Virgin" (1984), Cyndi Lauper's "True Colors" (1986), Whitney Houston's "So Emotional" (1987), and Heart's "Alone" (1987).

Steinberg didn't have the typical urban Jewish experience. He was born in Fresno in 1950 and moved to Palm Springs in 1958. His great grandparents were from Poland and Alsace-Lorraine, but his father, Lionel Steinberg, was born in Fresno and joined his stepfather's farming business, the David Freedman Company, growing table grapes. Besides being a grape grower, papa Steinberg was also an ardent Zionist who contributed to numerous Jewish causes in deed as well as financially. In 1959, Lionel Steinberg represented the state of California and Senator Clair Engle at a forty-nation World Farmers Conference in Israel. He made trips to Israel to teach grape-growing techniques, helped bring certain varieties of dates to Israel as a crop, and trained Israeli farmers on his California farm to grow grapes in the desert. He also sat on the board of trustees of Ben-Gurion University until his death in 1999.

Though the family didn't put a great deal of emphasis on religious observance, Billy's father's love and support for Israel fostered a strong sense of Jewish pride. "There was always a strong feeling in our home that we were, culturally speaking, proud of our Jewish heritage, and that we needed to help Israel in whatever way possible," Steinberg says. The elder Steinberg also taught his son a lesson right out of the Talmud about pursuing justice when, in 1970, Lionel Steinberg gave labor leader Cesar Chavez and the United Farm Workers their first contract. "My father was unusual as a farmer," Steinberg says. "He was Jewish and a Democrat while most other farmers were Italians, Armenians, or Slavs and staunch Republicans."

Observant or not, Billy Steinberg did have a bar mitzvah. "One thing I remember about it is all my gentile pals were sitting there, and of course I was feeling embarrassed and nervous," Steinberg says. But he remembers Rabbi Joseph Hurwitz giving "a rather out-of-the-ordinary preliminary speech to the audience, telling them some things about Judaism and bar mitzvahs because he realized most of the audience was not Jewish." Among those in attendance at Temple Isaiah were family friends Dinah Shore and Frank Sinatra's wife, Barbara. Steinberg still uses a pair of binoculars and a leather-bound dictionary he received as bar mitzvah gifts.

By his bar mitzvah, Steinberg already was a music aficionado, having fallen in love with songs from listening to the radio, older friends' records and his dad's blues collection, which included the music of Leadbelly, Josh White, and Sonny Terry and Brownie McGhee. In fact, by the age of eight, Steinberg already had a sizable singles collection. The Everly Brothers and Ricky Nelson were early favorites. Nelson's "Poor Little Fool" and the Everly's "All I Have to Do Is Dream" had "a plaintive, melodic quality that seemed to affect me," Steinberg explains.

From ages six through eight, Steinberg says, "I bought records whenever I could get my hands on a dollar bill. I drove my parents crazy listening to the same songs over and over, thirty or forty times a day." He still has every single he bought since 1958.

As a teen, Steinberg developed a love of language, much of it from playing frequent games of Scrabble with his mother, Louise, and began writing songs. By junior high school Steinberg was the lead singer in a band called the Fables, and in high school was in a band called Dirt. By the time he reached Bard College as a Literature major, Steinberg was in his folkie phase and had dreams of being the next Bob Dylan. (Donald Fagen and Walter Becker of Steely Dan fame were Bard seniors when Steinberg was a freshman.) "I liked everything about Dylan, the poetic quality of his lyrics, his vocal style. I think Dylan is very underrated as a singer. He has a very expressive way of singing."

After college Steinberg joined the family business, learning Spanish from farm workers and becoming fluent. In his spare time, however, he wrote songs on the guitar. "I never had any music lessons," he says. "My lessons were from the records I listened to, the concerts I attended, the bands I played in and the songs I wrote. My musicianship is the weakest link in my songwriting skills. That's why I seek out collaborators who are superior musicians."

By the late seventies, with New Wave the rage, Steinberg was fronting a rock band again and playing Los Angeles clubs on weekends as Billy Thermal (named after Thermal, California, the town where the family farm was located.) and pitching his songs to music publishers. By 1979, Steinberg had a recording contract with Planet Records. But if Linda Ronstadt hadn't heard one of his songs, Steinberg might be running his family's vineyard in the California desert. Steinberg's big break came in 1980, when a member of his band passed a demo tape to Ronstadt. Her rendition of Steinberg's rocker "How Do I Make You" became a hit that year. While Steinberg's dream of being the next Dylan was fizzling, his songwriting career took off. "The first song I ever had covered was a Top Ten hit for Linda Ronstadt. I got a music attorney and had instant credibility as a songwriter," Steinberg says.

His hits, most of them co-written with Tom Kelly, include the No. 1 songs mentioned above as well as the Bangles' "In Your Room" (No. 5 in 1988), Cyndi Lauper's "I Drove All Night" (No. 6 in 1989), Susanna Hoffs's "My Side of the Bed" (No. 30 in 1991), the Divinyls' "I Touch Myself" (No. 4 in 1991), and the Pretenders' "I'll Stand By You" (No. 16 in 1994). Over the years, Steinberg's songs also have been recorded by Roy Orbison, Phil Collins, Bette Midler, Tina Turner, and the brother-and-sister Celtic-pop band, the Corrs. Israeli singer Rita has recorded a Steinberg song and Steinberg collaborated on a song with Israeli singing sensation Noa.

Steinberg's songs are overwhelmingly recorded by women or female-fronted bands. He's not sure why, but it may be because he has the knack of looking at all the angles of love from a woman's perspective. He doesn't intentionally write for female voices. "I just write stuff that pops out of my head," he says, adding that, "I guess I'm in touch with my feminine side. I enjoy cooking. I collect beads, and I write pretty good songs for women."

The Steinberg-Kelly alliance began in 1981 after record producer Keith Olsen introduced the two at a party. Steinberg had the Ronstadt hit to his credit and Pat Benatar had just recorded a pair of his songs as well. Kelly had been making a name for himself as a versatile recording session backup singer for a variety of acts ranging from Barbra Streisand to Motley Crue and had performed as a backup singer with Toto, Dan Fogelberg, and the Eagles. While Kelly was known as a singer, his songwriting career was in its infancy. The partnership, says Steinberg, "was good for both of us. We wrote songs together that were better than either of us could have written separately. We're an odd couple—different as night and day. He's a laid-back golfing guy from the Midwest and I'm a bit more driven, a Jewish type if I do say so myself." But they had similar musical tastes, eventually figured out each other's writing strengths, and developed mutual respect for each other's instincts. (In the late 1990s, with Kelly scaling back, Steinberg began successfully collaborating with writers Rick Nowels and Marie-Claire D'Ubaldo.)

Steinberg has very particular writing habits. He carries student notebooks and writes whenever he gets an idea—possible song titles, poems, whatever comes to mind. He never uses a rhyming dictionary, or a typewriter or word processor. He has used the same Mount Blanc fountain pen for more than fifteen years, and he uses only black ink. "A fountain pen and a blank piece of paper is like a dream world for me," he says.

Steinberg's writing methods and creative muse continued to pay off during the latter half of the 1990s. He co-wrote and co-produced the title track of Celine Dion's 1996 album, *Falling Into You*, as well as Italian pop singer Robert Miles's 1996 European smash "One and One." In 1999, the songwriter's name seemed omnipresent, with three collaborations on the Pretenders' *Viva el Amor* album, two on heartthrob Enrique Iglesias's *Enrique* album, and a pair on former Spice Girl Melanie C's solo record, *Northern Star*. He also co-wrote Amber's 1999 No. 1 dance hit "Sexual (Li Da Di)."

But there is more to Steinberg's life than songwriting. He's married and the father of two sons. Growing up around a farm, he developed a love of the land, and today he contributes to a variety of environmental causes. He is president of the environmental group Friends of the Indian Canyons, which is dedicated to preserving land in the California desert, not far from where the family grape fields were located. It is his small way of repairing the world.

# Don Was
## of Was (Not Was)

**Songwriter. Multi-instrumentalist. Producer. Born Don Edward Fagenson,
September 13, 1952, Detroit, Michigan. Best known for co-founding
the soul-rock-funk band Was (Not Was) and co-writing the group's
Top Twenty hits, "Walk the Dinosaur" and "Spy in the House of Love."
Also credited with reviving the career of Bonnie Raitt as producer of her
hit-filled, multi-Grammy–winning albums *Nick of Time* and *Luck of the
Draw*. He won the 1995 Grammy Award for Producer of the Year.**

*Don Was embraces the morality of the Torah. (Photo courtesy Don Was.)*

*Was (Not Was) in 1988. From left, Sweet Pea Atkinson, Don Was, David
Was, Sir Harry Bowen. (Photo by Paul Natkin, Photo Reserve, Inc.)*

Don Was will always remember Rosh Hashanah of 1964, not for the religious experience he had, but for the musical experience he lost. At the time, he was twelve-year-old Donald Fagenson, and he had tickets (restricted view) to see the Beatles at Olympia Stadium in Detroit. His parents didn't realize Rosh Hashanah and the concert coincided until the eleventh hour, and forbade him to experience "Beatlemania." The Mop Tops from Liverpool were a little too mysterious and risqué for Rosh Hashanah. Instead, as a consolation, William and Harriet Fagenson took their son to the Michigan State Fair to hear the New Christy Minstrels, a folk group featuring Barry McGuire, sing its hit "Green, Green." The New Christy Minstrels, recalls Was, "were two degrees cleaner than the Beatles, and [his parents] thought that was observing the holiday." If missing the Beatles was in any way a motivating moment for Was, then it succeeded beyond anyone's expectations.

Similar to musician-songwriter-producer Al Kooper, Was has missed little of consequence in the world of popular music since the eclectic Was (Not Was) notched a pair of Top Twenty hits in 1988 and Don went on to produce singer-guitarist Bonnie Raitt's 1989 album, Nick of Time, which sold four million copies and won the Grammy Award for Album of the Year. That year, he also co-produced with Nile Rodgers (each was responsible for half the album) the B-52s' bestselling record, Cosmic Thing, which included the Top Five hits "Love Shack" (Was), and "Roam" (Rodgers). Those successes catapulted Was onto the short list of producers with the Midas touch. He solidified his reputation producing Raitt's Grammy-winning 1991 followup, Luck of the Draw, which included the Top Twenty hits, "Something to Talk About" and "I Can't Make You Love Me." Since then, the much in-demand Was has made records with childhood musical heroes, including Bob Dylan (Under the Red Sky), the Rolling Stones (Voodoo Lounge, Stripped, Bridges to Babylon), Beatles drummer Ringo Starr (Time Takes Time), and Willie Nelson (Across the Border Line). (Was planned an afternoon of the recording sessions for Dylan's 1990 album Under the Red Sky as "All Jews Day" with Dylan's supporting cast Was, Al Kooper on organ, drummer Kenny Aronoff, guitarist Waddy Wachtel, engineer Ed Cherney, and co-producer David Was.)

Was also produced numerous film soundtrack albums and songs, including the Oscar-nominated Randy Newman–Lyle Lovett duet, "You've Got a Friend in Me," from the 1996 film Toy Story. He also has served as musical director for special events, including the 1993 Rock and Roll Hall of Fame Awards Ceremony, ABC Television's Elvis Presley tribute in 1994, the *Kennedy Center Tribute to Willie Nelson* in 1998, the *Seventy-second Annual Academy Awards* in 2000, and the *Kennedy Center's Tribute to Chuck Berry* in 2000. He also established himself as a director of music videos and film documentaries, the most notable being the 1995 *Brian Wilson: I Just Wasn't Made for These Times*, about the creative force behind the Beach Boys.

Don Was began life as Donald Fagenson in a heavily Jewish section of Detroit. His paternal grandfather, Edward Fagenson, who had a fabric business, emigrated from a shtetl outside Kiev around the turn of the century and first settled in Omaha. He died about twenty years before Don was born. (Don's other grandparents were of Russian, Hungarian, and Polish decent.) His maternal grandfather was a Detroit butcher, and "not a terribly religious guy." His parents were both schoolteachers. His father, William, became a guidance counselor at Oak Park High School where Don was a student. His mother, Harriet, became an assistant principal at another area high school. Oak Park High, according to Don was about 80 percent Jewish, 10 percent black, and 10 percent "everything else." (His younger sister, Nancy Potok, is the chief financial officer of the U.S. Census Bureau.)

The family belonged to Reform Temple Emanuel, where Don went to Hebrew school and had a bar mitzvah with Rabbi Milton Rosenbaum officiating. Don describes the congregation as one that tried to melt into the dominant culture. The temple looked like a church, there was a choir in robes, no cantor, and most of the services were in English. He describes Hebrew school as one of his worst memories because though he learned to read Hebrew, he didn't learn the meaning behind the words. "My Jewish education was utterly void of anything significant. It was ritual without foundation," Was says. "I never learned the significance or importance of it. My Haftorah was something about a goat." He believes he and others of his generation were never instructed in the "whys" of Judaism, and thus became somewhat disconnected from it, because Jewish leaders were focusing on survival and maintaining tradition, rather than on meaning. "When you combine the immigrant need to disappear into the fabric of the new culture, not just Jews, but anyone who left any place for fear of their lives, with the political move of draining the mysticism and significance of our religion, then you've got a real problem." Was solved that problem for himself, and eventually for his children by "painting in broad strokes" and providing his eldest child, Anthony, with Judaism's core concepts and a more mystical outlook. "This can't-drive-on-Saturday doesn't play so well in Beverly Hills," Was says. But Jewish ethics, and responsibility, and the idea that every move you make has consequences, are important concepts to him.

Music was important, too, and was playing frequently in the Fagenson household. Harry Belafonte, Peter, Paul and Mary, and Alan Sherman comedy records were favorites. Don's mother was a fan of the TV program *American Bandstand* and Don enjoyed watching *Hootenanny*. ("There was a moment when that was rebellious, alternative music," Was says.) By age eleven, Don was in his first band, the Saturns, playing acoustic guitar. The band performed the Tokens' hit "The Lion Sleeps Tonight," at a school hootenanny, which also featured a singer named Moishe who taught guitar at the local Jewish community center, and a duo billed as Chuck Mitchell and Wife (her name was Joni). The week after the Beatles appeared on *The Ed Sullivan Show*, Don showed up at band practice with an electric pick-up on his guitar and an amplifier. He was louder than the rest of the band, prompting the other guitar player to buy an electric guitar. By seventh grade, the Saturns had evolved into a rock band, but because of group infighting didn't last long. (Was credits the Saturns' dissension with preparing him later in life to produce the Rolling Stones.)

Don met his future musical partner, David Weiss (born October 26, 1952, Detroit, Michigan), in junior high school. They both got in trouble in gym class, and the kindred spirits became fast friends. "David's the only person on earth who has gone through everything with me. We have identical roots," Don says. They spent lots of time collaborating on songs with Fagenson generally coming up with the music for Weiss's satirical, sarcastic, often out-in-left field lyrics. Weiss, a flute and saxophone player, eventually moved to Los Angeles where he wrote music reviews. Fagenson, whose primary instrument was now the bass guitar, began playing on recording sessions, and doing some production work and performing in lounges. But neither Don nor David found much satisfaction in their work.

In the early eighties the duo began collaborating on what would become their debut album. They added area musicians, most notably black lead vocalists Sir Harry Bowens, who delivered the velvet-toned ballads, and Sweet Pea Atkinson, who provided hard-edged soul with his gravel voice. It was like having Smokey Robinson and Otis Redding in the same band. Fagenson and Weiss dubbed the group "Was (Not Was)" after a word association game Fagenson's toddler son played at the time. They also became the Was Brothers. The band started to gain notoriety in 1980 for a dance single called "Wheel Me Out." The group followed that with its debut album, *Was (Not Was)*, in 1981. The band combined deep-grooved funk, sweet soul, rock, and even jazz influences with lyrics that ran from romantic to zany and titles that were simply strange, such as "Earth to Doris," and "Dad, I'm in Jail."

Other songs were sobering and provocative, such as "11 mph," about the assassination of John F. Kennedy. While the debut album received critical acclaim and was popular in dance clubs, it didn't sell well. They followed it in 1983 with the critically acclaimed *Born to Laugh at Tornadoes*, which earned as much attention for its odd assortment of musical guests—(Jewish) jazz singer Mel Torme and metal head Ozzy Osbourne, among them—as for the intriguing music the band delivered. But that record also failed to produce a hit song, and the group was dropped by its record company. Was (Not Was) waited five years to release its third album, but the wait was worth it. *What Up, Dog?*, released in 1988, was a hit not only with critics but with the public as well. It included a pair of Top Twenty hits, the driving R&B delight, "Spy in the House of Love," which reached No. 16 on the pop charts, and the funk-filled novelty, "Walk the Dinosaur," which made it all the way to No. 7. The record also featured Frank Sinatra, Jr., on a tune titled "Wedding Vows in Vegas," as well as a couple of solid pop songs that got lost in the shuffle: "Anytime Lisa," and "Anything Can Happen." The funk 'n' soul–filled Was (Not Was) returned in 1990 with *Are You Okay?*, which featured a rousing version of the Motown classic, "Papa Was a Rolling Stone," and more tunes with oddball titles such as "I Blew up the United States" and "Elvis's Rolls Royce." By the end of 1992, Was (Not Was) wasn't. Reports were that the band's demise stemmed from Don's rising star as a producer, creating tension between him and David. Was says it was a combination of self-inflicted intimidation at not being as good as his musical heroes, and record company pressure to deliver another hit like "Walk the Dinosaur." Says Was: "We stopped because we lost our voice."

David got involved with playing, producing, and serving as musical director on soundtracks for Broadway musicals (The Lion King), TV shows (The Wonder Years, X-Files), and films (The Flintstones, An American Werewolf in Paris). Don became one of the busiest producers in the record business. He developed a reputation for having the knack to put the right musicians together on the right songs, giving them enough leeway to add to the creative process, making the sessions enjoyable, and being versatile enough to produce almost any genre of musical act. His diverse credits include pop singer Paula Abdul, Mexican "rock en Espanol" stars Jaguares, Jamaican reggae band Ziggy Marley and the Melody Makers, South African World Beat star Johnny Clegg, Nashville icons Conway Twitty, Travis Tritt, and Clint Black, and blues legend B. B. King.

In 1998, Was (Not Was) regrouped and began working leisurely on a new record that had no timetable for completion. "We found our voice," Don says. He also kept busy as a producer as well as a performer, touring in 1998 with Bon Jovi guitarist Richie Sambora, whose album Undiscovered Soul he also produced. It also was the year of being a proud papa as son Anthony, the drummer in the rock band Eve 6, followed in his father's footsteps with a debut hit album, Eve 6, and Top Thirty single, "Inside Out." In 2000, albums with Was's production stamp included the Barenaked Ladies' Maroon as well as Bette Midler's Bette. That year, he wrapped up production on the latest Black Crowes album, Lions, released in 2001. And in early 2001 he became involved in social action, meeting with a group called the Progressive Jewish Alliance, whose primary mission is to repair the rift between Jews and blacks.

The strong social statement made by the black-Jewish alliance that remains at the core of Was (Not Was) has not been lost on Don. It crystallized for him in Mobile, Alabama, in 1990 when the band was at a low point, opening for dance and hip-hop acts on the Club MTV Tour. During a solo ride to the airport, his cab driver peppered his conversation with racist epithets, until he asked Was why he was in town. When Was responded that he was in town performing with his band Was (Not Was), the driver immediately apologized for his bigoted remarks. He was familiar with the band. The mere presence of white and black musicians onstage together made enough of a statement to cause the cabbie to ask forgiveness. "At that moment, I felt the power of the band," Was says. "It was a pivotal moment that attested to the power of the union of Jews and blacks in everything."

*Israeli singer Ofra Haza in 1992.*
*(Photo courtesy Shanachie Records.)*

Of the dozens of acts Was produced, few, if any, left more of an impression than Israeli singing star Ofra Haza. Haza (born Nov. 19, 1959 in Tel Aviv), began performing at age twelve, but her career took off in 1983, at age twenty-three, after winning second place at the prestigious Eurovision Song Contest with a song sung in Hebrew, "Ani Od Hai" (I'm Still Alive). Haza became a star when her song "Im Nin'alu," a love song based on a poem by seventeenth-century rabbi Shalom Shabazi, became an international hit in 1988. Haza, who gained popularity in the United States after rappers Eric B. and Rakim sampled the song on their dance hit "Paid in Full," based much of her music on ancient Jewish texts and prayers. (The rap group M/A/R/R/S also sampled her voice on its 1988 hit, "Pump Up the Volume.")

Besides releasing some two dozen albums in various international markets, Haza sang backup on records by Paula Abdul, Thomas Dolby, and Sisters of Mercy. She also performed in Oslo, Norway, in 1994 when Israeli prime minister Yitzhak Rabin, foreign minister Shimon Peres, and Palestinian leader Yasser Arafat were awarded the Nobel Peace Prize. In 1998, she sang the role of Moses' mother in the animated film *Prince of Egypt*.

Haza and Was met in 1989 at the Tokyo Music Festival. Was heard Haza during a sound check and was mesmerized and enthralled by the other-worldliness of her voice. He felt Haza was "channeling something that was ten thousand years old." Through Haza, Was discovered a form of Judaism with which he was unfamiliar. "She was so spiritually aware," Was says, "the Judaism she was describing to me was Judaism I didn't know about. It was non-American Judaism. It had nothing to do with who's going to be elected president of the temple next year. It had to do with a profoundly spiritual connection." They became friends, and Was produced Haza's 1992 album, *Kirya*, which was nominated for a Grammy Award in the Best World Music category and became a No. 1 record in Israel, where she was a superstar. The album, much of it based on traditional

Yemenite melodies, included a song influenced by the terror caused by Scud missiles raining on Israel during the Gulf War in 1991. Called "Trains of No Return," it is a prayer that the Holocaust never be repeated. In 1995, Haza and Was were set to make a documentary film of Haza returning to her parents' native Yemen to retrieve the body of a famous rabbi for reburial in Israel. She also was scheduled to perform a concert for Jews in Yemen, and perhaps help some of them return to Israel with her. Bringing the dwindling, oft-persecuted Jews of Yemen "home" to Israel and reuniting them with family members was one of Haza's missions in life. All those plans fell apart on November 4, 1995, with the assassination of Israeli prime minister Yitzhak Rabin as he left a peace rally in Tel Aviv. Any hopes Haza and Was had of making the documentary at a later date were dashed when Haza died unexpectedly at age 41 on February 23, 2000. "She was an extraordinary person," Was says. "When she died, I felt she had simply reached the uppermost levels. She couldn't be any more higher evolved and remain human. In a world with no time and multiple lifetimes, she was moving on to the next plateau."

# David Bryan
## of Bon Jovi

Keyboard player. Composer. Born David Bryan Rashbaum, February 7,
1962, Perth Amboy, New Jersey. Best known as founding member
of the rock band Bon Jovi. Hits include "You Give Love a Bad Name,"
"Livin' on a Prayer," "Wanted Dead or Alive," "Bad Medicine,"
"Born to Be My Baby," "I'll Be There for You," "Lay Your Hands on Me,"
"Bed of Roses," "Always," "It's My Life."

*David Bryan performing in Chicago during Bon Jovi's "big hair" days,*
*circa 1987. (Photo by Paul Natkin, Photo Reserve, Inc.)*

For years, David Bryan has proudly played the role of *baal tekiah*, or shofar blower, during the High Holy Days at Temple Emanu-El in Edison, New Jersey. In fact, Bryan calls himself "the Mark McGwire of *tekiah gadolahs*" and claims the temple record, if not world record, of thirty seconds for longest tekiah gadolah. "I challenge anyone in the world. I can beat out anyone," says Bryan, who co-founded Bon Jovi with Jon Bon Jovi in 1983. He also participates in the children's service on Rosh Hashanah and gets a thrill when "they all pull out their stop watches" to time him.

Bryan is a lifelong member of Temple Emanu-El. He attended Hebrew school, became a bar mitzvah, and was confirmed at the Reform synagogue. His children attend Hebrew school there (and join him on the bima when he is called to sound the ram's horn). Rabbi Alfred Landsberg, who officiated at Bryan's bar mitzvah, remains a guiding influence in Bryan's life. And Bryan remains rooted to his faith. On occasions when Bon Jovi has had to play on Yom Kippur, Bryan fasts. If he doesn't have to play on the High Holy Days, but is on tour, he seeks out a synagogue, no matter where the band is. On one occasion, he attended Yom Kippur services in a synagogue in Hong Kong. Fasting on Yom Kippur is important to him—he has been fasting on the holiday since he was eleven—especially as a member of a superstar act working at a frenetic pace. Performing or not, fasting triggers reflection and reassessment. He views Yom Kippur as an Etch-A-Sketch game of sorts. "You look at [your sins], shake them up, erase them, and start over again," he says. It has helped him maintain his balance in the pressure-packed, precarious world of rock stardom.

Bryan grew up in Edison, New Jersey. His father, Ed Rashbaum, the son of Orthodox Jews who fled Poland before the war, played trumpet in the fifties with a jazz man called Hot Lips Page before getting into the surgical supply business. Bryan was five when his father began teaching him the trumpet. He also studied violin in elementary school and began taking piano lessons at age seven. At thirteen, his father brought him a Farfisa organ and a Honer electric piano as bar mitzvah gifts. By age fourteen, Bryan was playing backyard parties and charity events in a band called Transition. A few years later, he met a singer and guitar player named John Bongiovi. While still in high school, the two put together a ten-piece band complete with horn section called the Atlantic City Expressway. The band played every club on the New Jersey shore within striking distance of returning home in time for school the next day.

After graduating from J. P. Stevens High School, Bryan enrolled at Rutgers University as a double major in pre-med and music. Bryan had visions of becoming an orthopedic surgeon, just like his father's best friend. Then, in his senior year, Bryan decided he wanted to be a classical pianist. He practiced eight to fourteen hours a day for months to pass the "cold, scary, ugly, don't-screw-up" ten-minute audition required to get into the Juilliard School of Music in New York. "My parents knew I was serious, and that anyone who worked that hard would succeed at something," Bryan says. He was accepted into the prestigious school, but before enrolling got a call from John Bongiovi telling him he'd landed a recording contract and inviting Bryan to form a band. "I told him he better not be lying," says Bryan. He turned down Juilliard, dropped out of Rutgers with a 4.0 grade point average, and joined his friend. The initial record contract was less than Bongiovi had described, and for a while the band had to scrape to get by.

Bryan and Bongiovi, however, were determined to make it. There was no Plan B. "If you have nothing to fall back on, all you can do is go forward," Bryan says. "There was no safety net. It was all or nothing. It was commitment beyond reality, dedication beyond what people really think is required." Bryan believes that much of his determination comes from his Jewish heritage, and a history of having to continuously overcome adversity. "Fighting against the odds is in our nature," he says, hoping that perhaps one day, his children won't have to.

By the time Bongiovi and Bryan began working on their debut record, John Bongiovi had become Jon Bon Jovi, the band's namesake, and Rashbaum was going by Bryan, his middle name. By the release of Bon Jovi's self-titled debut in 1984, the band comprised Bon Jovi, Bryan, guitarist Richie Sambora, drummer Tico Torres, and bass player Alec John Such. (The record deal meant Bryan could continue a friendly race to success with Temple Emanu-El's other up-and-coming Jewish keyboard player, David Rosenthal. Rosenthal was a couple of years older and already making a name for himself in former Deep Purple guitarist Ritchie Blackmore's band, Rainbow. Rosenthal went on to tour with Cyndi Lauper, then became a fixture in Billy Joel's backup band.)

Bon Jovi had been honing its blend of what the *Rolling Stone Encyclopedia of Rock and Roll* calls, "good hooks and good looks." It was anthemic, hummable, non-threatening hard rock coupled with a fashionable, carefully coifed, long-haired, but working-class, teen-idol look that would pay huge dividends on MTV during the golden age of rock videos. The band's debut included the modest hit "Runaway," (No. 39). The 1985 follow up album, *7800 Fahrenheit*, spawned a couple of lesser hits and sold half a million copies. The stage was set for a make-or-break third album of what would become known as pop-metal, and would give birth to a whole genre of eighties "big hair bands." The resulting look and sound was marketing genius; it appealed to suburban housewives as well as rebellious teens.

The band called in prolific hit songwriter Desmond Child to help hone the songs for the next album. The band also played the songs for local teenagers and polled the listeners for their favorite songs. Those moves paid off. The band's third album, *Slippery When Wet*, released in 1986, included back-to-back No. 1 singles co-written by Child, "You Give Love a Bad Name," and "Living on a Prayer," as well as the Bon Jovi–Sambora-penned Top Ten hit "Dead or Alive." The album sold nine million copies and, only three years after Bon Jovi's inception, established the band as a superstar attraction. "That's what happens when all the planets and the moon line up, and everything makes sense. Thank God I was a part of it," says Bryan. In 1987, between albums, the band backed Cher in the studio on a self-titled album that would include the hits "I Found Someone" (No. 10) and "We All Sleep Alone" (No. 14).

Bon Jovi would solidify its star status and add to its hit list with the 1988 release of *New Jersey*. Using *Slippery* as a blueprint, the album's first single, "Bad Medicine," co-written by Child, reached No. 1. Another four songs from the record also became Top Ten hits, and *New Jersey* sold five million copies. In the early nineties, Jon Bon Jovi spent time making music for movies. In 1992, the band regrouped to record *Keeping the Faith*, and in 1995 released *These Days*. While successful, neither were the blockbusters their predecessors had been. The band's popularity may have waned a bit at home, but it remained greater than ever abroad. In the later half of the nineties, while Jon Bon Jovi was making solo albums and acting in films, Bryan released his first solo album, *On a Full Moon*. Available only outside the United States, some of the music from the record was used at the 2000 Olympic Games in Sydney, Australia. By then, Bryan was one of the busiest musicians in the business, recording a new Bon Jovi album called *Crush* and following it with a world tour, releasing *Lunar Eclipse*, a sequel to his solo record, and polishing a pair of musicals, *Sweet Valley High* and *Memphis*, for production. The latter is based on the Memphis disc jockey Dewey Phillips, one of the first DJs to play black music on a white radio station.

The new Bon Jovi album, *Crush*, sold more than seven million copies worldwide and spawned the hit single, "It's My Life." With songs such as "Just Older," and a less bombastic delivery of its anthemic style, the band showed it was unafraid to mature and grow old gracefully. Fans responded positively, especially in Europe where during a stretch of twenty shows Bon Jovi played to one million people, an average of fifty thousand fans per concert. In 2002, the band released another album of new songs called *Bounce*. "It's a Cinderella story," says Bryan. "I'm the luckiest guy. I reached for a goal unreachable, worked my ass off, and got it. Many others work hard and don't get it." He is so grateful for his success, and so bereft of cockiness, that he has no problem sitting in with bar mitzvah bands back home. After all, his father always got up to sing "Sunrise, Sunset" at family events, and a cousin who played in the Miss America Pageant band played at Bryan's bar mitzvah. Bryan has kept the rock-star trip in perspective. "That's the path I walk," he says. "No ego. My ego comes from hard work. You learn that every man walks equally. No man is ahead or behind. I truly believe that, and I think that's a big part of my Jewish upbringing."

# Diane Warren

Songwriter. Born Diane Eve Warren, September 7, 1956, Van Nuys, California. Warren is one of the most commercially successful songwriters in contemporary pop music. She has written so many hits that at least three airlines offer a Diane Warren channel on their inflight music selections. Her staggering list of Top Ten hits includes "I Don't Want to Miss a Thing," "How Do I Live," "Un-Break My Heart," "Because You Loved Me," "I'd Lie for You (and That's the Truth)," "Don't Turn Around," "If I Could Turn Back Time," "Look Away," and "Nothing's Gonna Stop Us Now." About sixty of her songs have been used in films.

*Diane Warren, the most commercially successful songwriter of the nineties, supports several Jewish causes. (Photo by Erik Asla.)*

Diane Warren, a self-described "nice Jewish girl from the Valley," is legendary for the incredible amount of time she spends in her inner sanctum writing songs. She can go twelve hours a day, six days a week, and despite her unparalleled success, has veered little from that marathon pace since she notched her first Top Forty hit in 1983 with Laura Branigan's "Solitaire." She attributes her hustle and ambition to the same Russian-Jewish immigrant gene that drove thousands of Jews, including her grandparents, to the Land of Opportunity and pushed them to build a better life for their families. "I do feel like I'm carrying an immigrant hunger," says Warren even though her publishing company is worth millions. Though she didn't spend a lot of time in synagogue as a child, she has a preference for minor keys, and she wagers that "Havah Nagilah" probably influenced her in some way.

Warren grew up in the San Fernando Valley in a nonreligious household with Hanukkah the most memorable holiday. She attended Sunday school at Temple Beth Ami in Reseda, California, but usually cut classes in favor of spending the morning watching the ducks in the pond across the street. She "thankfully" didn't go to Hebrew school, and didn't become a bat mitzvah. During her early teens, Warren and her Jewish girlfriends turned their B'nai B'rith Girls social group into a mischievous gang where wild beach parties were a primary activity.

Still, Warren grew up with a strong Jewish identity, much of it instilled in the face of anti-Semitism. The time she was called a "dirty Jew" she was only seven and didn't understand the slur. What really grated was that her father, an insurance salesman born David S. Wolfberg, had had to change his name to make a living. As Wolfberg, few doors opened for her father and few phone calls were returned. As Warren, business picked up dramatically. Despite her minimal formal Jewish education, Warren was instilled with many Jewish values, including honoring your mother and father, the obligation of *tzedakah*, and the *mitzvot* of caring for the elderly and being kind to animals.

Warren spent her childhood listening to the rock records and Broadway musical soundtracks her two older sisters were always playing, as well as poring over the records' songwriting and production credits. She remembers hearing Buddy Holly music as a baby. She recalls as early as age five seeing vivid pictures in her mind when the music played. As one of the most sought after composers of songs for films, those early cinematic images were not lost on her. (Neither was the fact that her paternal grandfather, Jacob Wolfberg, was a film projectionist for a movie theater.) Seeing the Beatles on *The Ed Sullivan Show* and in concert at

Dodger Stadium in 1964, and the Hollywood Bowl in 1965, were also defining moments. She remembers "being blown away like the rest of the planet," after hearing the Fab Four.

Her father was a frustrated writer, and he encouraged Diane's musical interest by buying her a guitar when she was ten. Warren also learned to play piano but had little desire to perform. Her ambition was to write. By eleven she had written her first song. Her role models were the legendary songwriting teams of Jerry Leiber and Mike Stoller, Gerry Goffin and Carole King, and Barry Mann and Cynthia Weil, as well as the fabled songwriters at Motown Records. Warren, equally at ease with words and music, almost always worked alone. By age fifteen she was participating in songwriters' showcases, using her parents' and friends' connections to set up meetings with music publishers, and getting her father to chauffeur her to appointments. She also went to concerts and threw cassettes of her songs on stage hoping someone might call her. "I was a hustler," Warren says. "I'd just go for it. I wanted to make something of myself."

That same drive did not transfer to school where she was a passable, but bored student, who just wanted to get on with a songwriting career. Her father promised to pay her way through college if she enrolled. She attended Cal State–Northridge for two years, "B.S.-ing" her way through while writing lyrics in the back of her classes. A film studies class would later prove to be very helpful. A music theory class, which Warren didn't understand at the time, taken at Pierce College in Woodland Hills where she spent another two years faking her way through classes, also would come in handy.

In 1983, Warren finally landed a job as a staff writer for producer Jack White, who was working with singer Laura Branigan. White asked Warren to come up with English lyrics for a French song Branigan was going to record. The next day Warren turned in "Solitaire," which reached No. 7 on the pop charts later in the year. It was her next hit, for which she wrote the words and music, that Warren considers her real breakthrough. "Rhythm of the Night," from the film *The Last Dragon*, was a No. 3 hit for the group Debarge in 1985. The floodgates began to open. In 1987, Warren scored three Top Ten hits: "I Get Weak" by former Go-Go Belinda Carlisle; "Nothing's Gonna Stop Us Now" by Starship, and "Who Will You Run To?" by Heart. By then, due to a lawsuit with White, Warren had set up her own publishing company, Realsongs, and held exclusive rights to all her music. In 1988, the hits kept coming, with Chicago taking "I Don't Wanna Live Without Your Love" to No. 3 and riding "Look Away" to the top of the charts.

For those who hadn't heard of Warren by then, 1989 was a coming out party. More than a dozen of her songs hit the charts. "If I Could Turn Back Time" by Cher, "Through the Storm" by Aretha Franklin and Elton John, "Blame it on the Rain" by the infamous Milli Vanilli, "When I See You Smile" by Bad English, "Love Will Lead You Back" by Taylor Dayne, and "How Can We Be Lovers?" by Michael Bolton reached the Top Ten. At one point, seven of her songs were on the *Billboard* Hot 100 chart in the same week. Since 1983, more than eighty Warren-penned songs have charted in the Top Ten.

Warren does not write on demand for particular artists, but she does have a good notion of who should do a song once it's completed, and she pitches songs to singers with the same doggedness that she writes them. Believing that "If I Could Turn Back Time" was a perfect fit for Cher, who was reluctant to record it, Warren literally got down on her knees and begged the singer to do the song. Cher relented, and the song became one of her biggest hits. One reason Warren has had such stunning success with such a variety of acts, including rock, reggae, R&B, and country, is her universal approach to writing. Most of her hits are sweeping power ballads about falling in and out of love that can be adapted to almost any style. Singers and record company executives alike praise Warren for her ability to stir the emotions of the masses so consistently with her sentiments and melodies. Criticism that her songs were generic and overblown abated in the mid-nineties with smash hits such as "Un-Break My Heart," "How Do I Live," and "Because You Loved Me," which have more edge and depth than many of her previous songs.

The latter two songs, along with "I Don't Want to Miss a Thing," helped cement her reputation as a master of writing songs for films. Her songs have appeared in about sixty movies. Her work also has earned her five Best Song Oscar nominations, one Grammy Award (and multiple nominations), five ASCAP Pop Songwriter of the Year awards, one Country Songwriter of the Year Award, and numerous other film and music industry awards. In 1993, she also was nominated for a Dove Award, which the Gospel Music Association gives out to honor contemporary Christian music. Sitting in the audience in Nashville waiting to find out if "I Will Be Here For You," co-written with singer Michael W. Smith, was a winner, Warren couldn't help thinking, "I am definitely the only Jew here," and wondering if anybody knew. Warren also holds the record for the length of time a hit has stayed on the charts. "How Do I Live," from the soundtrack to the film *Con Air*, recorded by both Leann Rimes and Trisha Yearwood, spent sixty-nine weeks on the charts in 1997 (counting both versions separately). In 1998, crooner Johnny Mathis recorded a whole album of Warren's songs called, *Because You Loved Me: Songs of Diane Warren*. Warren considers "Because You Loved Me," written in memory of her father who died in 1987, and the Michael Bolton hit, "When I'm Back on My Feet Again," as her most spiritual songs. "Something was coming through me when I wrote them," she says.

In late 1998, the singer Brandy spent two weeks at No. 1 with the Warren-penned "Have You Ever?" In 1999, singer Gloria Estefan and vocal group 'N Sync took Warren's song "Music of My Heart," from the film of the same name, to No. 2 on the pop charts. In fact, the film's title was changed to match Warren's song. It was one of eight films in which Warren's songs appeared in 1999. *Notting Hill*, *Message in a Bottle*, *Detroit Rock City*, and *Runaway Bride* were among the others. In January of 2000, the entertainment trade publication *Daily Variety* published a sixteen-page tribute to Warren. In December of 2000, another trade magazine, the *Hollywood Reporter*, named Warren one of the fifty most powerful women in Hollywood, ranking her No. 43.

Despite the heady acclaim and achievements, Warren remains grounded, unpretentious, and grateful. Her success has allowed her to become involved in an array of charities, including several Jewish causes. In memory of her father, she founded the David S. Warren Weekly Entertainment Series at the Jewish Home for the Aging, which presents singers, dancers, and other performers. She also underwrites a pet-therapy program where dogs, cats, and other small pets are brought in to keep the residents company. Warren believes it is important to treat the elderly with reverence and respect. She is also a substantial contributor to the Simon Wiesenthal Center Museum of Tolerance in Los Angeles. "We have to remember the Holocaust," Warren says. "Imagine someone coming to your door and saying, 'We're taking all your things, and we're taking you.' You think it can't happen again?"

An animal lover, Warren is also a member of PETA (People for the Ethical Treatment of Animals). Among her pets are two Jewish cats, Alien and Rusty, and three pet birds, including a parrot named Buttwings, who "is Jewish, too." Warren is also a Buddy for Life at AIDS Project Los Angeles, and says contributing to these causes is a duty. "I just feel a need to do it. After all, I am a nice Jewish girl from the Valley."

# Eric Bazilian and Rob Hyman
## of the Hooters

Eric Bazilian, singer, songwriter, multi-instrumentalist. Born July 21, 1953,
Philadelphia, Pennsylvania. Rob Hyman, singer, songwriter, keyboards.
Born Meriden, Connecticut, April 24, 1950. Also, Rick Chertoff, songwriter,
producer. Born March 29, 1950, New York City. Best known for the
U.S. hits "And We Danced," "Day by Day," "Where Do the Children Go,"
"All You Zombies," and European hits "Satellite" and "Johnny B."
Also known for co-writing, playing on, and producing key albums
for Cyndi Lauper, Joan Osborne, and Sophie B. Hawkins.

*The Hooters in 1993. From left, Eric Bazilian, Mindy Jostyn, John Lilley,
David Uosikkinen, Fran Smith, Jr., Rob Hyman. (Courtesy of MCA Records.)*

In one of rock music's great ironies, the Hooters, a band led by two Jewish grad-uates of the University of Pennsylvania, achieved a great deal of their success in Germany. German audiences were buying their records and filling concert halls long after the Hooters' popularity in America had waned. Even more ironic was that one of the band's most memorable concerts in fifteen years of touring oc-curred in 1990 outside Nuremburg, Germany, at a site that had once served as a Nazi headquarters. Band co-founder Rob Hyman didn't know whether to laugh or cry over the band's German stardom. "It was a really great experience, but it was really eerie," Hyman recalls. "I kept thinking that fifty years ago my father was in the army and this was the enemy, and even though I'm not deeply religious, it stirred up stuff in me."

On May 11, 1990 the band set up shop at a concert venue called Serenaden-Hof. It was on the site of a huge unfinished stadium where the Nazis had held rallies. More than forty years later, young German entrepreneurs had created a beauti-fully landscaped open-air theater inside the stadium walls, which loomed as a stark backdrop. As four thousand fans danced, cheered and sang every word to every song, Hyman couldn't help wonder if they knew he and band co-founder Eric Bazilian were Jewish. "This location stirred up a lot of things. I wasn't ever worried, I was just curious," Hyman says. He had rarely, if ever, experienced a greater outpouring of emotion from a concert audience. Fan reaction fired up the band. The audience refused to go home, and urged the band on. Hyman thought he was witnessing the idealistic power of rock 'n' roll work magic. The band had played huge multi-act stadium shows for social and political causes, Live AID and Amnesty International concerts included, but nothing moved him like this. The audience shouted for more of the Hooters' special brand of melodica- and mandolin-driven folk-rock-reggae music even after the exhausted, sweat-soaked band had showered. The Hooters had played every song in its repertoire, but the members were pumped up enough to deliver one more song. They chose a fitting rock classic, Nick Lowe's "(What's So Funny) 'Bout Peace, Love and Understanding."

Hyman had been the only Jewish male in his Connecticut high school class. Though his family was not very observant, he grew up feeling that sense of being a minority. He had arrived at the University of Pennsylvania as a biology major, but really wanted to meet musicians. He had been tinkering on the family piano since he was four or five, and eventually began taking lessons. (He enjoyed study-

The walls of a stadium built by the Nazis dwarf the Serenaden-Hof concert stage outside Nuremberg, Germany. The Hooters performed there in 1990. (Photo from the collection of Rob Hyman.)

ing Hebrew for his bar mitzvah, because it reminded him of learning to read music.) By the seventh grade he had joined his first band, the Trolls, made his first fifty dollars playing music, and discovered that girls were attracted to guys in bands. It wasn't long after arriving at college that he met Eric Bazilian and Rick Chertoff. "They were the Jewish buddies I never had in high school," Hyman says.

Bazilian came from similar Eastern European roots as Hyman, and he grew up in a family where religion wasn't paramount but a Jewish identity was important. He attended Hebrew school, had a bar mitzvah, then went off to a Quaker school. He believes his Quaker education was more meaningful than a strictly yeshiva education as it exposed him to many other cultures and religions and, in the process, deepened his "love and appreciation for the rich heritage that is Judaism." The Jewish commandment of tikkun olam, of repairing the world, would inform much of his writing. God, Jesus and an array of biblical characters would make frequent appearances in his songs. "If anything, I feel that Judaism imparts a sense of compassion, not just from man to man, but between man and his creator, be that internal, external, or simply a futile attempt to fathom an otherwise unfathomable universe," Bazilian says. A Jewish sense of humor also influences his music. What other culture, he asks, could "produce a writer who, with love and sympathy, would call God 'a slob like one of us,'" he asks, referring to a lyric from his song "One of Us," which became a Top Five hit for Joan Osborne in 1995.

Bazilian began playing guitar at eight. He wanted to build rockets when he grew up and would major in physics at college—until he saw the Beatles on The Ed Sullivan Show in February of 1964. Within two weeks of that epiphany, he formed his first band. He was eleven. Two years later, he used his bar mitzvah money to buy the twelve-string Rickenbacker electric guitar that he would use to write and record "One of Us," his biggest-selling song.

Rick Chertoff came from a family that was fairly observant and quite active in Temple Beth-El, a reform congregation in Great Neck, New York. Chertoff was bar mitzvahed by Rabbi Jacob Phillip Ruden, and married years later by assistant rabbi Jerome Davidson. Both rabbis ardently supported the civil rights and antiwar movements in the sixties, and their social activism appealed to the Chertoff family. Chertoff calls his Jewish education and upbringing "an exceptionally positive experience." Passover at his home has evolved into a forty-person production complete with a "Seder orchestra" that performs such numbers as "Eliahu Hanavi" and "Go Down Moses." Chertoff calls the evening "an extraordinary redemptive experience." He credits his mother, a teacher of gifted first-grade students and a "great" piano player, with instilling in him a passion for music. By the time he enrolled in college as a history major he played bassoon, trumpet, and drums. When Chertoff, Hyman, and Bazilian formed a college band called Wax, Chertoff was the drummer.

Since then, the trio's friendship and creative chemistry has blossomed and endured. If their Jewishness has had anything to do with that chemistry, Chertoff says it's more likely "a hidden, mysterious piece of it." More importantly, they like each other and each other's musical compass. Still, Chertoff allows that as the trio has gotten older, "the Jewish part has deeper meaning."

After college, they formed a new band called Baby Grand, which recorded a pair of albums for Arista Records in 1978 and 1979. When Baby Grand broke up, Hyman and Bazilian continued to work together writing songs and doing session work. In 1983, Chertoff, who already had produced Air Supply's two-million-selling American debut *Lost in Love* in 1980, brought them in to help with a new singer he was producing for Columbia Records. The singer was Cyndi Lauper, and the record was *She's So Unusual*. Hyman and Bazilian played numerous instruments on the record, provided background vocals, and arranged and co-wrote songs with Chertoff and Lauper. Released in late 1983, the album sold five million copies, spawned five hit singles, including the No. 1 "Time After Time" co-written by Hyman, and earned Lauper a Grammy for Best New Artist.

In 1984, Bazilian and Hyman added drummer David Uosikkinen, guitar player John Lilley, bass player Andy King (replaced later by Fran Smith, Jr.), and formed the Hooters. The band moniker came from the slang term for the melodica, the combination horn-and-keyboard instrument that was a bedrock part of the band's sound. The band became a favorite in the Philadelphia area and released an independent album, *Amore*, which piqued the interest of the major record labels after it sold a hundred thousand copies. The Hooters secured a recording contract with Columbia Records and, with their friend Rick Chertoff producing and co-writing, released *Nervous Night* in 1985. The band's debut sold a million copies and included three Top Forty singles: "And We Danced" (No. 21), "Day By Day" (No. 18), and "Where Do the Children Go" (No. 38).

It was a tune that fell short of the Top Forty, however, that became the band's signature song. "All You Zombies," filled with biblical and Jewish references, had become a local fan favorite and concert-closer when the Hooters were still a Philadelphia bar band. The dramatic reggae-rock song opened with a slow, ominous instrumental mix of melodica, bass, drums, and crying electric guitar notes. Then the lyrics kicked in:

> Holy Moses met the Pharaoh.
> Yeah, he tried to set him straight.
> Looked him in the eye,
> 'Let my people go.'

Holy Moses on the mountain,
high above the golden calf.
Went to get the Ten Commandments,
yeah he's just gonna break them in half.
All you zombies hide your faces,
all you people in the street.
All you sitting in high places,
the pieces gonna fall on you.
No one ever spoke to Noah.
They all laughed at him instead.
Working on his ark,
working all by himself.
Only Noah saw it coming,
forty days and forty nights.
Took his sons and daughters with him,
yeah they were the Israelites . . .
The rain is gonna fall on you . . .

The song evolved quickly out of a jam session. The two co-writers didn't purposely set out to write a song about the birth of Judaism. (And they knew that chronologically the verses were backwards, because in biblical history Noah precedes Moses.) "There are the obvious Hebrew images contained therein, but I believe it's more an allegory for the Human Condition," says Bazilian, who believes in the healing power of music and tries to write songs about tolerance and social justice "without being warm and fuzzy."

Born of divine inspiration or not, "Zombies" was a career saver. It was the song fans began packing clubs to hear, and the song Philadelphia rock station WMMR began playing at a time when the band was considering calling it quits. "Zombies" helped the band get its recording contract, and it spearheaded the band's popularity in Europe. "I don't think we knew what we had," Hyman confesses. "We liked it, but it was a throwaway. It wasn't a set closer, but it became that."

The band's 1987 follow up album, *One Way Home*, sold half a million copies, but included no U.S. Top Forty hits. The song "Satellite, however, was a smash in Europe, and the anthemic "Johnny B" was a concert crowd-pleaser overseas. (Both were co-written with Chertoff.) In 1989, the band released *Zig Zag*, which was a commercial disappointment in the United States. The Hooters signed a new record deal with MCA Records and in 1993 released *Out of Body*. The record also fared poorly, but included an engaging up-tempo rocker featuring Cyndi Lauper, called "Boys Will Be Boys" and a song called "(Living in the) Shadow of Jesus," which, though not about how Jews feel in many parts of the world, could be interpreted that way. (The record also included a song called "Private Emotion," which sex symbol and singing sensation Ricky Martin recorded and included on his multi-million-selling debut album in 1999.)

Throughout the nineties, Bazilian and Hyman were in demand as songwriters and session musicians. They contributed to numerous projects, including albums by Belinda Carlisle, Cyndi Lauper, Taj Mahal, the Band, Johnny Clegg and Savuka, Wailing Souls, Willie Nelson, and Jon Bon Jovi, among others. They joined Chertoff for Sophie B. Hawkins's 1992 debut, *Tongues and Tails*, which included the Top Five hit, "Damn, I Wish I Was Your Lover." They teamed with Chertoff, whose production credits by now also included the Outfield, Mick Jagger, Patty Smythe, and the Band, for Joan Osborne's 1995 debut album *Relish*, which included the Bazilian-penned smash "(What if God was) One of Us." Bazilian wrote the song at home while trying to demonstrate a recording process to his wife. He had no idea where the song came from, but brought it to the Osborne recording sessions the next day as a lark. "I really feel like I'm an antenna. I wrote 'One of Us' in half an hour without any thought. It was like I told my brain to go to the other room. I put the recorder on, played the guitar, and that's what came out," Bazilian says. "I feel like part of a machine that's brought these things to earth."

In 1996, Bazilian, Hyman, and Chertoff, began work on what they thought would be another Hooters album. They added singer-songwriter David Forman as a collaborator. Forman (born March 31, 1949 in Brooklyn, New York) is the founder and lead singer of a popular contemporary doo-wop band called Little Isidore and the Inquisitors, a name only a nice Jewish boy with a warped sense of humor could conceive. "I though it would be fun to trash the Catholic Church a little bit," the former yeshiva student says.

The Hooters album-to-be evolved into a song cycle based on Czech composer Antonin Dvorak's late-nineteenth-century "New World Symphony." "Symphony" was inspired by Dvorak's two-year sojourn through America from 1892 to 1894. "Symphony" resonated with the four songwriters. It was about Dvorak's search for indigenous American music and his discovery that it was a blend of many colors: Celtic, folk, Native American, Shaker and Baptist hymns, but primarily black forms. It was something Hyman and the others felt they were a part of. "The black contribution is the blues and gospel vocal qualities. We all draw on that deep well," Hyman says. "The Jewish thing is the great songwriting craft." Their album titled *Largo* (Blue Gorilla/Mercury Records) picked up where Dvorak left off, evolving into a folk-rock opera tracking the immigrant experience into the twentieth century.

It included the song "Gimme A Stone," based on the biblical David's legendary showdown with Goliath. The couplet "Never had to fight such a real big man. / Gimme a stone and I'll do what I can," serves as metaphor for the Jewish immigrant experience. "It didn't escape me that four Jewish guys were putting this thing together," says Forman, who wrote the song's lyrics. Chertoff called the album "definitely our immigrant story, too," adding that though it may be impressionistic, much of *Largo* is about faith, and is spiritually based. The Hooters asked an all-star cast of singers and musicians who they'd worked with previously to help them make the record. Cyndi Lauper, Levon Helm and Garth Hudson of the Band, Taj Mahal, Joan Osborne, members of the Chieftains, and others, contributed. The album was released in 1998 to strong critical acclaim but didn't enjoy the commercial success it deserved. "I felt like this was a life's work," says Hyman. "I'm most proud of this record." After the completion of *Largo*, the four principals returned to working on various projects, including records by Ricky Martin, Canadian singer Amanda Marshall, Carly Simon, Jules Shear, and Dar Williams.

In 2000, a song co-written by Forman, Hyman, and Chertoff called "Christmas of Love," and released as a Little Isidore and the Inquisitors number, was featured in the hit holiday film, *The Grinch*. Earlier in the year, Bazilian released a solo album on his own Mousetrap Records label. As usual, the record had more than passing reference to God and spirituality. "I wish I really understood the songwriting process. The main thing is I'm just getting started, and I hope there's a purpose for it, and that there's *tikkun olam* in it," Bazilian says. "That's the whole point of songwriting. Without *tikkun olam*, it's just (pointless)."

# Peter Himmelman

**Singer. Songwriter. Guitar player. Pianist. Producer. Born November 23, 1959, Minneapolis, Minnesota. Best known for writing the music and original songs for the television program *Judging Amy*. He is one of the most compelling and engaging performers in popular music. He does not perform on Shabbat.**

*Peter Himmelman's folk-rock music is infused with the spiritual and influenced by the Torah. (Photo by Gary Hacking.)*

In 1987, Island Records was geared up to release Peter Himmelman's second album, *Gematria*. The company was excited about the potential of the gifted singer-songwriter. His first album, *This Father's Day*, released in 1986, though not a blockbuster, had set the stage for Himmelman. Reviews of both albums were positive. *Rolling Stone* and *Time* magazines, among others, heralded the rise of a bright new talent, comparing him favorably to Elvis Costello and Bruce Springsteen. Radio seemed receptive. Perhaps best of all, the company had arranged for Himmelman to be the opening act on Rod Stewart's 1987 tour. The exposure would be priceless. All the pieces were in place to catapult Himmleman to stardom.

Then Himmelman told the president of Island Records that he couldn't join Stewart's tour, as he had decided to become *shomer Shabbos*, Sabbath observant, and could not perform on Friday nights. Everyone thought he was joking. He wasn't. The record company had won the marketing battle for *Gematria* by convincing Himmelman to shave his long beard for an album cover photo shoot, but it had lost the war. Himmelman may have fumbled his first shot at commercial stardom, but he had won a personal spiritual victory. "When you set aside time and say this can't be violated, and you stick to it, it's a very rare and remarkable spectacle. It's nothing short of amazing," Himmelman says of how the decision made him feel. He doesn't view his strict Jewish observance as preventing him from having hit records. His music, he says, has been ahead or behind its time. "I was thinking about changing the world, bringing Moshiach, keeping Shabbos, I was trying to write about it, not proselytize, but nobody else was thinking about it," he says. (In 2001, another shomer Shabbos rock act, yeshiva grads Evan and Jaron Lowenstein, reached the Top Twenty with a radio-friendly pop-rock song called "Crazy for This Girl.")

Himmelman also refused to use his marriage to Bob Dylan's daughter, Maria, in 1988, for professional gain. His refusal to talk to the media about his wife and children, or his legendary father-in-law, cost him career-boosting profiles in national magazines. Since *Gematria*, he has released eight impressive albums (including a pair of children's records), brimming with well-crafted songs that grapple with timeless spiritual and religious questions. None of his songs has breached the charts to become a hit, though a sizable cult following across the country embraces his thoughtful, provocative song catalog, which is full of Jewish references. The album title *Gematria*, for example, refers to the search for alternative meanings in Hebrew words based on the numerical value assigned each letter of the Hebrew alphabet. The title of his 1991 album, *From Strength to Strength*, is taken from the Hebrew phrase "M'Chayil El Chayil," from the Book of Psalms, and is a blessing for those trying to elevate themselves to a higher spiritual plane. The album, which wrestles with good versus evil, the material versus the spiritual, and faith versus a lack of belief, includes "Impermanent Things," a song Himmelman says is his most Jewish.

The song's provocative chorus goes like this: "Why keep hanging on to things that never stay / Things that just keep stringing us along from day to day / All these impermanent things / Present yet elusive / Passive yet abusive / Tearing out the heart in utter silence / All these impermanent things / Well they point in all directions / Like second hand reflections / And they're leading us to subtle shades of violence." Himmeleman explains that the song "is not a renunciation of materialism. It's talking about the struggle of the soul in the physical world. I am fooled by it, but it is impermanent; it's not real. The struggle is to keep it all in check."

The 1992 album *Flown This Acid World* concludes with "Untitled," also known to fans as "The Taxi Song." It is a chilling, eight-minute tale based on a true story of being driven from an airport by an anti-Semitic cabbie who unabashedly tells his passenger that Hitler had the right idea. The title of his 1998 release, *Love Thinketh No Evil*, is taken from a passage in the Talmud. The album includes the song, "Seven Circles," which he wrote for his wife, Maria, as a first anniversary gift, refers to the part of a traditional Jewish wedding ceremony where the bride circles the groom seven times to symbolize her protective influences over him. The album's opening song, "Eyeball," includes the lyrics, "The river is red / there's frogs in your bed"—an obvious reference to the Ten Plagues from Exodus. In other words, though "Jew" or "Jewish" never appear as lyrics in any of Himmelman's songs, Judaism is an essential ingredient in the fuel that fires Himmelman's songwriting, resulting in spiritual-versus-material themes that are universal.

His fans also eagerly anticipate his concerts, which are known for being unpredictable, engaging, humor-filled events. (How many performers invite audience members who'd like a better seat to go back stage, carry a couch onto the stage, and watch from there? Or allow a fan to sing a song when Himmelman can't remember the lyrics, or make up a song on the spot about a stranger in the audience?)

Peter Himmelman was the third of four siblings born and raised in Minneapolis, a city in which, Himmelman says, Jews were made to feel very aware of their "otherness." Even his neighborhood, St. Louis Park, was pejoratively called "St. Jewish Park." In junior high and high school, he had to deal with anti-Semitic bullies practicing their hockey moves by selectively hip-checking Jewish students into hallway lockers. Peter's father, David, an ex-Marine and entrepreneur who created and sold businesses such as Silent Night Security Systems, is legendary for being expelled from the Minneapolis school system at age fourteen after punching a gym teacher who called him a dirty Jew. Peter's mother, Beverly, was an early "woman's libber," who went back to school to get a teaching degree when Peter was in the third grade, and became a teacher in a suburban school system's gifted program.

Himmelman grew up in what he describes as "a very Jewish household." He attended Hebrew school, learning to speak the language quite well. The family wasn't strictly kosher or *shomer Shabbos*, but his parents and maternal grandmother, family matriarch Rose Wexler, frequently spoke Yiddish, and his mother lit Shabbos candles every Friday evening. "That left an impression on me," he says. The family also celebrated most Jewish holidays and made its first trip to Israel in 1968 to visit cousins. Peter was moved "to the point of tears" by a visit to the Western Wall in Jerusalem. He was eight. His family returned for month-long visits in 1971 and 1974. The lengthy visits enabled him to become fluent in Hebrew. While Himmleman's repertoire includes no Jewish music, holiday songs such as "Adon Olam" and the minor key of so much synagogue music were very early musical influences. Other early influences included folk singer Burl Ives, classical conductor Leonard Bernstein, and records by jazz pianist Thelonius Monk, which his mother played while practicing modern dance. His father owned the city's first eight-track tape store, *Tape-O-Rama*, and brought Peter the latest releases by Jimi Hendrix, the Who, Herb Alpert, anything he thought his son would enjoy. "Music was always serious, really serious. I thought about it day and night," Himmelman says.

He was in the sixth grade when he started his first band, the Reflections, which filled its sets with Creedence Clearwater Revival songs and Himmelman originals. From there he joined a reggae band comprising Jamaicans and Trinidadians, called Shangoya. By age seventeen, he was making a name for himself as leader of the popular New Wave band Sussman Lawrence. The band included musicians he would record and perform with well into the nineties, his cousin keyboard player Jeff Victor, bass player Al Wolovitch, and drummer Andy Kamman, who were all Jewish, and Eric Moen, who was not. The group released a pair of albums regionally, *Hail to the Modern Hero* in 1980 and *Pop City* in 1984. Song titles such as "Naturally (You're Artificial)" and "Baby Let Me Be Your Cigarette" were harbingers of Himmelman's growing sense of humor and desire to be unconventional. In 1985, Himmelman independently released his first solo album, *This Father's Day*, dedicated to his father who died in 1983. A video of "Eleventh Confession," a song from the album, wound up on MTV, created music industry buzz, and led to Himmelman's big break. Island Records offered him a recording contract, and in 1986 re-released *This Father's Day*.

Around this time, Kenny Vance, a founding member of sixties hit-makers Jay and the Americans, took Himmelman to a class led by Rabbi Simon Jacobson, one of Lubavitcher Rebbe Menachem Mendel Schneerson's oral scribes. (Oral scribes were responsible for memorizing the rebbe's Shabbat speeches and writing them down after Shabbat.) Jacobson's class, Himmelman says, "delved into the deeper aspects of Judaism, and I was hooked." He did not, however, don the Orthodox mantle, and in fact eschewed labels such as Orthodox, Conservative, and Reform. He referred to himself as an observant Jew, and refused to judge others on how they manifested their Judaism.

He began davening with tefillin, took a trip to Israel, and also recorded his first album for Island Records, *Gematria*, released in 1987 to great fanfare. The critically acclaimed *Synethesia* followed in 1989, after which he parted ways with Island Records. He signed with Epic Records the following year and released what may be his overall best work, *From Strength to Strength*. The album, primarily heartfelt folk-rock, included "Impermanent Things" and fan favorites such as the full-throttle rocker, "Woman with the Strength of 10,000 Men" and the more delicate "Mission of My Soul." Himmelman followed *Strength* with two more provocative, rocking records for Epic: *Flown This Acid World*, and the concept album *Skin*. Both records were filled with a mix of propulsive, soul-stirring rockers tackling God, faith, and redemption, and heart-aching ballads and love songs, as well as something new from Himmelman: social commentary. *Skin*'s "Disposable Child" was the best example of this: "Have you seen the disposable child / With sunken cheeks and belly distended / Have you seen the disposable child / Exempted from grace / And left undefended? . . ."

When these records fell short of commercial expectations, Himmelman was once again without a recording contract. In 1996, however, he released a live, "unplugged" album, *Stage Diving* through a small independent label, Plump Records. He followed that in 1997 with a children's record called *My Best Friend Is a Salamander* (Baby Boom Records), featuring songs such as, "You'll Always Be You to Me" and "Larry's a Sunflower Now." In 1998, he returned to thematic form with *Love Thinketh No Evil* (Six Degrees/Koch Records), a more musically diverse album brimming with more spiritual questions, mortal observations and doubts, and triumphant declarations contained in poignant songs such as the wonderfully titled, "Gravity Can't Keep My Spirit Down." Like his previous records, critics thought this, too, would serve as Himmelman's commercial breakthrough, but it didn't.

During the nineties, he also contributed to Six Degrees Records' two contemporary Hanukkah releases. He performed a rock song with Israeli singer-songwriter David Broza that the pair co-wrote called, "Lighting Up the World," that appeared on *Festival of Light* in 1996. He wrote and performed "In the Embryo of Silence" and also wrote and produced the Neshama Carlebach contribution, "A Love Transcending" for *Festival of Light 2*, released in 1999. Throughout the decade, Himmelman also wrote music for films, fashion shows, and TV commercials, and in 1999 began scoring the music and writing original songs for the hit television drama, *Judging Amy*. He also recorded another children's album, *My Fabulous Plum*. In 2002, Himmelman was nominated for an Emmy for the song "The Best Kind of Answer" from an episode of *Judging Amy*.

The fact that he hasn't broken into the Top Forty hasn't deterred him, and he doesn't blame his religious practices for stardom's eluding him. "I still think I'm working on something big in a way I didn't envision as I was growing up," Himmelman says. He is less charitable toward the media and how it has depicted Jews in America. "There is something about the media portrayal of what it means to be Jewish in this country that just takes the testosterone out of a man," Himmelman told the *Jerusalem Report* in 1993. "I wish someone would tell me why it's cool to take your date for Cajun shrimp jambalaya, but not gefilte fish."

# 1990s and Beyond

**"Every-day we must dance, if only in our thoughts."**

**NAHMAN OF BRATSLAV**

# Victoria Shaw

**Songwriter. Singer. Pianist. Born Victoria Lynn Shaw, July 13, 1962, New York City. Best known for writing the No. I country hits "The River" and "She's Every Woman" recorded by Garth Brooks, "Too Busy Being in Love" by Doug Stone, and "I Love the Way You Love Me" by John Michael Montgomery.**

*Victoria Shaw watched Garth Brooks turn two of her songs into No. 1 country hits. (Peter Nash photo reprinted and used by permission.)*

Victoria Shaw didn't actually aspire to be a nice Jewish girl from New York writing hit songs for the biggest country acts in Nashville. Ever since she was a child, Shaw wanted to be a pop singer. Then again, she was practically born into the entertainment business. Her father, Ray Shaw, played Sky Masterson to Walter Mathau's Nathan Detroit in the first touring company of *Guys and Dolls*. Her mother, Carole Bergenthal, recorded for Verve and Capital Records as Carole Bennett, and also acted in theater and television. Bergenthal had been told by an agent to change her name because "Bergenthal sounded more like a disease than a name." Ray Shaw, also Jewish, didn't have that problem. His family name can be traced back to his paternal grandfather in England. "Everybody's always shocked that that's my real name," Victoria says. "Even my mother didn't believe it when she first met him."

The Shaw family moved to Los Angeles to escape the cold, settling in a small house in the San Fernando Valley when Victoria was about five. Aside from acting and singing, her parents were dreamers and doers, conceiving one project after another, including starting the first fashion magazine for large women, *Big Beautiful Women (BBW)*. "My mom was a pioneer in helping large women," Shaw says. The Shaws attended synagogue on the High Holy Days, and Victoria went to Sunday school for five years. Though she didn't become a bat mitzvah, she recalls going to her friends' bar and bat mitzvahs just about every weekend in the heavily Jewish-populated Valley. During her teens, the family occasionally attended the Synagogue of the Performing Arts where she saw actors such as Henry Winkler, Walter Mathau, and Shelly Winters. "It made me feel proud, and feel cool. It made me connect," Shaw says. Anti-Semitism was practically non-existent in the world in which Shaw grew up. "I didn't have to think about being Jewish—we just were," she says.

From the time Victoria was born, her mother, fluent in Yiddish, was singing Yiddish lullabies and Broadway show tunes to her. The family's frequent car trips were filled with singing. "We didn't have lots of money, so we did lots of driving to places like Las Vegas," Shaw recalls. By seven, she was taking piano lessons, and by thirteen, formed her first band. The band, called Solace, earned money playing weddings and bar mitzvahs on a regular basis. "There was never a doubt in my mind that [singing] is what I would do. I just didn't know I'd be a songwriter. I wanted to be a star," she says. As long as Victoria wasn't playing in bars, and was home shortly after the event, performing in the band was fine with her folks. Especially since Victoria was in the gifted program in high school.

It hit her parents hard, however, when she decided to quit school at sixteen. "I really hated school. I wasn't stimulated," Shaw says. She loved to read, however. *The World According to Garp* and *Time and Again* were favorite books. Dorothy Parker and Fay Weldon were favorite authors, in great part because of their off-the-wall wit. Shaw's appetite for fiction, ear for dialogue, and powers of observation would serve her well as a songwriter. In the meantime, after leaving school, she worked in a bakery by day and played in bands by night. Her parents understood her passion, and were her role models. They had always made something out of nothing, had never given up on their dreams, and earned a living in the entertainment business. To placate her mother, Victoria took the GED exam and studied shorthand and typing in case she couldn't forge a career in music. "I am a great typist," the hit songwriter says.

In 1981, Shaw moved back to New York and got a job managing a recording studio and performing at night in piano bars. In her spare time, she began writing songs, and says, "they came out sounding country, which is really bizarre." She half-jokingly credits the TV programs *Hee Haw* and *The Barbara Mandrell Show*, and a Kenny Rogers album she owned, for instilling in her the country influences she didn't know she had. A Brooklyn boyfriend also had introduced her to the music of Merle Haggard and Hank Williams, Jr. The more she heard, the more she fell in love with country music. "I loved it because it was real. I was truly country when country wasn't cool," Shaw says. In 1982, she began traveling to Nashville several times a year in search of a recording contract. She'd rent a house, network, write songs, then return to her piano bar gigs in New York. Brimming with confidence, she thought she'd have her pick of deals. Recording contracts didn't materialize, but songwriting offers did. Thinking she would have to become a famous songwriter to become a famous singer, she relented and signed her first publishing contract in 1989—seven years after relentlessly seeking a recording contract.

Shaw's life was about to change dramatically. Her very first song released on record was "The River," which Garth Brooks rode to No. 1 in 1992. Her second song released as a single, "Too Busy Being in Love," became a No. 1 hit for Doug Stone in 1992. Her third single, John Michael Montgomery's version of her tune, "I Love the Way You Love Me," reached No. 1 in 1993 and won the Academy of Country Music "Song of the Year" award. Credited with writing three consecutive No. 1 hits, Shaw was suddenly the hottest name in town. In 1993, Shaw won the Music Row Breakthrough Award. "I couldn't get arrested before that," she says. "I felt like God said, 'Enough. You paid your dues.'" The following year, Warner Brothers Records offered her a recording contract.

In 1995, Shaw's debut album *In Full View* was released. It didn't produce any hit singles, but Garth Brooks scored another No. 1 hit with Shaw's "She's Every Woman," which he had included on his album *Fresh Horses*. After that, more Nashville acts, including Lorrie Morgan, Tanya Tucker, Trisha Yearwood, Suzy Boggus, and Bryan White, began recording songs Shaw had penned, or co-written with songwriters Gary Burr, Skip Ewing, and Chuck Cannon. Shaw's second album, *Victoria Shaw*, was released in 1997. Brimming with smart, well-crafted songs sung with passion, that album surprisingly also failed to generate a hit.

At the same time, Shaw was experiencing success in an unexpected quarter, soap operas. She was nominated for an Emmy Award for "All for the Sake of Love," which appeared in *As The World Turns*. In 1999, her song "Love is a Gift," sung by Olivia Newton-John and also featured in *As The World Turns*, won an Emmy for Outstanding Original Song. Shaw released her third solo album that year, *Old Friends New Memories*, on her own Taffeta Records label. The fourteen-song record included her versions of "The River," "She's Every Woman," "Too Busy Being in Love," and other hits, as well as new songs. In 2000, Shaw won the Emmy for Outstanding Original Song for "When I Think of You," featured in *One Life to Live*. The year continued at a busy pace with Latin-pop crossover superstar Ricky Martin ("Livin' La Vida Loca"), including "Nobody Wants to be Lonely," written with Gary Burr and Desmond Child on his new album, *Sound Loaded*. The song was released as a single featuring Martin duetting with pop star Christina Aguilera. A song co-written with Burr and Joe Henry, "Wave to the World," was used as the title song for an album promoting the Paralympic Games. Shaw also produced a new album for country icon Patti Page, and she was writing with actor Kevin Bacon and the reunited female trio, Wilson Phillips.

Perhaps most satisfying was that "Cryin' Time," a song from Shaw's third solo record, had become a country hit in Europe. The song is a prime example of Shaw's ability to paint vivid, emotional portraits of human behavior: "I put the saddest song on my stereo, / turned all the lights in the house down really low. / Poured myself a glass of wine. / Oh yeah, this is cryin' time. / Took the phone off the hook, built a fire. / Burned your letters one by one and watched the flames get higher. / I know by heart every single line. / Oh yeah, this is cryin' time . . ."

In the midst of her hot writing career, Shaw took time to do her part to repair the world. In 1998, she wrote a song called "One Heart at a Time" for the Cystic Fibrosis Foundation and rounded up Nashville friends and colleagues Garth Brooks, Faith Hill, Michael McDonald, Neal McCoy, Olivia Newton-John, and others to sing it. She donated all of the proceeds, and one hundred percent of her royalties to the Foundation. What began as a way to help friends raise money and awareness to fight the disease became much more personal when her father died of a heart ailment during the making of the record. "One Heart at a Time" has sold more than 250,000 copies since its release. "I feel like I do good. I try to live a good life," Shaw says of the project.

Part of trying to live a good life includes embracing Judaism. "I'm not married to a Jewish man. I always thought I would, but I didn't. But Robert (husband and manager Robert Locknar) is an incredible human being. I do believe in my heart of hearts that God brought him into my life, and that I would have been a fool to pass up that relationship. I'm lucky he wanted to have a Jewish household. We had a Jewish wedding, and we're raising our children Jewish. Robert is now more Jewish than I am. We're active in temple, and we go to dinner with the rabbi."

# Julie Gold

**Songwriter. Piano player. Born February 3, 1956, Philadelphia, Pennsylvania.**
**Best known for writing the international hit "From a Distance."**

*Julie Gold believes God had a hand in helping her write the classic "From a Distance." (Photo by David Rodgers.)*

From a distance
The World looks blue and green
And the snow-capped mountains white.
From a distance
The ocean meets the stream
And the eagle takes to flight.
From a distance
There is harmony
And it echoes through the land.
It's the voice of hope
It's the voice of peace
It's the voice of every man . . .

Julie Gold, the daughter of founders of a Philadelphia synagogue, says she was simply the vehicle God used to deliver "From a Distance" to planet Earth. Gold was a struggling but determined songwriter working as a secretary for HBO in New York when she began sketching out the words to the song in 1985. Country singer Nanci Griffith was the first to believe in Gold's peace anthem, which pointed out our common bonds rather than our differences. Griffith recorded it in 1986 for her *Lone Star State of Mind* album. The song quietly took hold in Ireland where Griffith is a popular concert attraction. But it was singer-actress Bette Midler's version that shot to No. 2 on *Billboard*'s singles chart in November of 1990, won Gold a Grammy Award for Song of the Year, was heard worldwide, and became an international standard recorded by a wide range of acts. (Even folk-rock band the Byrds included "From a Distance" as one of four new songs for the band's 1990 self-titled retrospective boxed set.) The song has been used at the Olympic Games, beamed to astronauts in space, and in 1999 was turned into a children's book illustrated by British artist Jane Ray and published by Albion Press. "From a Distance" rightfully has taken its place in the canon of pop music evergreens, songs that have a timeless, universal appeal and never wear out their welcome.

The huge success of the song focused attention on the rest of Gold's catalog. Singers as diverse as Kathy Mattea, Patti LaBelle, Cliff Richard, Judy Collins, Jack Jones, and Jewel have recorded Gold tunes. Success also allowed Gold to perform and record. She has an award-winning cabaret act, her limited voice rendered practically unnoticeable by her ceaseless enthusiasm, good nature, and warm rapport with audiences. In 1997, Gold released a CD of her songs called *Dream Loud*, which includes her interpretation of "From a Distance." The title song was adopted as a theme song by Girl Scout troops throughout New England. In 2000, a second CD, *Try Love*, was released.

Gold explains the Jewish influence in the writing of "From a Distance" this way: "I have a Jewish sensibility, so that is how I write. I think that God saw me as a diligent fisherman and saw how devoted I was, and allowed me to reel in a whale, and of course I love whales." While Gold takes credit for writing the lion's share of her songs, she credits some of them to God. "They just come through you; this is one of those songs. It was all about my heart and my pen, not grandiosity, but humility and wonder. How long did it take me to write? Thirty years and two hours."

Much of those thirty years were filled with Jewish experience. Gold's maternal grandparents were poor. They arrived in the United States from Russia in 1930 with their five children, including Gold's mother, Ann. Gold's maternal grandfather, Nathan Olinsky, an Orthodox rabbi who came to America to take over a small congregation in Philadelphia, died before Julie was born. Her maternal grandmother was killed while on the way to a charity function when struck by a drunk driver. Julie was about seven at the time. She knows little about her paternal grandparents. They emigrated from Romania and, as owners of movie theaters and some real estate, realized the American Dream. Gold's mother spent her career as a secretary in the Philadelphia school system. After retiring, she became a Yiddish teacher in her retirement community. Her father, Aaron, who died in 1992, worked in the personnel department of a whisky manufacturer, and later in the safety department of the Philadelphia police department.

When her Orthodox mother married her Conservative father, the couple became a founding family of Philadelphia Mainline Reform Temple Beth Elohim. Julie attended Hebrew school, Sunday school, and, during summers, a Reform Jewish camp in the Pocono Mountains. She also went on a National Federation of Temple Youth–sponsored high-school-in-Israel summer program in 1973, just before the outbreak of the Yom Kippur War. While she would have appreciated the trip more had she been older, she remembers "an incredible feeling of being in the land of my people and being where these founding events took place. I remember thinking that I may not believe that this is where Moses re-

ceived the Ten Commandments, but under the water I would have believed that
this was the Garden of Eden."

Music was always being played in the Gold home. Gold's father was a serious
fan of Broadway musicals; her older brother (by two years) was tuned into Top 40
AM radio stations, filling the house with the Beatles' Mersey Beat and the Motown Sound. Gold was seriously drawn to music at age four when her father took
the family to a production of *My Fair Lady*. The musicians in the orchestra pit, not
the actors, left the biggest impression. Gold began strumming a plastic toy
guitar to birds, bees, and butterflies in her backyard. She also played a fife-sized
melody flute in school, prompting her first-grade teacher to recommend that
Julie take piano lessons. Gold became Rae Goldberg's youngest pupil and began
an enduring student-teacher relationship. "I love and revere her," Gold says. "I
feel she liberated me and gave me the keys to expressing myself through music."

Gold was on her way to becoming a classical pianist when her brother introduced her to rock 'n' roll, pop, and soul music via AM radio. She spent less time
practicing lessons and more time playing along with the radio. She wondered
where the songs came from and "how you could get to do that." By the seventh
grade she was trying to write original tunes. By her sophomore year at Temple
University, Gold was playing once a week at a Philadelphia bar called the Khyber
Pass. By that time, Gold wanted to drop out of college to try to make it in New
York as a songwriter. At the urging of her parents, she finished college, graduating with a B.A. in English. "All through college, I sang in bars and never missed
a class. I owe that to my parents. All my parents did from the minute they saw my
commitment was encourage me," Gold says. "Imagine the pride I have that they
both lived to see me reach my dream." Gold moved to New York in 1978 and took
a series of odd jobs, including vacuum cleaner salesperson, to pay the rent while
pitching songs to music publishers.

Gold's songs are born in a place where folk and pop meet Tin Pan Alley. The
lyrics are smart, the melodies catchy; the stories poignant, often bursting with
promise, hope, euphoria and simple goodness. God is a recurring character; so
are biblical references and Jewish touchstones such as Anne Frank and Ellis Island. "I have always had a relationship with God. Always," Gold explains. "I can't
see a flower and not say, 'Nice work, God,' or see some of the work we humans
do and say, 'I'm sorry, God.' We're the only things he created that screwed up.
Humans live in God's masterpiece and do it with disrespect. I love being alive,

and love God's creation, and I am in constant touch with him. For me, being Jewish is a key element of being, but it is more about God than religion for me."

While "From a Distance" gets all the glory, other Gold tunes trumpet similar themes of brotherhood. In "The Human Experiment," for example, Gold sings:

> Jew and Arab look the same.
> Point the rifle and take aim.
> Spill the oil on the sea.
> Life is costly, death is free.
> And God has heard so much of this
> for years and years and years.
> He cries his eyes out all the time.
> The oceans are his tears . . .

With its opening line of "My mother came to America, sailed through the harbor of hopes and dreams," *Goodnight New York* pays tribute to her immigrant family and their courage and determination to make a better life in America. Her family is as much a rock for Gold as her faith. Her parents encouraged her every step of the way. Their positive outlook on life inspired her. (Gold describes her mother as one who "rejoices in her portion.") She shows her mother as well as her publisher every new song, and she never goes onstage without her father's lucky stone. "It possesses magical powers for me," she says. As a thirtieth birthday gift, her parents sent Julie the piano she had played throughout her childhood. The first song she wrote on it was "From a Distance."

"From a Distance" had been brewing. Gold describes it as a song about the difference between appearance and reality and the way things could and should be. "When I finally sat at the piano, these majestic chords came out of me and the words followed. All this," she adds, "is something that I prayed would drop down from heaven, and did." She continues, she says, to live her slogan: "Working, playing, pitching, praying."

# Marc Cohn

**Singer. Songwriter. Guitar player. Piano player. Born July 5, 1959, Cleveland, Ohio. Best known for the hit "Walking in Memphis," and for winning the 1991 Grammy for Best New Artist for his debut album *Marc Cohn*.**

*March Cohn, who won the Best New Artist Grammy in 1991, has used his music to explore his Jewish identity. (Photo by Paul Natkin, Photo Reserve, Inc.)*

Throughout much of the nineties, Grammy-winning singer-songwriter Marc Cohn explored a Jewish heritage and faith that had become distant and neglected. Nowhere are the results of that exploration more evident than on his 1998 album, *Burning the Daze*. The album's opening song, "Already Home," ebullient horn-driven rock 'n' soul, initially sounds like a simple declaration of finding oneself. And it is. But for Cohn that meant coming to the realization that after a long, widespread search for identity and spirituality, he found it right where he started, in the cradle of Judaism. "Already Home" is Cohn's way of trumpeting his revelation. It's there in the song's chorus: "This is where I lay my hat. / This is where they know my name. / This is where they show me that, / a man's not so alone. / Maybe I'm already home . . ." And it's hammered home in the final verse: "Why it had to take so long. / Just had to find a place that really feels, / this must be where I belong. / Thinkin' about it, all I had to do was click my heels."

If there's any doubt that Cohn is rediscovering his Judaism, the subject subtly rears its head again in the beautiful, soulful ballad "Healing Hands," and even more directly in the album's closing acoustic ballad, "Ellis Island." The song is not only a visit to a monument and journey through his people's past, but an awakening, attested to in the song's final verse: "But as the boat pulled off the shore. / I could see the fog was liftin'. / And lights I'd never seen before, / were shining down on Ellis Island, / shining down on Ellis Island." As Cohn told an interviewer in 1998, "There was a very strong sense of identity, even spirituality, that I gained from visiting there . . . It wasn't that long ago that relatives of mine were there under incredible duress and uncertainty." Cohn tried to recreate his family's experience for himself. While he doesn't make a habit of interpreting his work, he admits the songs that book-end the album, "Home" and "Island," are related, and he doesn't refute the interpretation that the songs are part of a Jewish identity reclamation project. "The record is the beginning of some kind of waking up," he said when the record was released.

It is not the first time he has made statements about his Jewishness. His interpretation of "Rock of Ages" ("Ma'oz Tzur") opens the 1996 album *Festival of Light*, a compilation of traditional and original songs recorded by Jewish and non-Jewish acts for Hanukkah. For Cohn, the invitation to participate in the project was *beshert*, meant to be. At a time when he was exploring his heritage, it was an avenue for him to connect to Jewish celebration. The album's producers described Cohn as earnest, serious, and committed to making the song as good as it could be. Sad and celebratory, it is one of the most striking and heartfelt tracks on the record, gathering strength, beauty, and momentum as it goes. Cohn's contribution to the record was also a statement about the importance of Judaism in his life. He could have played it safe, and declined the invitation. After all, he was a Grammy-winner and writer of a substantial hit in "Walking in Memphis," a song that some consider a rock classic. Even in "Walking in Memphis, Cohn hinted that a nice Jewish boy was at work. The clue is in hearing a singer named Cohn howl the sly, playful verse, "Now Muriel plays the piano, / every Friday at the Hollywood. / And they brought me down to see her, / and they asked me if I would— / Do a little number, / and I sang with all my might— / And she said, 'Tell me are you a Christian, child?' / And I said, 'Ma'am I am tonight.'" He told an interviewer in 1994 that the song wasn't just about Memphis as a place. "It has something in it about a kind of spiritual awakening."

Cohn's quest to research and perhaps reclaim his Jewish identity issued from his childhood and continued through his adulthood. He grew up in the Shaker Heights and Beachwood sections of Cleveland. The family was not well off. His mother died suddenly from a brain aneurysm when he was two; his father, who operated several pharmacies, remarried, then passed away when Marc was twelve. (The song "Saints Preserve Us" from Burning the Daze deals with his mother's death.) The youngest of four brothers, he began writing songs as early as age ten. An older brother taught him a little piano. By junior high school he also was playing guitar and had joined a band called Doanbrook Hotel, in which he performed through high school. After graduating from Beachwood High School, where he began writing songs influenced by Van Morrison, James Taylor, Joni Mitchell, and Jackson Browne, he enrolled at Oberlin College. There he majored in psychology, taught himself more piano, and began performing his songs at local coffeehouses. He transferred to UCLA, where he earned his psychology degree, and continued performing in supper clubs for a hundred dollars a night.

In the mid-eighties, he moved to New York to work in recording studios as a backup singer, appearing on albums by B. J. Thomas and Tracy Chapman, as well as lending his voice to the soundtrack record for the Andrew Lloyd Webber musical Starlight Express. He also put together a fourteen-piece party band called the Supreme Court. The group had the distinction of playing at Caroline Kennedy's 1986 wedding, having been recommended to Jackie Kennedy Onassis by singer Carly Simon. Cohn also began refining his songwriting and in 1989, on the strength of a tape that included "Walking in Memphis," he was offered a recording contract with Atlantic Records. After a false start with a producer he wasn't comfortable with, Cohn's self-titled, acoustic piano-based record was released in late 1991 at a time when grunge and alternative rock ruled. It became the surprise hit of the year. The album sold more than a million copies on the strength of the soul- and gospel-flavored "Walking in Memphis," which reached No. 13 on the charts. (Acts such as Tom Jones and Cher have since recorded the song.) The album also was a hit in the United Kingdom, spawning a second hit as well in "Silver Thunderbird," a song that grappled with his father's unfulfilled dreams.

Cohn's "overnight" success with his debut album also was the beginning of the end of his marriage. From 1991 through 1994 Cohn was almost always on the road touring and promoting the record as well as its followup, *The Rainy Season*, released in 1993. He returned home to New York and spent much of the next four years vainly trying to repair the marriage, going through a divorce, raising his two children, Max and Emily, and writing the songs that would make up *Already Home*. Between albums he remained popular as a session vocalist singing on records by Roseanne Cash, David Crosby, Carly Simon, Jimmy Webb, and Kris Kristofferson. His songs also were recorded by Crosby, Art Garfunkel, and country chanteuse Jo Dee Messina, and they were featured in the TV program ER and the film *Message in a Bottle*.

It was during this period that he also contributed "Rock of Ages" to the Hanukkah album *Festival of Light*, setting the record's glowing tone. It is no coincidence that Cohn's contribution is followed by an original instrumental composition by songwriter, producer, and multi-instrumentalist John Leventhal. Leventhal played guitar, bass, and even Irish bouzouki on Cohn's debut album, and produced and played a variety of instruments on *The Rainy Season*. Leventhal is better known as co-writer and producer of Shawn Colvin's 1997 Grammy-winning, Top Ten hit "Sunny Came Home." His song on *Festival of Light*, titled "1902" for the year his father was born, is almost more noteworthy for the explanation that accompanies it. His father, the son of Russian immigrants, was born in New York City, grew up in a Yiddish-speaking household, but distanced himself from his Jewish roots as he grew older. He married a Catholic. "By the time my sister and I came along, my father always claimed not to be able to remember any Yiddish at all," Leventhal wrote. "My sister and I were brought up neither Catholic nor Jewish, but when it came to the holidays, we celebrated

Christmas. There was always a Christmas tree, but never a menorah. My father instilled in us a secular sense of pride in our cultural Jewish heritage, but in his later years . . . I really sensed a feeling of loss and regret that he hadn't involved us more in the rituals that he himself had lost touch with. So this is for all those lost Hanukkahs and also for the ones he had on the Lower East Side. It was easy to write—like realizing you knew something all along."

Already re-examining his Judaism, it is more than likely that Cohn took a lesson from Leventhal's childhood experience, or lack of Jewish experience. As a Jew and a father, Cohn did not want to wake one day with similar regrets. Cohn's third album was already in progress when he scrapped it to work with Leventhal again. The result was a record that opened with funky horns proudly blaring, "I'm already home," and closed with the quiet but vivid homage to the courage of his ancestors: "Mothers and bewildered wives, that sailed across a raging sea. Others running for their lives, to the land of opportunity. Down on Ellis Island."

# Mike Gordon
## of Phish

**Bassist. Vocalist. Band co-founder. Born June 3, 1965, Boston, Massachusetts. Phish is best known as one of the most popular and commercially successful concert attractions of the nineties.**

At the suggestion of Phish bass player Mike Gordon, the band includes "Avinu Malcanu" and "Yerushalayim Shel Zahav" in its repertoire. From left: guitarist Trey Anastasio, Gordon, keyboard player Page McConnell, and drummer Jonathan Fishman. (Photo by Danny Clinch, © Phish.)

Whenever Phish, the daring, eclectic rock quartet from Vermont, and one of the most popular concert attractions of the nineties and the new millennium, performs "Avinu Malcanu" ("Our Father, Our King") or "Yerushalaim Shel Zahav" ("Jerusalem of Gold") in concert, bass player Mike Gordon pays closer attention to the audience. "I always look to see if there are Jewish fans out there perking up—and you can see people reacting," says Gordon. Phish, the band most cited as inheritor of the Grateful Dead's crown of improvisational folk-rock-jazz jamming, includes a pair of Jewish songs, sung in Hebrew, in its vast repertoire. Gordon brought the songs to the band because he wanted to "revisit something Jewish, and with the band into being eclectic and learning from different cultures, it wasn't totally out of line. We've done it with bluegrass, Latin music and jazz. The others were really into it." Gordon adds, "'Avinu Malcanu' has that sort of deep, lurking, familiar melody and I think [Jewish fans] feel something. It's a part of my heritage and I feel a real warmth because of their reaction."

Considering the band's extraordinarily wide repertoire, "Avinu Malcanu" has been performed fairly frequently in concert. Part of the High Holy Day liturgy, "Avinu Malcanu," more prayer than song, admits wrongdoing and humbly asks God to show mercy and inscribe "us" in the Book of Life for another year. During Phish concerts, the song is usually heard as part of a medley between original tunes written by lead guitarist Trey Anastasio. "We gave 'Avinu Malcanu' a place to live in the Phish concert world," Gordon says. "We sing it—one verse— with the original melody. It's a little more upbeat than you hear it in temple and on rare occasions some rabbis are offended. I always knew that that would be a possibility, but other times Jewish fans and rabbis are very happy we do it. We bust it out sometimes if there's something Jewish-related going on."

"Jerusalem of Gold," written by Israeli Naomi Shemer for a song contest shortly before the Six Day War in June of 1967, is a concert rarity. The band performs the song, which has become an unofficial second Israeli national anthem since the Israeli capital was reunited after the Six Day War, using an *a cappella* choral arrangement. About a minute of the song concludes the group's 1994 album *Hoist*, and a lyric from the song, "*Halo l'chol shiraich ani kinor*" (In all your songs I am a violin), written in Hebrew, is included in the CD cover liner notes. When Phish first performed the song in concert, at Great Woods in Massachusetts in the early 1990s, the band worked hard to get it right to impress Gordon's grandmother and other Jewish relatives who were in the audience.

The original plan was to perform the song with instrumentation, but a friend from Gordon's Jewish day school years found a choral arrangement of the song. Since the band had been performing barbershop quartets such as the classic "Sweet Adeline" to break up its sets, the group decided to try "Jerusalem of Gold" with vocals only. The hardest part was teaching the Hebrew lyrics to the non-Jewish band members, guitarist Anastasio, and keyboard player Page McConnell. (Drummer Jonathan Fishman, born February 19, 1965 in Philadelphia, had attended Hebrew school and is a bar mitzvah.) Serious about getting it right, the band learned the song with the help of a voice coach. The result, Gordon says, was "good enough to move people."

Gordon's Jewish roots run deep. His maternal and paternal ancestors emigrated from the Leningrad area of Russia around 1885 and settled near Boston. His father's side of the family was in the "rag business" with a mill, fabric store, and stitching room. Mike's father, Robert Gordon, was a businessman who eventually ran Store 24, a chain of convenience stores, and served as chairman of the National Association of Convenience Stores. He also became heavily involved in helping refuseniks—Soviet Jews who had been denied permission to emigrate—leave the former Soviet Union. As president of the Union of Councils of Soviet Jews, he traveled frequently to the former Soviet Union to meet with refusenik leaders such as Natan Sharansky, now a political leader in Israel. "My dad was one of the world leaders of that, and one of my many jobs during high school was updating the list of refuseniks," Gordon says. "The way my father talked about it, he wanted to do something for his people. He wanted to avoid another Holocaust."

Passover was, and is still, a major family event, and the annual building of a sukkah at school or in a neighbor's yard remains a fond memory. Believing it was important for their son to have a Jewish identity, Gordon's parents sent him to the Solomon Schechter School in Newton, Massachusetts, from kindergarten through sixth grade. The family also belonged to Temple Beth-el in Sudbury.

Gordon wasn't the perfect student, and he found Hebrew difficult to learn. He rebelled at the one-hour commute and intense Jewish education by neglecting his homework and falling behind in class. "I'd be sitting at home with my dad with the *Tanach* and an English-Hebrew dictionary while the rest of the class could read Hebrew fluently. Foreign languages came hard, though I was a communications major in college [after initially majoring in electrical engineering].

"In retrospect," he adds, "I'm glad for all of it. It was a religious and cultural identity that has become part of me. It doesn't always get played out, but I feel like it gives me a deeper identity and enriches my character. Everything from the songs we sang in class to the stories in the Torah . . . have given me roots and traditions I value."

A Jewish education and upbringing also helped him come to terms with the ideas of faith and God. "Even though I didn't know what God meant, or if I believed in God, all those hours talking about it, about a concept so big, ubiquitous, abstract, formed me into a person with more faith in the unknown, the concept of God, even biblical stories and the idea of miracles. I do think it's a miracle that we're alive at all," Gordon says.

Much of Gordon's approach to music is faith-based. For him, playing music is literally a religious experience, one that Judaism helped him explore and cultivate. "I think that that background gave me a way of thinking and pondering and existing that led to looking for a sense of spirituality in my adult life. And a lot of that has come from music, letting my ego get out of the way and letting my instrument be played for me, I guess, by God. I like to be in touch with the spiritual nature of what I do and I think my Jewish upbringing led to that sensitivity."

Gordon's first formal musical training was in the form of piano lessons at age six. He also remembers hearing Beatles albums, especially *Abbey Road*, playing in his home. At age twelve or thirteen, during a family vacation, Gordon became enamored of the vibe and vibrations of the bass guitar while listening to a calypso band. The bass, he decided, was the instrument for him. When he became an electrical engineering major at the University of Vermont even his parents didn't believe engineering fit his creative personality. His parents, in fact, would become wholehearted Phish fans—better known as Phish Heads.

Phish began taking form in 1983 when University of Vermont philosophy major and guitarist Trey Anastasio joined Jonathan Fishman, a drummer and chemical engineering major, and guitarist Jeff Holdsworth, and Gordon answered their notice seeking a bass player. The lineup solidified in 1985 with the departure of Holdsworth and the addition of keyboard player Page McConnell. By the time Phish released its first album on a major label, *A Picture of Nectar* (Elektra Entertainment) in 1992, the band was well on its way to becoming one of the most proficient, creative and fan-friendly acts of the nineties. Without a hit song, relatively little mainstream media attention, and less-than-platinum album sales, the band annually ranked among the top fifty concert attractions in the United States, and had a growing fan base in Europe and Japan.

The group is marked by a dogged work ethic, musical boldness, unpredictable, jam-packed concerts where anything goes musically and otherwise (including using a vacuum cleaner as musical instrument and arriving on stage via a giant flying kosher hot dog). Early use of the Internet to communicate with young fans and favorable comparisons of the band to the Grateful Dead also helped boost the unpretentious Phish to stardom. Having ice cream mavens Ben & Jerry name a flavor after the band, Phish Food, in 1997, didn't hurt either. (All of Phish's proceeds from ice cream sales go to charity.) The band's musicality and personality have not only drawn an unusually high number of Jewish fans, but an Orthodox rabbi as well. Since 1995, Rabbi Shmuel Skaist, who has his own group called the Gefilte Fish, has attended numerous concerts offering spiritual guidance to fans and has even held Shabbat services near concert venues.

Annual New Year's Eve concert celebrations and oddly named, multi-day concert extravaganzas (the Clifford Ball, the Great Went, Lemonwheel) at off-the-beaten-path locations (old Air Force bases in New York and Maine) have consistently drawn 60,000-plus fans. These "concerts" have become legend as much for their peacefulness and sense of community as for the music. The band's New Year's spectacle at the Big Cypress Seminole Indian Reservation in South Florida from December 30, 1999, through January 1, 2000, drew 79,000 fans from across the country and cemented its reputation for being fun-loving, innovative, and fan-friendly. (And for having fans that actually cleaned up after themselves during the weekend.) It also positioned Phish as a cutting-edge band for the new millennium, unfettered and undeterred by market trends or musical boundaries. During the first half of 2000, the band released *Farmhouse*, its seventh studio album on the Elektra label, and toured Japan and the United States. In 2001, the band took a hiatus from touring and recording, but continued to mine its archives and release collections of concert recordings to satiate hungry Phish Heads. On New Year's Eve 2002, the band ended its long "vacation" with a sold-out concert at Madison Square Garden.

For Gordon, who has an interest in Jewish mysticism, New Year's '99 remains a musical, and spiritual and religious peak. "I felt I was more myself than ever, less ego, and more connected to the world. I was totally in the moment. I want to live knowing those experiences are possible. So it makes sense that I gravitated to the mystical, and return to my roots and look at the Jewish take on things. I've got a lot of pride and connection to Judaism and just try in my own way to stay connected to it."

# Lisa Loeb

**Singer. Songwriter. Guitar player. Born March 11, 1968, in
Dallas, Texas. Best known for the No. 1 hit "Stay (I Missed You),"
from the soundtrack to the 1994 film *Reality Bites,* as well as
the Top Twenty hits "Do You Sleep?" and "I Do."**

Lisa Loeb was the first pop singer to reach No. 1 without a recording contract.
(Photo by E. Patino, courtesy of Geffen Records.)

Lisa Loeb is in the vanguard of young Jewish performers who, in the nineties, began to unselfconsciously exhibit Jewish pride and publicly demonstrate an ease with their Jewish identity. Since 1994, when Loeb made pop music history by becoming the first performer without a recording contract to score a No. 1 hit, Loeb has refused to compromise her Jewish soul in exchange for possible career advancement. Some of her actions would have been unthinkable only decades earlier for Jewish pop and rock stars seeking mass appeal. Once asked during a television interview what she was planning to do for the Christmas holiday, she answered that she celebrated Hanukkah, not Christmas. When a radio station asked her to wish its listeners a Merry Christmas, Loeb, uncomfortable with the idea, politely declined. She has wished concert audiences a happy Passover and Easter when the holidays fell at the same time, she says, "even though they have nothing to do with each other." Perhaps her boldest move in proclaiming her Jewishness was setting it down in black-and-white in her official record company biography. In a paragraph detailing her early performing experiences, Loeb noted that she played the part of Linus in *You're a Good Man Charlie Brown* at the Jewish Community Center in Dallas.

Loeb has not hidden or glossed over her Jewish identity when it would have been more convenient to do so, because, she says, "people have become more proud of their differences; they're not afraid to stand up and say who they are." She also is proud enough to speak up when people make anti-Semitic remarks, letting them know that she is Jewish and didn't appreciate what they said. Their response, she says, is usually "'You don't look Jewish. I didn't know.'" Her answer to that: "Well, it just shows your ignorance."

Loeb is not alone in her honest take-me-for-who-I-am stance. Since including her performance at the Dallas JCC in her record company bio, a wave of acts rising on the national scene have unabashedly let their audiences know, in one way or another, that they are Jewish. The Rosenbergs, a power-pop quartet from the New York area, do it through their band name (though only two of the members are Jewish and neither is named Rosenberg). The Boston-based acoustic rock trio Guster offers obvious clues on its Web site, and performs "The Dreidel Song" in concert. Los Angeles–based singer-songwriter Dan Bern reclaimed his family name, now calls himself Bernstein, and peppers many of his mainstream folk-rock songs with Jewish references. Singer-songwriters Judith Edelman and Jen Cohen, both Nashville-based, let their Judaism out of the bag during between-song banter at their shows, especially when performing in the Bible Belt. And Atlanta-bred twins Evan and Jaron Lowenstein request kosher food backstage and will not perform on Shabbat.

Loeb, one of four siblings, grew up in a close-knit family that had deep roots in the Dallas Jewish community. Both her maternal and paternal grandparents were raised in Texas. The family celebrated all the Jewish holidays, with Passover, Rosh Hashanah, Yom Kippur, and Hanukkah, especially important. The family belonged to Temple Emanuel, a Reform congregation, where Lisa attended Sunday school from kindergarten through tenth grade. "I was bat mitzvahed, confirmed, consecrated, everything. I had a pretty Jewish upbringing," Loeb explains. She also had a very musical upbringing. Her mother, Gail, studied ballet and modern dance in college, and playing piano was a serious hobby for her father, Peter. The four Loeb children, two boys, Ben and Philip, and two girls, Lisa and Debbie, all took years of piano lessons. The sisters also had dance lessons. The children learned art appreciation, often visited museums, and were frequently taken to the theater. "I think education in the arts is a Jewish tradition," Loeb says. Lisa and her sister sang along to the latest Olivia Newton-John and Elton John records, and to Broadway musical soundtracks playing in the house, and Lisa participated in the annual school play, as well as shows at the Dallas JCC.

At fourteen, with the family piano drawing a crowd, and older brother Benjamin showing world-class potential on the instrument, Lisa switched to guitar. She began writing songs regularly a year later, influenced by David Bowie and Jimi Hendrix, and new wave rockers such as the Police and the Cure. Her first effort was an instrumental called "Fried Eggs." After graduating from high school, Loeb enrolled at Brown University, where she formed a group called Liz and Lisa and spent the majority of her time writing songs, performing, and recording. She eventually developed a playing style that included simultaneously strumming with a flatpick and finger picking with her other three fingers. Her songs, more like confessions, confrontations, and conversations with intimates, were wrapped in a folk-pop-rock-jazz hybrid style coated with breezy vocals, and later on record, enriched with orchestral arrangements.

Loeb's parents were shocked when she announced that she wanted to become a professional musician. Lisa responded that with music playing in the house all the time, years of music theory and piano lessons, and exposure to musical theater, her parents shouldn't have been so surprised. It was a natural course to follow. In 1990, Loeb moved to New York and continued playing area nightclubs and coffeehouses as the duo Liz and Lisa as well as with a band called Nine Stories. After Liz and Lisa amicably parted, Lisa recorded an untitled acoustic collection of songs that became known as *The Purple Tape*, which she sold at her shows. She also used *The Purple Tape*, as well as a collection of songs recorded with her band Nine Stories in 1993, to showcase her music to record company talent scouts. The latter collection included a gentle, wistful song of longing called "Stay (I Missed You)." Loeb's friend, actor Ethan Hawke, took the tape to actor Ben Stiller who was directing the film, *Reality Bites*. Stiller thought "Stay" was just right for the film, which was released in 1994.

A video of the song was made to promote the film and the accompanying RCA Records soundtrack album. Both song and video struck a chord with the public. The video was ubiquitous on MTV and other music programs, and the song spent twenty-five weeks on the charts, three weeks at No. 1, and sold 750,000 copies. Loeb and Nine Stories were nominated for a Grammy Award for Best Pop Performance by a Group and won a Brit Award for Best International Newcomer. All of this was an unheard-of accomplishment for a singer and songwriter without a recording contract. Loeb signed on with Geffen Records and, with Nine Stories, recorded and released her debut album, *Tails*, a year later. She took her brand of breathy, breathless, alternative folk-rock on the road and toured heavily with her band and as a solo performer. The rigorous schedule paid off with a second hit single, "Do You Sleep?" in the fall of 1995. With a pair of hits on her résumé, Loeb was invited to tour with acts such as Lyle Lovett, Sarah McLachlan, and Counting Crows. She also landed a spot on the all-female Lilith Fair tour. But touring in Germany and other European countries was uncomfortable for her. "I'd be working out in a gym, and I'd think that the older people being nice to me were probably around during the Holocaust, and it made me nervous to talk about Judaism there," she says. It was probably coincidence that the first single from Loeb's 1997 followup album, *Firecracker*, was a liberating, up-tempo tune about finally refusing to be pushed around in a relationship. Titled "I Do," the song became Loeb's third Top Twenty hit.

Loeb is not certain of a specific Jewish influence in her work. Most of her songs, on a conscious level, center on telling stories of interpersonal and romantic relationships. But with a life steeped in Jewish spirituality, tradition, and

Bible stories that she finds simultaneously romantic and sad, and full of imagery and symbols, she says, "everything filters in." She's more certain that the value Jews place on education has resulted in an obsession with getting the songs just right. "I feel some kind of responsibility to do a good job," Loeb says. "I don't know if that's family or Judaism." Loeb's songs, many of them orchestrated by older brother Ben, have found a place on numerous film and television sound-track albums since "Stay" made her a star in 1994. In 1995, her song "How" was featured on the *Twister* soundtrack, and used again in the 1998 film *Jack Frost*. Loeb also landed a song, "All Day," on the soundtrack to *Rugrats: The Movie* in 1998. In 1999, concert versions of "I Do" and "Falling in Love' were featured on a pair of CDs that chronicled the Lilith Fair tour. "Falling in Love," a fan concert favorite, also was featured on the compilation CD, *Where Music Meets Film: Live from the Sun-dance Film Festival*. Her song "I Wish" appeared in the Susan Sarandon–Natalie Portman film, *Anywhere But Here*. The song "Summer" was included on *Friends Again*, a soundtrack companion to the hit TV comedy, and it also was used on *Music for Our Mother Ocean, Vol. 3*, a benefit for an ocean preservation group. Loeb also participated in Music Bridges Around the World, a program that sent a four-dozen-strong contingent of American songwriters to Havana for a week to write with Cuban counterparts. In 2000, Loeb's signature song, "Stay," was included on the VH1 compilation, *Welcome to Storytellers*, which also featured tunes by Ste-vie Nicks, Natalie Merchant, Jewel, and James Taylor. Playing against type, Loeb participated on an Ozzy Osbourne tribute CD, *Bat Head Soup*. In 2001, Loeb was making forays into television, appearing on *The Chris Isaak Show*, and released her third studio album, *Cake and Pie*. One of her new songs, "We Could Still Belong Together," was featured in the film *Legally Blonde*.

Judaism remains an important part of Loeb's life, perhaps best illustrated by her voracious appetite for books on Jewish subjects. That's partly from her own thirst to learn more about her religion, and partly from being thrust into the role of "rebbe" by her many non-Jewish friends who frequently question her about Jewish holidays and traditions. Loeb believes the reason more Jews don't talk about Judaism is from embarrassment stemming from a lack of Jewish knowl-edge. She encourages her Jewish friends and fans to overcome any embarrass-ment, for that only maintains ignorance. "They don't want to talk about religion because they don't think they know enough about it," she says. "But instead of not talking about it, I think they should go as far as they can with it."

# Dan Bern, a.k.a. Bernstein

**Singer. Songwriter. Guitar player. Harmonica player. Born Mount
Vernon, Iowa, July 27, 1959. Best known for dramatic, unpredictable
concert performances, and thought-provoking songwriting unafraid
to tackle any subject. One of the most important new voices
to arrive on the music scene in the nineties.**

*Dan Bern returned to using his father's family name, Bernstein, after visiting Lithuania where most of
his father's family perished during the Holocaust. (Photo by Patricia Masisak, courtesy Dan Bern.)*

In June of 1999, several years after his father's death, singer-songwriter Dan Bern decided to visit his father's birthplace of Skuodas, Lithuania, and learn about the family members he never got to know. His father, born Yehuda Bernstein, and one brother, Leon, were the only members of a family of seven to survive the Nazi invasion of Lithuania. They had fled Lithuania in 1939 after Hitler's pact with the Soviet dictator Joseph Stalin. Yehuda eventually made it to Palestine, while Leon joined partisans in the forests of Eastern Europe and the former Soviet Union. Bern's mother, Marianne, was a German Jew who, along with a sister, made it to England in 1939 by way of *kindertransport*, the now-famous train that was allowed to leave Germany for England carrying thousands of Jewish children. Her parents made it to England three weeks later.

Bern's father's family wasn't as fortunate. On June 22, 1941, the Nazis invaded Lithuania with a plan to eradicate the country's 225,000 Jews by Yom Kippur. The village of Skuodas was in the path of the Gestapo's deadly Einsatzkomando 2 unit as well as Lithuanian Nazi collaborators. In village after village, the men and women were separated, the women locked in synagogues and used as slave labor, lent to farmers and forced to work in their fields. All males over the age of sixteen were marched into the woods in groups of fifty or more, forced to dig large pits, then shot, and buried in mass graves. This continued relentlessly for days until nearly every male Lithuanian Jew over the age of sixteen had been killed. The women and children were murdered later. Only 10,000 of Lithuania's Jews escaped the slaughter.

Fifty-eight years later, Bern, along with an Israeli cousin, visited Skuodas (as well as the sites of the Vilna and Kovno ghettos), searching for a part of his past he never knew, and for a part of his father's past he wanted to better understand. With the help of a guide, he and his cousin found people who remembered their family and the location of the family's shoe factory. They spoke with a man who recounted the Nazi occupation of the town and described hearing the shots that killed hundreds. Bern's trip back in time was emotionally overwhelming. "I went back to get my house in order, to make peace with my past, to face it and look at it," Bern says. "It was a very profound experience." A major result of the trip was the reclamation of his family name. "A women we met in Skuodas knew the name Bernstein, and from that moment I felt I was Bernstein [pronounced Bernstine]." Returning home, singer-songwriter Dan Bern became simply Bernstein, even dropping his first name. He changed the message on his answering machine, welcoming callers with "Bernstein here," and changed his Web site home page to read "Bernstein a.k.a. Dan Bern." It strengthened his sense of identity, and his connection to his family. "Now, when I say 'Bernstein,' I feel something every time," he says. He continues to use Bern as his professional stage name.

Bern's family history and Jewish identity fuel much of his songwriting and form much of his world view and conduct, which includes, to a great degree, championing the talmudic commandment, "Justice, justice you shall pursue." His songs are fearless and unafraid, often politically incorrect, always insightful, and, like master storyteller Randy Newman, filled with irony, sarcasm, humor and wit as well as a variety of characters who help him make his often scathing points. Where Newman prefers an economy of words, Bern veers into early Bob Dylan territory spinning tales and spitting words in an aggressive stream-of-consciousness style, accented by a driving, percussive guitar. Songs such as "Jerusalem," "One Thing Real," "Hannibal," and "Wasteland," are among those in his catalog that reference Judaism, religion, and the evil of Nazism.

In "Hannibal," Bern takes on Holocaust deniers, among other things, with the verse, "Hitler never hurt a soul / I read it in a book / That I finished up just this morning / I was happy and I couldn't wait to tell the good news / To all of my dead uncles." The song "Oh, Sister" is a tribute to his older sibling, Jennifer, a cantor at a Norfolk, Virginia, synagogue.

His most autobiographical and cathartic song, however, is "Lithuania," a song of profound loss and painful triumph, written before his 1999 trip: "These are my ghosts: My uncle Emanuel, uncle Eli, aunt Mia / And my grandparents, Jenny and Tobias, / none of whom I ever met / I saw some letters once that they wrote my dad in Palestine in 1940 / Not too long before they were all shot . . . / Sometimes I want to dance on Hitler's grave / And shout out (the names) Groucho Marx, Lenny Bruce, Leonard Cohen, Philip Roth, Bob Dylan, Albert Einstein, Woody Allen, Abbie Hoffman . . ." The song continues with, "I say Kristallnacht is over! / The only broken glass tonight / Will be from wedding glasses shattered under boot heels . . ."

Dan Bern was born in Mount Vernon, Iowa, in 1959. His parents had met in Israel around 1950. His mother, Marianne, had been assigned to work there for the World Jewish Congress. Marianne and Yehuda returned to England for about a year, then immigrated to the United States in 1954 where Yehuda Bernstein changed his name to Julian Bern. The family spent time in New York, then Chicago, before Julian, a pianist and composer, found a job as a professor of music at Cornell College in Mount Vernon. Dan and his older sister, Jennifer, were the only Jews in the Mount Vernon public schools.

His parents drove him to nearby Cedar Rapids for Hebrew school and bar mitzvah lessons. While he grew up in a house filled with musicians playing Mozart (everybody played piano), music didn't truly resonate for him until around age twelve when he discovered storytellers such as blues man Lightnin' Hopkins, folk singer Woody Guthrie, and, of course, master raconteur Bob Dylan. "When I heard that," Bern says, "I found the right setting for myself." It wasn't long before he picked up a guitar, and ideas, stories, and commentary began spilling from him. After graduating from Lawrence University in Wisconsin, where he spent much of his time playing tennis, practicing guitar, and writing songs, he headed to Chicago and began performing seven nights a week in the city's clubs. He also began playing at midwestern colleges. He even performed in Germany while visiting his sister, who, ironically, was studying to be an opera singer in the country her mother had been forced to flee.

He moved to Los Angeles in 1986 in his quest for a recording contract. He spent years doing odd jobs that included club bouncer and performing in coffeehouses and at open mike nights in clubs. In 1991, record producer and studio engineer Chuck Plotkin, known for his work with Bob Dylan and Bruce Springsteen, heard him and began trying to get Bern a record deal. In 1995, Bern gave up on a recording contract to pursue what he loved best: performing. He traded in an apartment for a van, and began a seemingly endless tour of the country, earning a following in the process. In 1996, Bern was offered a recording contract with a division of Sony Music called The Work Group. The record label released Bern's self-produced, six-song EP, *dog boy van* that year, to critical acclaim that heralded him as "the Bob Dylan for the skateboard generation." (Though rocker Elvis Costello and satirist Lenny Bruce are also fair comparisons.)

Bern's been making waves, provoking listeners, and winning fans ever since. And he's been doing it with that "next Dylan" millstone around his neck. Initial comparisons are unavoidable: Both are guitar-strumming, harmonica-blowing, midwestern Jews who sing with a nasal whine, have a poet's way with words, and the ability to express an idea as it's never been expressed before. But unlike Dylan, Bern has an in-your-face punk-rock streak in him, is more autobiographically blunt in song, and is more communicative with concert audiences. In 1997,

Bern followed *dog boy van* with the Chuck Plotkin–produced, eleven-song album, *Dan Bern*, featuring the song "Jerusalem," in which Bern questions the coming of the Messiah by revealing that he is the Messiah. "Yes I think you heard me right / I am the Messiah / I was gonna wait 'til next year / Build up the suspense a little / Make it a really big surprise / But I could not resist," he sings. In 1998, Bern released *fifty eggs*, a twelve-song bittersweet onslaught of incisive social commentary produced by singer-songwriter and kindred spirit Ani DiFranco. The prolific Bern followed that in 1999 with *Smartie Mine*, a 27-song, double CD that maintained his high caliber of writing. In the midst of this flurry of recordings, Bern also independently published a pair of paperback books, *Dan Bern's Big Book of Songs, Stories and Pictures*, which included the lyrics to his first two releases and showcased his cartoon-style drawings, and *Ted the Cow*, again peppered with his artwork.

Bern is always provocative, and he can be quite profane on record and on stage. In fact, he has been banned from some folk festivals for using a few too many expletives. He explains that there are two kinds of folk music: that which makes listeners feel good and gives them a respite from the world grind, and music that provokes listeners to question their world. Bern prefers the latter. "I try to put it (the world) in some kind of perspective, whether it's humorous, raunchy, sad, whatever, and that has its place, too. Sometimes festivals want to be all soft and cheery. The irony is they cloak it in some kind of family values. For me there's nothing better than to give a family something to think about."

Bern is as much news commentator as he is chronicler of family history and social behavior. Current events such as the 1995 bombing of the federal building in Oklahoma, the Los Angeles riots, the suicide of rock star Kurt Cobain, and the epidemic of shootings in the nation's high schools during the nineties, were all catalysts for songs. "Kids' Prayer" was written after the shootings of students at a Springfield, Oregon, high school in 1998, but released on CD after the slaughter at Columbine High School in Littleton, Colorado, in 1999. The song urges parents to "Talk to your kids / Play with your kids / Tell them your dreams / and your disappointments / Listen with your kids / Listen to your kids / Watch your kids / Let your kids watch you." Historical icons and pop culture celebrities fill many of his songs. It's a device he uses to create universal shared experiences in an era when niche marketing and programming afford the public less common ground than ever before. Santa Claus, Marilyn Monroe, Muhammad Ali, Vincent

Van Gogh, baseball player Pete Rose, and Jesus Christ are all subjects of, or characters in, his songs.

He pulls no punches in "One Thing Real," cleverly using Jesus to question the role of savior assigned to him. "Jesus, he comes up to me / Jesus he sits down / Says take this f-----g cross off my back / I'm goin' downtown / I said, aw but ain't that your uniform / He offers me a toke / Says 2,000 years is long enough for this particular joke . . ."

Blunt or not, Bern sees himself as more than a contemporary folk singer. He views himself as a descendant of a centuries-old Jewish (and Irish and English) tradition of storytelling. Incorporating ancient talmudic debate that encourages questioning authority and wrestling with God, he is a modern-day wandering minstrel spreading news and often uncomfortable, but perceptive, views. He believes the difference between himself and his musical forebears is that they didn't have the technology to record music and thus leave a legacy. "Who knows what great balladeers there were in the Ukraine in the 1600s?" Bern wonders. "We don't know about them because they never walked into a studio and banged out their twelve best songs." In late 2001, Bern released *New American Language* and toured with a backup band he dubbed the International Jewish Banking Conspiracy." In 2002, the prolific Bern released a five-song CD called *The Swastika E.P.*

# Rami Jaffee
## of the Wallflowers

**Keyboard player. Songwriter. Producer. Born March 11, 1969, Hollywood, California. Band formed in Los Angeles in 1990, best known for the hit singles "6th Avenue Heartache," Grammy-winning "One Headlight," and "The Difference," from the album *Bringing Down the Horse*.**

*The Wallflowers shortly after the release of their 2002 album Red Letter Days. From left, bass player Greg Richling, singer and guitarist Jakob Dylan, drummer Mario Calire, and keyboard player "Rabbi" Rami Jaffee. (Photo by Marina Chavez.)*

In December of 1999, when the Wallflowers were recording *Breach*, the follow-up to their Grammy-winning, four-million-plus-selling album, *Bringing Down the Horse*, Rami Jaffee, the band's keyboard player, arrived at Sunset Sound studio in Hollywood with a backpack full of extra gear. Instead of recording equipment, however, Jaffee pulled from the bag a Hanukkiah, candles, yarmulkes, and copies of the Hanukkah candle-lighting prayers. Before the recording session began, Jaffee assembled band members, guest musicians, producers, engineers—Jewish or not—passed out the yarmulkes and prayers, and led a service for the opening night of Hanukkah. Each night, for the duration of the holiday, the Hanukkah candles were lit before the recording sessions began. The Jews in the studio were appreciative, but few were surprised at Jaffee's dedication to celebrating Jewish holidays, especially the other two Jewish members of the Wallflowers, lead singer and guitarist Jakob Dylan (Born December 9, 1969, New York City) and bass player Greg Richling (Born August 31, 1970, Santa Monica, California).

For years, whether on concert tours or making records, they watched Jaffee make time to welcome Shabbat, even if it was shortly before going onstage for a show. They often shared the moment with him. "They light up when we do it. All it takes is a nudge and the kippas are on," Jaffee says of his bandmates. With the philosophy that it's the thought that counts, Jaffee has said Kiddush over Pepsi and recited the Motzi using potato chips when kosher wine and a challah, or any wine or bread for that matter, could not be found. He's also drawn Stars of David on cups and wine glasses to add to the spirit of the occasion. The important thing, Jaffee says, "is to spend a second remembering you're Jewish, to do what it takes to feel Jewish." In 1997, during recording sessions for a solo album by Richie Sambora, the lead guitarist for Bon Jovi, Jaffee was dubbed "Rabbi Rami" by Sambora's co-writer Richie Supa (born Goodman). Jaffee encouraged everyone in the studio to honor Shabbat and remember their Jewish roots even though they were about to go to work. Sambora's backing group could have been called the Jewish All-Star Band. When Sambora appeared on *The Tonight Show* to promote his record, *Undiscovered Soul*, his band included "Rabbi Rami" on keyboards, Supa on guitar, the ubiquitous producer-musician Don Was (born Fagenson) on bass, and the irrepressible Kenny Aronoff on drums.

Jaffee grew up in a Conservative Jewish home in Hollywood, California. His family, which includes an older brother and sister, celebrated Shabbat. The house was kosher down to two sets of dishes, and even a third set for Passover.

Rami's father, Marty, was from New York, the son of Ukrainian Jews. His mother, Regine Benyayer, a Sephardic Jew from Morocco, had moved to Israel in 1959 while in her twenties, to work on a kibbutz. Marty and Regine met in Israel in late 1961 and married early the next year. Marty, a computer expert, had been on assignment in Tel Aviv teaching programming to the Israeli Department of Defense. After that assignment, the couple lived in New York for three years, then, upon acceptance of a new job in the aerospace industry, moved the family to the Los Angeles area in 1965, settling in the heavily Jewish Fairfax section of Hollywood, where Rami was born. Rami attended the Institute of Jewish Education, a nursery school where his mother worked, and went on to attend Hebrew school three days a week at Conservative Temple Beth Am, where he became a bar mitzvah. (He continued to attend Hebrew school even after his bar mitzvah.)

He began taking piano lessons at age five after hearing his father dabble at home on the family piano and watching his older sister take lessons. By ten, he was in his first band. The band knew only three songs—"Bye-Bye Love" by the Cars, "Surrender" by Cheap Trick, and "Cars" by Gary Numan—but got a chance to perform them at a school talent show. In the seventh grade, Jaffee's junior high school principal asked him and his friend, drummer Sean Franks (son of musician Michael Franks), to perform at a Masons' meeting. They played an instrumental version of "Stairway to Heaven," with just piano and drums. Jaffee called it "the weirdest duo in the world," but it helped him realize his life's direction. At thirteen, he took his bar mitzvah money and bought a Casio keyboard. He also switched piano teachers, dropping his classical training in favor of studying jazz. He played in a series of bands throughout high school, including an early version of Warrant, a pop-metal band that would score a string of hits in the late eighties and early nineties. By 1989, Jaffee was gaining a reputation as a dependable session player and, to achieve the elusive goal of a recording contract, was in several bands simultaneously, even accompanying El Vez, "the Mexican Elvis."

That year, he also began dating Alicia Backer. A non-Jew, she was curious about Judaism, and when Jaffee found he couldn't answer a lot of her questions, the two enrolled in introductory Judaism and Hebrew classes in 1990. They fell in love, Alicia converted to Judaism, and the couple married in 1993. They have a daughter named Tovy. When Jaffee's not on tour or stuck in the studio they celebrate Shabbat, often with Wallflowers bass player Richling and his wife, Shana, who live nearby.

Rami Jaffee on his bar mitzvah day. (Photo courtesy of Rami Jaffee.)

The Wallflowers were cooked up in a delicatessen in 1990. (At one point in its early stages the band had a short-lived all-Jewish lineup.) Band leader Jakob Dylan still needed a keyboard player when a mutual acquaintance spotted Jaffee waiting in line to get into the popular Los Angeles eatery Canter's Deli. Dylan and the rest of the band, then known as the Apples, often hung out in a small bar off the main room called the Kibbitz Room, where it was less crowded and the beers were cheaper. The two were introduced; Dylan played Jaffee a three-song tape, and Jaffee was won over by the blues-based tunes. Jaffee was already playing just about every night in different bands, sometimes two the same night, all with different styles. Unfazed, he began rehearsing with the Wallflowers the following day. He had no idea that his new pal, Jakob, was the son of Bob Dylan, and didn't find out until months later. What was more important, and established within the first few minutes of meeting in the Kibbitz Room, was that at that point four out of five band members were Jewish. "It's more of a brotherhood, same tribe kind-of-thing. It's not necessarily religious," Jaffee explains of the landsman bond. Jaffee loved the Wallflowers' roots-rock sound. Still, he hedged his bets by remaining in several other bands. He was sure one band eventually would be offered a recording contract. He never figured it would be the Wallflowers. "I thought this was probably the last band that was going to get me somewhere," recalls Jaffee, "but it felt so good. This was great just for my heart."

The meeting at the Kibbitz Room not only launched a band, it gave birth to a celebrated Tuesday night jam session immortalized in the song "Rocking in the Kibbitz Room," by Chuck E. Weiss. What began innocently as a birthday party for Jaffee unintentionally ballooned into a wacky, weekly oddball jam session when a crowd showed up the following Tuesday expecting more of the same "schmaltzy, campy, two-chord jams," Jaffee and his friends had delivered the previous week. Contrary to many accounts, these were not Wallflowers rehearsals, though various Wallflowers participated. The deli manager, recognizing an opportunity, asked Jaffee to host Tuesday nights at the Kibbitz Room. As word spread, members of rock 'n' roll royalty were drawn to the cramped stage, Neil Young, Jackson Browne, Melissa Etheridge, and U2 lead singer Bono among them. One night, Jaffee recalls, former Monkee Peter Tork quietly arrived through a back door, plugged in his guitar, enthusiastically played three songs, then left without saying a word. From 1991 through 1994, the jam sessions were the talk of the town, with a host of rock stars dropping in to hang out or play on the cramped stage in the seventy-five-seat room.

In 1991, the Wallflowers also got their first record deal, and, in 1992, released their self-titled debut album. With Jakob Dylan refusing to do much record promotion, or talk about his relationship with his famous father, the record drew little interest. The problems didn't end there. Bob Dylan fans began showing up at Wallflowers concerts wearing Bob Dylan T-shirts, eyeing Dylan junior like a curiosity and shouting requests for daddy Dylan's songs. Such requests were not honored. Disillusioned with the lack of commercial success, band members began to quit. Jaffee delivered pizzas and worked in a shoe store to make ends meet while the band regrouped and polished its act.

In 1995, when a new record deal was secured, only Jaffee and Dylan remained from the original lineup. New members were added after the two already had begun recording the band's followup record, *Bringing Down the Horse.* Jakob Dylan's songwriting had matured and, cryptic and dense, was reminiscent of his father's early work. Jakob's voice was gruff and gravely, more Bruce Springsteen than Dad. The band's sound pleasingly fell somewhere between the muscular folk-rock of Tom Petty and the Heartbreakers and the laid-back country-rock of the Jayhawks. Jaffee's keyboards were prominent in the mix on just about every track. The album was released in May of 1996, and with strong radio support and relentless touring, spawned three hit singles: "6th Avenue Heartache," "One Headlight," and "The Distance." By early 1998, *Horse* had sold more than two million copies. The Top Ten hit, "One Headlight," won Grammy Awards for Best Rock Song and Best Rock Performance by a Group or Duo. (Like son, like father, Dylan senior won three Grammys for his album *Time Out of Mind*, including Album of the Year.) In 1998, the band also was featured on the film soundtrack to *Godzilla*, performing a version of the 1977 David Bowie hit "Heroes." That song also became a hit for the Wallflowers, reaching No. 27 on the charts.

The Wallflowers toured incessantly, then finally returned to the studio in 1999 to record its third album, *Breach*, released in September 2000. By then, the band had coalesced, and the three Jewish members had formed a special bond. "There's a certain spirituality in what we do that keeps us at it," Jaffee says. "It's more of a subconscious feeling that we're brothers and tribe members. To the others in the band it's a novelty." Throughout the nineties, Jaffee also remained active as a session musician, adding his touch to a stylistically diverse array of acts from El Vez to the rock trio Everclear. In 1999 alone, Jaffee's album credits included Garth Brooks's *In the Life of Chris Gaines*, Melissa Etheridge's *Breakdown*, Macy Gray's *On How Life Is*, and the film soundtrack to *Anywhere But Here*. In the summer of 2002, the Wallflowers were back in the studio recording a new album called *Red Letter Days*. No matter the recording session, 'Rabbi Rami' hosted Shabbat in the studio for whoever wanted to participate. "I'd rather celebrate Shabbat at home, but since I'm not home let's still do it, and spread it to other guys in the band," Jaffee says. "Jews are always wandering, so you've got to make the best of it."

# Remedy

**Songwriter. Rapper/MC. Producer. Born Ross Filler, November 4, 1970, Staten Island, New York. Best known for the song "Never Again," one of the most powerful statements about the Holocaust and its aftermath ever written and recorded.**

*The Jewish hip-hop artist Remedy is not shy about infusing his songs with Jewish pride. (Photo courtesy Ross Filler.)*

White Jewish rapper and MC Remedy became internationally known among Jews and non-Jews alike on the strength of an emotionally gripping Holocaust rap on the 1998 compilation hip-hop album, *Wu-Tang Presents the Killa Bees: The Swarm.* The album was compiled and produced by RZA (pronounced rizzuh), a member of the popular Staten Island hip-hop group Wu-Tang Clan, with whom Remedy often works. (Because of his affiliation with Wu-Tang Clan, Remedy is also known as "Jew-Tang.")

Four minutes and nine seconds long, the song, titled "Never Again" not only expressed the sorrow, loss, shock, and anger wrought by the Holocaust, but also a new-found defiance and vigilance. "Never Again" is a tidal wave of vivid, chilling, overpowering imagery and poetry that combines ancient Hebrew prayers with "Hatikvah," the Israeli national anthem, and Remedy's spitfire Holocaust history rap. The chorus creates goose bumps: "Never again shall we march like sheep to the slaughter. / Never again leave our sons and daughters. / Never again shall our children be stripped of our culture, robbed of our names, / Raped of our freedom and thrown into the flames, / Forced from our families, / taken from our homes, / Pulled from our God, / and burned of our bones. / Never Again." Since the song's release and its embrace by Jewish youth, Remedy has spent hours in Jewish day schools and Hebrew schools talking about the importance of remembering the Holocaust, and serving as a role model for Jewish pride.

Ross Filler grew up on Staten Island hearing a much different song, an anti-Semitic one that he recalls, went like this: "Collecting, collecting the *Daily News.* You got pennies, give 'em to the Jews." He heard that taunt, and others like it, so often as a child that for a while he was ashamed to admit he was Jewish. Though he attended Sunday school and Hebrew school, his parents' divorce, when he was about ten, set back his Jewish education and weakened his Jewish identity. At thirteen, he had what he describes as a "low key" bar mitzvah. In the late eighties, he attended Staten Island's New Dorp High School, where future members of the Wu-Tang Clan also were enrolled. Filler was a fan of metal acts such as Ozzy Osbourne and Iron Maiden, and was a member of the KISS Army, the band's fan club, from age nine. But at his interracial high school he was exposed to rap music, which was beginning to gain commercial acceptance. The Beastie Boys (a white Jewish hip-hop trio with street credibility), KRS-ONE, and Run DMC were early influences.

Filler became the self-described black sheep of his family. Instead of following in his father's footsteps and attending Cornell University, as his older brother and sister did, Filler immersed himself in hip-hop culture, spending most of his time in recording studios learning how to make rap records. He also entered local talent shows. In 1987, he dubbed himself MC Remedy, choosing the name to broadcast that he was part of the solution to society's ills, not part of the problem. He dropped the "MC" a few years later when the overused term was no longer fashionable as part of a name. In 1992, Remedy met Robert Diggs, better known as RZA, the leader of Wu-Tang Clan, who became a friend and mentor. (The nine-member Wu-Tang Clan began to gain fans in 1992 with a "gangsta"-as-warrior image based on kung fu movies, video games, and comics. Since then, the group's albums have sold in the millions, and that success has spawned a clothing line, comic books, and a bestselling video game.)

Around 1995 Filler became curious about his Jewish heritage and began to research his roots as well as Jewish history and belief. He called it "a search for the truth." He learned from his paternal grandmother, Gertrude Filler (probably derived from Phila), an immigrant from Hungary, that a great uncle and his family were killed in the Holocaust. The more he read about the Holocaust, the angrier he became that it was not taught when he was in high school. The more he read about Jewish history, the prouder he became about the resiliency, determination, accomplishments, and mission of the Jewish people. The child who was once afraid to admit being Jewish, now believed strongly in it, and was vocal in saying so. "I think Judaism definitely helped give me a sense of security," he says.

Filler, recast as Remedy, became a savvy hip-hop act who made no secret of his love of Judaism. He wore his Jewish pride in the form of a fist-sized Star of David emblazoned with a "Chai" on a thick gold chain around his neck. This took more chutzpah than one might imagine, as some of the members of Wu-Tang Clan belonged to the Five Percent Nation of Islam, which is known to be anti-Semitic. But Remedy says the Wu-Tang members respect him for standing tall as a Jew. "They know I'm dealing with equality, and truth, and justice for my people," he says. Aside from "Never Again," other song titles include "Rueven ben Menachum" (his Hebrew name) and "Judaic by Genetics." While Remedy has incorporated Jewish pride and awareness into his music as few others have, he considers himself a mainstream hip-hop act looking to appeal to the masses. "I'm Jewish, and I take pride in it," he says, "but I'm a rapper, and I'm human, so first things first, I deal with humanity."

In 1997, Remedy's first single for public consumption, "Seen it All," a sting-
ing commentary on racism, earned critical praise. In 1998, Remedy was invited
to submit a song for a compilation that featured performances by acts associated
with the Wu-Tang Clan. Remedy submitted "Never Again," a song he says was
easy to write "once [he] decided to do it." He already had composed the music,
which he describes as ominous, and was looking for a dramatic story to go with
it. He had seen the film *Schindler's List*, which many of his non-Jewish peers and
acquaintances didn't realize, or even believe, was based on a true story. Remedy
felt someone of his generation had to say something to Jews and non-Jews alike.
He decided to begin his song the same way the film began, with a family saying
the blessings over the wine and bread when the Nazis kick in their door. (The *kiddush* used in the song's opening is sampled from the film.)

"I did this song from my heart, " Remedy says, adding he had no idea the song
would affect so many people, from children to Holocaust survivors, so deeply.
Even black youth have told him that "Never Again" is the best track on the *The
Swarm* CD, and that they learned more about the Holocaust in four minutes than
they'd ever learned before. Shortly after the song's release on *The Swarm*, Remedy
was invited to Los Angeles by Rabbi Sam Jacobs to perform the song for his
Woodland Hills, California, congregation during Yom Kippur services. Remedy
also attended a dinner for Holocaust survivors during his visit.

In April of 1999, he was among Jewish acts from the United States, Israel,
England, and the former Soviet Union invited to perform in Moscow at "To Russia with Love," a rally and concert to fight fascism and anti-Semitism. The day-
long affair also marked the fifty-first anniversary of the founding of Israel and
the opening of the second Solomon Mikhoels Moscow Arts Festival. The festival
is named in honor of the Jewish actor and director who co-founded the State Jewish Theater in Russia to keep Jewish culture alive there. (His death in a 1948 car
accident is believed to have been directly ordered by Stalin.) Remedy also traveled
to Tel Aviv for a concert that year, and he was invited to perform in Paris after a
French record company included his song "The Anthem" on a compilation CD.

The following spring in celebration of Israel Independence Day, Remedy performed for five thousand people at Israel 2000 at the Greek Theatre in Los Angeles. During the past few years Remedy has made a point of visiting Jewish
day schools and Hebrew schools and playing role model. He doesn't want the
students to ever feel ashamed of being Jewish as he once felt. Nor does he want

them to drop their guard. Holocaust survivors won't be around much longer, and schools don't always do a good job of Holocaust education, so Remedy has made it part of his mission to reach and teach children about the Shoah through music. To help educate black children about the Holocaust, and illustrate parallels between racism and anti-Semitism, the video for "Never Again" uses images of slavery. Remedy continues to educate himself about Judaism as well. He reads Jewish biographies, books on Jewish custom and ritual, and keeps a copy of the Torah by his bed.

In April of 2001, to coincide with Yom Hashoah (Holocaust Remembrance Day), Remedy released his debut full-length CD, *The Genuine Article*, on his own independent Fifth Angel label. The CD included "Never Again." This time around, he was aware of the song's power. "If I never get the big record deal," he says, "at least I did 'Never Again' for the people."

# Evan and Jaron

**Singers. Songwriters. Guitar and piano players. Evan and Jaron Lowenstein, born March 18, 1974, Atlanta, Georgia. Best known for the 2001 Top 20 hit, "Crazy for This Girl."**

*Evan (acoustic guitar) and Jaron Lowenstein performing in Florida in 2001. (Photos by Tom Craig.)*

When Evan and Jaron broke out of the pack in 2001 with the hit single "Crazy for This Girl," the fast-rising pop-rock duo were more than just Atlanta favorite sons; they were also sons of the Atlanta Jewish community. Raised on Orthodox Judaism *and* rock 'n' roll, the twin brother act existed on secular and religious planes. The combination of a Top 20 hit and the fact that they were rocking up the charts while keeping kosher and observing Shabbat, made Evan and Jaron Lowenstein twin beacons for Jewish observance, not to mention pioneers in the pop music world, though that was not their intention.

The crunchy guitar- and silky harmony–laden "Crazy for This Girl," the first single from their self-titled sophomore album, fashion model looks, and a life-style unique to rock 'n' roll, garnered the twins an avalanche of media attention. They were featured on MTV and in *People, Rolling Stone, Entertainment Weekly, Vogue*, and other national publications. To keep the emphasis on their music instead of their religious beliefs, they did fewer interviews with the Jewish press and stopped performing at Jewish venues and functions. It didn't matter. Nearly every article included the twins' commitment to Jewish observance, highlighting that they had a "Sabbath clause" in their recording contract stipulating that they did not have to work on Shabbat.

Evan's theory for the heavy media interest was, he said, "because rock 'n' roll is about a lack of structure, about chaos, and religion is all about structure. People go around saying, 'Sex, drugs, and rock 'n' roll,' not 'Mitzvah, Torah, and rock 'n' roll.' It's two worlds that collide." The Lowensteins, however, not only avoided a collision, they proved that the term "religious rocker" wasn't an oxy-moron, and that observant Jews could thrive in the unforgiving world of secular rock. The handsome Lowenstein boys, without a tattoo or nose ring between them, were indeed rebels, rocking and rolling on their own terms, terms bound by a tight connection to Judaism.

The twins' sharp wit, which belied a slight annoyance with journalists' irrev-erent approach to their Jewish story, occasionally shone through in interviews: "Remember when we wanted to form a band with two other guys and call it Fourskin?" *Rolling Stone* quoted Evan asking Jaron during an interview. And when *Entertainment Weekly* asked, "How much would your yarmulke go for on eBay?" Evan responded, "on heBay or eBay?" Jaron answered with, "Probably not as much as a round of Hide the Afikomen with Evan and Jaron."

On a more serious note, when asked by the *Jewish Journal of Greater Los Angeles* how keeping the Sabbath affected the band's career, Evan touted its benefits: "It affects us in a positive way. The most unbelievable thing is to have a consistent day off, just on a physical level. We know there's no phones. I don't do interviews, or radio, no shows. On a mental level it's nice—after answering questions about ourselves all week—it's nice to step down, take attention off us, and focus somewhere else. It's very easing on the mind."

Despite their telegenic good looks, the media wouldn't have been interested in their Jewish background if the twins didn't deliver on the music end. The pair's second major label release, *evan and jaron*, was filled with infectious, hard-driving folk-rock and pop-rock. Critics who dismissed the duo as just another pretty boy band delivering sweet harmonies to lovesick teens missed the boat.

Like the twins themselves, the album could be viewed in secular and religious terms. On the surface, the record brimmed with muscular, hummable, hook-filled pop-rock. Song after song, especially "Crazy," "Done Hanging On Maybe," and "From My Head to My Heart," were pop radio programmers' dreams. All were tuneful, thick with shimmering harmonies, instantly ear-grabbing, and of their time; they fit smoothly with what was on the air and in the air.

But anyone who names their publishing company "Tzitzis What We Do Music" has got to be thinking deeper than simply being "crazy for this girl." As it turned out, the Lowenstein brothers ran deeper than radio-friendly teeny-bop pop. The chugging rocker "Make it Better" was about more than healing broken bones or hearts. The lyrics, "I've fallen down a time or two, / but no one was looking, / so I'm not telling you . . . / I've got to find me a ladder to reach the light," are as much about God and faith as anything else. The same case can be made for "Pick up the Phone," a mid-tempo plea for good council in the midst of faith that has been shaken. "If you know everything that's happening to me," the brothers sing, "why do I have to ask you for things that I need? / And what about people who don't even call, / because they don't have your number, / do you help them at all?" "Phone" is a prayer disguised as a rock song.

On its surface, "From My Head to My Heart" sounds like a typical break-up song, but it is just as easily about temptation to stray from Torah as the sirens of secular success beckon. "You've got everything I could ever want . . . / and we've been close from the start, / but the furthest distance I've ever known is from my head to my heart." Listen closer (with a Jewish sensibility) to "Wouldn't It Be

Nice to Be Proud." The song isn't just about believing in yourself, it's about remaining committed to your religious beliefs, and living by them, no matter what others say. With these songs, Evan and Jaron accomplished the difficult feat of composing an album that succeeded on two levels.

A look at the Lowensteins' family history might predict a career in music. The brothers' parents, however, were not making any predictions when they named the younger twin (by a few minutes) Jaron, which in Hebrew (Ya-ron) means "He will sing." Music courses through the family tree. The boys' maternal grandmother sang in clubs with big bands in the 1930s and 1940s. Their paternal grandfather worked his way through college playing piano in a band. An uncle's high school band included Max Weinberg, future drummer for Bruce Springsteen's E Street band. Parents Chuck and Leslie play instruments and sing, too. And with an older brother and sister in the house playing records by everyone from the Beatles to Black Sabbath, Evan and Jaron were exposed to the gamut of rock and pop music.

A love of Judaism is also apparent in the Lowenstein family. The twins and their three siblings grew up in a kosher home and attended a Jewish day school and yeshiva. Their older brother, Lee, is a rabbi and principal of a girls' yeshiva in Baltimore. Older sister Andrea is married to a rabbi and lives in Jerusalem. Still, it looked like the twins were headed for a career in professional baseball. Each excelled at several positions and were such talented players as young teens in their JCC league, they were not allowed to be on the same team. By sixteen, they were traveling around the country playing semi-pro baseball.

A trip to Israel changed that. Shortly after graduating early from Atlanta's Yeshiva High School in 1992, Evan went to Israel to continue Jewish studies at Yeshiva Neve Tzion outside Jerusalem. Jaron joined him a few months later. After a year at the Yeshiva, they not only had become more committed to Jewish observance; they had begun to hone their act. "They discovered themselves as singers together. That's really where it happened," says their father, Chuck Lowenstein.

When they returned home in 1993, they began performing in area clubs. In 1994, they formed their own record company, A Major Label Records (because radio stations would only play songs by acts on "a major label"), and released *Live at KaLo's Coffeehouse* and, later, *Not From Concentrate*. The "buzz" increased, and word of the duo spread beyond Atlanta. After hearing Evan and Jaron at one of his clubs, Jimmy Buffett brought them to the attention of Island Records founder Chris Blackwell. The band signed with the label in 1997 and released *We've Never Heard of You Either* the following year.

Unfortunately, the album and the twins' recording contract were jettisoned in a corporate shuffle. Undeterred, the duo relocated to Los Angeles, signed with Columbia Records, and began recording what would be their breakthrough record a year later. They also were invited to participate in Music Bridges in Havana, Cuba, a cultural exchange program at which North American, British, and Cuban songwriters write and perform together.

To help promote the album's release in September of 2000, Evan and Jaron embarked on a "We'll Play Where You Say" tour, a contest for fans in which the prize was an Evan and Jaron concert in the winner's "backyard." With a heavy touring schedule, and with "Crazy for This Girl" being played on television shows such as *Dawson's Creek*, as well as on radio, the song rolled into to the Billboard Top 20. Perhaps the biggest compliment to their talent, and another sign that they had arrived, was being invited to perform on the star-studded TNT cable network's *An All-Star Tribute to Brian Wilson of the Beach Boys*, which aired in July 2001. The twins shared the bill with Paul Simon, Elton John, and Billy Joel, among others.

In 2002, the brothers began writing songs for a followup album. "They've had an impact on a lot of people," says Chuck Lowenstein. "They didn't set out to be role models. They want to be successful performers. If Jewish people increase their observance because of them, great, but they're not out there to do that."

As much as Evan and Jaron want fans and media to focus on their music, and as reluctant as they are to be Jewish role models, the music they make is the result of how they live and what they believe—and is undeniably connected to their faith.

Evan's wife, Kassi, offers an illuminating word here. "The music business is so arbitrary," she says. "There's no rhyme or reason to who gets a hit. One group gets tons of publicity and goes nowhere; another comes out of nowhere and has a hit. Evan and Jaron believe they got a hit single because they believe in a higher power. They believe in something beyond the business."

374